·KIEV·

A PORTRAIT,

1800-1917

A PORTRAIT, 1800-1917

Michael F. Hamm

PRINCETON UNIVERSITY PRESS

PRINCETON, NEW JERSEY

Library of Congress Cataloging-in-Publication Data
Hamm, Michael F.
Kiev: a portrait, 1800–1917 / Michael F. Hamm
p.   cm.
Includes bibliographical references and index.
ISBN 0-691-03253-X
ISBN 0-691-02585-1 (pbk.)
1. Kiev (Ukraine)—History.
DK503.935.H36   1993
947′.715—dc20   93-16290 CIP

This book has been composed in Sabon Typeface

Princeton University Press books are printed
on acid-free paper and meet the guidelines
for permanence and durability of the Committee
on Production Guidelines for Book Longevity
of the Council on Library Resources

Fourth printing, and first paperback printing,
with new preface, 1995

Printed in the United States of America

5   7   9   10   8   6

CONTENTS

ILLUSTRATIONS AND TABLES

ILLUSTRATIONS

TABLES

PREFACE TO
THE PAPERBACK EDITION

SINCE *Kiev: A Portrait, 1800–1917* first appeared in 1993, Ukrainians have suffered horrendous inflation, steep declines in industrial and agricultural production, and a deteriorating standard of living. Responding with apathy, many Kievans refused to vote in the November 1994 elections, rendering the results invalid in sixteen of eighteen voting districts. Political gridlock between the president and parliament has stalled efforts at economic reform, and the state sector still accounts for sixty percent of Ukraine's production. However, in recent months Leonid Kuchma has strengthened the powers of the presidency, brought down inflation, and increased real wages. Ukraine's future as a stable, independent country looks promising at this point, but Kuchma warns that at least another year or two will be required for Ukraine to recover from its economic crisis.

The paperback edition of *Kiev: A Portrait* contains only a few changes and corrections from the 1993 edition. I wish to thank Lady Alexandra F. Harris of Oxford, England, a descendant of Mark Brodsky, for material from her family archive enabling the changes found on pages 122, 153, and 170.

Michael F. Hamm
Centre College
Danville, Kentucky
September 1995

PREFACE

THE RULING CENTER of Kievan Rus, the largest political entity in medieval Europe, and the early stronghold of Eastern Slavic Christianity, Kiev has long held a special place in Ukrainian and Russian history. Destroyed by the Mongols in 1240, and sacked again in 1416 and 1482, Kiev fell under Lithuanian, Polish, and ultimately Muscovite Russian rule. Although it retained some importance as a religious, educational, and trade center, it did not recover the size or significance it had enjoyed as the capital of Kievan Rus for many centuries, and, in fact, did not regain its thirteenth-century population of fifty thousand or more until the middle of the nineteenth century. In 1800 one visitor described Kiev as little more than three barely connected, "village-like" settlements: Podil, Pechersk, and High City. "Kiev," he asserted, "could barely be called a city at all."

At the beginning of the nineteenth century, Kiev had a continuous population of about twenty thousand people. By 1869–1870, when the railroad connecting the city with Moscow and the Black Sea port of Odessa was completed, Kiev's population had grown to seventy thousand. By 1914 it had become a major metropolis with more than six hundred thousand inhabitants. *Kiev: A Portrait, 1800–1917* is the story of the city's transformation and renascence during these decades of exceptional growth.

In exploring the changing world of late-imperial Kiev, I have been as comprehensive as my sources permit. My examination of the city's political culture, for example, includes discussions of burgher attempts to defend the autonomy provided them in medieval times by the Magdeburg Rights; the policies and priorities of the propertied elite empowered by the tsars to manage municipal growth and development after 1870; the rise of the city's socialist movement; and the upheavals of 1905, which shook the foundation of the imperial order. I devote considerable attention to the ethnic and ethnoreligious composition of the city and the extent to which various ethnic groups helped shape its character. Although most Kievans came from the Ukrainian lands that bordered Kiev Province, Kiev became an important center of Russian culture and authority.

During the nineteenth century, in fact, it came to be thought of as a "Russian" city. However, Poles contributed mightily to its culture and economic life, and Polish national goals were a prominent concern of Kiev authorities, at least until the insurrection of 1863. After long periods of exclusion, Jews reestablished a sizable community in the city under Alexander II. The resulting tensions quickly came to overshadow all other ethnic issues during the remaining decades of Romanov rule, and brutal pogroms decimated the Jewish community in 1881 and 1905.

The tensions and conflicts found in Kiev existed in other cities too, but in some ways Kiev was distinctive. The Ukrainian cities of Odessa and Kharkiv, for example, were also Russified in the nineteenth century, but Poles contributed less significantly to the cultures of these cities, and Polish national objectives remained peripheral to their politics. Odessa had a large Jewish population and a history of pogroms, but unlike Kiev was located within the Pale of Settlement. Odessa's Jews did not face the nighttime roundups and expulsions that made late-imperial Kiev notorious.

I have tried to capture the color and flavor of everyday life in Kiev. I depict changes in the city's main neighborhoods—Podil, Khreshchatyk, Shuliavka, and others; profile some of the personalities who dominated its political, cultural, or economic life—the one-armed Governor-General Dmitry Bibikov and the wealthy Jewish entrepreneur Lazar Brodsky, for example; and describe a variety of its subcultures, including the raucous university students who were frequently targets of Bibikov's wrath, the Ukrainian day laborers and servants who congregated in its bazaars in search of work, the so-called vagabond artel that hauled freight to and from its port, and the anonymous ghetto Jews who hoped to find opportunity among its inhabitants, many of whom disliked or resented them. What it was like to live in Kiev, how Kievans amused and entertained themselves, and the diversions the city provided are among the topics addressed in this book.

Central to the historian's craft is the ability to tell a story. *Kiev: A Portrait, 1800–1917* tells the story of a frontier town's transformation into a large metropolis; as such, it should contribute to a deeper understanding of urban development in the Russian Empire as a whole. My analysis of Kiev's political culture and the accomplishments and shortcomings of its political institutions should enhance our understanding of the strengths and weaknesses of that empire. Examination of an environment where Ukrainians, Russians, Poles, and Jews lived side by side should help us comprehend the dynamics of ethnic and ethnoreligious relationships in Eastern Europe as a whole.

Arguably, Kiev was the most prominent city in the Russian Empire after Moscow and St. Petersburg. Today it is the capital of independent

Ukraine, the largest state in Europe outside of Russia. Because of Ukraine's size and its fifty million people, its fate is critical to the prospects for stability in Eastern Europe. In light of Kiev's storied medieval past, its historic importance to Ukrainians and Russians, its prominence in Imperial Russia and the Soviet Union, and its importance as a world capital today, the story of Kiev's transformation and renascence in the nineteenth and early twentieth centuries deserves to be told.

A NOTE ABOUT NOMENCLATURE AND TERMINOLOGY

Kiev: A Portrait, 1800–1917 will be of interest to scholars of Russian, Ukrainian, and Eastern European history, but it will also be read by nonspecialists, by undergraduates taking courses in Russian, Ukrainian, and Eastern European history, for example, and by individuals simply interested in the history of cities. With the nonspecialists in mind, I have simplified the transliteration of Russian and Ukrainian. In so doing, I follow the pattern used in Orest Subtelny's panoramic *Ukraine: A History*. In the text I have dropped the apostrophe, used to denote soft and hard signs, as well as the long forms of the adjectival endings in surnames. The Ukrainian name Sadovs'kyi thus becomes Sadovsky; the Russian name Shul'gin, simply Shulgin. I have retained the longer forms (Sadovs'kyi, Shul'gin, Zakrevskii) in the endnotes, however, since the notes are intended for scholars who know the Slavic languages.

In the interest of general readability, wherever possible I avoid using Slavic words in the text. Thus, "province" is used instead of *guberniia*; "nobleman" instead of *dvorianin*; "burghers" instead of *meshchane*. I use commonly recognized, Anglicized names such as Kiev, Moscow, and Odessa whenever logic dictates. For towns and areas in Ukraine that do not have commonly recognized English forms, I use the Ukrainian names even though they were not used officially during tsarist times. Thus, the reader will find Kharkiv, Lviv, Berdychiv, Katerynoslav, and Kaniv instead of Kharkov (or Khar'kov), Lvov, Berdichev, Ekaterinoslav, and Kanev, except where the name appears in quoted material. For Kiev neighborhoods where the old names continue to be used, I use simplified Ukrainian names: the reader will therefore encounter Lukianivka and not Luk'ianovka, Podil (or the Podil) and not Podol (or the Podol). I use the original Russian where there does not seem to be a Ukrainian equivalent today (for example, Ploskaia District) or where the name is used in common by Ukrainians and Russians, as in the Kiev factory district Shuliavka. In instances where Russians and Ukrainians share a common historical figure from medieval times—for example, Vladimir (Volodymyr) the Great of Kievan Rus—I generally use the term that appears most commonly in English-language publications (in this case, Vladimir). I use the original Russian name for Kiev's university (St. Vladimir), for the name did not survive the revolution, and as far as I can tell, the Ukrainian name (St. Volodymyr) was rarely if ever used.

When referring to places outside of Ukraine, I use currently preferred designations such as Belarus (and Belarusian) rather than the older Belorussia (and Belorussian). Latvia and Estonia are used instead of their tsarist near-equivalents, Lifliand and Estliand Provinces, for example, and Vilnius is used instead of Vil'no or Vilna, for the current names are much more familiar to readers who are not specialists in the field. Where appropriate I provide the alternative name parenthetically.

I have tried to use the Ukrainian and Polish names of individuals who were Ukrainian or Polish (or who saw themselves as such), even though their names almost always appeared in Russianized forms in late-imperial times. In the text the name of the eminent scholar Dmytro Bahalii, for example, is used in the Ukrainian, for he saw himself as a Ukrainian. In the endnotes Bahalii is cited as Dmitrii Bagalei, for this was the Russianized version of his name required in publications at that time. Because of the restricted use of Polish and Ukrainian, particularly between 1863 and 1906, I often had to convert names from Russian into Ukrainian or Polish. I have taken great care in doing this, often consulting with specialists whose linguistic or historical knowledge surpasses my own, but there still may be inconsistencies and mistakes.

SOURCES AND ACKNOWLEDGMENTS

As I began to organize and edit a collection of essays on Russian and Soviet cities, published in 1976 under the title *The City in Russian History*, I became acutely aware of the need for detailed biographies of individual cities. Without them, the study of the urban history of Russia, Ukraine, and the adjacent regions could not progress very far. In the late 1970s and early 1980s, several studies by American and Canadian scholars of Moscow and St. Petersburg appeared, but the provincial cities continued to be ignored. Consequently, I organized another group of scholars in order to profile the history of eight of Imperial Russia's largest cities from the Great Reforms of the 1860s to the collapse of the Romanov dynasty in 1917. These essays were published in *The City in Late Imperial Russia* in 1986. Since then, works have appeared in English on Odessa, Riga, and Warsaw. Kiev, however, remained without a biographer.

There are abundant sources for the study of late-imperial Kiev. Prominent residents—for example, Governor Ivan Funduklei and historian

Nikolai Zakrevsky—wrote about its charms and character in the first half of the nineteenth century. Relying on records from church parishes, Kiev statistician Ivan Pantiukhov compiled and published data on public health, mortality, and marriage for certain years before 1870. The Ukrainophile *Kievskaia starina* (Kievan antiquity, 1882–1907) published many documents and scholarly articles, often in an effort to capture fragments of the color of city life. The works of one of its contributors, V. S. Ikonnikov, constitute an important source for the study of Kiev's history prior to the Great Reforms.

Kiev produced many memoirists. They wrote in Russian, Ukrainian, and Polish about their student years, their participation in local political struggles, or simply about life in the city they loved. Among the most interesting are the recollections of the journalist Sergei Iaron, who called himself "Starozhil" (Old-timer), on the character and characters of the 1880s, and those of the Ukrainians Hryhory Hryhorev, Volodymyr Samiilenko, and Maksym Slavinsky.

For the latter decades of the period under study, city directories, yearly provincial surveys, and reports from Kiev's municipal administration provide useful information. The publications of the Kiev Stock Exchange chronicled the city's commercial growth. The Literacy Society, the Society to Promote Sobriety, the Ukrainian organization *Prosvita*, and other groups published materials about life in the city from a variety of different perspectives.

The 1920s brought an outpouring of publications in Russian and Ukrainian, much of it recollections about Kiev's revolutionary movement. More recent Soviet histories stress the development of the labor movement and the class struggle, while minimizing the role of ethnic and ethnoreligious tension in the city. Pogroms, for example, are largely passed over in Soviet works. Nevertheless, Soviet scholars provide many useful details. Particularly notable are the works of G. I. Marakhov on the Polish insurrection of 1863 in Kiev and Right-Bank Ukraine, and *Istoriia Kieva. Kiev perioda pozdnego feodalizma i kapitalizma* (The history of Kiev in the late feudal and capitalist periods), published in 1983 by the Ukrainian Academy of Sciences under the editorship of B. G. Sarbei. Polish historians continue to write about the city. Leszek Podhorodecki's *Dzieje Kijowa* (History of Kiev) and Jan Tabiś's study of the Polish students at St. Vladimir University are two recent Polish works that contributed to this study.

As I pursued my research on Kiev, it quickly became apparent that the most informative source materials, at least for the years after 1870, were the massive newspaper collections available in Russia and Ukraine. In the 1870s and 1880s *Kievskii telegraf* (Kiev telegraph) and *Zaria* (The dawn) covered local politics, the arts, and public concerns of all kinds. Although some topics could not be fully examined because of censorship, one could read, for example, about the condition of local streets and bazaars, the rapid growth of Jewish ghettos, the repression of the Ukrainian language, and the inadequacy of the city's welfare institutions. Newspapers published statistics, some of them official, some compiled by local reporters. As time passed, the number of city newspapers increased, and coverage of local news expanded. Journalists added "all over town" columns— "Kievskaia zhizn'" (Life in Kiev), "Memuary," (Memories), and "Obo vsem" (About everything) are three examples—which brought to life the personal stories behind the statistics and official reports. As longtime residents of the city, columnists were particularly well equipped to write about continuity and change. Their back-page portraits and vignettes offer unique perspectives and vivid glimpses of local life.

Newspapers from around the Russian Empire were also helpful. Zhytomyr's *Volyn'* (Volyn), Kishinev's *Bessarabskaia zhizn'* (Bessarabian life), Kharkiv's *Utro* (Morning) and *Iuzhnyi krai* (The southern region), Rostov-na-Donu's *Donskaia rech'* (Talk of the Don), and Saratov's *Saratovskii listok* (Saratov leaflet), among others, offered insights on topics ranging from concerns about crime to local amusement preferences. They provided details on pogroms and other disturbances. By reading through newspapers from Riga to Baku, I studied a score of municipal elections, which enabled me to understand more fully those issues and grievances that local people considered important. Occasionally, in distant newspapers I uncovered stories about Kiev that I had not found in Kiev's press.

Needless to say, there were drawbacks to this research strategy. Reading through nearly five decades of newspapers from Kiev and elsewhere consumed a great deal of time. Coverage of specific issues was often anecdotal rather than systematic. Nevertheless, the newspaper collections available in the libraries of Moscow, St. Petersburg, and Kiev provided a richness of detail that I found in no other set of sources. They were invaluable for this study, and they are invaluable, I believe, for the historian of late-imperial urban life.

I am indebted to the International Research and Exchanges Board (IREX), which on two occasions funded research for this project, and to the Fulbright-Hays Faculty Research Abroad program, for the grants they provided enabled me to spend thirteen months in the libraries and archives of the former Soviet Union. I found a rich collection of materials in the Moscow library then called the State Lenin Library. The Central State Historical Archive in St. Petersburg holds many censuses and tax rolls for Kiev and surrounding towns, data on the fiscal posture of various cities, plans for developmental projects, and reports by police and officials on a wide variety of matters.

My five visits to Kiev between 1977 and 1991 reflect the changing character of the city in recent times. In 1977, after months of productive research in Moscow and St. Petersburg, I traveled to Kiev, only to be told upon arrival that Moscow had not provided the proper papers to permit me access to a local archive. For nearly a week I wandered about the city, enjoying the sights, before local authorities told me to return to Moscow. In the early 1980s, when I took students from Centre College to the Soviet Union on a study tour, our Intourist courier guide, an Estonian woman, came to my Kiev hotel room one night to implore that I stop asking questions of the local Intourist guide about the city's history. Although my questions had been nonpolitical and inoffensive, she tearfully explained that Kiev's KGB had a particularly notorious reputation and that the city was a very intimidating place for guides. In the spring of 1986, when *glasnost* and *perestroika* were beginning to unfold, I continued to have difficulty getting Moscow's bureaucrats to approve a research trip to Kiev. In December 1991, however, I encountered a completely different city. Friends welcomed me warmly and without fear. I watched as a couple of hopeful entrepreneurs in a small single room equipped with only a bare table and a telephone traded in scarce commodities ranging from sugar and butter to steel. Local scholars, archivists, and museum curators were eager to meet with me and accommodate my needs. One afternoon I discussed the American concepts of academic freedom and tenure with a class at Kiev University. An organization invited me to return as soon as possible to give public lectures on the city's past.

Completing a study as large and complex as this one presents many problems, and I owe a debt of thanks to many people. I have already acknowledged the International Research and Exchanges Board and the Fulbright-Hays Faculty Research Abroad programs. Although I worked in several major American libraries, the Summer Research Laboratory at the University of Illinois at Champaign-Urbana deserves special mention for the opportunities it provided, as does the Slavic Reference Service at Illinois for its assistance. Centre College gave me several research grants, time off for writing, and a subsidy to help print the photographs of old Kiev. Most of these prints were obtained through the services of Kiev's Mystetstvo Press, whose director, Valentin Kuzmenko, granted me permission to use them. Some of these photos can also be found in the stunning pictorial collections published by Mystetstvo. The city map was drawn by Stuart Arnold of Danville, Kentucky, and based largely on a map of Kiev published on page 80 of *The City in Late Imperial Russia* (Bloomington: Indiana University Press, 1986).

Many individuals provided bibliographical assistance, personal insights, or help with translating or interpreting difficult passages. They include Barbara Szubinska and Renata Maryniak, both of Warsaw; Serhii Bilokin of the Kiev Academy of Sciences; Leonid Cherkassky of Kiev's State Ukrainian Museum for Theater, Music, and and Film; June Pachuta Farris of the University of Chicago; Dmytro Shtohryn of the University of Illinois at Champaign-Urbana; Laura Souders of the Library of Congress, and Zenon Kohut, who was then at the same institution; Henry Abramson of the University of Toronto; and Danae Orlins and Ken Keffer of Centre College.

I give special thanks to Orest Subtelny of York University in Toronto, who read much of the manuscript in draft stage, and to Lauren Osborne and Lauren Lepow of the Princeton University Press for their support and assistance. Stephen Corrsin of Brooklyn College, John Klier of University College, London, Richard Stites of Georgetown University, Frank Sysyn of the Canadian Institute of Ukrainian Studies at the University of Alberta, and Christine Worobec of Kent State University all read drafts of individual chapters and offered valuable comments and suggestions for further research. Above all others, special thanks go to my wife, JoAnn Hamm, who read many drafts of the entire manuscript, offering countless suggestions for stylistic and organizational improvement, and to my friends Sergei Basarab and Vikenty Shimansky, both of Kiev, whose valuable assistance expedited the completion of this manuscript.

Michael F. Hamm
Centre College
January 1993

·KIEV·

A PORTRAIT,

1800-1917

· CHAPTER I ·

The Early History of Kiev

THE ORGANIZING center of Kievan Rus, the first great Slavic state, Kiev arose in the ninth century as a commercial hub on the trade routes connecting Europe, the Eastern Christian empire known as Byzantium with its capital at Constantinople, the glorious Abassid Moslem empire ruled from Baghdad, and the Khazar state of the lower Volga and northern Caucasus. At its zenith in the eleventh century, Kiev was the ruling center of the largest political entity in medieval Europe and one of the world's most splendid cities. Its population for the year 1200 has been estimated at fifty thousand or more. By comparison, Paris had about fifty thousand inhabitants at that time, while London had an estimated population of thirty thousand.[1]

Situated at the meeting point of the pine forests common to the north and the oak and hardwood forests common to the south, Kiev grew on the steeply sloped west bank of the Dnipro River (Dnepr in Russian), along the hills, ravines, and floodplains shaped by that river and the smaller Lybid (Lybed) and Pochaina rivers. Called "the mother of the towns of ancient Rus," Kiev's origins are obscure and enshrouded in myth. According to the chronicler Nestor, three brothers from an ancient Slavic tribe settled on separate hills and built a city in honor of the eldest brother, Kyi.[2] The name Kiev followed. Archaeological excavations headed by Petro Tolochko indicate the probability of commercial activity in Kiev's Podil (Podol) District in the seventh or eighth century. However, dendrochronological analysis of the remnants of Podil's log dwellings provides evidence of settlement only as far back as 887, and, according to Omeljan Pritsak, archaeologists have proven "beyond any doubt that Kiev as a town did not exist before the last quarter of the ninth to the first half of the tenth century."[3] Iron metallurgy, blacksmithing, jewelry making, and stone and bone carving existed in Podil in the ninth and tenth centuries, and fragments of imported goods, including tenth-century Byzantine coins, indicate the probability of international commercial contact.[4]

˙KIEVAN RUS

By the time Kiev's burghers signed an advantageous trade pact with Constantinople in 911, the city had become the capital of the great state called Kievan Rus, the origins of which are also controversial. Relying on a passage from an ancient chronicle, several eighteenth-century German scholars concluded that this state was organized by Varangians, a Germanic-Scandinavian people known in the West as the Vikings or Normans. Slavic historians have rejected this so-called Norman theory because it implies that their ancestors needed outside help to organize their state, but they have not produced a definitive alternative explanation. In his encyclopedic *Ukraine: A History*, Orest Subtelny argues that the warrior-merchant Varangians "rapidly assimilated the East Slavic language and culture and were probably too few in number to bring about important changes in native ways." He notes, however, that "either by politically organizing the Slavs over whom they gained control or by posing a threat and forcing the Slavs to organize themselves more effectively, the Varangians acted as catalysts for political development." Thus, Kiev's rise was not "the exclusive achievement of one ethnic group or another," but resulted from "a complex Slavic/Scandinavian relationship."[5]

In examining the history of early Kiev, one should note the accomplishments of Sviatoslav, who ruled Kievan Rus from 962 until 972 and seized control of the Volga River, bringing all the East Slavic tribes under his authority. Writes Subtelny: "His Slavic name, Varangian values, and nomadic life-style reflected a Eurasian synthesis. His reign marked the culmination of the early, heroic period of Kievan Rus'."[6] The Kievan state ultimately took in territory that would now include St. Petersburg and Lake Ladoga, Moscow, Vladimir, and Riazan.

Vladimir the Great (Volodymyr in Ukrainian), who ruled Kievan Rus from 980 until 1015, was more intent on addressing the needs of his subjects and establishing a cohesive state. Having married into the royal family of the Christian Byzantine Empire, Vladimir converted to Christianity and converted his subjects as well, baptizing en masse a large number of Kiev's inhabitants in a Dnipro tributary in 988. Kievan Rus thus became Christian Europe's eastern flank, and not the northern flank of the Islamic caliphate. In the words of Subtelny, "The importance of Christianity coming from Byzantium and not from Rome cannot be overestimated. Later, when the religious split between these two centers occurred, Kiev would side with Constantinople and reject Roman Catholicism, thereby laying the groundwork for the bitter conflicts that Ukrainians would have with their closest Catholic neighbors, the Poles."[7]

The reign of Iaroslav the Wise, who ruled from 1036 until 1054, represents a high point for Kievan Rus, for during these years peace prevailed and hundreds of churches were built, among them St. Sophia Cathedral, modeled after Constantinople's Hagia Sophia. From his death, however, Kievan Rus began a process of decline, aided by the demise of its trading partners, the Abassid Caliphate, which fell prey to the Mongols, and Byzantium, sacked by the crusaders in 1204. During the twelfth century, at least a dozen hereditary principalities emerged, among them Novgorod and Vladimir-Suzdal (which included the settlement of Moscow). As these principalities, related by language, religion, and dynastic ties, became independent of one another, the territorial base of Kievan Rus shrank and its power declined accordingly. Kiev itself was sacked in 1169 and 1203.[8]

In 1240 the city of Kiev was destroyed by the Mongols, whose leader, Batu Khan, is reported to have boasted: "I will tie Kiev to the tail of my horse."[9] In the ensuing centuries, Kiev and the surrounding territory continued to be the target of Tatar raids. From 1450 to 1586, for example, eighty-six raids were recorded, and from 1600 to 1647, there were seventy more.[10] Crimean Tatars sacked Kiev in 1416 and again in 1482. Kiev was not ravaged again until the mid-seventeenth century, but even during this long period of comparative peace, it did not recover the size or importance it had enjoyed as the capital of Kievan Rus. According to one set of figures, Kiev had about three thousand residents early in the fifteenth century. Lviv (Lvov), Ukraine's largest town at this time, had about ten thousand.[11] In 1474 one Venetian visitor described Kiev as "plain and poor."[12] Statistician Ivan Pantiukhov estimates that its population averaged no more than ten thousand inhabitants from the fourteenth through the seventeenth centuries.[13]

"THE HISTORIC KIEV"

If the actual city of Kiev remained "plain and poor," various leaders competed for the right to claim themselves successors to "the historic Kiev." Charles Halperin notes that "Kievan literature, art, folklore, law and politics received new life in Suzdalian Russia long after Kievan Rus' had ceased to exist."[14] Suzdalian princes claimed to be the rightful heirs of Kievan Rus and called their principality "The Russian Land." After defeating the Mongols at Kulikovo in 1380, Muscovite Russia made the same claim as it absorbed rival principalities. Muscovite princes were directly descended from Kiev's princes. They assumed the "pose of Kievan mythic models," Halperin notes. Kievan saints protected Moscow, and Kievan culture did in fact serve as the basis for Muscovite culture.

Contrasting "the historic Kiev" with the actual city of Kiev, which passed into Lithuanian hands, Halperin concludes: "The city of Kiev that now existed in the fourteenth and fifteenth centuries had no claim upon the Kievan inheritance, which no longer resided in Kiev, but in Moscow."[15]

KIEV UNDER LITHUANIAN AND POLISH RULE

As Mongol rule receded, the Grand Principality of Lithuania, a loose congeries of independent tribes ruled from Vilnius (Vilna), absorbed Kiev. Although the Lithuanians initially failed to protect Kiev from Tatar raids, they built a fortified settlement called Vladimir's Town on the hill overlooking Podil. Eventually, this fortification was named for a Polish governor (*voevoda*), Adam Kisel, and came to be known as Kyselivka. Within its walls—which were defended by fifteen six-cornered, three-story towers, seventeen cannons, and one hundred long muskets—stood thirty barracks for soldiers, the homes of the city's administrative elite, three Orthodox churches (the most important of which was the Castle Church of St. Nicholas), and a Catholic chapel for those occasions when a Catholic governor was put in charge of the city. The Lithuanian princes fostered the economic recovery of Kiev by allowing its burghers unrestricted trade anywhere in their state. Armenian and Genoese merchants established settlements in Podil, as caravans of silks, tapestries, oriental rugs, saffron, pepper, and other spices came to the city from the Crimea and the Muslim world. Kievans came to control much of the region's trade in German and Russian silk, paper, wool, iron, furs, linen, taffeta, dyes, beef fat, beeswax, and salted fish.[16] Kiev's goldsmiths and furriers became particularly famous, and local craftsmen also established reputations for manufacturing high-quality rifles, saddles, bows, and metal, eagle-feathered arrows, which were often sold to Tatars in return for salt.

The most important legacy of Lithuanian rule, however, was the granting of the Magdeburg Rights to Kiev between 1494 and 1514, which enabled Podil's burghers to govern themselves as a semiautonomous jurisdiction. Common throughout medieval Europe, these rights, modeled on the principles of free self-government established in the thirteenth century by the German city of Magdeburg, had also been extended to several other towns in the region, including Lviv. They provided Kiev's burghers with tax exemptions and allowed for the creation of a burgher magistracy, which took on full administrative and judicial authority. A mayor (*voit*) was elected, usually for life. Initially, the magistracy was elected by all of Podil's residents "in accordance with their reason, capability, and virtue," and city business was transacted informally, by word of mouth. Justice was swift, if not always fair, and the accused did enjoy the right to

defend himself.[17] Over time, however, the magistracy became a hereditary aristocracy of powerful burgher families.

Efforts by Lithuanian and Polish authorities to interfere in Kiev's affairs did not altogether cease, but Kiev's burghers succeeded in maintaining their privileges, and the Magdeburg Rights were affirmed many
times.[18] From 1654 Russia's tsars also honored these rights, although
officials appointed in St. Petersburg took on more and more authority,
especially during the reign of Catherine the Great (1762–1796).[19] In 1835
Tsar Nicholas I (1825–1855) finally abrogated the Magdeburg Rights.

Supported by land-hungry nobles, rich Cracow burghers who hoped to
secure control of the Dnipro trade routes, and the proselytizing Catholic
church, the Polish kings, beginning with Casimir the Great (1333–1370),
tried to conquer Ukraine. The Lithuanians were able to thwart the early
Polish campaigns, forcing the Poles initially to settle for control of Galicia, but in 1385 Lithuania and Poland established a dynastic union, and
the Lithuanian monarch adopted Catholicism. Although Lithuania reasserted itself under Vytautas in the 1390s, in 1452 Volyn, just to the west
of Kiev, was occupied and transformed into a joint Lithuanian-Polish
province, and in 1471 Kiev and its environs met the same fate.

At the Union of Lublin in 1569, Poland and Lithuania merged into a
common state, but as the stronger of the partners Poland took control of
Lithuania's Ukrainian territories. As demand in Western Europe for grain
increased, huge estates, "unknown in Poland proper or in the western
Ukrainian lands," came to dominate Poland's frontier in the Dnipro
basin.[20] One rich magnate, Jeremi Wiśniowiecki, owned an estimated
230,000 peasants on 7,500 estates in the Kiev and Poltava regions. The
size of these landholdings was unmatched "anywhere else in Europe. Because these magnates controlled more territory and population than
many West European princes at the time, they were often referred to as
'kinglets.' "[21]

Polish penetration of Ukraine resulted in a fierce struggle for souls between the Orthodox and Catholic churches, a struggle that Kiev could
not escape. A Catholic bishopric was established in the city early in the
fifteenth century, and a Catholic church was built in 1433. In 1455 the
Polish king Casimir IV commanded that no new Orthodox churches be
built in Kiev and that existing churches not be repaired.[22] Jesuits established collegia in Lviv and elsewhere. Piotr Skarga and other polemicists
"castigated the alleged doctrinal fallacies and the cultural backwardness of the Orthodox in sermons and open debates. In his famous work
'The Unity of God's Church,' Skarga argued that the state of Orthodoxy
was so hopeless that its adherents' only alternative was union with
Rome."[23]

In response to the pressure from Catholic proselytism, the Uniate church, which retained the Orthodox ritual and the Slavonic liturgical language while recognizing papal authority, was created in 1596 and backed by the Polish government. Sensitive to allegations of backwardness, Subtelny argues, Ukrainian noblemen quickly converted, leaving the Ukrainians "without the class that normally provided political leadership and purpose, patronized culture and education, supported the church, and endowed a society with a sense of ethnopolitical identity." To be Ukrainian was henceforth to be lower class, an object of scorn. "Henceforth, ambitious, talented Ukrainian youths would constantly be forced to choose between loyalty to their own people and traditions and assimilation into the dominant culture and society. Usually they opted for the latter. Consequently, the problem of a Ukrainian elite, or rather, the lack of one, now emerged as yet another of the central and recurrent themes in Ukrainian history."[24]

Uniates captured many of Kiev's monasteries, but the Cave Monastery (Pecherska lavra), which escaped capture in 1596 and 1598, and the Epiphany (Bohoiavlennia) Brotherhood fought back, and Kiev again became "the undisputed cultural and religious center of Ukraine."[25] In 1632 the Kiev Epiphany Brotherhood and the Metropolitan See organized the Kiev Collegium (later Kiev Academy). Petro Mohyla (d. 1647) became its leading intellectual force, introducing Latin scholasticism on the Jesuit model. The Kiev Academy attracted students from Serbia, Bulgaria, Greece, and even the Christian communities in the Arab lands. For more than a century, it served as a major conduit of Western ideas into the Russian Empire. At the peak of its influence early in the eighteenth century, it had more than eleven hundred students. By 1780 its library had accumulated twelve thousand volumes.[26] By this time, however, St. Petersburg's Academy of Sciences, founded in 1725, and Moscow University, founded in 1755, had surpassed it in stature. The Kiev Academy began to lose students and in 1817 became a theological seminary. In summarizing its significance, Alexander Sydorenko contends that until the mid-eighteenth century, the Kiev Academy ranked as "the foremost intellectual center of the Eastern Slavic world" and was comparable in influence, perhaps, to the universities at Prague and Cracow.[27]

Under Polish rule Kiev became a battleground for competing religious faiths. One notable victim was the Kobyzevich family, Christianized Tatars who had been resettled as boyars in Mozyr Region by a Lithuanian prince. Ivan Kobyzevich came to Kiev in the sixteenth century and grew rich. Joined by his relatives, the family became the wealthiest landowners in the Kiev region, changed its name to Khodyk, and gradually transformed the burgher magistracy into a kind of family empire. After purchasing the nearby village of Krynychy, the Khodyks took the name of Khodyk-Krynytsky. The Khodyk-Krynytskys embraced the Uniate movement as a means of showing support for the Poles (they wrote all documents in Polish, including official acts). During a bitter fight, Fedor Khodyk-Krynytsky was apparently quartered and dumped into the Dnipro, but his sons carried on until mid-seventeenth century, representing Uniate interests in Kiev.[28]

Polish kings did affirm the city's Magdeburg Rights, however, and local burghers still had forty-seven specific privileges when Fedor Kurakin was appointed Kiev's *voevoda* by Moscow in 1654, signaling the demise of Polish influence in the city. Poles would again become influential in Kiev in the 1790s. In 1793, during the second partition of Poland, Russia seized the Right-Bank Ukrainian lands, and in 1796 Kiev was made the capital of the newly created Kiev Province. Poles owned most of the rich farmland on the Right Bank and assumed many of the local offices. In 1797 the Contract Fair (so named because of its numerous land and agricultural product transactions) was moved to Kiev from Dubno, bringing thousands of free-spending Polish landowners to the city each winter. Symbolic of these changes, a small wooden Catholic church was built in Kiev's Pechersk District in 1797 to accommodate the sudden influx of Poles.[29] Nicholas I greatly reduced Polish influence in the city and the region, but the Contract Fair and Kiev's St. Vladimir University, founded in 1834, continued to serve as centers for Polish political intrigue until Polish national aspirations were suppressed in the insurrection of 1863.

PODIL: KIEV'S COMMERCIAL HUB

Medieval Slavic cities were often characterized by a central aristocratic and administrative district (*ditynets*, *detinets*, and later *kreml* in Russian), where princes and high ecclesiastical officials exercised their authority, and surrounding trade and craft sections called *posady*.[30] Kiev's *ditynets* was called Vladimir's Town, and later High City or Old Kiev. Podil, the floodplain that lay beneath Kiev's great hills along the Dnipro and Pochaina rivers, was its principal *posad*, its commercial hub. Near the center of medieval Podil was Merchant Square, flanked by two great Byzantine-style single-cupola churches. According to the Nestor Chronicle, a wooden bridge was built across the Dnipro from Podil, possibly around 1115.[31] For the most part, Podil's inhabitants did not involve themselves in the politics of Kievan Rus, which were centered in Vladimir's Town.

Fishermen, food growers, and craftsmen lived in Podil's narrow, one-story, thatch-roofed wooden homes, which were surrounded by gardens and said to be constructed in the "Moscow style." Trade brought Greeks, Armenians, Italians, and Jews, as well as Slavs from Great Russia and surrounding Ukraine, to Podil. In the fifteenth century, Armenians were said to be Podil's wealthiest merchants, and an Armenian church was built there in 1433. Early in the 1600s Podil had thirteen Orthodox churches and three Catholic churches, but in 1604 part of it was taken over by the Catholic bishop and called Bishop's City.[32] Beginning in the 1690s, Magistracy Hall was constructed in the late-rococo style. Like the great halls in Prague, Moscow, and Novgorod, it had a famous clock with a golden inscription, "God watches over the city of Kiev, 1697." On a high balcony trumpeters and drummers performed daily at daybreak, noon, and nightfall, and in summer musicians played late into the evening. A large city coat of arms was displayed on the clock, and when the Archangel Michael (since ancient times the city's protector) struck the snake, sparks cascaded downward. Magistracy Hall remained the symbol of Kiev's burgher rights until it was destroyed in the great fire of 1811. Its bricks were used to build the Contract Hall, where the Contract Fair was held during the remaining decades of the nineteenth century.

From the destruction of the High City by the Mongols in 1240 until the early decades of the nineteenth century, Podil was Kiev's population center, and, in fact, Kiev and Podil were virtually synonymous. Ivan Pantiukhov provides estimates, averaged by century, of the three barely connected settlements that would ultimately become the core of modern Kiev (table 1.1).

TABLE 1.1
Estimated Average Population of Kiev by Century

Century	Old Kiev	Podil	Pechersk	Total
9th	8,000	1,000	—	9,000
10th	15,000	2,000	—	17,000
11th	25,000	3,000	100	28,100
12th	25,000	5,000	300	30,300
13th	10,000	3,000	400	13,400
14th	6,000	3,000	500	9,500
15th	4,000	4,000	500	8,500
16th	2,000	5,000	2,000	9,000
17th	1,000	6,000	3,000	10,000
18th	1,500	8,000	6,000	15,500

SOURCE: I. Pantiukhov, *Opyt sanitarnoi topografii i statistiki Kieva* (Kiev: Kievskii gubernskii statisticheskii komitet, 1877), 114.

UPLAND KIEV: OLD KIEV (HIGH CITY)
AND PECHERSK

Vladimir's Town, built on high ground but away from the Dnipro bluffs, had been the political and ecclesiastical center of medieval Kiev. It was named for Prince Vladimir who built a strong fortress surrounded by a deep moat and earthen and wooden ramparts, with gates leading to Podil, Pechersk, and the St. Sophia Cathedral, founded in 1037. Fortifications were expanded by Iaroslav, and the new ramparts had three gates, Lviv, Polish, and the famous Golden Gate, built in 1037 and named for the Golden Gate in Constantinople. Initially, the Church of the Annunciation was built on top of the Golden Gate, which served as a passage through a two-story log wall built atop an earthen rampart. Until it was destroyed by the Mongols in 1240, it was the main fortified entrance to the old city.[33] Periodic Tatar raids hindered efforts to restore the great hilltop churches, and Vladimir's Town, which came to be more commonly called High City or Old Kiev, remained a sparsely populated area notable mainly for its ruins. Traveler Reinhold Geidenshtein reported in 1596 that of the great churches that had once stood there, only St. Sophia was functioning and that even there services were not being held because of the destruction.[34]

Old Kiev was never granted Magdeburg autonomy, and the area was administered by St. Sophia and St. Michael's of the Golden Domes Monastery. After 1654 their authority was shared with the Russian troops who were garrisoned there, and in 1782 Russian officials assumed full fiscal and administrative control. Old Kiev would grow significantly in the nineteenth century, but when St. Vladimir University was founded there in 1834, it was still a mostly empty land of ruins and ravines.

The third of Kiev's settlements, Pechersk (called Bishop's City by the Poles), was the hilly embankment overlooking the Dnipro and surrounding the labyrinth of underground cells and passages that had been turned into hermitages and then monasteries by the early Christian population. The famous Cave Monastery was founded here in 1051. Aside from the monastery, Pechersk remained very sparsely populated. A bazaar and trade community were established early in the seventeenth century, but significant growth came only after Peter the Great (Peter I, 1682–1725) decided to build the Russian fortress in Pechersk. The Russian governor-general shared administrative responsibility over Pechersk with the Cave Monastery and the Ukrainian Cossack state known as the Hetmanate. As in High City, the Russian state assumed full control over the area in 1782.

By then Pechersk had 1,131 homes, 36 of them owned by the Russian government. Even during the nineteenth century, Pechersk remained an odd amalgam of soldiers, monks, and religious pilgrims.

COSSACKS AND RUSSIANS

In the seventeenth century Poles, Russians, and Ukrainian Cossacks waged a fierce battle for control of Ukraine. An egalitarian organization of free frontiersmen, many of whom lived on the Right Bank to the south of Kiev, Cossacks had their headquarters "beyond the rapids" in the so-called Zaporozhian Sich (Sech), just to the south of the future site of Katerynoslav (Ekaterinoslav, today Dnipropetrovsk). To one historian, the Cossacks were "exceptional people," adventurers who left "the security of communities where families had lived for generations . . . , setting out for a borderland known in the folk tales for its bloodthirsty infidels, the cruelty of its winters, the loneliness of its vast plains."[35] Some were runaway serfs from Russia or escapees from the Ottoman slave ships, but most were probably from Ukraine. Only Jews were reportedly unwelcome in the ranks of these aggressive frontiersmen, who became notable as "an army of mercenaries and freebooters."[36]

The Zaporozhian Sich functioned as a state and had relations, for example, with the pope. Under the leadership of Hetman Petro Sahaidachny (1614–1622), the Cossack army took the side of the Orthodox population in its struggle against the Catholics and the Uniates, and the powerful Zaporozhian army joined ranks with the Kiev Orthodox Brotherhood. Under Sahaidachny's leadership, Kiev had the potential to become the capital of an Orthodox Ukrainian state, and when he died in 1622, "the population of Kiev turned out en masse."[37]

Beginning in 1648 the Cossack hetman Bohdan Khmelnytsky (1595?–1657), said to be "Ukraine's greatest political and military leader,"[38] led a massive rebellion that initially drove most of the Poles from Ukraine and slaughtered tens of thousands of Jews as well. Khmelnytsky destroyed Kiev's Catholic monasteries, and in 1649 the city's Orthodox hierarchy welcomed him "as 'the second Moses' who had 'liberated his people from Polish slavery.' "[39] With the help of Lithuanian troops, Poles regained Kiev in 1651, and in August of that year fire destroyed much of the city (including the documents certifying its ancient privileges). In 1654 Khmelnytsky sought the protection of the Muscovite Tsar Aleksei (1645–1676), and at Pereiaslav took an oath of loyalty to him, thereby linking Ukraine's fate inextricably with Russia's. Aleksei affirmed virtually all of Kiev's privileges, and in the next few years Poles, Jews, and Armenians were expelled from the city. Cossacks, loyal to Russia, settled in devastated and depopulated Podil to ensure against a resurfacing of pro-Polish sympathies.[40]

During the decades following Khmelnytsky's death in 1657, Cossack armies, some loyal to Poland, some to Russia, battled each other; the resultant period of devastation in Ukraine is often called "The Ruin." Exhausted by warfare, Russia and Poland reached an agreement at Andrusovo in 1667, which left Russia in control of the Left-Bank provinces and the city of Kiev, and in 1686, after further fighting initiated by the Cossacks, the agreement won international recognition. That same year Kiev's metropolitan was subordinated to the patriarch in Moscow. Peter the Great affirmed Kiev's privileges in 1700 and 1710, and in 1701 a new road was begun to forge a better link between Podil and Pechersk. In 1706, during a visit to Kiev, Peter laid the groundwork for the construction of his great fortress, and the city took on new importance as part of a fortified line designed to expand the Russian Empire to the south and west, while protecting its flanks from Poles, Swedes, Ottoman Turks, and steppe nomads.

"GOOD MEN BECOME BAD"

In the eighteenth century Kiev continued to be a frontier city with a frontier blend of peoples, a fortress city with soldiers from many places. The city even acquired a reputation as a nerve center, where spies intent on learning what they could about Russia, Poland, the Ottoman Empire, and the Crimea congregated. Eastern Europeans, many bound for the open lands of New Russia and the lower Volga, came through Kiev, and some stayed. In 1726 Kiev had at least twenty-two Greek merchants. Around midcentury, Serbs settled in the city and helped manage the state vineyards. These Balkan peoples helped establish Kiev's silk industry and its reputation as a center for cooked and candied fruits. In 1758 more than a thousand Montenegrins came for the purpose of forming a hussar regiment. Under Catherine the Great, who encouraged foreign colonization in the empire, at least a hundred Germans settled in Kiev. Religious pilgrims also poured into the city, and sometimes "ordinary people traveled south simply as a diversion, much in the way one would now visit a foreign land."[41]

Podil continued to be the burgher stronghold (in 1785 they owned 1,974 of the quarter's 2,110 homes),[42] but throughout the century Kiev's burghers had to wage a persistent, and only partially successful, battle to maintain their autonomy against encroachments by Cossacks and the increasingly powerful Russian state. More than principle was at stake. Officeholding had become very profitable. In the eighteenth century the mayor received one hundred vedros of *horilka* (distilled spirits), mead, and beer annually, as well as one hundred pine logs, one hundred carts of firewood, and hay, and more spirits at Christmas and Easter. He was given a city-owned hut and still, hayfields, and a fishing lake for his personal use. Underlings were also paid in smaller quantities of *horilka*, beer, mead, and firewood. In addition, the ruling oligarchy came to view the various sources of city income as its own.[43]

One of the magistracy's rights and obligations that was altered with the onset of a Russian presence in the city was that of self-defense. Kiev's burghers had their own martial tradition. In medieval times the city's population had been grouped into units called *sotni* (hundreds), which provided an organizational basis for raising a militia, collecting taxes, and carrying out projects related to public welfare. The size of the burgher militia is unclear, and may have changed over time, but it was large enough to defend the city, escort trade caravans, and chase Tatar marauders into the steppe. In 1624 the Polish king Sigismund III (1587–1632) released the militia from the obligation of pursuing Tatar raiders unless they actually came into Kiev's territory.[44] After 1654 defense of the city fell to regular Russian troops, but old traditions died hard, and the corps, a symbol of Kiev's ancient rights, continued to mobilize when the city was threatened and for important ceremonies.

Peter the Great required Kiev's burghers to assist in the construction of the Pechersk fortress and in the provisioning of Russia's troops, who numbered about three thousand in 1708.[45] In 1736 burghers were excused from this obligation. In 1743 local rights were again affirmed, but the city was subjected to general taxes for the maintenance of imperial troops. Subsequent actions by the Senate restored the local exemption, but in the 1760s the issue of state prerogatives versus local rights again came to a head, this time over whether burghers could be forced to quarter a Moldavian hussar regiment posted in Kiev. Friction intensified when some of the hussars opened taverns, infringing upon the burghers' right to monopolize tavern trade.[46]

Although Moscow had established control over Cossack Ukraine, the Cossack Hetmanate continued to operate with considerable autonomy, especially during the reign of Elizabeth I (1741–1762). Between 1750 and 1764 the leader of this state was Hetman Kyrylo Rozumovsky, a personal favorite of Elizabeth. Few Cossacks actually lived in Kiev—in 1752 only 28 of the 2,140 homes in Podil were owned by Cossacks[47]—but the Cossacks had a special love for the city, "where the source and beginning of our religion glitters, where the holy places are preserved with great pomp."[48] In 1737 Cossacks had helped Russian officials arrest Kiev's burgher mayor Pavel Voinych for refusing to obey a state directive. Carried out in a public way, the arrest dishonored Voinych and threatened Kiev's independence. Under Rozumovsky tensions between burghers and Cossacks escalated, partly over who was responsible for maintaining the Khreshchata "road," at this time a network of dirt paths through the Khreshchata ravine that connected Podil, High City, and Pechersk. In 1751 Rozumovsky tried to have Ivan Sichevsky appointed mayor even though Sichevsky was not a member of the magistracy. Above all, burghers and Cossacks battled over distilling rights.

The importance of alcohol in the culture of Russia and Ukraine has been noted by many, and tavern trade had long played an important role in Kiev's commerce and public life. Lamented one early graffito-writer in St. Sophia Cathedral: "I drank away my clothes while I was here."[49] In 1474 the visitor Kontarini observed that by three o'clock in the afternoon Kievans were already in the taverns, where they would stay until night-time. Needless to say, brawls were common.[50] In the seventeenth and eighteenth centuries, if not before, the city derived almost all of its income from the making and selling of spirits. The magistracy paid the Imperial Russian government for the right to protect its distilling monopoly, and the Russian government reaffirmed the magistracy's monopoly many times. Neither the monasteries nor the Cossacks respected this privilege, however. Cossacks enjoyed distilling rights outside of Kiev. Why should Kiev be different? The main monasteries had numerous stills. In the 1750s monks from the Cave Monastery ran fourteen taverns in Pechersk, one on each street.[51]

The fact that Cossack leaders recruited local burghers, who in turn were accused of being lazy turncoats wanting nothing more than to live off illegal trade in *horilka*, also added to the tension. The "free life" of the Cossacks carried a certain fascination and was widely respected. The wife of the burgher Maksym Gorbanenko, for example, had been previously married to a Cossack and fervently wanted Maksym to join their ranks. After conspiring to get her unfortunate husband drunk, she enrolled him in the Cossacks against his will, or so he later claimed. Gorbanenko fled to the vagabonds who lived along the Dnipro banks, but was captured again by the Cossacks. Disputes of this kind usually ended up in court and provided further pretext for brawls.[52]

On the matter of distilling rights, the Russian Senate tended to back the burghers against Cossack encroachments. Illegal distilling nevertheless continued, as did feuds and deadly brawls. In the 1760s, of eighty-four farmsteads near Kiev cited in one survey, sixty-two were involved with distilling,[53] and Hetman Rozumovsky himself warned that Ukrainians were neglecting their land and livestock, exhausting the supply of firewood, and deforesting the countryside, all for the sake of distilling. A few decades later, in 1816, Tsar Alexander I (1801–1825) would observe:

"Distilling has completely exhausted Little Russia; it resembles a weakened man."[54] As for the city itself, for all of Kiev's "miracle-working icons," ran an eighteenth-century lyric, "its men, though charitable to the poor, are in the end destroyed by the taverns. They become stingy. Good men become bad."[55]

THE CENTRALIZING REFORMS OF
CATHERINE THE GREAT

More than any other Russian ruler before her, Catherine the Great sought to bring a centralized, uniform administration to the empire, and the autonomy of Kiev and the rest of Ukraine diminished accordingly. In 1764 Catherine boldly abolished the Hetmanate, appointing a governor-general and an administrative body known as the Little Russian College to administer its territory. The Cossack companies were phased out, and the Orthodox church was brought fully under Moscow's control. Evaluating the position of Kiev's burghers during the early years of Catherine's reign, Zenon Kohut contends that their concerns included "the high taxes in support of Russian troops; the cost of quartering Russian officials and officers; foreigners, particularly Greeks and Vlachs, trading in the city without payment of municipal taxes; and the all too familiar problem of Cossacks and their officers competing with the burghers in trade."[56] Requesting that the Cossacks either be expelled from the city or be forced to pay municipal taxes, Kiev's burghers fought to defend their Magdeburg autonomy, but in 1785 Catherine's Town Charter introduced a new city council (duma), which was to oversee day-to-day management of municipal affairs. Policy-making power and supervision of the police were given to the governor, appointed in St. Petersburg. Russia's military presence in Pechersk continued to be extensive. During the Russo-Turkish War of 1768–1774, for example, Kiev became the main supply base for the Russian army, and in 1784 construction of the Arsenal, which manufactured supplies for the Russian army, was begun. Some historians have concluded that the magistracy lost virtually all of its power under Catherine, and that from 1785 it functioned mainly as a judicial body.[57] Kohut takes a different approach, noting that the 1785 Town Charter's "provisions were skillfully blended with local traditions. Magdeburg Law remained in force, and the Kievan patriciate maintained control over government and finances, even reinstituting a traditional part of Kievan administration, the militia."[58]

As part of an effort to undo his mother's reforms, Catherine's successor, Paul I (1796–1801), sought to restore Kiev's traditional administrative structure. Under Paul, Kiev became the capital of a new province carved out of territory taken from Poland during the second partition. At best, Paul's initiatives produced two overlapping and conflicting structures, neither of which could balance the city's books. Magdeburg Rights were affirmed again in 1802 by Alexander I, but the magistracy had become a shadow of its former self. By the turn of the nineteenth century, the groundwork for the full absorption of Kiev into the empire, and the subsequent Russification of the city, was in place.

• CHAPTER II •

The Growth of Metropolitan Kiev

ON HER WAY to the Crimea, Catherine the Great visited Kiev from January 29 until April 22, 1787. "From the time I arrived, I've looked around for a city, but so far I've found only two fortresses and some outlying settlements," she complained. "In all of these ruins of what they call Kiev, I can only think about the past grandeur of this ancient capital." Wrote another from Catherine's entourage:

> From a distance Kiev conveys great beauty. The green and golden cupolas on the bluffs are particularly charming, but that charm disappears when you enter the wretched place. The timber, the merchandise—everything that comes by water—has to be carted from Podol [Podil] to the high areas which often are without drinking water. Podol itself is deep in dirt; the streets are paved with planks and burn along with the houses when fire breaks out during dry spells. In Pechersk I saw a carriage pulled by a team of horses bog down in the mud, and another time a team of six horses could not pull a carriage from the muck. Pechersk has only one beautiful stone house, which was built by monks and now belongs to the state. The Palace in Kiev, at the Tsar's Garden, is beautifully sited, but it is built of wood and poorly maintained. . . . In winter the simple women of Kiev wear boots; in summer they walk about barefoot. At the slightest rain or thaw the city becomes impassable; in summer the dust is unbearable.[1]

Catherine was not without her prejudices, one of which was a great dislike for the urban poor, for she feared that municipal upheaval might undermine her regime. Kiev was full of poor people and beggars, and she appeared to see the city much as she saw Moscow, as "a seat of sloth," only smaller and less dangerous. Plague riots had occurred in congested Moscow in 1771. Thus, Catherine sponsored efforts to redesign the city with straight streets, great squares, and classical buildings. In cutting "official culture loose from its religious roots," Catherine "substituted the city for the monastery as the main center of Russian culture," in the words of James Billington. For Kiev this meant a general plan, drawn up in 1787 by Artillery-General Miller and Count Shuvalov, which sought to eliminate Podil and move its inhabitants to the high ground of Old Kiev and Pechersk, all in the name of military security, public health, and an end to incessant flooding. This assault on Podil was not implemented, and in 1797 it was still the site of the magistracy, twenty-six of Kiev's forty-six churches (excluding the Cave Monastery), and 40 percent of the city's 2,672 private homes.[2] In 1811 a great conflagration consumed much of Podil; as in Moscow in 1812, fire opened the way for redesign in Kiev.

More favorable was the view of another visitor, Prince I. M. Dolgorukov, who in 1810 called Kiev "a great, well-built city with many tasteful homes . . . and more than ten fashionable shops, music, and book stores including the 'Cabinet de lecture.'" Each house had three or four signs advertising its various workshops, he continued, noting that Gubarev's store in Podil, which had glass, china, bronzes, and "all kinds of surprises," was the equal to any shop in Moscow. "Don't come at Lent . . . when the city is overrun with pilgrims," he warned, "or during the Contract Fair when raucous Poles transform Kiev into a carnival."[3]

Gubarev's store was well stocked largely because the Contract Fair, held in Lviv until 1774 and then in Dubno, was brought to Kiev in 1797 by Paul I. Traditionally, Kiev had six fairs, three of which were considered important by the standards of the times. They occurred during the second week of Lent, in May, and in August. The Contract Fair brought together Polish landowners, Great Russian and Jewish merchants, Ukrainian ox-carters and peasants, Catholic priests and Orthodox monks, and a medley of soldiers and foreigners, and it quickly dwarfed the other fairs. According to one account, visitors choked Podil with itinerant dentists, Kazan soap boilers, Tula samovar smiths, Berdychiv booksellers, and hawkers of exotic delights from Persia, Bukhara, and the Caucasus. Matias came to peddle Albanian tobacco and eau de cologne, Zhorgo his new sweet-smelling soaps and dyes for graying hair. They were joined by Choko the vaudeville violin master; Gypsy bands and trained birds; pickpockets and prostitutes; an albino bear that did number tricks; and "bluebirds," the myriad con men and opportunists. Yiddish, German, Armenian, Tatar, and Turkish combined with Polish, Ukrainian, and Russian in an unusual cacophony amid a background provided by Jewish musicians playing wooden harmonicas. The fair began in mid-January and lasted for about three weeks. During these weeks, private homes were turned into shops, and sometimes into hotels, and the city's economy boomed.[4]

At the turn of the nineteenth century, however, Kiev still impressed visitors as being little more than three barely connected settlements,

1. Photograph of Podil taken from the Tsar's Garden probably in the late nineteenth or early twentieth century. Destroyed by fire in 1811, Podil was rebuilt with straighter, less congested streets.

2. Contract Hall in Podil. Site of the annual Contract Fair. Photo is from the 1870s.

3. Scene from the Grain Market near Podil harbor. Kiev's main market from the fifteenth century.

Podil, Pechersk, and Old Kiev, each "village-like" in appearance, each surrounded by earthen or wooden walls as if to underscore old functional distinctions. Said one visitor: "Kiev hardly deserves to be called a city at all."[5] After midcentury, no one would make this claim. Dramatic changes, particularly in the latter decades of the century, transformed the city. Commented one Pole late in the nineteenth century: "Whoever knew Kiev thirty years ago wouldn't even recognize it now."[6]

In 1797 Kiev had about 19,000 residents, although at fair time its population swelled to 30,000. By 1817 the city's population had grown by about 20 percent, to 23,514. The great fire of 1811 and the reduction of trade caused by the Napoleonic Wars slowed its growth. To underscore the fact that Paul I and Alexander I had reaffirmed Kiev's autonomy, a new magistracy hall was built of stone on the Dnipro bank between 1802 and 1808, along with a monument to the Magdeburg Rights. But state officials continued to complain about the city's inability to balance its budget and reduce its debt. Several commissions tried to bail the magistracy out of its financial quagmire, and a new property tax was levied in 1820. Kievans complained about the new tax, and about the high cost of quartering troops mandated by the state. In 1828, 3,593 Kiev homes were used to quarter 8,000 troops. When a new barracks was built, the city had to pay for part of its cost.[7]

The magistracy was further weakened by a twenty-year war led by a butcher, V. N. Kravchenko, who had tired of the local oligarchy's corrup-

4. As many as eighty thousand pilgrims came annually to the Cave Monastery.

tion and favoritism and of justice that "depended on who could pay the most." Kravchenko argued that for years the magistracy had not employed proper fiscal procedures and that discriminatory taxation was reducing the burghers to penury. The destruction of many records in the 1811 fire contributed to the confusion.[8] Not surprisingly, tsarist officials came to argue that only a state-imposed administration would bring financial order and administrative fairness to Kiev.

THE END OF MAGDEBURG AUTONOMY

Perhaps Tsar Nicholas I, who visited the city in 1829, saw Kiev as others had seen it, as a city notable for its blind, crippled, and poor, for its "terrible multitudes of the strange." Wrote a German visitor: "To the shame of the monasteries, the indigent sit on the streets of Kiev and everywhere else in the towns of Ukraine. Many could be earning their keep in workhouses. But a great number are blind; they ought to be cared for by the government."[9] The influx of countless pilgrims contributed to the large number of cripples and beggars in the city. Some, feigning poverty, came in order to take advantage of the charitable handouts by the monks and the pilgrims themselves. Kiev Academy students had also earned a reputation for skillful beggary, going from house to house with panegyrics, psalms, recitations, and short plays. This practice caused considerable conflict with the townspeople and began to disappear in the eighteenth century.[10]

Perhaps Nicholas I saw in Kiev the city described by Ivan Sbitnev:

Most of the huts are decrepit, whether in Pechersk, the Kreshchatik, or Old Kiev, and crowds of Jews greatly mar the appearance of the city. If you take away the great monasteries, the buildings at the fortress, the *gymnasium* [secondary school], and a score of private homes, Kiev is without significance. Only Podol can really be called a city. It's hard to believe that this populous place on such an important waterway, our ancient capital for so long a time, existing for fifteen centuries and visited by people from all over Russia, could look so bad. Khar'kov, six times younger, has greatly surpassed Kiev in its private homes.[11]

Ever since Alexander I visited the city in 1816, it had been rumored that St. Petersburg again wanted to enlarge the Pechersk fortress because of its strategic location relative to the Ottoman Empire and central Europe. In 1830 Nicholas I began that project, which was not finished until 1852, and which included an army hospital capable of handling eighteen hundred patients. As a result, new neighborhoods emerged on Pechersk's slopes, and the woods and ravines that separated Podil, Old Kiev, and Pechersk gave way to development. Kiev was beginning to fuse into a single urban community. Governor-General Wasilij Lewaszew (Levashov, 1783–1848) opposed further expansion of the city's garrison, and Nicholas no doubt listened, for he loved the city, became personally involved in plans for its beautification, and even thought about making it "a third capital." Between 1832 and 1852 Nicholas visited Kiev nine times.[12]

On November 23, 1835, purportedly in the interest of promoting Kiev's economic development, Nicholas I abolished the magistracy and the city militia once and for all. A new municipal council (duma) was introduced, and most of the old administrative positions disappeared. An imperial decree of March 8, 1835, had already offered Russian merchants a three-year tax exemption for resettling in the city. Governor-General Dmitry Bibikov (1792–1870), appointed in 1837, quickly became a commanding presence in Kiev. However, even though its ancient privileges disappeared forever, one can surmise that the city's more influential burghers continued to exert considerable influence in local affairs.

SUGAR TO THE RESCUE

Plagued by flood, fire, and political discord, Kiev was somewhat overshadowed in the early nineteenth century by Kharkiv, where a regional university had been founded in 1805. Kharkiv's fairs continued to grow very rapidly. In these decades its Khreshchenska, or Epiphany, Fair was the largest in Ukraine and the third largest in the empire. To the south, another competitor, Odessa, where a great port was built, drew a substantial portion of Ukraine's ox-cart trade. Of Ukrainian products brought to Odessa between 1858 and 1862, for example, 40 percent came from the Right-Bank lands near Kiev.[13] Later, from the 1870s, the developing rail network would further enhance the importance of Odessa and the Black Sea ports.

Economically, for Kiev sugar came to the rescue. Stimulated by short-ages resulting from the blockade of Russian ports during the Napoleonic Wars and by the subsequent decision of Alexander I to establish high protective tariffs, the empire's beet sugar industry burgeoned, and Kiev became its capital. Count Lev Potocki built the first sugar beet refinery in Kiev Province in 1834. By 1846 there were forty-nine refineries, twelve of them steam-powered; most were located on the estates of large landown-ers who supplied the capital, sometimes with the assistance of Jewish moneylenders.[14] By the mid-1850s, Kiev Province accounted for half of the empire's beet sugar production, and by 1860, 60 percent of all Ukrainian "workers" were employed in the beet sugar industry.[15] By the turn of the twentieth century, the offices of more than one hundred sugar enterprises had located in the city. In 1870 the city erected a monument to Count A. A. Bobrinskoi, underscoring the city's debt to the sugar industry.[16]

The sugar industry helped boost the importance of the Contract Fair, and the volume of fair trade continued to grow, doubling between 1842 and 1847. The fair gave a quick fix to the city economy every winter and enabled many local craftsmen to survive; yet it was never as important to the city's commerce as the great fairs were in Kharkiv, for example. In 1854 it required sixty thousand carts and wagons just to get salable prod-ucts to Kharkiv's Khreshchenska Fair! At least three of Kharkiv's four major fairs did more business than did Kiev's Contract Fair.[17]

Officially, Kiev grew from 23,514 in 1817 to about 29,000 by 1835, and 50,137 by 1845. During much of the year the population was consid-erably larger, however, for there were more than 13,000 permanently stationed troops and 40,000 summer trainees. An estimated 200,000 people visited the city yearly in the 1840s. Of that number, 50,000 to 80,000 were pilgrims (the number fluctuated in accordance with the qual-ity of the harvest), and 40,000 to 50,000 were Jewish traders who were allowed to stay in special quarters for limited periods of time.[18]

THE EMANCIPATION OF THE SERFS

Since death rates exceeded birth rates, virtually all of the growth resulted from migration. Even before the emancipation of the serfs in 1861, the surrounding area abounded in potential migrants. According to the fig-ures of N. N. Leshchenko, in Poltava Province one-half of the peasants owned by landowners were landless by the end of the 1850s. In Chernihiv (Chernigov) Province, the other Left-Bank territory bordering Kiev Province, one-third were landless. Throughout the region there were thousands more state-owned serfs who would not receive land in 1861.[19] During the first decade after the 1861 reform, no fewer than 600,000 people left annually in Kharkiv, Poltava, Chernihiv, Kursk, and Orel Provinces. Many went south. The Poltava zemstvo estimated that in the 1880s, 100,000 left annually to look for work, 150,000 by the beginning of the twentieth century.[20] Belarusians also migrated to the south in great numbers.

Records for Kiev indicate a population of 70,050 for 1861, only 68,424 for 1863, and 70,591 for 1870.[21] Assuming consistency in the method of census taking (the size of the population could fluctuate significantly from season to season, for example), these figures suggest that Kiev's population fell slightly after the emancipation of the serfs. The emancipation does not even warrant a reference in the history of the city written in the mid-1860s by Nikolai Zakrevsky. New neighborhoods had emerged, but nothing fundamental had changed in the city in the past thirty-five years, he contended. It still had the same charming hills, splendid churches, and zealous pilgrims; in its population, "simple-hearted Little Russians (Ukrainians)" (*prostodushnyi Malorusskii tip*) continued to prevail, and there were still the "indefatigable" Jews. "In short, Kiev is the most eternal of cities—our eternal Rome."[22]

The emancipation of the serfs did cause difficulties for enterprises that had depended on serf labor, particularly since there were few credit facilities to ease the transition to wage labor. Between 1860 and 1862, 130 beet sugar enterprises in the region closed down, including the respected Iakhnenko and Simirenko firm. Hard times were probably responsible for the short-term decline in Kiev's population. Kiev benefited from a quick resurgence in the sugar industry, however, and sugar production quintupled between 1863 and 1873.[23] By the census year 1874, Kiev had 127,000 people, but much of this growth appeared to come in the early 1870s with the building of the railroad.

NEIGHBORHOODS OLD AND NEW

Kiev continued to expand outward, and the open spaces between its historic districts filled in. Steam-powered machinery first appeared in the city in 1848 and was used in the construction of the chain bridge, designed by English architects and built between 1848 and 1856, Kiev's first modern and permanent bridge over the Dnipro. In 1856 most of the remaining city wall in Old Kiev was taken down. Bridges and paved roads brought the three main districts together; there were thirty-two wooden bridges in

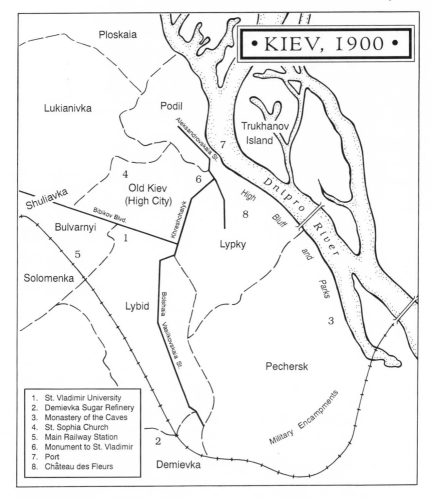

• KIEV, 1900 •

Ploskaia

Lukianivka

Podil

Trukhanov Island

Aleksandrovskaia St.

7

4

6

Old Kiev (High City)

Shuliavka

Bibikov Blvd.

Khreshchatyk

High

Dnipro River

Bluff

and

Parks

8

Bulvarnyi

1

Lypky

5

Solomenka

Lybid

Bolshaia Vasilkovskaia St.

3

Pechersk

Military Encampments

1. St. Vladimir University
2. Demievka Sugar Refinery
3. Monastery of the Caves
4. St. Sophia Church
5. Main Railway Station
6. Monument to St. Vladimir
7. Port
8. Château des Fleurs

2

Demievka

the city by midcentury, and the first stone bridge was constructed in 1847 in Podil.

By 1874 two outlying districts, Lybid (Lybed) and Ploskaia, each had more than 20,000 inhabitants. A few decades earlier they had consisted of sparsely populated farms and woods. Old Kiev, site of St. Vladimir University (founded in 1834; see chapter 3), and Pechersk each had nearly 20,000 people. Podil had 14,518 residents, followed by Lukianivka (Lukianovka, 9,806), Lypky (Lipki, 8,885), and Kurenivka (Kurenevka, 4,664). Ploskaia included the flatlands beyond Podil and the Obolone port. Sometimes called Meshchanskaia for the artisans who worked there, it had a large Jewish population. Cholera epidemics often began in

5. Spring floods were a frequent problem for low-lying areas. This photo was probably taken in Podil or Ploskaia.

this low-lying area. Lybid also had a burgeoning Jewish neighborhood. Along with Bulvarnyi (Boulevard) District, which would later grow from the main rail station to the Shuliavka factory district, Lybid was a good example of the city's outward growth. Lukianivka was named for a Podil guildmaster and began to grow after the great flood of 1845 forced many inhabitants to higher ground. Lypky grew between Pechersk and Old Kiev. Taking its name from the lime trees on its hillsides, it became the city's premier high-rent district. It was sometimes called Dvortsovaia (Palace) because the palace had been built there by Elizabeth I for use by the royal family during visits to Kiev. Outlying Kurenivka, named for the *kurin* (Cossack barracks) that had existed there until the eighteenth century, continued to be a largely rural area with a predominantly Ukrainian-speaking population. Other parts of the outskirts would soon be settled by railroad and factory workers, and would become centers of political unrest. They included Demievka (pop. 3,554 in 1874), Solomenka (3,910), and Shuliavka (2,003).[24] Shuliavka would become the headquarters of a radical workers' "republic" in December 1905.

Old Kiev and a new district called Novoe Stroenie, which connected Old Kiev with Lybid, grew rapidly, partly because of the growth of St. Vladimir University. Most of the owners of the 533 homes destroyed by the expansion of the Pechersk fortress between 1832 and 1846 relocated in these neighborhoods. On the other hand, Podil, victimized by flood, fire,

TABLE 2.1
Kiev's Electorate by District, 1902

	# *Voters*	# *Councilmen*
Bulvarnyi	221	5
Lukianivka	579	14
Lybid	647	15
Lypky	276	6
Old Kiev	817	19
Pechersk	162	4
Ploskaia, Kurenivka & Priorka	357	8
Podil	382	9

SOURCE: *Kievskie otkliki* (Kiev), December 2, 1905.

and the abrogation of the Magdeburg Rights, had lost its role as Kiev's main commercial and residential center. Although it was rebuilt after the great fire of 1811 with straighter, less congested streets, many of its inhabitants settled in other areas. The Contract Fair became much less important to Kiev's economy with the advent of railroads in the last third of the century, and the commercial potential of Podil was further restricted by the failure of the Southwestern Railway (or the city) to build a rail spur between Podil's river port and the main railway line.

Pechersk also declined in importance over the century. Some of its military buildings fell into disrepair and others were replaced by parks as the fortress grew less central to the life of the city. Shops moved away from Pechersk's Moscow Street, known in the 1840s for its Siberian furs and gems and considered by some the city's elite shopping area.[25]

The relative decline of Podil and Pechersk as centers of local economic power is reflected in the numbers of eligible voters for city council elections by district (table 2.1), for after 1892 the vote was given only to those with substantial income-producing real estate, residential, commercial, and industrial.

THE KHRESHCHATYK

With the decline of Podil and Pechersk, the Khreshchatyk (Kreshchatik in Russian)—built along a wooded ravine and creek favored by hunters, trappers, and anyone who could put up a distilling shack—became the commercial center of Kiev and one of Imperial Russia's most famous main streets. *Khreshchatyk* comes from a Ukrainian word meaning crossroad, and the Khreshchatyk was indeed a series of intersecting ravines. A creek ran through the main ravine. *Khrest* (Ukrainian) and *krestiny* (Rus-

6. View of Old Kiev (High City), ca. 1850.

7. Scene from the Khreshchatyk, ca. 1851.

8. Scene from the Khreshchatyk, ca. 1900. Note the electric tram and the horse-drawn cabs. The large marquee advertises a pharmacy that dispensed medicines for the university clinic. In front of it is a sign, "S. B. Shenfeld, Notary."

9. The National Hotel on the Khreshchatyk near the Bessarabka Square. Photo from 1906.

10. This 1888 engraving shows the hill-and-ravine terrain that characterizes much of Kiev.

11. Houses in Shchekavitsa District, 1888.

sian) also mean baptism, and one legend held that Grand Prince Vladimir baptized his twelve sons here.[26] The first wooden homes in the ravine were built in 1797. Around midcentury Ukrainian historian Mykola Kostomarov (1817–1885) lived on the Khreshchatyk, and his apartment became a meeting place for the Cyril and Methodius Society (see chapter 4). In the early 1880s wooden buildings with small restaurants and taverns, including the *krantsa*, the skittles alley where the city's German community congregated, still predominated, but four- and five-story homes with shops, many of them stone, were already going up. The Khreshchatyk came to be called "the only real street in Kiev," and, along with the great churches and monasteries, became the city's center of attraction.

Unlike the churches, however, the Khreshchatyk symbolized the modern. The best shops and the large department stores located there, as did the Grand Hotel and the European Hotel. In 1874–1876, on a part of the Khreshchatyk formerly known as Goat's Bog, the new city hall was constructed. A statue of Archangel Michael, Kiev's patron saint, stood on one of its towers. Other buildings that located there were the Merchants' Hall (which could accommodate one thousand people), the concert hall, the post office, and the Club for Polish Noblemen, built by Maurycy Poniatowski. The offices of the sugar magnates and the great banks that financed the city's growth also located on or near the Khreshchatyk. In 1868 Kiev had only one real credit facility, an office of the State Bank. That year the Kiev Private Commercial Bank and the Kiev City Mutual Credit Society located on the Khreshchatyk. They were followed by the Kiev Stock Exchange (1869); the Kiev Industrial Bank (1871); the Kiev branch of the St. Petersburg Industrial Bank and the Volga-Kamsk Bank (both 1871); the Kiev Land Bank (1877); the Mutual Insurance Society for Sugar Producers (1877); and the Kiev branch of the Russian Bank for Foreign Trade (1894). Gaslights appeared on the Khreshchatyk in 1872, electric lights in the 1890s. In 1897 it was still the only street in the city with electric lights. Cobblestoned in 1888, in 1892 it carried Russia's first electric tram to Podil. (Horse-drawn trams had first appeared in Kiev in 1869, steam-powered trams a few years later; both had difficulty coping with the city's hills, and Kievans had come to fear runaway trams.) In 1905, as Kiev's new symbol of commercial affluence and political influence, the Khreshchatyk became a center stage for public demonstrations.[27]

INDUSTRIAL KIEV

Kiev never became an industrial center like Moscow or St. Petersburg. Until the 1870s it had almost no large industrial enterprises. Peter the Great had established a silk mill, and the Arsenal had been built between

1784 and 1801 (with captured cannons and pyramids of cannon balls atop its walls) opposite the main gate of the Cave Monastery. In the first half of the nineteenth century, it manufactured ammunition and artillery mechanisms, employing about 700, mostly soldiers and serfs. Between 1809 and the 1830s the state also operated a cloth works in Kiev, mostly for the manufacture of canvas and army uniforms. In the 1830s leather and candle enterprises, financed by private capital, were founded in the city, and in the 1840s Kiev had eleven brick manufactories, the largest of which, the Eisman brickyard (founded in 1833), employed 150. Eight of the brickyards were privately owned; two were run by the state, and one by a monastery. The Dekhterev plant, the first great Russian enterprise lured to Kiev by the tax incentives provided by Nicholas I, was founded in 1836. Employing up to 250 during the summer, it made caldrons and presses for the sugar industry. In all, some seventy-three manufacturing enterprises employed about 7,000 Kievans at midcentury.[28]

In the 1870s and 1880s new factories quickly came to be the city's largest employers. The South Russian Machine Works, formerly Donat, Lipkovsky & Co., was initially built in 1858 and modernized in 1870. It produced cast-iron boilers for the sugar refineries, the distilleries, and the mills. The Pole Termen established a plant on Kuznechnaia Street in 1873 which produced a variety of products for these same industries and for the water, sewer, and steam heat lines that began to appear in the more affluent neighborhoods. The Termen plant was expanded in 1876 and renovated in 1887, and its owner would later develop the city's greatest brewery, importing its equipment from the famous Czech brewery at Plzen (Pilsen). Greter & Krivanek opened in Shuliavka in 1878, expanding in 1885. It produced machinery, mostly for the sugar industry, and sometimes built entire refineries. Along with South Russian, it would become the citadel of revolution in 1905.

The huge Alexander refinery in Demievka, built in 1868, was part of the economic empire of the Brodsky family. In 1880 the Pole Nicki built a mill on Kiev's Kirillov Street that made iron and copper caldrons and tubing for the distilling industry. Shantz, which made cast iron products and scales, located in Shuliavka in 1885. Baron M. B. Shteingel's sheet-metal works (1885) and the Polish mill Zarębscy & Felaner (built in the 1880s to produce milling machines) also deserve mention. By 1884–1885 Kiev had 104 enterprises employing 4,100 workers and a total population that exceeded 155,000. By 1897 it had 100 plants that employed at least 100 workers each. Large enterprises accounted for an estimated 72 percent of Kiev's industrial product and employed 60 percent of its workers.[29]

Even so, when compared with the capitals, Kiev could not be considered industrial. In 1897 Moscow had 153,200 industrial workers, and St. Petersburg 144,400. Riga followed with 32,600 workers; then came

Odessa (24,200) and Ivanovo-Voznesensk (20,900). Kiev, Kharkiv, and Iaroslavl each had slightly more than 13,000 industrial workers, and Tula and Rostov-na-Donu followed with about 10,600 each.[30]

COMMUNICATIONS AND TRANSPORTATION

Kiev's first postal service apparently opened around 1725, but its frequency of contact with the outside world is unknown. In the 1820s, when mail left three times a week, it still took about ten days for mail from Kiev to reach St. Petersburg. In 1835 Kiev's mayor opened a stagecoach line in Podil, offering mail and occasional passenger service to Moscow and St. Petersburg. Electric telegraph service with St. Petersburg and Odessa, and points in between, began in 1856, and continuous passenger stagecoach service to St. Petersburg began on the mail coaches in 1861.[31] Daily stagecoach service to Zhytomyr still existed at the turn of the twentieth century.

Far more significant, in 1869 Kiev's rail link to Moscow, via Kursk, was finished, and in 1870 the continuing link to Odessa was completed. In 1873–1874, amid cries that "the iron horse is devouring our forests," rail service was extended through Brest into Poland. In 1901 Kiev was linked with the Donets Basin to the southeast, and in 1902 with Kovel near today's Polish-Belarusian border. The main railway station was built in 1868–1870 (construction of a new station began in 1914 but was interrupted by World War I; the current station was built in 1927–1932). The Main Railway Shops, established in 1867, quickly became the city's largest employer.

Kiev's significance as a river port also continued to grow. By the 1840s, 2 passenger boats operating regularly on the Dnipro were bringing 108,000 people to the city or past it. In 1855 there were still only 6 steamers operating on the Dnipro. By 1882 that number had grown to 32, by 1894 to 194, at least 60 of which were run by the two Kiev steamer corporations. A new boat-building and repair facility was finished in 1873, employing 200. In 1883 steamers transported 304,614 passengers and earned 392,000 rubles in receipts. In 1893 they transported 1,209,804 passengers and earned 1.12 million rubles. Boat freight quadrupled in ruble value between 1869 and 1894.[32]

From the 1870s the nature and limits of Kiev's growth depended substantially on decisions made in the transportation sector. For example, early in the century the imperial government had built the Oginsky Canal connecting the Prypiat River (a tributary of the Dnipro) with the Neman, which flowed to the Baltic. The Prypiat was also joined to the Western Boh (Bug), the Berezina to the Western Dvina. But with the new commit-

12. The main railway station, completed in 1870.

ment to railroad building, the government found it unnecessary or financially impossible to further develop its water transport system. Though the technology was available to make the rapids below Katerynoslav navigable, this was not done, and the Dnipro's potential for cheap transportation was left largely untapped.

As a rail center Kiev was hostage to the government and the Southwestern Railway. It had a long shoreline and a natural bay at Obolone, which was used mainly for small boats and for the city baths. It was never developed as a major port, partly because its land connection was deemed too narrow and flood-prone. Furthermore, the Southwestern Railway never built a rail spur from the freight depot to the existing port in Podil, which meant that freight had to be carted by humans or animals over hilly terrain from rail to port, or port to rail. For items such as bricks, wood, and grain, this slow and expensive method of cartage added 7 to 15 percent to the price of the commodity. The Southwestern Railway also reserved the right to ship grain westward by the cheapest, most direct route. Kiev was bypassed, and the city's potential to become a major center for grain milling and wood products was never realized. Kremenchuk (Kremenchug), Katerynoslav, and even Cherkasy drew business away from Kiev, for they had rail depots close to their ports. The first two cities, consequently, became important milling centers.[33]

Kiev's merchants did petition the Ministry of Ways of Communication to build the spur and improve the port. In 1883 the ministry approved a plan to widen and improve the port at Obolone, and in 1889 authorized the Southwestern Railway to raise money for the spur and other needs. The military supported these initiatives, for Kiev could still be used as a mobilizing center for men and matériel should confrontations arise in the

Balkans or Central Europe. In her study of Odessa, Patricia Herlihy has argued that support of the military was politically important. She believes that no overall plan governed the construction of railroads, and that strategic, rather than commercial, factors often dictated rail routes. The Kiev-Odessa line, consequently, had a huge bulge that lengthened the distance by two hundred kilometers, and it actually became cheaper to ship grain from the Kiev region to Königsberg, in East Prussia, than to Odessa.[34]

Regardless of the army's support, a modern Dnipro port was not built in Kiev until 1899. During the First World War local entrepreneurs were still hoping that Kiev might become a major inland port, but by then hopes centered on the possibility that a projected canal from Riga to Kherson might be routed through the city.

Thus, Kiev's potential as a major milling and agro-processing center did not fully materialize. In the mid-1890s there were only two significant wheat mills in the city, the largest run by Lazar Brodsky, and seven rye mills, including one run by the state and another by the Cave Monastery. In 1894 Kiev had but three sawmills, one operated by the Cave Monastery; Katerynoslav had nineteen, Kremenchuk seven, Cherkasy and Kherson six each. Merchants from Briansk closed their warehouses in Kiev, for the railway system diverted the shipment of wood away from Kiev. A textile industry also failed to develop; cotton, linen, and woolen production remained concentrated in the small sweatshops.[35]

SELF-GOVERNMENT RETURNS TO KIEV

In 1846 a form of self-government was given to St. Petersburg, and voting rights were given to about seven thousand residents with property incomes of one hundred rubles or more. But the imperial government remained fearful of local initiative and public revelation of controversy, and thwarted efforts in the 1860s to publish an empirewide newspaper devoted to city and zemstvo affairs. In 1863 the St. Petersburg city council began to publish news from other cities, foreign and Russian, in its semi-monthly *Izvestiia* (News). A year later Odessa's council increased the frequency of its *Vedomosti Odesskogo gorodskogo obshchestvennogo upravelniia* (News of the Odessa city government) to three times per week and included complete transcripts of the sharp council debates. Kiev's city government subscribed to this publication. Also in 1864, Rostov-na-Donu tried to publish a paper that would address current issues and needs, but the state disallowed it, forcing the council to restrict publication to official announcements. Even so, and with fewer than a hundred subscribers, it remained the only newspaper in Rostov-na-Donu until the mid-1870s.[36] St. Petersburg, Odessa, and Rostov-na-Donu were the only city governments to publish periodicals until 1871, when they were joined by Kazan and Iaroslavl. The Moscow council did not publish a periodical until 1877, and Kiev did not follow suit until the 1880s.

Behind the scenes, debate over fundamental questions of local governance persisted. Who should participate in city government? Who should control the police? To what extent should cities be expected to finance the huge developmental needs of their burgeoning populations, not to mention the quartering of troops and other state needs? When the 1870 statute on municipal self-government was announced, it evoked great hopes, for city governments were given a great deal of local autonomy. State officials were to interfere mainly to determine whether a particular city regulation conformed to state law. But there were drawbacks; for example, city tax rates had to conform to rates set by the state, and cities could not independently institute new taxes.

Initially, the 1870 statute was applied to 45 cities, including Kiev. Gradually it was extended: to Moscow, St. Petersburg, and Odessa in 1872; to the Caucasus in 1874; and to the rest of Right-Bank Ukraine and the western provinces in 1875. By the time of the 1892 "counterreform," it had been extended to 621 cities. The franchise was based on payment of taxes; it provided for a small electorate subdivided into three curiae. Three percent of St. Petersburg's and Odessa's residents could vote, 4 percent of Moscow's, and 7 percent of Kharkiv's. In Kiev 3,233 residents could vote, and data for one early election indicate that 532 (less than 1 percent of the populace and 16 percent of the electorate) did vote.[37] Voting was by paper ballot (*shar*), and voters dropped their ballots either in a box to the right (in favor of a candidate) or in one to the left (against). This cumbersome process sometimes required days. In the first election in Kiev, the first curia was selected on January 4, while the third curia was not selected until January 22. The process was simplified when black ballots came to be used for negative votes, although the practice of voting separately for each candidate continued. If a black ballot was not deposited, a vote was registered for the candidate. *Peterburgskii listok* (Petersburg leaflet) noted that in one third-curia election, of 140 candidates whose names began with the letters *A* or *B*, only three got enough votes to be elected! Not surprisingly, about half of those who bothered to vote sent proxies to cast their ballots.[38]

Mayors were powerful figures under this system, and the office went mostly to merchants, industrialists, or "honored citizens" (designations given to prominent and affluent subjects). Kiev's first mayor was Petr Demidov, a factory owner who tried unsuccessfully to get the electorate broadened. Demidov was also known as Prince San-Donato, a title he inherited after the death of an uncle who owned the principality of San Donato near Florence. St. Vladimir University history professor N. K.

Rennenkampf, a nobleman who owned a home in Kiev and one thousand acres in Kursk and Chernihiv Provinces, followed Demidov as mayor. Gustav Eisman, of German extraction and the owner of a large brickyard, and the merchant Ivan Tolli, a descendant of Odessa Greeks, both extremely wealthy, held the office in the 1880s, as did Kiev Academy professor Stepan Solsky. Other mayors included the Pole Józef Zawadzki, Podil physician V. N. Protsenko, and Ivan Diakov. The anti-Semitic Protsenko presided over the "hooligan council" in 1905 (see chapter 8). The conscientious Diakov, whose leadership dominated city politics in the years before the First World War, once refused to cut off debate in a council meeting even after receiving reports that his house was on fire![39]

The 1870 statute excluded apartment renters from the electorate, thereby denying many of the community's most talented professional people the right to participate in city affairs. Merchants were favored in this system, and in Kiev and elsewhere they acquired a reputation for opposing developmental projects, especially if these involved spending large sums of money. Merchants and members of the State Council (the advisory body to the tsar that had existed since the days of Alexander I) predominated in the two upper curiae in Kiev in the 1870s. The third curia comprised at least seven professors (including the prominent historian Volodymyr Antonovych), three physicians, and six civil servants. Apparently no Jews were elected ("a big deficiency," said the local newspaper *Kievskii telegraf* (Kiev telegraph). Still, there was considerable optimism, and the paper expressed hope that the councilmen would defend rich and poor alike, and that streets in outlying districts would finally get paved.[40]

A decade later expectations had not been fulfilled. *Kievskii telegraf*'s successor, *Zaria* (The dawn) reported on June 11, 1881, that notwithstanding the seventeen professors among its members, the council had shown little interest in education or public health; it had accomplished nothing more than had the city council in Saratov, where a local newspaper had complained about the Saratov council's dearth of educated men. Yet, despite perennial revenue shortages, self-government did bring amenities to Kiev, albeit slowly. Privately owned water and gas companies were established in 1872. The council elected in 1887 proved to be particularly energetic. It sat for seven years because the changeover to a new electoral system in 1892 delayed the scheduled elections. Telephones appeared for the first time in 1888. (By 1900 there were 1,300 phone subscribers.)[41] An electrical utility was constructed in 1890, and electric lights were soon introduced in the better neighborhoods. Electric streetcars (the first in the empire) appeared in 1892. The council also rebuilt the city theater, and constructed a slaughterhouse, new public parks, and a storm sewer along the often-flooded Khreshchatyk. In 1892 it laid the city's first sanitary sewer lines. Sewers and other amenities boggled the

13. Andreev Slope just below St. Andrew's Church. Note the bulb-topped electric utility pole and the gaslights across the street.

minds of many a villager, whose countrified ways were targeted in the press, as in the case of the fictional bumpkin from "Tarakanovka" (Cockroachville) who came to Kiev during the Contract Fair "to do some hard drinking." Upon passing Kiev's sewage treatment plant, this innocent assumed it was an oil gusher, probably brought to the fair "by two Armenians from Baku." Told what it was, the astonished visitor replied that "in Tarakanovka our sewage just flows. They don't gush it out of a fountain."[42] Amenities, of course, were concentrated in the central high-rent districts of the city, for the outlying districts were too poor to be adequately represented.

MUNICIPAL "COUNTERREFORM"

Municipal self-government suffered a setback when the "counterreform" of 1892 further reduced the electorate's size while facilitating state officials' interference in city affairs. In 1902, with a population of about 319,000 people, Kiev had only 2,821 eligible voters. However, thirty-six of the seventy-eight councilmen elected in 1902 had some higher education. There were thirteen lawyers, eight physicians, seven professors, six engineers, four teachers, and seven military officers (six of them retired).[43] The main issues in this election were poor fiscal management and ongoing controversy over the lucrative contracts given to the privately held companies that provided water and electricity. Complaints that the horse-tram network had not been widened and that the *kanava*, the open drainage-sewerage ditch in Podil, had not been covered were also registered. The press called for the election of new faces, and one writer cited the defeat of Tammany Hall, "the dark forces, the Black Hundreds of New York," as evidence that change for the better could occur.[44]

It took at least ten days to get a new council elected, and only thirty-four of the eighty councilmen elected had served in the previous council (nine others had served prior to 1898). New faces did not mean a new sense of activism or commitment to reform, however, and Kiev continued to suffer from an absence of bold, energetic leadership. New York's new mayor was Columbia University president Seth Low. Kiev's was V. N. Protsenko, an anti-Semitic physician who would preside over the disintegration of city government in 1905.

Until the end of the Russian Empire in 1917, Kiev's city council was pilloried in the city's progressive press, often with good reason. In 1903 one columnist wrote: "Even *Birzhevye vedomosti* [The Stock Exchange news] in Petersburg is more interested in Kiev than is Kiev's city council." "The good half of our councilmen ought to resign on the grounds of incompetence, and the other half long ago should have refused the honor of sitting with them."[45] Judging from voter participation records, except in Riga and the smaller towns of what is now Latvia and Estonia, most municipal voters simply ignored city politics. Kiev's voter turnouts were, in fact, quite respectable when compared with those of other cities of the empire (table 2.2).

MUNICIPALIZATION AND MODERNIZATION

Between 1870 and the early 1900s, Kiev's annual budget grew steadily and impressively, from 200,000 rubles to more than 3,000,000 rubles. City officials boasted that while Kiev's population quadrupled between 1870 and 1905, its budget grew tenfold, and its per capita spending grew by 2½ times.[46] Yet as the tsarist empire drew to a close, Kiev seemed in poor fiscal health. About one-third of city expenditures continued to go toward meeting mandatory state needs such as police salaries and the cost of quartering troops. That Kiev continued to rely almost exclusively on private concessionaires to provide services and utilities contributed significantly to the city's financial difficulties.

TABLE 2.2
Voting Turnout for Selected Cities, 1900–1914

	Ukraine		
Berdychiv	1903: 30%	1907: 24%	1913: 36%
Kharkiv	1902: 23%	1906: 23%	1910: 35%
Kiev	1902: 45%	1906: 45%	1910: 59%
Mykolaiv	1905: 28%	1909: 29%	1913: 37%
	Other Areas		
Kazan	1905: 34%	1909: 40%	1913: 35%
Moscow	1904: 23%	1909: 43%	1913: 34%
Riga	1905: 79%	1909: 69%	1913: 87%
Samara	1905: 22%	1909: 32%	1913: 35%
Tbilisi (Tiflis)	1902: 23%	1907: 16%	1911: 38%
Vilnius (Vilna)	1901: 42%	1905: 40%	1909: 45%

SOURCES: Tsentral'nyi gosudarstvennyi istoricheskii arkhiv (TsGIA), *fond* 1288, *opis'* 5, *delo* 170, p. 135 (Kiev); *opis'* 5, *delo* 170, p. 152 (Berdychiv); *opis'* 25, *delo* 78, p. 173 (Mykolaiv); *opis'* 95, *delo* 77, p. 82 (Kharkiv); *opis'* 25, *delo* 41, p. 48 (Moscow); *opis'* 25, *delo* 24, p. 57 (Kazan); *opis'* 25, *delo* 56, p. 55 (Samara); *opis'* 25, *delo* 8, p. 76 (Vilnius, known then as Vilna); *opis'* 25, *delo* 36, p. 363 (Riga); *opis'* 25, *delo* 70, p. 31 (Tbilisi, known then as Tiflis).

In 1889 Kiev's council opened its own slaughterhouse, and the income from this enterprise enabled the city's budget to grow sharply. However, the council declined to move further in the direction of municipalization and, in fact, borrowed only 627,000 rubles between 1883 and 1898, mostly for street paving. Between 1898 and 1910, Kiev borrowed about 7,500,000 rubles for a variety of purposes, still a small sum for a city of that size.[47]

Comparative data for 1910 indicate that Kiev's per capita spending was the *lowest* of the empire's major cities, about half that of Odessa, Kharkiv, Saratov, or Baku, and less than one-third that of Riga, Moscow, or St. Petersburg (table 2.3).[48]

The issue of municipalization separated the "progressives" from the "conservatives" in city politics throughout the empire. Municipalized services enabled cities to determine how services would be provided, and at what rates, while enabling the municipalities themselves to realize the profit from these enterprises. Failure to municipalize carried a big price. In 1910 Mayor Ivan Diakov estimated that if the city bought its privately owned tram system, it could net up to 300,000 rubles annually, even after loan payments. In 1913 Kiev earned a paltry 55,000 rubles per year from its tram contract; Warsaw earned more than 1,000,000 rubles from its city-owned system! Kiev made nothing from its water utility; Warsaw

TABLE 2.3

Expenditures of Provincial Imperial Russian Cities in 1910 and 1913 (in Millions of Rubles) and Per Capita Expenditure (1910)

	Expend. 1910	*Expend. 1913*	*Population 1910*	*Per Capita 1910*
Baku	6.7	12.4	232,000	29.0
Samara	2.8	3.2	145,568	19.2
Saratov	3.9	5.4	217,418	18.0
Riga	6.2	8.2	370,000	16.7
Odessa	8.6	9.7	620,143	13.9
Kharkiv	3.3	6.0	244,526	13.5
Warsaw	10.2	14.9	781,179	13.1
Kiev	3.7	4.7	527,287	7.0
Tbilisi (Tiflis)	2.1	3.1	303,150	6.9

SOURCES: *Gorodskoe delo* 4 (1914): 202. 1910 population data are from Thomas Stanley Fedor, *Patterns of Urban Growth in the Russian Empire* (Chicago: University of Chicago Department of Geography, 1975), 183–214.

received 2,000,000 rubles. Kiev *paid* the privately owned electric company 129,000 rubles to light its streets; Astrakhan earned a profit of 67,000 rubles from its lighting system.[49]

Progressives also hoped to follow the European example and build staffs of professionals to solve municipal problems. Congresses of city officials were convened so that mutual problems and possible solutions could be discussed. The first congress was held in Odessa in 1910. Kiev sent three representatives, but the meeting was poorly attended because Odessa was in the midst of a plague epidemic. Moscow and Warsaw sent no one, and Riga's councilmen drew lots to see who would have to go.[50] In September 1913 Kiev hosted a ten-day congress, which was attended by nearly two hundred delegates and chaired by Mayor Diakov. The governor made sure the congress stuck to the narrow, preapproved agenda of fiscal issues. Those who tried to suggest ways to change the 1892 statute were accused of being "political," and police threatened to disband the congress if such matters were brought up. Thus, moderate and sensible proposals, to tax apartment renters and give them voting privileges, for example, were ruled out of order. One liberal spokesman from the Constitutional Democratic (Kadet) Party noted that it was permissible everywhere—*except* at the Kiev Congress—to recommend changing the statute. Branding the congress a complete failure, the progressive Moscow paper *Utro Rossii* (The Russian morning) published a lengthy parody of one of its sessions and warned that it reflected neither the needs nor the mood of urban residents.[51]

Finally, in 1912, Kiev negotiated to buy its privately run electric utility, although the two sides remained far from agreement on price.[52] In March 1914 the city municipalized its waterworks after two decades of struggle with the private water company. During the war Kiev's application to borrow money to purchase its tram network was approved. Borrowing money was difficult, however, and not only because of the war. By 1913 more than half of Moscow's budget of 48 million rubles came from city-run enterprises, and almost all of its debt had gone to finance productive and profitable enterprises. Moscow's bond issues, consequently, were attractive to investors.[53] Kiev had no such track record.

All of the empire's cities were handicapped by the fiscal and electoral limitations imposed by the 1892 statute, but Kiev ranked among the least successful in taking advantage of the opportunities that did exist. In 1913 Kharkiv, half the size of Kiev, earned five times more income from city-run enterprises than did Kiev. Kiev continued to rely heavily on property taxes for revenue; yet its property tax rates also ranked among the lowest of the empire's major cities. In fact, property taxes generated about the same amount of revenue in Kharkiv as in Kiev at this time.[54] City business in late-imperial Russia, it was said, was often "conducted blindly, unsystematically, and only occasionally with talent, honesty, idealism and sacrifice." Beyond that, Kiev's reputation was particularly notorious. Fiscally, its affairs were "surrounded by scandal."[55]

THE RIVER: THE LIFE AND DEATH OF THE CITY

Because local politics were controlled largely by fiscal and political conservatives who refused to establish citywide municipal utilities and expand the city budget accordingly, progress in the area of public health was not as rapid as it might have been. The ongoing controversy over the quality and quantity of water remained the central public health issue right up to 1917.

At least as early as the sixteenth century, the Dnipro was regarded as an unhealthful source for drinking water, and Kievans drank home-brewed beer or bought spirits at one of two taverns owned respectively by the city and the Polish Catholic bishop. The Cave Monastery began to pipe water (apparently from wells) in the seventeenth century, and Podil soon followed suit. In the eighteenth century, the city laid wooden water conduits and assumed the burden of maintaining wells. Data for 1874, however, indicate that only 147 homes were supplied with piped water. Water sellers continued to be common on Kiev's streets in the final decades of the nineteenth century.[56]

Writing in 1902, A. N. Gusev described Kharkiv's sluggish Kharkiv and Lopan rivers as "rivers of mold," which at times were covered with thick layers of green vegetation or "a green, bubbly slime." Kharkiv's *Iuzhnyi krai* (The southern region) echoed that the rivers and streams in the countryside were becoming just as foul.[57] The Dnipro at Kiev probably looked and smelled better than Kharkiv's rivers. It was wider and deeper, and its current was faster. Officially, Dnipro water was regarded as potable, except during floods, and, since wells frequently went bad or dry, many Kievans continued to drink it in addition to water from smaller streams and springs. In 1887 a newly established sanitary commission relieved the police of some of the burden for supervising public health, but it moved slowly, recommending only in 1907 that people be prohibited from using water directly from the Dnipro.

During the intervening years, the progressive faction in the city council battled the privately owned water company in a largely unsuccessful effort to get it to lower its rates, construct a better filtration system, and extend its lines to the outskirts. The water company hid behind the very advantageous terms of its contract with the city, arguing that it was not legally obligated to improve or extend service. At times complaints about water quality and shortages flowed to the city council almost daily. Even amid the revolutionary upheavals of 1905, protesting homeowners appeared with a bottle of drinking water described as "reddish yellow sewage [*zhizha*]." Claimed one: "Horses stand and look at it for a long time and accumulate great thirsts before drinking it."[58] Nevertheless, the majority in the city council continued to favor cheap water instead of pure water.

After the cholera epidemic of 1907, the city decided to rely entirely on artesian wells as its water source, but the water system did not reach many of the outlying districts. In March 1914, when about 40 percent of Kiev's residences still lacked running water and some schools had to close periodically because of shortages, the city council bowed to pressure from the state and resolved to buy the water company, though it failed to act on another proposal to build an auxiliary system to use river water for fire protection and sanitary use. Paris and Vienna had built similar systems, and one Kievan noted with sarcasm: "Kiev certainly is not Vienna, but its residents do want water."[59]

ILLNESS IN KIEV

Epidemics are as much a part of history in Kiev as they are elsewhere in the world. Between 1348 and 1351 bubonic plague appeared in the city, although the details of its impact are unknown. Polish sources record at least forty-six major epidemics in the sixteenth century, most of them probably typhus. Plague reappeared in the seventeenth century. People abandoned the city during these epidemics in favor of the forests. Famine often followed epidemics, wars, or shortfalls in the harvest. Pantiukhov writes that in 1282, 1283, 1312, 1315, 1319, 1440, and 1570, hunger was so intense that instances of cannibalism were recorded.[60]

Organized health and welfare services in the eighteenth-century Russian Empire were spartan at best. However, because of Kiev's growth and the heavy influx of religious pilgrims, Catherine the Great's Little Russian College resolved to build a hospital and a botanical garden for medicinal herbs, and to move the pharmacy that had been operating in Lubni (Lubny) to Kiev. The army brought in its own medical personnel, but civilian Kievans often relied on itinerant Hungarian traders for medicines. The only alternative was the folk cures of "*baby* [old women] quacks." In 1764 there were two "frontier doctors," presumably paid out of public funds, and several private physicians in the city. The absence of good roads and bridges between Podil, Pechersk, and Old Kiev made delivery of medical care difficult, and at times impossible.

Supervision of public health was largely in the hands of the police. City policemen were in charge of cleaning the streets, for example, but only the most important streets were maintained. A request in 1786 to buy twelve pair of oxen, presumably to pull the cleanup carts, was rejected for financial reasons. Ikonnikov notes that streets were cleaned, bridges were repaired, and drunks were quieted mainly when a visiting dignitary was scheduled to appear in the city.[61] Epidemics continued to be a fact of life. Of 600 prisoners under guard in Kiev in 1768, almost all died of unnamed causes in a thirteen-week period. In 1770–1771, when plague struck, the main burden fell on the army doctor Lerkhe. According to official data, 3,631 of the approximately 20,000 inhabitants died, and the epidemic nearly produced a riot. An almshouse for families victimized by illness was founded in 1771. Subsidized partially by the city and partially by private charity, it housed about 75 indigent Kievans in the 1780s. Kiev's first city cemetery was also founded after this epidemic (previously people were apparently buried in land owned by monasteries and churches).[62]

In 1833 Governor Lewaszew established the Office for Public Care, the same year that the Society to Assist the Poor was founded. A mineral water facility was built in 1834, and the city opened two shelters for homeless children in 1845. The presence of a large garrison in Kiev was a mixed blessing. The military brought equipment and expertise to its hospital, which was opened in the 1830s and equipped to handle 1,800 patients, but in 1826–1828 and 1831, for example, outbreaks of particularly bad epidemics were associated with the movement of troops into the city.

For the period for which I have data (through the 1870s) deaths generally exceeded births, meaning that the growth of the city came entirely
from migration. In 1851–1855, for example, 10,674 were born, while
15,054 died. In only one of these years (1852) was the number of births
and deaths about the same. The number of births remained steady during
the five-year period, fluctuating between 2,084 and 2,164; but the number of deaths fluctuated between 2,106 in 1852 and 4,254 in the cholera
year of 1855.[63] As was true elsewhere, child deaths accounted for much
of the mortality. Children between the ages of six months and one year
were particularly at risk because at that point the child was weaned. In
the 1830s, of every 100 deaths in Kiev, 32 were of children under one;
another 17 were of children between one and five. Thus about half of all
deaths were of children under five. Between 1867 and 1870, children
under five continued to account for 47 percent of all deaths in Kiev.
Smallpox and scarlet fever were particularly dangerous killers of children
at this time.[64]

Toward the end of the nineteenth century, Kievans benefited from the
development of the germ theory of disease by Louis Pasteur (1822–1895)
and the application of this theory by the German bacteriologist Robert
Koch (1843–1910), the Englishman Joseph Lister (1827–1912), and others. The advent of municipal self-government in 1870 provided the opportunity for practical application of this new knowledge. St. Vladimir
University's medical faculty and clinics greatly enhanced the quality of
medical care in the city, and a rapidly increasing literacy rate and advances in educational opportunity late in the century helped raise public
awareness of health issues. Thus, the number of epidemic victims declined
on a per capita basis toward the century's close, but epidemics continued
to afflict the poorer parts of the city.

Cholera epidemics, first recorded in Kiev in 1830–1831, broke out twelve
times between 1830 and 1872. Pantiukhov implies that up to 15 percent
of the city population died from these outbreaks, but his data do not seem
to support this figure. For example, during the bad epidemic of 1848,
1,798 of the city's 52,000 inhabitants got the disease, and 931 (52 percent of them) died. This figure represents only 2 percent of the city's population. In 1831 perhaps 4 percent of the populace died of cholera.[65]

Early nineteenth-century Europeans were unaware that impure water
contaminated by human waste was the primary source of the disease. In
1830–1831, Kievans were warned not to eat fruit, especially if it was
spoiled or unripe. Plums, gooseberries, and mulberries, as well as mushrooms, were said to be particularly dangerous. Police checked the bazaars
for suspect fruit, and Kievans were warned, more wisely than anyone

realized, not to consume unboiled drinks except vodka, especially after eating fruit or salted fish.[66] Cholera death rates ranged from two or three per thousand during mild epidemics to thirty per thousand in 1848, twenty-five per thousand in 1844, and twenty-one per thousand in 1855, the three worst years. In 1871–1872, the last epidemic years recorded by Pantiukhov, the death rates were about twelve per thousand. In 1848 death rates in the poor, congested Kudriavsko parish were eight times higher on a per capita basis than they were in the more affluent hilltop parishes in Lypky and Old Kiev.[67]

From the early 1820s through the 1870s, smallpox epidemics occurred in Kiev about two years out of every three. Cholera epidemics brought more fatalities, but smallpox was a consistent killer, perhaps accounting for 6 to 9 percent of all deaths in the city during these years. Fatalities were sometimes fifteen times higher in Ploskaia than in Lypky. Typhus also raged, often decimating groups of pilgrims. During one epidemic in May of 1866, 529 were hospitalized with typhus in various city medical facilities, while another 234 were sick in facilities owned by the Cave Monastery.[68]

Syphilis, described in fifteenth-century Polish and sixteenth-century Russian sources, was also a major public health problem. A home for victims of venereal disease was built in 1787. In 1847 there were 1,680 reported cases of syphilis in the city, and 990 related deaths. In the 1870s an estimated one-third of all Kievans suffered from venereal disease.[69] Rightly or wrongly, criminal acts were sometimes blamed on the effects of syphilis. One example was the case of the nobleman Grebnev (a member of the notorious Union of Russian People), who had returned from Ufa to Kiev, where ten years earlier he had killed a railway official. In 1907 Grebnev killed a woman and then himself, "splattering blood and brains about the apartment. Advanced syphilis was blamed."[70] Another consequence of advanced syphilis was blindness. Famed St. Vladimir surgeon Vladimir Karavaev ran an eye-disease clinic for more than forty years that attracted patients from throughout the empire. Subsidies from a local merchant enabled the eye clinic to operate during the summer when the university was closed, and in 1886 Shuliavka Street was renamed after Karavaev.

PERSONAL HYGIENE

We know little about the hygienic habits of Kievans, but anecdotal evidence suggests that the level of personal hygiene was not high. In the 1880s imperial administrators complained that residents were throwing human waste into the streets along with "soapy water" (bath and wash water for clothes and dishes). The city council not only declined to address the issue, it lodged its own complaint—against the administration! Newspapers sometimes complained about the poor state of local public bathhouses. Although I could find no information on Kiev's baths, one newspaper reported from Kharkiv in 1881 that the five local commercial baths were in such bad shape that "residents go only out of habit," particularly on Saturdays and before big holidays when it was almost impossible to get in. The baths were open only during warm weather and used foul river water, but for most they remained the main alternative to the summer's "heat, dust, and filth." The importance of bathing in clean water was stressed by the paper, which concluded that the "skin, lungs, kidneys, and digestive tract all work in close harmony; as soon as one of these organs grows lazy, for whatever reason, pressure is inevitably put on the other organs." The Dutch were cited as a people who had learned that personal cleanliness *and* hard work, accuracy, honesty, and "purity of morals" went hand in hand. Paris, which had four thousand baths by 1850, was cited as a model of hygiene well beyond the wildest dreams of urban Russia.[71]

Kiev's first sewerage system was completed in 1892 by private concessionaires. It served the central neighborhoods; outlying districts remained without this expensive improvement. Untreated sewage continued to be pumped into the Dnipro. In 1907–1908 the city borrowed money to extend the sewers and constructed a new sewage field below the city, which unfortunately threatened to further foul the water for those who lived downstream.[72] Calling in vain for massive infusions of spending on public health and sanitation, and declaring the urgent need to educate the public about such matters, one reformer noted with resignation: "Meanwhile, we can only wait and die." During epidemics newspapers instructed readers to "boil water, take baths often, and disinfect clothing." Said one writer: "It is not surprising that Kiev is famous for its scandalous lack of sanitation, nor is it surprising that our death rate and incidence of illness is greater than that of any other Russian city."[73]

The journalist Sergei Iaron suggested that the practice of bathing together in the Dnipro, apparently common in the 1880s, had disappeared by 1910 because public morals had changed. The fouling of river and stream that accompanied the growth of industry and population may also have contributed to this change. On the eve of the First World War, the city council was still squabbling over whether to cover open sewerage ditches in heavily populated areas. All too common was the attitude of Councilman Iasnogursky: "Why should we worry about cholera when all around us we have plague, diphtheria, scarlet fever, and syphilis."[74]

HOUSING

After the great fire of 1811, the burning wooden splinters formerly carried for light gave way to candles surrounded by hurricane lamps, and then to oil lamps. Tallow candles were made locally and used for night-time lighting, and in 1840 a stearin candle manufactory was established by the German Finke. Kiev remained a predominantly wooden city, however, although old photographs reveal that many houses had a kind of exterior plaster. In 1845 there were only 281 stone or brick houses in the city, compared with 4,040 wooden houses. Another 1,374 wooden houses sat on stone foundations, and 174 homes had a stone first story and a wooden second story. In 1845 Kiev had eighty streets and thirty alleys. About thirty of these roads were at least partially paved (with stone or wood), mostly in Pechersk and Podil. Although Podil was rebuilt after the fire, it remained among the most congested and least sanitary parts of the city.[75]

Fire proved to be the most consistent counter to congestion, for Kiev never experienced the systematic slum clearance and urban redesign that dramatically transformed midcentury Paris, for example. The fact that the city had many open spaces to absorb its growing population also helped in the battle against crowding, but many of late-imperial Kiev's inhabitants appear to have been poorly housed. Rapid population growth drove rents upward and created great differences in the cost of living among the various city neighborhoods. In the 1870s an apartment cost 410 rubles a year on average, a room 85 rubles. These figures were said to be 20 to 35 percent more expensive than those for St. Petersburg. Rents for apartments in Lypky averaged about 850 rubles per year, those in Old Kiev 690. Rooms cost about 120 rubles per year in either district. Thus, much of the population was driven to the outlying neighborhoods such as Ploskaia or Lukianivka, where yearly rents averaged about 150 rubles for an apartment, 45 rubles for a room. These areas had virtually no services or amenities and were ravaged by epidemics.[76]

Data compiled by a local physician around the turn of the twentieth century indicated that 3 percent of Kiev's population lived in basement apartments, most of them damp, dark, and unhealthy, and that one-room worker's flats typically housed 4.6 people. Rents often consumed 30 percent of a worker's wage. The city had the legal responsibility to combat contagion but seldom did so. In 1902 the city council had twenty-six committees, but not one was intended to deal primarily with welfare or social services.[77] In mid-1903 the council established a committee to investigate basement apartments, but it may never have met. In January

1905, a couple of days before Bloody Sunday, it was noted that of all the council committees, only two dealt with the problems of the poor: the Committee on Doss Houses and Cheap Apartments, and the Committee on City Pawnshops. Neither had met a single time in 1904! The council did discuss basement apartments in May 1904 but buried the issue in committee.[78]

Committees of public care called *popechitel'stva* were established in 1902, but a 1904 editorial alleged that thus far, "society has paid them little heed," in part because volunteers received too little recognition for their efforts. Some *popechitel'stva* were successful: in Old Kiev one raised two thousand rubles for a child shelter and a doss house, but in some parts of the city, as in heavily Jewish Lybid, the poor viewed the *popechitel'stva* "with fear and mistrust." What was needed, it was argued, was fresh blood and a new spirit of volunteerism.[79] A 1912 account reports that five child shelters were operating in the city, the first of which had opened in 1875, but they served only 356 children. The shelters were supported by N. I. Greter, N. A. Tereshchenko, and other industrial magnates, and helped children learn bookbinding and bootmaking. Child shelters received little support from the city council and relied heavily on revenue generated by the Merchants' Club lottery. They suffered a blow when, in 1912, lotteries generating more than fifteen hundred rubles were made illegal.[80]

In 1904 a columnist for *Kievskaia gazeta* bemoaned the problems with syphilis, scarlet fever, diphtheria, and typhus, pointing out that the victims were mainly poor, "crowded into basements and corners, especially in the outskirts, where epidemics often begin." Even in the city proper, along the tracks, there is still a place "where they dump excrement, garbage, and every conceivable kind of junk, all of which is enveloped in a great stench. It attracts stray dogs and children who are lured by the junk and the prospect of finding a kopeck."[81] Inadequate municipal funds contributed to these problems, but so too did the absence of an ethos that viewed public welfare as a priority concern for city government. Many of Kiev's wealthy and prominent residents gave generously to charitable causes, but these same affluent voters saw the church and the private charities—not the organs of municipal government—as the rightful purveyors of welfare services.

Rapid population growth, the fiscal and electoral restrictions of the 1892 counterreform, the financial limitations of the state as a whole, and a generally unconcerned and inept imperial leadership beginning with Nicholas II (1894–1917) all contributed to Kiev's problems, which appeared to some to be worsening as the insurrectionary year 1905 approached. Rightly or wrongly, in 1904 *Kievskaia gazeta* cited the city council as the single most important cause of Kiev's rising cost of living, which was "conservatively" estimated at 10 to 15 percent over the past five years. In order to keep taxes on real estate low, the council raised taxes on trade, including bazaar stalls; the resulting price increases hurt the poor.[82] Unresponsive to basic issues of human welfare, in 1905 city government would condone a pogrom and essentially disintegrate.

SOME CONCLUSIONS: CONTINUITY AMID GROWTH

Late-imperial Kiev had all the signs of a boom town. Many of the open spaces and much of the greenery, so noticeable a generation earlier, disappeared as the city grew haphazardly, with little order or harmony. Some houses were set close to the streets, others were set back at various distances. Street paving was generally done by the German method of setting stones in concrete, as asphalt was deemed too expensive. By the 1870s about one-third of the streets were paved, but Kievans continued to complain about the condition of their streets and bridges. In 1910 one city council faction justified its paving expenditures with the argument that, according to midwives, walking and riding along rutted streets and bridges were "major sources of female ailments."[83] Congestion and sprawl aptly describe late-imperial Kiev, but the natural beauty of its hilltop vistas and splendid churches had not been diminished. As one Polish count put it, the city's "disorderly" character had a kind of artistic quality to it.[84]

For all the growth, however, the city's economic structure changed little over the century. Late-imperial Kiev was a major rail and water transport center, but overland and river trade had always been important to the city. In 1900 Kiev's economy continued to be driven by the needs of the region's agriculture, particularly sugar, and by small workshops producing consumer items, much as it had been decades earlier. Fancy shops and department stores were appearing on the Khreshchatyk, but small traders and craftsmen still predominated in the city. In the 1890s, 3,700 permanent retail stalls and kiosks were operating in the city's nine major bazaars.[85]

The educational sector, long a driving force in Kiev's economy, expanded substantially. The 1892 statute had charged the municipalities to oversee the development of public education, but the exact responsibilities of the cities, as opposed to those of the state, remained unclear. In 1908 the state began to provide subsidies for the salaries of elementary school teachers. By 1911 Kiev, which had had virtually no primary schools a century earlier, had 139 elementary schools of all types, although fewer than half were publicly funded. In 1914 primary school attendance reached 14,000, but another 11,000 children were either denied enrollment for lack of space or chose not to attend.[86]

Secondary education also grew very slowly over the century. Eight *gymnasia* for men and women enrolled only 3,677 pupils in 1895 (at a time when Kiev had 240,000 residents). After the 1905 revolution, the number of secondary schools grew rapidly, mainly because the new spirit of reform had encouraged women to seek an education. Almost all of the new secondary schools were privately funded, however. Higher education continued to contribute mightily to Kiev's culture and economy. Although the Kiev Academy had lost its influence as a center of learning in the late eighteenth century, St. Vladimir University, founded in 1834, enrolled about 2,300 students in 1895, 5,300 in 1915. By the advent of the First World War, there were ten institutions of higher learning in Kiev, with a total enrollment of more than 15,000. Aside from St. Vladimir, the largest were the Commercial Institute, with 4,000 students, and the Polytechnical Institute, with 2,300. Some forty institutions, most of them private, taught everything from stenography and accounting to foreign languages and midwifery.[87]

Perhaps the decline in the relative importance of the Pechersk garrison represented the main long-term change, for Kiev's economy was no longer geared to the needs of taming the steppe or defending the empire against Cossacks and Poles, Tatars and Turks. Kiev was no longer a frontier outpost.

Many improvements occurred in the nineteenth century in public health and medical care, but many pressing problems remained. Enforcement of hygienic standards continued to be haphazard and was attempted mainly when officials, having heard about epidemics elsewhere, began to worry that contagion might spread to Kiev. The Sanitary Commission, established in 1887, stopped issuing reports in 1898. Property owners feared that their findings might force the implementation of rudimentary plumbing codes and other expensive improvements. In 1904, although the city mayor was a physician, V. Protsenko, and several councilmen were doctors, the Sanitary Commission, by now consisting of "one old sanitary physician" and four assistants, was allowed to dissolve.[88] By imperial standards, Kiev had plenty of physicians (one per 701 inhabitants in 1904, compared with one per 837 in Moscow and Odessa, and one per 3,175 in nearby Zhytomyr),[89] but the city continued to be short of hospital beds. Aside from the army hospital, four small hospitals had provided only 268 beds in the 1860s. In 1875 the municipal Alexander Hospital was built, and the total number of available beds in the city reached 723. About half of the 190 beds at Alexander were free of charge. Complaints appeared in the press about the ignorance and ineptitude of hospital personnel; some were said to be "rough to the point of cruelty to the sick."[90]

THE CITY AS FORTRESS

In his study of the nineteenth-century Russian city, Daniel Brower observes that the introduction of public health measures moved Russia's cities

> from the category of "Asian" city, where epidemics raged uncontrolled . . . closer to the "cities of light" of Western Europe. . . . Municipal public works, in other words, were part of a progressive agenda shaped by Western models of the city. . . . The heightened concern for local needs was the product of a new awareness of the public interest, increasing respect for scientific discoveries in such areas as public health, and the threat that mass urbanization posed to public order.[91]

Science and self-government did indeed make Kiev less Asian and more European, if by Kiev one means the historic central districts. The outskirts were left out and, in fact, were seen as places to dump problems that had surfaced downtown. In the early 1870s the council discussed a proposal to build a special "suburb" that would serve as a holding area for Jews without residence permits. The community would have its own water supply, hospital, slaughterhouse, markets, and parks. Pilgrims could also be detained here, for they were regarded as a particularly dangerous "source of infection and disorder." Although nothing was done, the idea resurfaced frequently.[92]

The lower classes were also encouraged to move to the outskirts. In rejecting a request by a worker's artel for free land so that private homes could be built, Councilman Dobrynin acknowledged that while home-ownership might reduce drunkenness, since Kiev was "a city of 300,000, 200,000 of them poor," the council could hardly afford to set a precedent by giving away land. "Let them look outside the city for land," he concluded.[93] During a 1904 typhus epidemic, which was blamed on hunger and cold, and on the fact that the city's water supply still did not have proper filters, Councilman P. A. Zalevsky revived the idea of a holding area in the outskirts, telling the council that "only people who can pay for their apartments and feed their children should be allowed to settle in Kiev." Maybe "a Chinese wall" could be built around the city, one newspaper replied sarcastically, but Zalevsky's idea drew some attention. The doss houses could be moved out of town, he suggested, in order to create a "plague barracks" (*chumnoi barak*) for the teeming migratory masses.[94] Complaints about brothels also brought suggestions that they simply be moved to the edge of town.

Meanwhile, the outskirts continued to be virtually unrepresented in the council because of the property qualification required of voters, and some districts remained for years in unincorporated limbo. Demievka's petition to join the city was rejected by the Ministry of the Interior in 1904. By then it had twenty industrial enterprises and 20,000 people. Hilly Solomenka, where many railway workers lived, was annexed in 1907. In 1910 it had but two recognizable streets. Garbage, collected only during half of the year, filled its ravines. In 1913, when the city population as a whole surpassed 600,000, Solomenka's 30,000 inhabitants had only three schools serving 350 children; they had no doctor, hospital, or organized medical service. Hooligans shut down the community at night.[95] During the cholera epidemic of 1907, an angry resident of Shuliavka's partly annexed factory district asked whether authorities "even knew where Shuliavka was."[96]

The affluent who controlled the local power structure saw the older, central districts of Kiev as a kind of fortress, barricaded against the mounting problems of the poorer outskirts. This attitude, and the glaring inequities between advantaged and disadvantaged neighborhoods, must have given visible reinforcement to socialist rhetoric on class oppression, adding tensions to a city that had already experienced ethnic conflict fueled by Polish nationalism and by the Judeophobia which was deeply imbedded in the culture of Kiev and Ukraine.

· CHAPTER III ·

Polish Kiev

AT THE TURN of the nineteenth century, "politics" in Kiev revolved primarily around attempts by various guilds and burgher factions to defend parochial economic interests against one another, while staving off further encroachments by the Russian state. During the course of the century, however, national consciousness and conflict grew increasingly important as determinants of the political climate of the city, as they did elsewhere in the Russian Empire and Europe. Poles were the first to challenge authority, and their discontent came to dominate local politics until the insurrection of 1863. Largely as a result of Polish insurrectionism, the imperial government tried to Russify Kiev and the surrounding region. During these same decades, the age-old question of whether Jews could reside in Kiev also surfaced with a vengeance. In the 1790s a Jewish community took root in Kiev, only to be expelled in 1827. From the 1860s, however, it would grow rapidly, and Jews would be horribly victimized by pogroms in 1881 and 1905. Around midcentury the Ukrainian national movement began to become an irritant to the Russian state. Although the Ukrainian cause came to be centered in Habsburg Lviv, Kiev became the most important center for Ukrainian cultural and political activities in the Russian Empire.

It is important to note that not every issue came to be viewed through the prism of national consciousness. National aspirations helped fire the upheavals of 1905, but they were not the main source of those disorders, at least in Kiev. As the twentieth century progressed, however, national issues would become increasingly important to the politics of Kiev and Ukraine, and it is therefore useful to examine Kiev's ethnic communities and their aspirations in the period under study. Because Poles had considerable influence in Kiev and Right-Bank Ukraine in the early nineteenth century, and because their aspirations resulted in upheaval, I will turn my attention first to the city's Polish community.

In the sixteenth century Polish kings saw Kiev as a fortress against Moscow, an outpost for the further rooting of Catholicism, and even as a kind of model frontier community. Craftsmen and merchants were encouraged to settle there. After Poland lost Kiev to Russia in 1667, Polish influence in the city diminished but did not cease, for Kiev remained the most important outpost on the Russo-Polish frontier. After the partitions of Poland and the creation of Kiev Province in 1796 out of Right-Bank Ukrainian territory formerly held by Poland, flamboyant Polish noblemen frequently came to Kiev, "noisily" electing their provincial officials in a private home (probably in Pechersk, where the Polish magnates tended to live) inscribed with "Dworzańska kommissja" (Noblemen's Committee) in huge golden letters. Poles owned most of the land in Right-Bank Ukraine and assumed most of the local offices. In 1812 there were 43,677 Polish noblemen in Kiev Province, compared with only 1,170 "Russians" of noble or civil-servant rank.[1] Polish landlords often wintered in Kiev, and some of Warsaw's finest families also had homes there. One example of Polish economic power in Kiev at this time was Count Branicki, a landowner and sugar magnate who owned Kiev's largest grain and flour warehouse, a four-story stone structure built on the river.

Virtually all of the landowners in Right-Bank Ukraine visited Kiev each January in order to attend the Contract Fair, held in and around Podil's Contract Hall, which was designed by the Pole Andrzej Melenski (1766–1833), Kiev's most important early nineteenth-century architect. Table 3.1 provides one breakdown of the fair's visitors. Most of the landowners who frequented the fair were Poles, for even in 1861, on the eve of the emancipation of the serfs, 87 percent of the landowners in Kiev Province, 89 percent in Podil (Podol) Province, and 93 percent in Volyn Province were Polish. As much as 90 percent of the arable land in the Russian Empire's new southwest region belonged to Poles.[2]

TABLE 3.1
Visitors to the Contract Fair

	1835	1846	1862
Landowners, nobility	944	1,597	1,357
Merchants	78	118	287
Foreigners	39	115	130
Jews	1,656	1,731	1,805
Servants (*prislugi*)	1,936	3,486	3,905
Groomsmen, drivers, smiths	3,813	10,130	7,100

SOURCE: V. S. Ikonnikov, *Kiev v 1654–1855 g.g.* (Kiev: Imperatorskii Universitet Sv. Vladimira, 1904), 199.

Some noblemen came to strut, for the fair provided the supreme opportunity to display the latest European fashions or simply the pride and arrogance befitting a count. Money poured into Kiev. Count Mieczyslaw Potocki paid four thousand rubles just to rent a wooden home for two weeks.[3] Great balls were held twice a week, often for charity, and it was not unknown for a Polish gentleman to purchase a glass of champagne with a hundred-ruble note. At one Polish haunt, Ogniwo, hundred-ruble notes were hurled down as ante in card games. All-night orgies began at wealthy Polish homes, or at the Grand Hotel or the Hotel François (owned by the Pole Gołabek who had transformed a small confectioner's shop into a fortune). At midcentury they often ended with a sleigh-ride to the chain bridge.[4] Wealthy Russians and Ukrainians may have conducted themselves in similar fashion, but the impression left is that during the Contract Fair Poles from the countryside were a singularly raucous bunch.

Poles wore their national dress and danced the mazurka, and it was said that they sometimes clashed with local "Russians." The extent to which flamboyant Polish behavior caused hard feelings in Kiev is hard to gauge. Sometimes clashes resulted simply from the fact that civilians were required to quarter soldiers in their often-cramped homes. In any case, local distress was surely assuaged by the huge amount of income generated by Polish spending. Ikonnikov notes that when a rump Polish state, the Duchy of Warsaw, was created in 1807, the "mood" of the regional Polish nobility became more militant,[5] and the bizarre panic that followed the great fire of 1811 reflects the character of the ethnic tensions that began to mount.

THE GREAT FIRE OF 1811

The fire began on July 9 in an open area near the Grain Market. Church bells from around the city sounded alarms, but the fire spread rapidly and Podil soon became an inferno. Many perished as thousands watched its destruction from the bluffs above. Soldiers began to plunder. The historian Zakrevsky remembers "our house on Black Dirt Street being filled with soldiers and rabble [*chern*] in rags. They raided our larder, carrying off cans of preserves and other foods, smashing up dishes, brawling. . . . In a matter of minutes our larder and cellar were empty. Then they went after our furnishings. Soon we had nothing left except for a few things my father had managed to hide." After they left, fire consumed the house. "It was like the panic in the chronicle when the Mongols came."[6]

The fire burned out of control for three days, leaving only a small neighborhood beyond the drainage canal unscathed. Police quickly rounded up several Poles, Jews, and Frenchmen, blaming them for the fire. Rumors of gangs of arsonists were fanned by the alleged appearance of a letter, written in verse, threatening further damage. When Tsar Alexander I formed an investigative commission, rumors expanded in scope and number, and what had been half-believed now became gospel. "Fables, formerly unthinkable, grew like mushrooms after a rain," as one adventurer after another came forth to tell his own dramatic tale. A certain David Molenko claimed he had captured two Great Russians and two Jews with incendiary powders in a nearby forest. The four "confessed" that they were part of a gang of five thousand arsonists financed by Frenchmen and Poles and led by three colonels dressed as women. Molenko was arrested for spreading false rumors.[7] In mid-August three more fires occurred, but investigators who had arrived from St. Petersburg on August 12 attributed them to human carelessness, the usual cause of fires in the city.

In September a Volyn nobleman calling himself Paul Trzszałowski "confessed" that he was part of a gang that had set more fires in and around Kiev than he could remember. The group was headed by a Polish general with lots of money to hire Poles, Jews, Tatars, and Germans to carry out its evil deeds, he insisted. It was a fear that the gang members were hirelings of the Duchy of Warsaw, or of France itself, which convinced St. Petersburg to establish another investigative commission, this one headed by Lieutenant-General Ertel. After failing to catch the conspirators, who supposedly wore bits of green cloth so that they could recognize one another, Trzszałowski changed his story, supplying new names and details.

Kiev "became an armed camp." Cossacks demanded that homeowners build chimneys in their huts and remove their stacks of hay. Locals were expected to detain anyone who looked suspicious. Since frontier Kiev was full of runaway serfs and army deserters, there were many potential detainees, but Jews and Tatars were particular targets. Antonio Rio, an Italian merchant who for years had sold prints and paintings throughout the region and who in fact had been given burgher status in Zhytomyr, was accused of being Anton, the infamous German arsonist and gang leader. Fortunately, he was sent to Kiev, where many merchants recognized him. Catholic priests were also suspect, and the witch-hunt continued until it was overshadowed by a new panic in 1812 caused by the burning of Smolensk and Moscow in the struggle with Napoleon.[8] Not one of Trzszałowski's alleged arsonists was ever caught, and Trzszałowski turned out to be a nineteen-year-old former brewery worker and army deserter, Pawel Grodski. Another self-confessed leader of a gang of Polish arsonists, Szymon Kowalski, also turned out to be a fraud and was allowed to escape punishment by joining the Russian army.

INSURRECTION AND THE CONTRACT FAIR

From 1816 Pavel Pestel, S. G. Volkonsky, M. F. Orlov, and others met frequently in Kiev and won considerable support for their ideals among local soldiers and the region's nobility. The famous poet Alexander Pushkin (1799–1837) participated at times in this conspiratorial activity, some of which took place at Kiev's Green Hotel. In 1818 Polish noblemen helped organize the Masonic Society of the United Slavs in Kiev. It apparently had about seventy members, although hundreds of Poles made contributions to it while in Kiev for the Contract Fair. Hoping to unite Polish and Russian Masons, the society had as its insignia a cross with the Polish inscription "Jedność Słowiańska" (Slavic Unity).

In 1821 the secret Southern Society was organized. Between 1822 and 1825 it met at the Contract Fair, thrashing out its republican program, which included the emancipation of the serfs and the equality of all before the law. Representatives of the Northern Society also came to Kiev to conspire, and the insurrectionists came to see St. Petersburg, Moscow, and Kiev as the most important targets for seizure. Since Poles and Russians from far and wide had an excuse to be in the city at this time, the Contract Fair provided the perfect conspiratorial cover.

National issues were discussed as well. In 1824 Colonel Seweryn Krzyżanowski (1787–1839) came from Warsaw to meet with Russian conspirators to discuss various Polish goals, and in 1825 Prince Antoni Jabłonowski conducted similar talks with Russian dissidents at the fair, but no agreement was reached. Thus, when Alexander I died unexpectedly in December 1825, Russian "Decembrists" rose unsuccessfully, and without significant Polish help. Although members of the Chernihiv Regiment rose in a nearby village, Kiev itself remained quiet. In an effort to save his land, Jabłonowski betrayed the others, and Krzyżanowski was tried for treason. A few years later, Poles would use the Contract Fair to help organize their own revolt.[9]

Thus, although Poles probably did not constitute more than 10 percent of Kiev's population at this time, Russian nationalists came to view the city as a den of Polish insurrectionism and its fair as a "convention spot" for revolutionaries. Nationalists accused "Jewish contrabandists" of bringing insurrectionary literature to the fair and argued that the southwest region had become so "Polonized," petty noblemen had come to see themselves as Poles even though they could not speak Polish. The response to Polish political activism came in the form of "intensive Russification," which, in the view of one Polish historian, began around 1818.[10]

THE POLISH CONTRIBUTION TO EARLY
NINETEENTH-CENTURY EDUCATION

The tsarist government had done little to develop educational facilities in Ukraine, relying instead on church parishes to teach basic literacy skills. Kiev's first "people's school" (*narodnaia shkola*) had opened in 1789 in Podil, offering five levels of instruction. German, Latin, physics, and architecture were among the subjects that advanced students could take. In 1791 it had 164 pupils, including 33 girls, although girls could apparently enroll only in the lower classes where reading, writing, and religion were taught.[11] Thus, Poles took much of the initiative in developing educational facilities in Right-Bank Ukraine. One indication of Polish importance in local education came in 1787 when the Kiev Academy received the right to open a print shop at the Cave Monastery. Its first publication, in 1791, was a Polish grammar.[12] Under the influence of Tadeusz Czacki (Chatsky, 1765–1813), Poles founded about 150 schools in the region between 1803 and 1813. Born in Volyn Province, Czacki attributed the "ignorance and low standard of living" in the Right-Bank towns to the absence of educational opportunity. In Kiev Czacki was disturbed to find that many students knew Polish poorly, if at all, and lacked access to Polish books. The children of Kiev's more prosperous families were often tutored privately, usually by Germans, or sent to Uman or Kaniv (Kanev) for their education.[13]

In 1806 a three-class district school was opened in Podil, and on January 30, 1812, with great fanfare (and a 101-gun salute), Kiev's first *gymnasium* opened as well. It offered a four-year course with an additional and optional preparatory year. Regional noblemen contributed heavily to the school, which soon acquired a reputation for quality. By 1828 it had 119 students; in the 1840s its enrollment fluctuated between 250 and 350. Polish was its language of instruction, although German, French, Russian, Latin, and Greek were also taught. Poles dominated its student body, and textbooks, supplied by the Ministry of Education or by the universities at Kharkiv and Vilnius, were all in Polish.[14] Basic literacy could also be acquired at one of Kiev's thirteen Orthodox church or monastery schools or at one of its private schools. In 1812 the British-sponsored Russian Biblical Society opened a branch in Kiev. It sought to "educate" prisoners, the blind, and Jews, among others. But until the 1830s, aside from the church schools, education in Kiev seemed to be largely Polish in sponsorship.

INSURRECTION AGAIN

Influenced by the success of Greek revolutionaries in winning their independence from the Ottoman Turks, and by Louis Philippe's successful revolt against the Bourbons in France, Poles rose again in November 1830. In Warsaw rumors circulated that the Russian tsar might use his armies to crush uprisings in France and Belgium, and on February 5, 1831, in the midst of a strike in Warsaw against factory conditions, a Russian punitive force attacked the agitated Poles. "By this act, a local rebellion was transformed into a national war."[15] It lasted for 325 days.

The Polish historian Leszek Podhorodecki argues that "a great part" of Kiev's inhabitants supported or were sympathetic to the uprising, but I could find no evidence either confirming or refuting this view.[16] Another Polish historian, Jan Tabiś, observes that a number of Kiev's "academics"—presumably *gymnasium* students and instructors—joined the revolt, a fact that must have reinforced Nicholas I's belief that a *Russian* school system had to be developed in the southwest region, headed perhaps by a flagship *Russian* university in Kiev.[17] One Pole recalled that among Kievans, "there reigned a sense of excitement unseen anywhere else."[18] Polish newspapers published false rumors that Kiev's Poles had taken the city and its fortress, and that city mayor G. I. Kiselevsky flew Polish flags from the city walls awaiting the arrival of Polish troops. In reality Warsaw was the center of the rebellion, and Polish magnates in the Kiev region seemed to be caught unprepared. In Kiev proper, Kiselevsky seems to have mobilized the city militia against the possibility of Polish attack. It patrolled the city and its outskirts but saw no combat, for apparently there was no uprising in the city in 1830–1831. Soon to be abolished by Nicholas I, the militia was twice honored for its efforts and zeal.

If nothing else, the Polish Insurrection of 1831 underscored the absence of a strong *Russian* culture in Kiev and the surrounding region. Kievans relied on Polish calendars, published in Berdychiv. These did list Russian holidays but, at least until 1829, used the Polish orthography. Ukraine's publishing industry, such as it was, was concentrated in Kharkiv. Between 1805, when its university was founded, and 1815, some 210 books and pamphlets were published in Kharkiv, and the journal *Ukrainskii vestnik* (Ukrainian herald), which included articles on a variety of subjects, was also published there from 1816 until its suppression in 1819. There were no locally published journals in Kiev in the 1820s. Even the Kiev Academy did not publish its moral-spiritual *Voskresnoe chtenie* (Sunday reading) until 1837.[19]

Ivan Sbitnev recalled the flaming patriotism of the Polish nobility, their despotism within their homes, and the charm, gentility, and beauty of their wives. "In general they were affable and devout, with a high standard of morality." But nationalists such as Shulgin, claiming that a single absentee Catholic bishop from western Ukraine owned 6,200 serfs and about 115,000 acres of land in Kiev Province alone, accused the Poles of seeing "the peasantry not as people but as things, and treating them as colonial slaveholders would."[20] Thus, the insurrection of 1830–1831 and the image of the Pole (and the Jew) as exploiters made it easier for Nicholas I to move ahead with plans to Russify the region in administration, finance, and language.

In 1836 the region's most important bank, the Polish bank in Berdychiv, was closed, and in 1840 the Kiev Commercial Bank, a Russian bank modeled after the Commercial Bank branch in Odessa, was opened. Kiev's mayor was to be selected from among the Great Russian merchants who were lured south by tax incentives. But the most dramatic changes came in education. In 1836 a second three-class district school and a second *gymnasium* were established in Kiev. Russian replaced Polish as the language of the schools. Governor-General Lewaszew remained sympathetic to the local Poles, and in 1838 established a school for 200 daughters of impoverished regional noblemen, but overall some 245 schools in the region were closed (only 19 remained open), and the university at Vilnius was closed except for its medical-surgical course.[21] To create a Russian counterweight to Polish influence, St. Vladimir University was opened in Kiev in 1834.

THE FOUNDING OF ST. VLADIMIR UNIVERSITY

The first petition for a university in Kiev came in 1764 as part of an attempt to regain ancient rights for "Little Russia." Petitions also came in 1765 and 1767 from gentry and Cossacks, partly because Kiev Academy had lost its egalitarian character and had become a staunchly Orthodox institution.[22] A new movement to create a university in Kiev began around 1802 but came to nothing. It was proposed that the lycée at Kremianets (Kremenets, Krzemieniec), which was closed after the Polish Insurrection, be moved to Kiev, but Lewaszew argued instead for the creation of a new institution for the training of civil servants. A commission was set up in 1833, and Nicholas I decided to found a university.

14. St. Vladimir University ca. 1845. Note the open spaces.

Until 1842 the "university" was scattered in buildings throughout the city. Since one of its main functions was to train civil servants, St. Vladimir initially comprised faculties of philosophy and law, and political reliability was an important consideration in hiring decisions. A medical faculty was added in 1841; medicine would become its forte during the nineteenth century, and German professors from Derpt (Dorpat University, now Tartu in Estonia) would come to predominate there. In the early decades academic standards were not high, and faculty accomplishment was modest. Earning a doctorate, however, was a cumbersome process. Doctoral theses had to be defended in front of academics and the literate public. In its first thirty years, St. Vladimir gave only forty-two doctoral degrees, twenty-eight in medicine, and forty-four *magister* (master's) degrees. Faculty were given broad authority except in budgetary and police matters. They elected the rector and deans and had responsibility for curricular and personnel decisions.[23]

Out of necessity St. Vladimir's draft statute permitted instruction in Polish and the creation of a separate chair in Catholic theology. However, St. Vladimir was to be a *Russian* university, and Polish was apparently taught only until 1836. Although initially the university had to rely heavily on Polish academics, many of whom were well-known scholars, all but one were released in 1839. From that point "Russian" professors predominated. Of the 129 faculty who taught between 1834 and 1863, only 23 were Poles, 76 were "Russians" (no distinctions were made between Russians and Ukrainians), and 25 were Germans. Most of the Poles came from the upper nobility, reflecting Nicholas I's hostility to the lower gentry. In area of origin, 38 professors came from ethnically Russian provinces, 51 from Ukraine (33 from the Right Bank, 18 from the Left Bank), 14 from the Baltic lands, 2 from the Kingdom of Poland, 1 each from Belarus and Galicia, and 11 from foreign countries.[24] On the other hand, Poles would continue to predominate in the student body for decades. In 1856, 413 of St. Vladimir's 806 students were Catholic (overwhelmingly Polish), 336 were Orthodox (Russian and Ukrainian), 33 were Jewish, and 13 were Protestant.[25]

Polish secret circles existed at the university virtually from its beginning. In 1836 *Stowarzyszenie Ludu Polskiego*, the Polish National Union, had about 46 members. In order to avoid decimation by betrayal, it subdivided into eight small groups so that most members knew only a few of their brethren. "Faith, hope, and love" was the slogan of these moderates, whose organizational headquarters seems to have been the boarding-house for students run by Piotr Borowski.

Conspiratorial activities intensified with the arrival of Szymon Konarski (1808–1839). His Young Poland movement sought to stir revolutionary fervor with support from local peasants without waiting for problematic backing from other European states. Under Konarski's leadership, the organization spread into the army. The group survived various arrests, but in 1837 a Kiev student denounced it, and Nicholas I came to Kiev. Of the 274 students at the university, 251 were expelled and many were forcibly inducted into the army. St. Vladimir was closed for one year, reopening in September 1839 with a new student body. Kiev's Polish professors were removed; Professor Aleksander Mickiewicz (1801–1871), brother of the famous poet Adam Mickiewicz (1798–1855), for example, was transferred to Kharkiv. The ever-vigilant Nicholas came again in 1839, but St. Vladimir was turned over to the lazy Prince S. I. Davydov from 1839 until 1845. Known for his penchant for drawing heads on scraps of paper, he took little interest in university affairs.[26]

It is impossible to know how many of those arrested in Kiev were actually revolutionaries. Some had participated simply out of a love for reading and studying Polish. Others were attracted because Polish culture was under siege in Kiev. Konarski's group gave underground seminars in the history of the Polish national movement and offered assistance to political prisoners passing through Kiev on their way to Siberia. Kiev's Poles did have a secret library that got clandestine literature from France through the Kiev booksellers Lauron and Mieville. This underground library was very popular and helped students maintain their skills in literary Polish at a time when the language was under attack. One should not overestimate the extent of Polish influence or activity in Kiev, however. The regional headquarters of the Polish conspiracy was in Berdychiv, and not in Kiev, for Berdychiv had fewer Russian officials and soldiers. Tabiś notes that purely local efforts to organize Kiev's Poles had failed, and that without the help of outsiders like Konarski, a large Polish organization in Kiev would not have developed.[27]

THE ORDERLY KIEV OF DMITRY BIBIKOV

The leading spirit of Kiev in the Nicolaevan era was its governor-general, Dmitry Bibikov, appointed to that office in 1837. Having lost an arm at Borodino, Bibikov was remembered by Count Tadeusz Bobrowski as a man of great poise with a keen sense of humor. He could also be "brutal, cynical, and unscrupulous. In every Pole he saw a potential revolutionary."[28] Weary of Berdychiv's reputation as the favorite meeting place for Poles, even from distant Galicia and Poznań, and its legendary card games that attracted Poles from far and wide, Bibikov took direct control of this "nest of conspiracy" in 1844, eliminating its "indulgent authorities," "unruly assemblies," and its "disorders." Bibikov read (but could not speak) French and German, and had an avid interest in the region's history and archaeology. The works of his subordinate, the scholarly Ivan Funduklei (1804–1880), appointed Kiev's governor in 1839, remain among the most important sources for the city's and the region's history for the first half of the nineteenth century. Having accumulated great authority, Bibikov served as the region's governor-general until 1852, when he became minister of internal affairs. Reluctant to forcibly Russify the Poles, he believed that the poorer Polish nobility would gradually become Russianized if not coerced. In 1852, however, he directed all noblemen eighteen and older who were not Orthodox and whose parents owned fewer than one hundred serfs to serve either in the Russian military or in state service in a Russian province. Prominent Polish noblemen were also sent into service in Great Russian provinces and taxed heavily if they refused.[29] From the time of Bibikov onward, public business in Kiev was conducted in Russian. At midcentury Poles continued to hold many regional offices, speaking Polish among themselves but using Russian in official business.[30]

Bibikov was obsessed with order and cleanliness, and police were given more enforcement authority in Kiev than in other cities. They often patrolled in fives—three on foot, two on horseback. They maintained order

15. Dmitry Bibikov, governor-general of Kiev from 1837 until 1852.

and ensured fair prices in the bazaars. Seletsky recalls that "thievery and robbery were extremely rare in Kiev. One can say this was unprecedented. Kievans enjoyed complete security." Recalled another from the 1840s, at eleven o'clock at night Kiev was "quiet as a cemetery."[31] Not all agreed that Kiev was this quiet and safe, but Bibikov's authority and concern for order at least created that impression.

The temporary closing of the university in 1839 reflected Bibikov's insistence on enforcing standards of proper behavior at all educational levels. "Barracks rules" and corporal punishment for minor offenses prevailed. The gentlemanly arts of dancing and gymnastics were included in the educational regimen, and Bibikov cruised about the city with two Cossacks in search of students improperly attired or found to have buttons missing. In January 1843 students were prohibited from appearing in public places after ten o'clock at night, except for theaters, concerts, and the major social clubs. Students were forbidden to enter any drinking establishment except for the tavern at the Contract Hall and were disciplined for making too much noise in the theater, for yelling "Vivat mazury" and "Vivat Krakowiak" (references to Poland's beloved Masurian Lakes and Cracow), for excessive gambling (1851), and for demonstrating against one of their colleagues (1853). Forty different kinds of punishment were prescribed for students, including birching. Political offenses could mean five hundred strokes. A punishment cell with bread and water was used in extreme cases; students could be sent to the cell for up to eight days.[32]

Who were Kiev's students? Recalled one:

> The Poles were slim and gracious, dandies with their cocked hats, thin, turned-up mustaches, and self-assured gait. The Jews, sharp-featured, moved quickly and stuck close together. They spoke quietly, but with animated gestures. Some, from wealthy homes in Odessa, wore massive golden chains. Their distinct Russian accent made you uncomfortable. The Little Russians were hefty, well-built, strongly featured people who spoke in loud, animated national speech. They laughed loudly, were a bit rude, even cynical. There were only a few Russians, and they kept to the background. Poles predominated, then Little Russians, then Jews. Polish was the predominant language. Many of the students, whatever their nationality, were well-washed, slicked-down aristocrats with English haircuts, stylish narrow pants, and French accents. Exactly opposite was the well-tanned democratic element who wore shabby suits and old hats but no gloves. A different breed, the seminary students were serious, austere, and kept to themselves.[33]

Unimpressed with St. Vladimir, the Russian nationalist Shulgin reported this conversation between a newly arrived Bibikov and a Polish magnate:

> "Votre Excellence! j'ai l'honneur . . . " (the magnate begins).
> "Chto vam ugodno?" (What can I do for you?), Bibikov replies.
> "Votre excellence . . ."
> "Chto vam ugodno?" (I speak only Russian.)
> "Mais . . ." (But I don't know Russian . . .)
> "Then how do you speak to your peasants?"
> "Well, with them we use the *muzhik* [peasant] language."
> "Well, with me you use that same *muzhik* language. I am Russian just like your peasants. As they speak, I speak."[34]

Duels and orgies remained much in style at midcentury. Recalled one student about life at St. Vladimir:

> I remember sometimes
> Merchants calling me at midnight
> Wanting to beat me up.
> But I beat the hell out of one,
> And cracked open another with a bottle.
> Like a madman, he staggered for a long time.
> I returned home, beaten but triumphant.[35]

A legal Polish annual, *Gwiazda* (The star), published once in St. Petersburg and three times in Kiev between 1846 and 1849, asked that students end their wastrel ways and take a more serious attitude toward political and social issues. It presaged the so-called Purist movement, which would culminate in the 1863 insurrection. Many of these more serious-minded students had come from the *gymnasium* in Minsk, and in 1846–1847 some of them organized a group that supported agrarian reform, political democracy, and insurrection. The year 1848 brought revolution throughout Europe, and in Kiev calls for liberating the city "from the grip of the vile Tatar Bibikov," a reference to Bibikov's proud claims that he descended from Mongols. At least one hundred villages in Kiev Province experienced disturbances in 1848, but these remained localized and calm was maintained in Kiev and throughout urban Russia.[36]

In 1846–1847 Taras Shevchenko (1814–1861) and others formed a circle to pursue the ideas of Mykola Kostomarov, who had recently been given a chair in history at St. Vladimir. From this effort emerged the Cyril and Methodius Society, discussed in chapter 4. Said one student:

> We were the only secret organization at the university. We were divided into the aristocrats and the poor. Whatever their nationality, the aristocrats were interested mainly in having a good time. The poor imitated them. The Poles loved to talk about Poland, read Polish books, and nourished a secret hope that the great Polish kingdom would be restored. As a group they had no unity. Smaller in number, the Little Russians [Ukrainians] read Little Russian books and loved to recall the Hetmanate, but that was about the limit of their political activity. The Russians stuck mostly to their studies. There was little unusual about them. Kiev students tended to be more interested in psychology and billiards than in politics.[37]

The organization had perhaps one hundred members, mostly from St. Vladimir, and was predominantly liberal and Pan-Slavic in spirit. Only a few of its members (notably Shevchenko) were proponents of revolution, and Tabiś gives credit to Poles and their contact with European politics for these revolutionary stirrings.[38] For all the emphasis on order and proper behavior, local authorities often winked at student rowdiness, viewing it as an outlet for youthful energy that might otherwise be turned to politics. Bibikov, in fact, once told the university's medical students: "Dance, gamble, and chase women, but do not involve yourselves in politics." Such a dictum, of course, only served to challenge the more militant students, especially the Poles. One *gymnasium* student recalled that students did not divide along national lines but instead found solidarity in a common hostility toward the university administration, Bibikov, and the authoritarian Russian state.[39]

Given the objectives of Nicholas I, Bibikov was an ideal official, and Kiev remained one of Nicholas's favorite projects. Besides founding St. Vladimir and expanding the fortress, he established the Kadet Corps, a military school, in 1852, and linked the city physically with the Left Bank and the Russian lands beyond by building the chain bridge across the Dnipro. In 1887 the city council authorized the erection of a monument to Nicholas on Nicholas Square across from the university. Alleged damage to this monument would figure heavily in the "justification" for a pogrom against the city's Jews in October 1905.

On the other hand, neither Bibikov nor Nicholas succeeded in pacifying Russia's Poles, who occupied a sensitive geographical position in an empire that from midcentury found it increasingly difficult to defend itself against the rapidly developing Western European states. In the aftermath of the Crimean War of 1853–1855, Alexander II became convinced that concessions would have to be made to this restive population in order to avert an uprising. The Polish Medical Academy was thus reopened, Poles still in Siberia as a result of the 1831 insurrection were amnestied, and the views of Polish landowners were solicited in the debate over how best to reform the institution of serfdom. Reinforced, perhaps, by the knowledge that change was possible, Poles throughout the empire again began to organize, and ultimately the authorities panicked. During a crackdown, five demonstrators were killed in Warsaw in February 1861. One hundred more would die in April. Further concessions were offered. Labor service for Polish peasants was abolished in 1862 in favor of money payments. The Main School in Warsaw began admitting students into its medical, mathematics, and philosophy faculties. But with the spirit of revolt in the air, Count Aleksander Wielopolski (1803–1877), head of tsarist Poland's civil administration, decided to conscript thirty thousand young Poles into the tsar's army on the assumption that as soldiers of the tsar, they would have little opportunity to organize a revolt. The so-called *branka* (conscription), scheduled to take place on January 14, 1863, catalyzed the Poles to action. Thousands of resisters led the formation of guerrilla units that would keep the Russian army at bay for sixteen months.

KIEV'S ROLE IN THE 1863 INSURRECTION

In 1858 Kiev's political winter began to thaw with the appointment of the surgeon Nikolai Pirogov (1810–1881) as the superintendent of the Kiev educational region. Having served in a similar capacity in Odessa for twenty years, Pirogov had become convinced of the need to humanize the educational system and eliminate its most coercive features. As his liberal views were implemented, one Pole asserted that "Polish political life moved to Kiev virtually in its entirety."[40] While this statement probably exaggerates the city's role in the Polish insurrectionary movement, the student body at St. Vladimir University was still composed predominantly of Poles, and the atmosphere at the university was changing.

In October 1856 an organization calling itself "The Purists" formed around the Polish student Fortunat Nowicki (1830–1885). Its publication *Bigos* (Sauerkraut stew) poked fun at the raucous lifestyle of the rich students. The Purists held benefit theater and concert performances, particularly during the Contract Fair, raising money to assist poorer students. Illegal literature found its way to Kiev, especially through Odessa, where Polish conspiracy could flourish amid the crowds of foreigners. The ideas of Alexander Herzen (1812–1870) were particularly influential at this time, and thousands of his essays were hand-copied.

Town-gown relations were one source of hard feelings. In 1856, after fights between students and army officers left a Polish student dead, a certain Colonel Brinken stopped a student in the street and slapped him in the face. Outraged, four hundred students signed a petition demanding an apology from Brinken, who refused. Students then accosted Brinken as he left the theater, slapping him publicly. Police arrested ninety-three students, forcing those in their final year to take their exams in prison. Efforts to divide the students by claiming that protests were simply a front for Polish insurrectionism failed, and students of all nationalities participated in the Brinken protest.[41]

The Purist movement grew as a result of such incidents, drawing in artists, writers, professors, and even army officers, some of them veterans of the Crimean War. Notable for his influence was medical professor Ludwik Gorecki (1825–1885), a graduate of St. Vladimir during its "epicurean years." Gorecki refused to involve himself in politics, but his conscientious approach to learning served as a role model. Notable too was anatomy professor Izydor Kopernicki (1825–1891), an 1849 graduate of St. Vladimir and an army surgeon who had served in the Crimea with Pirogov. Kopernicki had taught at the Jagellonian University in Cracow and had married a Ukrainian; one memoirist recalls that their home, on Kuznechnaia (Blacksmith) Street—a quiet street near the Khreshchatyk where "neither the noise from the wheels of the gentlemen's carriages nor the sensitive ears of the police could penetrate"—had become a gathering place for the whole Kiev intelligentsia. Kiev's student underground also made contacts with a similar movement in Kharkiv.[42]

Kiev's Polish academics were by no means uniform in their ideals or objectives. Ksawery Pietraszkiewicz, for example, had been sentenced to military service in 1838, returning to Kiev in 1845, where he opened his own private high school. Conservative in outlook, he influenced numerous students by his honesty and seriousness. Count Tadeusz Orzechowski (1837–1902), a medical student from Podil Province, typified the aristocratic element in Kiev's Polish politics. Along with law student Włodzimierz Milowicz (1838–1884) and others, he left Kiev in 1859 to work in the Polish insurgency movement in Paris. Significant too were Leonard Sowiński (1831–1887) and Volodymyr Antonovych (Włodzimierz Antonowicz, 1834–1908) who hailed from the same small village. From petty *szlachta* stock, Sowiński married a peasant girl and worked for peasant rights, though he had no land of his own. A powerful speaker with democratic views, he published poetry in Kiev in 1860 and later wrote a history of Polish literature. Sowiński was one of the first translators of Taras Shevchenko into Polish. Antonovych, modest and shy, had a passion for history. He cut his ties with the revolutionary element and had nothing to do with the upheaval that would come in 1863. From a Polonized Ukrainian family, he converted to Orthodoxy, stressed the need for peasant emancipation, and helped found the Ukrainophile movement. Some attacked Antonovych as a Polish "outcaste" because he had argued that Poles had been more oppressive of Ukrainians than had Great Russians.[43]

The Brinken affair helped catalyze the creation of five circles in Kiev called *gminy* early in 1857. Student circles had generally formed around common social rank, common regional background, or around friendships forged in secondary schools, and initially, the *gminy* reflected these preferences and included members of all national groups. Given the highly charged political atmosphere that followed Russia's defeat in the Crimean War and the permissive policies of Pirogov, the *gminy* quickly became politicized. The *korona* (crown) group favored the restoration of the old Polish empire with prepartition borders. Regional groups from Kiev, Volyn, and Podil Province, and from Lithuania, tended to be more democratic. Some of the *gminy* further divided into factions, and the Kiev group took on Ukrainophile sentiments. Each wore a different-colored sash, except for the Kiev group, which did not wear sashes. A steering committee was formed to coordinate activities among the *gminy*.[44]

Kiev's *gminy* were strengthened by the arrival of compatriots who had been expelled from Kharkiv in the spring of 1858 and by the return from exile of individuals implicated in the conspiracies of 1825 and 1831. The Kiev Secret Society, sometimes called Związek Trójnicki (Trinity Union), formed from among the *gminy*. Highly secretive (each member knew only two other members), its origins and activities remain obscure, but it may have been responsible for forging links between the university and the Polish populace in the region. The use of the word *Trinity* may have reflected the hope of fusing the three Right-Bank Ukrainian provinces into a common, independent state.[45] In any case, in Pirogov's Kiev the smell of impending insurrection became as pervasive as the scent of the city's famous spring lilacs. In the summer of 1860 General M. A. Domontovich, sent to lecture on military tactics, observed that "Kiev seemed to be preparing for an uprising. There were proclamations in the Catholic church. Whole squadrons of Polish university students openly trained in military formation and with arms. They moved through the crowded streets on their way out of town for target practice."[46] Even if Domontovich was exaggerating, Kiev was clearly abuzz with politics.

On September 14, 1859, Kiev University students petitioned Pirogov to open a Sunday school in Podil where the sons of artisans might acquire basic literacy and arithmetical skills. Pirogov assented, and other schools throughout the city and region followed, numbering more than three hundred in the empire by 1862, one hundred in Ukraine alone. Kiev's Podil Sunday school grew from 125 students in 1859 to 818 in 1862. Students and professors gave open lectures on Tuesdays and Thursdays, on topics ranging from popular mechanics to literature, to an audience that ranged in age from seven to thirty. Poles were more active in the countryside than in Kiev itself, but overall these Sunday schools provided a cover for political agitation and undermined Pirogov's position. St. Vladimir history professor Platon Pavlov (Pawlow), who supervised the Sunday schools, was fired from the university and banished from Kiev. Under pressure, Pirogov departed in 1861. However, civil authority in Kiev tended to be "apathetic and lacking in civic consciousness and courage" in the early 1860s. Governor-General Prince I. Vasilchikov (1805–1862) seemed unequal to the task and upon his death was replaced by the inept Prince N. N. Annenkov, "an old duffer" who knew so little about the region that he often confused it with Galicia![47]

Although Warsaw was the headquarters of those who conspired to rise against the tsar, Kiev's Contract Fair continued to provide a convenient place for Poles from around Europe to gather, cement ties, and coordinate strategies. The Society for the Education of Polish People, which ran secret schools in Right-Bank Ukraine, for example, elected its ruling committee of twelve annually at the fair. St. Vladimir professors were active in this organization, which ran a library for young children in Kiev. Most of the schools taught democratic values, much to the chagrin of nationalistic, but more politically conservative, Polish noblemen. Adam Mickiewicz was often read by Poles. His son, Władysław-Józef Mickiewicz (1838–1926), spent time conspiring in the homes along Kuznechnaia Street, helping to organize schools in churches, factories, and other places where detection could be avoided. Ivan Krylov (1768–1844) was popular with the Russians, Taras Shevchenko with the Ukrainians. Although salaries for "teachers" were often paid in firewood or some other commodity, special agents traveled about collecting substantial amounts of money, often in a box with the inscription "Jałmużna dla biednych" (charity for the poor).[48]

The Polish conspiratorial leaders called themselves "The Central Committee in Rus," and outside of Warsaw their activities seemed to be concentrated mainly in St. Petersburg and Kiev. In August 1862 they reorganized themselves into "The Provincial Committee in Rus," which planned the uprising for the three Right-Bank provinces. Edmund Różycki (1827–1893), the son of 1830–1831 insurrectionary Karol Różycki (1789–1870), headed this group whose leaders also included Kopernicki, St. Vladimir student Antoni Juriewicz (1839–1868), a priest, and two Kiev *gymnasium* students. Another participant, Stefan Bobrowski (1840–1863), the uncle of the writer Joseph Conrad, was sent from Warsaw in 1860 to coordinate activities with the center, and his death early in 1863 complicated these efforts. Władysław Rudnicki, university riding master Romauld Olszański (1826–64), and Second Lieutenant W. Borowski were also very active in Kiev, organizing some 3,550 men within Kiev Province into infantry and cavalry units. Olszański's home and stable were primary meeting places, for students and others often came there to ride or take instruction in horsemanship. Olszański had an illegal printing press where copies of the *Golden Gramota*, promising land to supportive peasants, were printed, and on his property caches of arms and provisions were hidden. As if to underscore their disdain for local authorities, conspirators met in the apartment of Lieutenant Borowski, located in the home of the famous architect V. Beretti, in the orangery in the Tsar's Garden, in the garden of the governor-general himself, and in the flat of the lover of Kiev's notoriously cruel policeman, Officer Tur! Because of the relationship between Tur and his mistress, her house was not under surveillance.[49]

The Cave Monastery also played an unintended role in the conspiracy. A certain Gustaw Hoffman, who had come from Warsaw, managed to get a job in the monastery's print shop, where in 1861 he and Stefan Bobrowski began to publish an illegal Polish paper, *Odrodzenie* (Rebirth). Influenced by Alexander Herzen, it called for the emancipation of the serfs, the liberation of Poland, and self-determination for Ukrainians. They managed to print only a handful of issues, as well as one hundred copies of a leftist St. Petersburg paper called *Velikoruss* (Great Russia) before their discovery and arrest in 1862. These publications were illicitly distributed at the Contract Fair.

In February 1861 troops fired on a Warsaw demonstration, killing five. In March the families of those killed participated in a requiem mass in Kiev that turned into a political demonstration. That same month, Polish student Konrad Paszkowski was arrested for walking past a public reading of the tsarist emancipation decree without doffing his cap or putting out his cigarette. His expulsion from the university for "disrespect" sparked more political demonstrations, and Paszkowski was allowed to return to the university. Students carried clubs, intimidating and sometimes beating up police and suspected informers. They also had contacts with sympathetic or bribable guards who provided assistance to compatriots who had been jailed. Large demonstrations, which began at the Catholic church, occurred in the fall of 1861. On October 9 demonstrators marched down the Khreshchatyk, broke windows, and destroyed a portrait of Alexander II at the university. Sixty were arrested. Police seemed unable to deal with large demonstrations, but fear of police infiltration remained very real, and suspicion of spying quickly led to duels. Governor-General Vasilchikov considered closing the university and declaring martial law (martial law was declared in Zhytomyr after an estimated one thousand participated in a demonstration there), but instead chose the more moderate course of requiring students to sign pledges that they would not demonstrate, expelling those who refused. In all, 429 demonstrations were recorded on the Right Bank in 1861. They reflected the growing militancy of Polish nationalism, but in Kiev, at least, politically dissatisfied Russians and Ukrainians commonly joined these protests.[50]

In 1862, in preparation for the uprising, 176 St. Vladimir students stopped paying tuition. Another 236 declined to pay in 1863. The government tried to get these students to reenroll and even committed financial aid to them, feeling they could be better supervised if enrolled at the university.[51] In 1861 Poles, Lithuanians, and Ukrainians had started to wear national costumes to class, and reports from 1863 indicate that despite the threat of arrest, Kiev's taverns and confection shops were filled with people symbolically dressed in national attire.

In tsarist Poland insurrection broke out on January 23, 1863. In Kiev officials predicted its imminence, as did insurrectionary leaflets that appeared on city streets. "I received ten copies [of a leaflet], and gave two out to people unknown to me whom I met on the street and one to the university riding-master Olszański," one student recalled.[52] Fortress Kiev provided good opportunities to purchase black-market weapons. This particular student had purchased a pistol from a Jewish soldier, and canteens and cartridge belts were readily available in local bazaars.

However, in Kiev the insurrection did not begin until April 26 when Antoni Juriewicz led a detachment of twenty-one men into the surrounding villages, trying to win peasant support. Archival sources indicate that up to five hundred insurrectionaries, mostly students, left Kiev in the ensuing days, usually in small detachments which mobilized at Olszański's stable. About eight thousand Poles lived in Kiev at this time, and perhaps three hundred of the city's six thousand homeowners were Poles. No doubt many were seasonal residents who spent summers on their rural estates. Podhorodecki asserts that most of Kiev's Poles were sympathetic to the uprising, and he is probably correct, but within the city itself there seem to have been no disorders. On April 29, in fact, Annenkov reported to the tsar that "in Kiev, peace has not been violated." In June "Orthodox" Kievans attempted to form a city militia to protect themselves, presumably from Poles. Their request, which must have smacked of reviving the banned city militia, was denied.[53]

News of the rising spread quickly in the surrounding countryside, and many peasants living on land owned by Polish magnates turned out in village squares to listen to the rebels. Some joined the insurrection, but most did not. Juriewicz's unit was quickly ambushed in a village. Twelve were killed, and nine were wounded, including Juriewicz himself. Attacked by government troops, thirty-four men in Olszański's unit were killed and sixty-eight were taken captive in a two-hour battle. Only a handful escaped into the woods to join up with Władysław Rudnicki, who had rallied some local peasants, calling himself the "Cossack Savva." In general, around Kiev, Polish units had only isolated successes and suffered from the absence of a carefully coordinated overall military plan and from inadequate arms. Some insurrectionaries carried only sabers and hatchets. Units were sometimes unable to find one another. A telegram from Annenkov to Alexander II on April 29 reported fighting in five districts in Kiev Province but pointed to another reason for failure: the local peasantry remained loyal to the government. One anecdote suggests why hostility between peasant and lord had not been overcome. In the midst of the insurrection, when a peasant swore at a Pole in a tavern, "the impertinent *chłop*" was charged with witchcraft and sentenced to Siberia. Not surprisingly, in Berdychiv District peasants were said to have captured one hundred insurgents. Meanwhile, anti-Semitism rose as Jews were accused of helping finance the disorder and of contributing to the general panic by buying up and hoarding copper coins.[54]

In all, perhaps six thousand men took up arms in Kiev and Volyn Provinces, an estimated 90 percent of them Poles. In Podil Province, the insurrection never got off the ground.[55] Some eighty thousand to one hundred thousand Poles, many from Ukraine, were ultimately exiled. Estates were seized, and many families lost everything. Olszański was captured and shot, while Rudnicki managed to escape to Austria. Amnesty for Poles involved in the 1863 uprising was not granted until 1896. At least twelve hundred Poles were imprisoned in the Pechersk fortress, at least for a time before their exile. On their way to exile, captives were led through Kiev's streets to be taunted and humiliated, though Podhorodecki notes that the city's Polish community came out to display public support for these unfortunates, an act which must have required courage in a city riven by ethnic tension.[56]

After 1863 Kiev continued to serve as an underground center of a network that smuggled letters, diaries, money, memoirs, and political literature to and from the exiles. In September 1863 Kazimierz Bobrowski, brother of Stefan, was arrested on a boat in Kremenchuk while carrying a packet of written materials. He convinced local authorities not to open the letters because they were personal and might compromise the reputations of young women.[57] Sympathetic officers at the Kiev garrison and university students helped some Poles escape, generally through an underground network to Odessa, then to Constantinople where a secret agent at the Russian mission provided money and assistance.

Archival reports indicate the extraordinary role St. Vladimir students played in the insurrection on the Right Bank. Of a total enrollment of 900, 600 participated in the revolt. Of the 1,336 convicted in Kiev Province for their role in the affair, about 400 were university students. As a result, the university's enrollment was cut back to fewer than 600 students, and admission was commonly denied to Poles. By 1878–1879 enrollment had risen to 805, but 593 were Orthodox, only 136 were Catholic (Polish), and 76 were Jewish.[58]

THE DECLINE OF POLISH INFLUENCE IN KIEV

Prior to 1863 Kiev's Polish community was small in number but, as a whole, prosperous and influential. In the 1850s Ivan Aksakov observed that "in Kiev the Polish element is still very strong." Kiev is "a mixed city" of scholars, monks, soldiers, and traders, of Poles, Russians, Ukrainians, and Jews, "among whom there are striking differences in dress."[59] Some Poles looked upon everything Russian with scorn, but then again so did some Russians at this time. Clashes, even duels, occurred, often between civilians and army officers, but there is no evidence that these duels commonly grew out of grievances that were ethnic in nature. Count Buturlin, then living in Kiev, recalled that "with few exceptions, Poles and Russians got along well in Kiev's high society." Polish

and Russian professors were honored guests at the homes of local officials, and Russian and Polish students from appropriate backgrounds
also traveled in Kiev's beau monde. "In Kiev we lived in a continuous
social whirl," Buturlin recalls.[60] Kiev's social elite may have talked more
of debt than of national issues, for more than two-thirds of the province's
landowners and more than half of the peasants were in debt in 1856.[61] It
all seemed very civilized, and the uprising must have presented a real
dilemma for many Kiev Poles who perhaps harbored deeply patriotic
thoughts about independence, but who otherwise seemed much at home
within the city's cosmopolitan elite.

According to the census of 1874, very few Poles were employed in the
"physical" crafts such as carpentry. Of 7,498 Polish speakers (in a city
population of 127,000), nearly half were said to belong to the "privileged
classes," nearly one-fifth were soldiers, and nearly 400 were secondary or
university students.[62] Of the Polish craftsmen, 247 were tailors who
owned their own shops and employed 86 additional Poles. Fifty-seven
Poles owned carpentry or furniture shops, and there were 26 Polish physicians and 42 midwives. Poles could be found in almost all occupations,
but only 23 were listed as having agricultural professions, an indication,
perhaps, that some Polish noblemen had been exiled from the city or had
lost their land.[63]

In her study of St. Petersburg, ethnographer N. V. Iukhneva found that
affluent Poles joined the wealthy of other nationalities in prestigious high-
rent districts; middle civil servants congregated in their own neighborhoods; working-class Poles joined their proletarian brothers in the outskirts near the factories.[64] In Kiev as well, wealth and occupation were
probably the most important determinants of where one lived, but it is
also true that Poles tended to reside in certain neighborhoods. In 1874
more than half of Kiev's Poles lived in the upscale Old Kiev or Lypky
Districts, constituting about 15 percent of the population of each. This
fact indicates a high level of Polish prosperity in Kiev, but it probably
indicates as well that many Poles sought to settle in neighborhoods where
there were other Poles. Although I found no references to identifiably
Polish neighborhoods in Kiev, Kuznechnaia Street was one example of
what seemed to be a "Polish street" that, prior to the insurrection, served
as a center of Polish political intrigue.

Already small in size, the Polish community was dwarfed in the latter
decades of the century by the influx of Ukrainian peasants and Jewish
traders and craftsmen. Poles no longer dominated St. Vladimir's student
body. With the advent of the railroad, the Contract Fair declined in size
and importance. The flaming sense of honor, which had helped foment
insurgency, gave way to realism, and realists kept quiet.

Despite the repression that followed 1863, some Poles continued to involve themselves in political activities. Kiev's Union of Polish Youth resurfaced in the 1870s as a continuation of the student movement of the 1860s. Socialist tracts were translated from Russian to Polish and Polish to Russian. A Polish woman, Helena Kowalska, was important in the organizational efforts of the South Russian Workers Union in Kiev in the late 1870s, and in 1878, of 134 students expelled from the university for political activity, several dozen were Poles. At the end of the 1870s, Kiev's *gmina* published an underground leaflet, *Voice from the Ukraine*, which was characterized as "patriotic" (nationalistic). The *Voice from Lithuania*, published in Vilnius, was said to be more socialistic, urging struggle against both the tsar and Polish capitalists. In 1883 some Kiev Poles tried to organize a ball on March 1, the anniversary of Emperor Alexander II's assassination. Local officials talked them out of it. In Zhytomyr a sugar refinery owner named Gurowski tried the same thing, and Governor-General Alexander Drenteln (1820–1888) expelled him from the region.[65]

By the 1890s an estimated twenty-five small Polish circles of various political shades operated in the city, and Poles were very visible in the early socialist movement. Student sympathies divided between the Social Democrats and the more nationalistic Polish Socialist Party. In 1894 Kiev's leftist underground was strengthened with the arrival of radical students from Warsaw who had been exiled for commemorating the 1794 uprising. Polish Social Democrats merged into a common Marxist organization in 1897 and do not appear to have acted as a significant separate political force in Kiev after that time.[66]

In examining the Polish community in late-imperial Russia, R. F. Leslie observes that

> the Kingdom of Poland could not provide the opportunities for a *déclassé szlachta*, which constituted about 10 percent of the population, but the great Russian empire with its slowly evolving industry required a managerial class. The Polish colonies began to expand in all the major Russian cities, especially St. Petersburg, Moscow, and Kiev, as a result of the influx of engineers, technologists and commercial representatives, bringing with them a host of tailors, shoemakers, valets and pastry cooks.[67]

Kiev's Polish population grew from 16,500 in 1897 to 44,000 in 1909, although Poles made up about 7 to 9 percent of the total population throughout the period. Skilled Polish workers were highly competitive in Kiev's labor markets, and migration eastward had become easier because of Russia's expanding railway network. There were, in fact, many Polish railway workers in Kiev. The city's Catholic church, St. Alexander, had

Кіевъ.—Kiev. № 89.
Польскій костелъ.—Eglise catholique.

16. The St. Alexander Polish Catholic Church.

been built between 1817 and 1842 and could accommodate only two thousand parishioners. In response to the growing Polish population, a second Catholic church, St. Nicholas, was built in the Gothic style in the 1890s, and a third (St. Joseph) was started but never completed.

Poles continued to exert considerable economic influence in Kiev. Warsaw factories had branches in the city, as did fine Warsaw shops. According to the tax rolls for 1913, Poles owned 10 percent of Kiev's most valuable real estate.[68] At this time 40 percent of all sugar refineries in Ukraine still belonged to Poles, and one of the greatest in Kiev belonged to the family of Count Władysław Branicki.

According to Podhorodecki, Poles continued to form "a social and intellectual elite" in Kiev. In city government, however, they played a very insignificant role. Józef Zawadzki, a publisher and bookstore owner who had founded the Kiev Stock Exchange, served as mayor in the 1890s, but there were few Polish councilmen. In Minsk and Vilnius Poles dominated local politics, but in Kiev only six of the eighty councilmen elected in 1910 were Poles.[69]

Data identifying Kievans as ethnic Poles are by no means precise, for many Poles could speak enough Russian to be counted as Russians in late-century censuses. In St. Petersburg, Orthodox Belarusians often called themselves Russians, while Catholic Belarusians called themselves

Poles.[70] There is no reason to assume a different pattern for Kiev, and some of the new "Polish" migrants may have been Catholic Belarusians who identified themselves as Poles.

Each spring tens of thousands of Belarusians poured into the south looking for agricultural work. Many floated down rivers on rafts that often foundered on shoals. The trip from Pinsk to Cherkasy could take from five to eleven weeks! Although the Belarusian land was poor and overpopulated, these multitudes returned in late September and early October to spend their winters chopping wood and building new rafts. Railways added extra fourth-class cars but could not accommodate them.[71] Countless Belarusians must have stopped in Kiev every year, staying temporarily with relatives or fellow villagers, hoping to find some kind of job, adding yet another language to the polyglot culture of the bazaars and further clouding the statistical picture of ethnic Kiev.

During the spring of the revolutionary year 1905, Warsaw was described as "the most lawless city in the Empire"; according to the French consul-general, it was "terrorized by anonymous groups of veritable brigands . . . [who] avail themselves of every opportunity to provoke violent disorders."[72] Although Polish organizations were active in Kiev, none of the city's strikes in 1905 was specifically Polish in inspiration or participation. During the mass meetings at the university in the fall, some orators did call for the attainment of Polish national goals. Following the October pogrom against Jews, rumors persisted that a secret society of Orthodox hooligans would attack Poles on a Catholic holiday or if they demonstrated.[73] *Kievskie otkliki* (Kiev comments) noted that the Poles were the only ethnic group in the city to help their own as unemployment mounted late in the year. A Polish newspaper, *Dziennik Kijowski* (The Kiev daily), started up at the year's end. Its editors were said to hope for independence, but they came out publicly for autonomy and rights for all nationalities in a secure constitutional order, and against chauvinism and pogroms.[74] A more radical paper, *Goniec Kijowski* (Kiev courier), was published for a brief time, but the specifics of its outlook are unknown.

Many Kiev Poles continued to back Ukrainian aspirations for cultural freedom. Poles were active in the Kiev Society for the Friends of Peace, for example, founded in 1909 and headed by Count Michał Tyszkiewicz (1860–1930). Such cooperation only fueled the paranoia of Kiev's small but active Russian Nationalist Club. Prior to the city election of 1910, this organization demanded that local assessors tax the property of Poles and Jews at twice the rates used to tax the property of Russians.[75]

On the eve of the First World War, Kiev's Nationalist Club continued to rail against Polish separatism, and the governor-general continued to report to Nicholas II that Catholic proselytism "was set on Polonizing the population of the entire region."[76] In the minds of Russian nationalists, little had changed since the days of Bibikov. In reality, Polish influence had waned in Kiev since the insurrection of 1863, and, although the Polish question had not disappeared, it had lost its centrality in local politics. Dwarfed by the growing challenge of socialism and by heightened Judeophobia, by the turn of the twentieth century it had become a comparatively insignificant political issue in the city.

· CHAPTER IV ·

Ukrainians in Russian Kiev

IN AN EFFORT to end Ukrainian autonomy, in 1782 Catherine the Great divided the Cossack Hetmanate into three provinces (*namestnichestva*), one of which had its capital in Kiev. As a result, Left-Bank Ukrainian landowners, dressed in the "untidy" manner of the Zaporozhe Cossacks and differing little from the peasantry in language and custom, became prominent in the city, assuming many of the offices created by Catherine's reform. By 1787 all twenty-two officers of Kiev's civil court were Ukrainians, as were all but one of the twenty-one officers of the superior court called the *zemsky* court. Ivan Vyshnevsky, who owned 1,668 serfs in rural Kiev Province, presided over criminal court; the two sons of this sophisticated man studied in Vienna. Hryhory Ivanenko, who had commanded a Cossack unit in the Turkish wars, and Demian Demianovich Obolonsky were among the other Ukrainian landowners who held high judicial offices in the city. Obolonsky, also a veteran of the Turkish wars, had 3,411 Ukrainian serfs and spent summers on his country estate. In winter he held lavish banquets twice a week to which the entire city was invited! These feasts lasted most of the day, and according to the memoirist Vigel, Obolonsky came to Kiev in the winter primarily to feed the poor.[1]

Some "Little Russian" patriots such as Vasyl Kapnist, provincial marshal of Kiev's nobility, lobbied for the restoration of the Cossack companies, but more commonly the Ukrainian gentry, similar to their Russian counterparts in language, culture, and religion, accepted the imperial system.[2] Kiev's burghers continued to defend their Magdeburg privileges. They feared the power of the Russian state, but they had no reason to cherish the memory of the Cossacks with whom they had struggled for decades.

Catherine's successors, Paul I and Alexander I, affirmed Kiev's autonomy in 1797 and 1802 respectively, but during their reigns Poles assumed many of the provincial and regional offices. Poles became very prominent in the city, especially in high society. The imperial Russian army quartered in Pechersk represented the interests of the tsar, and Kiev's burghers maintained only minimal and "official" ties with it.[3] Nicholas I brought the city firmly under Russian control, and from the 1830s Russians became increasingly prominent in Kiev. For all of these changes, as historian Nikolai Zakrevsky would observe in the 1860s, Kiev remained predominantly a city of "simple-hearted Little Russians."

In the early decades of the nineteenth century, the term *Russian* was used to designate both Great Russians and "Little Russians" (Ukrainians), for it was commonly assumed that Little Russians were a branch of the Russian people. In addition, *Russian* often denoted loyalty to the tsar more than it did any kind of deeply felt sense of ethnic identity. Among educated Ukrainians, the idea that reunion with Russia had been a high point in their history had a certain appeal, for it played to their sense of distinctiveness while enabling them to affirm their loyalty to the tsar and his powerful empire.[4] As the nineteenth century unfolded, national self-consciousness became increasingly important, and Kiev came to be considered "a Russian city." By the end of the century, a majority of its inhabitants spoke Russian, or at least a heavily Russified blend of Russian and Ukrainian. By the turn of the twentieth century, Kiev could no longer be called a Ukrainian city; neither could it be considered fully Russian.

The terms *Little Russian* and *Ukrainian* also were associated with the ways and manners of the countryside, for nearly all of the region's peasants spoke Ukrainian. Among the peasants, a sense of Ukrainian nationality did not exist, and the word *Ukrainian* was not understood. Peasants referred to themselves as *khakol* or *muzhyk* (colloquial terms for peasants), or as "Orthodox." However, the peasant never lost "his sense of separateness from the Russian (moskalia)." If you called him a Russian or a "*moskal*," he denied this with repugnance.[5]

Obviously, not all Little Russians were country bumpkins; indeed, Ukrainians were very much a part of the local beau monde. The home of the widow Iuliia Veselytska, a Ukrainian who had married a Russian envoy to the Crimean khan, was the center of Kiev's social whirl around the turn of the century.

> Her home was as gay as her name itself. Her vibrant nature, sense of humor, and Ukrainian language made her an original, pleasant for everyone. Her hospitality knew no limits. At her table gathered the customs and outlooks of all of Rus—east and west, Great and Little. Her Little Russian relatives— the Ivanenkos, Hudymas, Masiukovs, and others—came to visit and went nowhere else, for at her home you could see all of Kiev. Having paid a visit there, they simply returned home.[6]

In the entrepreneurial world, the importance of the Ukrainians Iakhnenko and Simirenko to the beet sugar industry has already been mentioned. Natives of Kiev Province, the Iakhnenko brothers came from an industrious serf family noted for its trade in leather, bootmaking, and melons. They had been owned by Count Samoilov in Smila (Smela). Fedor Simirenko had been a serf of Count Vorontsov in Horodyshche (Gorodishche). After their freedom had been purchased by their fathers, probably in the 1820s, the sons capitalized on their ties with the families of their former lords and prospered in the buckwheat-milling business. They began to market leather, cattle, and grain products at fairs from Warsaw to Odessa. By the time they built the first steam-powered sugar refinery in Ukraine in 1843, they had become first-guild merchants in Odessa and had amassed a million rubles of capital. Their refinery in Horodyshche (in Kiev Province) was equipped to produce steam-powered machinery for the milling and water transport industries as well. Seven stories tall, it operated a good-quality factory barracks, credit facilities for its employees, and shops that sold good merchandise at fair prices. The technical and managerial staff, some of them Europeans, had private homes (about 150 in number), each with its own garden and orchard. The enterprise provided gas lighting for the whole community, a six-class school, and a hundred-bed hospital. At its peak in the 1850s it employed more than eleven hundred people. Its cafeteria served as a common meeting place for local landlords, Muscovite merchants, Jews, Poles, and Europeans. Until it collapsed in the early 1860s, the Iakhnenko-Simirenko enterprise was said to be both a model social community and a splendid example of early Ukrainian entrepreneurial success.[7]

Other examples of Ukrainian entrepreneurs included the industrialist Krivanek (probably shortened from Krivanenko), a co-owner of one of Kiev's largest machine-building plants from the 1870s, and sugar barons Mykola and Fedor Tereshchenko and their heirs. By 1914 they owned about 432,000 acres of land in eight provinces, nine sugar refineries, a distillery, and a flour mill. The Tereshchenko home in Kiev, which housed a rich collection of paintings by artists from the Russian Empire, was one of the city's most beautiful, as was the home of Bohdan Chanenko, a Tereshchenko son-in-law who was also a noted art collector.[8] The Tereshchenko and the Kharitonenko families joined the Jew Brodsky, the Russian Bobrinskoi, and the Pole Jaroszyński in a cartel that eventually controlled most of the empire's sugar production.

THE GUILDS

Key to the relationship between Kiev and the Russian state in the early decades of the nineteenth century was the ancient question of Podil's Magdeburg autonomy. The struggle to protect its autonomy had always been partly economic in nature, for burghers had long fought to retain their monopoly over local trade against encroachments by outsiders. Traders from Great Russia often came to Kiev. In 1474 the visitor Ambrosia Kontarini reported that Russians came to trade in furs.[9] Tensions mounted in the seventeenth century with the establishment of Muscovite political control over the city, and Russian soldiers complained bitterly that Kievans refused to provide them with adequate housing and that many consequently died.

Important to the struggle for autonomy were Kiev's guildsmen, who numbered about two thousand in 1742, four thousand in 1762. Guilds generally had their own yards, halls, and pubs. Wealthy guilds such as that of the butchers had splendid halls and enough capital to serve as lending institutions for their members. Guildmasters were elected for one year and were supposed to be literate (a requirement that could not always be met) and abstain from heavy drinking and from trade in alcoholic beverages. One of their functions was to maintain good relations with the burgher magistracy, which theoretically controlled the guilds by reviewing their account books and setting various fees and regulations. In the latter decades of the eighteenth century, however, the magistracy had difficulty making its decisions stick. In the 1770s, for instance, it gave the bakers' guild the sole right to sell bread without paying a special tax. The tailors, furriers, shoemakers, and weavers protested, for they had writs going back to the Polish king Sigismund III in 1591 giving their wives the right to sell bread. The magistracy relented but allowed bakers the sole right to ensure that bread standards were met by all sellers. In 1772 the magistracy joined the boat builders and millers to the coopers' guild even though the three crafts had nothing in common. The boatmen and millers resisted and often failed to show up at guild meetings, indicating that the magistracy had either little power to enforce its rules or little interest in doing so.[10]

Many of the guilds were also declining at this time. The potters' guild, for example, was only half as large in 1797 as it had been in 1786, when it had fifty-eight members. Some of the potters' rows at the market stood empty or were rented to cattle dealers. Traditionally, potters had enjoyed the right to make stoves, and stovemakers were supposed to have certificates verifying their competence because of ongoing problems with fire, but the guild lacked the power to enforce these rules. It also had great difficulty in making enough money to pay for the bread and other commodities that were commonly used to earn favors. Litigation in 1783–1784 over a disputed land purchase, and the consequent need to bribe everyone from a hired architect to court officials, had profound financial implications for the beleaguered guild. As profitability declined, so did discipline, and in 1792 the guild finally established a code of behavior that called for strict punishments, including beatings. Complaining about the guild without good cause could result in twenty-five whacks with a rod and/or a heavy fine.[11]

The prosperous fishermen's guild was subdivided into smaller units, which had formed voluntarily around skill and place of residence. The absence of good roads and bridges meant that Kurenivka and Podil, for example, remained distinct, barely connected settlements, and a separate unit, or *kurin* (a word used also to designate a Zaporozhian Cossack company), grew in each. Kiev fishermen had a monopoly on fishing rights on a certain stretch of the Dnipro, and fishing was done, mostly in the spring, with large and expensive nets. One *kurin*, usually comprising ten men, pulled the net through the water, another extracted the catch, another salted the catch, and so forth. In the fishermen's guild, the *kurin* seemed to make most of the entrepreneurial decisions—for instance, whether or not to hire outside labor.[12]

Guildsmen were expected to participate in various city festivals, and the burgher militia with its great gonfalons and brass band led these impressive celebrations, which are described in chapter 6. In earlier times the militia had fulfilled a real defense function, and it continued to drill every week for both ceremony and combat. During the Napoleonic invasion in 1812 it was mobilized to help defend the city. At full strength it was supposed to include a two-thousand-man infantry and a five-hundred-man cavalry, but only about one thousand infantrymen, about half the number marshaled in 1796, could be mobilized at this time, possibly because the great fire of 1811 had destroyed burgher homes, shops, and weapons, forcing many burghers to leave Podil. In 1800 the militia had nine cannons, which were maintained and fired by members of the barbers' guild. At least two cannons, some long rifles, and about six hundred pikes were found in the rubble of the magistracy building after the 1811 fire. During the Polish Insurrection of 1830–1831, the militia could mobilize only about two hundred burghers, and a small burgher cavalry watched the roadways. The independent spirit of this small militia was reflected in the fact that it continued to wear traditional uniforms and use its distinctive set of commands.[13]

Thus, Kiev's guilds had served a variety of functions. They guaranteed protected markets, notably at the main trade row (*gostinnyi dvor*). A new trade row, built in 1809 in the classical style, retained the long yellow and white facades typical of trade rows all over the empire. Rebuilt several times because of fire, the market's six gates led to about fifty shops grouped by commodity. The magistracy had its shops here, and the butchers' guild, for example, had eleven shops along butchers' row. Each shop had an underground warehouse, and individual craftsmen often lived in houses rented from either the guilds or the magistracy. Traders from outside Podil could sell their product to an appropriate guild but could not engage in retail trade on their own.[14] The guilds also adjudicated noncriminal disputes among their members. In their ceremonial and defense functions, they helped maintain Kiev's traditions and spirit of autonomy. In so doing, they helped delay the abrogation of the Magdeburg Rights.

The erosion of city autonomy and growing economic competition caused the guilds to decline, however. At least some of the guilds experienced a rapid turnover in their membership. For example, the fishermen's guild numbered only 75 to 100 members in 1797, but 193 new members had joined, at least for a time, during the previous eight years.[15] In 1807 all guild revenues were transferred to the magistracy and became part of the city's general revenue, reflecting the imperial government's desire to streamline local governance and destroy pockets of local resistance.

THE TRANSFORMATION OF BURGHER KIEV

How Ukrainian were Kiev's guildsmen and burghers? They have been called "the last Ukrainian stronghold" in the Russian Empire,[16] but individuals from many different places made up their ranks. For example, of the 193 newcomers to the fishermen's guild cited above, only eighty (41 percent) were Kiev burghers. Thirty-five (18 percent) came from the ranks of serfs or state peasants, and sixty-two (32 percent) were Poles. Two were merchants from Kiev, two were from Moldova (Moldavia), and twelve were of unknown origin.[17] Jews were excluded, and, because of the threat of Russian control, efforts to exclude Great Russians apparently continued. Nevertheless, both groups were already establishing footholds in Podil early in the nineteenth century.

In their cultural patterns, Kiev's early nineteenth-century burghers probably differed little from the peasants of the surrounding Ukrainian countryside. Significantly, according to Pantiukhov, the burghers spoke a Ukrainian language that was identical to the language spoken in Chernihiv and Poltava Provinces. In appearance, however, having descended from the many and varied conquerors and settlers of the past, they did not resemble even the Ukrainian peasants who lived just outside the city.[18] And when they donned their traditional attire to honor visiting dignitaries (which was permitted until 1830, when Nicholas I required them to wear Russian dress), it is likely that they did so to celebrate Kiev's traditional liberties rather than to flaunt a broader Ukrainian identity.

In 1835 burgher autonomy formally ended when Nicholas I established a new city council (duma). Russian law officially took precedence over local custom; a governor-general, appointed by the tsar, and the police were given authority to administer the city. Kohut notes that the only known protest literature from the burghers came from Kiev. Written anonymously in Ukrainian and blaming loss of independence on corruption and gambling, "The Lament of the Kievans on the Loss of Magdeburg Law" asked whether "the native Kievan's only recourse is to leave his wife and house and flee the city."[19] Quite probably, such protestation reflected less the emergence of a Ukrainian national identity than it did some Kievans' sorrow over losing the centuries-old fight to maintain the city's autonomy.

After 1835 the conflict over burgher autonomy seems to have quickly disappeared from Kiev's political scene. Although there is little information about specific burgher families, it is likely that most survived the advent of Russian ascendancy with little difficulty, and that many continued to enjoy considerable political as well as economic influence. There are indications that the Kobtsa family remained a powerful force in leather-goods manufacturing for many decades, for example. The entrepreneurial Chokolov brothers also descended from an old Kiev family, probably from Podil burghers. They remained prominent in local business circles and, after 1870, in city government. The guildsmen faced a challenge that had little to do with the coming of the Russians, however, that of free-market competition. In 1833, 618 guild-craftsmen turned out 78,600 rubles worth of product, while a mere 76 nonguild competitors produced half as much, 39,300 rubles worth![20] The archaic values of the guildsmen, with their collective restrictions on production and pricing, could not survive the growth-oriented ethos of laissez-faire capitalism.

If romantic visions of past autonomy remained at midcentury, they surely disappeared as the emancipation of the serfs, the construction of railroads, the appearance of large industrial complexes, and the rapid growth of the population dramatically changed the face of Kiev. And by the mid-1860s, both Russians and Ukrainians would find a new source of competition as thousands of Jews began to pour into Kiev from the impoverished ghettos of the Pale of Settlement.

CRAFTSMEN AND THE RUSSIFICATION OF KIEV

Traditionally, traders and entrepreneurs from Russia and elsewhere had led a kind of cloistered life within their own shops and markets, for continuous trade in Podil was denied them. In 1686 Russian soldiers occupied the upper portions of the city over the protests of the metropolitan and other clergy. The construction of the Pechersk fortress by Peter the Great laid the foundation for the further intrusion of Russian troops and collateral personnel. In 1719 the archimandrite of Pechersk, Ioaniky

Senytovych, wrote that although the name Pechersk remained, everything else had changed. Few former residents were to be found, and, symbolically, Pechersk's central street was renamed Moscow Street.

Ultimately, Russians bought property in Podil under false names, and a late-eighteenth-century regulation allowed burghers to hire Russians. Intermarriage, though apparently uncommon at this time, also contributed to the ability of Russians to get a foothold in Podil.[21] The loss of Magdeburg privileges meant that Russians could settle anywhere in the city, and by 1845, of 6,048 skilled craftsmen in Kiev as a whole, 2,089 had come from elsewhere in the empire, many to meet the city's growing construction needs.[22]

Burgeoning cities throughout the empire attracted people with critical skills, often from specific clusters of villages. In some districts of Russia's Iaroslavl Province, for example, nearly all of the eleven- and twelve-year-old boys left for St. Petersburg, and Iaroslavl peasants came to dominate the tavern trade in the capital. Peasants from the Tver region established good reputations as carpenters and bootmakers.[23] Even in the mid-1890s, when Kharkiv's giant locomotive works was under construction, skilled workers were imported from Moscow, St. Petersburg, and Riga, but particularly from the Briansk and Kaluga regions because of their reputations for craftsmanship and loyalty to the enterprise.[24]

By 1845 native Kievans dominated only the food, clothing, and most consumer goods industries, as table 4.1 illustrates. Outsiders were especially prevalent in the building trades. Reflecting what was probably a Great Russian view, Ivan Funduklei, who served as governor from 1841 until 1853, contended that Kievans had been spoiled by the Contract Fair and that local craftsmen did not have to work hard at improving their skills because they could always sell mediocre products at high prices at the fair.[25] In the 1840s it was said that native carpenters worked slowly, took long breaks when they got bored, and failed to finish construction jobs. Contractors thus imported Great Russian carpenters. They were paid twice as much, but they got the job done.

Recruited from serf estates and formed into artels usually consisting of six to twenty (and sometimes as many as fifty) workers, these peasants had little or no money. Contractors supplied some tools, personal necessities, and transportation, and assumed responsibility for passports and for meeting financial (*obrok*) obligations to their workers' lords. Collective dependency kept labor costs low. Young boys, fifteen and sixteen years old, were not paid at all during their first year as they learned their trades, and individuals were often hired who had large families, or no family at all, for they were likely to have fewer financial responsibilities to relatives at home. Artel workers were housed together in an apartment,

TABLE 4.1
Place of Origin of Kiev Craftsmen, 1845

	Kiev Natives	*From Outside Kiev*	*Total*
Carpenters	64	1,227	1,291
Stonecutters, stonemasons	11	1,099	1,110
Cobblers, bootmakers	889	64	953
Bakers	501	42	543
Tailors	418	63	481
Joiners	377	0	377
Plasterers	5	325	330
Fishermen	278	0	278
Blacksmiths	250	10	260
Hatters, capmakers	130	5	135
Furniture makers	97	34	131
Jewelers, goldsmiths, watch-makers, silversmiths	118	11	129
Roofers	0	118	118
Icon painters	111	3	114
Carriage makers	31	74	105
Wheelwrights, cart makers	91	0	91
Bookbinders	66	6	72
Chimneysweeps	40	27	67
Metal craftsmen	62	0	62
Barbers	61	0	61
Coppersmiths	48	0	48
Saddlemakers	45	0	45
Gunsmiths	29	0	29
Tinsmiths	20	6	26
Piano builders	0	12	12
Makers of other musical instruments	12	0	12

SOURCE: Ivan Funduklei, *Statisticheskoe opisanie Kievskoi gubernii* (St. Petersburg, 1852), pt. 1, 378–79. Data include apprentices and student craftsmen in each category. Some categories with few members are omitted.

usually near the construction site, and brought back scraps of wood from the site for use in cooking and heating (logs for firewood were very expensive). Workers were paid irregularly, usually when they needed new tools, before major holidays, or for family emergencies. They received most of their wages as winter set in and their eight- or nine-month contracts ended. After the foundation for a house was dug or sited, a priest was called to bless its four corners, and the owner gave gifts to the contractor and the artel workers (often kerchiefs) and treated them to a meal. As each stage of construction was finished, or about every two weeks, workers received five kopecks from the owner for the public baths and for vodka. Upon completion of the house, the owner again provided gifts to the contractor and his workers. Of the roughly 4,500 rubles required to build a house in 1845, about 2,660 rubles went for materials, half of that for wood, and much of the remainder was spent on wages for the work crew. Of the 1,830 rubles typically spent for labor, a substantial amount went to Russian artel laborers.[26]

Thus, contractors bypassed local craftsmen, and the massive construction needs of nineteenth-century Kiev were generally met by imported Russian workers with reputations for superior skill, work habits, and, according to Funduklei, comparative moderation in drinking. Contractors also imported stonecutters and masons from Russia, especially from Meshchovsky District in Kaluga Province, to build large buildings such as banks and churches, and to expand the Pechersk fortress. Skilled and unskilled Russian workers were imported to build the suspension bridge over the Dnipro, which was begun in 1848. In 1874, when a census was taken, 80 to 90 percent of the city's carpenters, glass cutters, and plasterers, and half of its stonemasons, came from Great Russia. Belarusians were strongly represented in the distilling and brick-making trades, while native Kievans were prevalent only among fishermen (90 percent), wax-candle makers, specialty bakers, market farmers (about two-thirds), bakers of black bread, bootmakers, and painters (about half). Ukrainians from outside the city dominated the hotel, tavern, and inn trade, and constituted about half of the brewery, distillery, tobacco, and brickyard workers. Of the women who worked, most were employed in the clothing and food trades.[27]

COMMERCE AND THE RUSSIFICATION OF KIEV

In the 1820s Governor Lewaszew asked that Kiev's Russian merchants be given the same benefits as the merchants in Kremenchuk, namely, full exemption from payment of taxes for five years and payment of 50 percent of taxes for the following five years. Factory builders, it was suggested, should be exempted from taxes for ten years. Initially, the Ministry of Finance declined, claiming that Kiev already had enough trade advantages, but on March 8, 1835, in an effort to attract Great Russians to the city, Nicholas I offered these incentives to Russian entrepreneurs. Even so, merchants were slow to take advantage of this new opportunity. In 1797 there had been 347 male Christian merchants (local data indicated religion but not nationality) and three Jewish merchants. In 1845 the number of Christian merchants was only slightly higher (358), and since Jews had been expelled from the city in 1827, no Jewish merchants appeared in the statistics.[28]

We know little about these Kiev merchant-entrepreneurs as individuals. One enterprise notable for its longevity was the Barsky department store, founded in 1723 in Podil by the Pole Iakim Barsky. Having moved to the Khreshchatyk in 1851, it was still in operation at the turn of the twentieth century, specializing at this time in paper goods, office supplies, and printing. Of the Russians who came during the reign of Nicholas I, some of the most prominent were Old Believers, and local tongues wagged about the hard-drinking habits of their wives. One Old Believer, Mikhail Dekhterev, established Kiev's first large machinery plant and became its first mayor under the new laws. Other Russian newcomers included the Bogatyrev family, descendants of state peasants in Tula Province, who established a booming hardware business, and the family of Fedor Ditiatin. One of the Ditiatins later served for twenty-five years on the city council, distinguishing himself by his continuous silence. Once, after being recognized by the chair for the first time in ten years, Ditiatin rose amid a hushed house but said simply, "I refuse to speak."[29]

Commercial penetration by Russian merchants thus came slowly and belatedly to Kiev, and in this sense Kiev differed from Kharkiv, which had no tradition of Magdeburg privileges to keep Russians out. Furthermore, there were few Jews and even fewer Poles in eastern Ukraine. Great Russians came to dominate Kharkiv's continuous trade in manufactured goods in the eighteenth century, while the local Ukrainian population was content to trade in farm products, particularly in wine and vodka. "The Little Russian is a poor industrialist and prefers to trade that which is close at hand—namely, farm products," observed historian Dmytro Bahalii (Dmitry Bagalei), himself a Ukrainophile.[30] Many of Kharkiv's entrepreneurs had originally come because of the city's great fairs. The family of Akim Pavlov, an Old Believer from Kolomenskoe, near Moscow, originally hawked *prianiki* (baked goods) at the fairs before branching into soap boiling, candle making, and finally into retail trade. Pavlov's store in Kharkiv "became a market in miniature." Customers got free tobacco so that they could sit and smoke while their orders were being filled.[31]

In Kiev the Contract Fair brought thousands of rubles to the local economy, and numerous Russian traders, especially from Moscow. During the fair's heyday, between 1843 and 1849 for example, Moscow city merchants brought about 1.8 million rubles' worth of merchandise to the fair, more than all other traders from beyond Kiev Province combined. Local Kiev merchants (we do not know their ethnic breakdown) brought about 1.1 million rubles' worth of product, and they were followed in importance by the mostly Jewish traders from Berdychiv (793,000 rubles), and by Russian traders from St. Petersburg (667,000 rubles) and rural Moscow Province (210,000 rubles). Armenians from Tiflis accounted for 175,000 rubles, traders from Warsaw 147,000, and from Volyn Province 109,000.

During these seven years, the fair's most significant markets were wool, silk, and cotton fabrics (which accounted for 35 percent of its sales) and jewelry (which accounted for 21 percent).[32] Kiev merchants dominated much of the fabric business, particularly in cotton and domestic woolens, and the markets for fish and caviar, school and art supplies, and mirrors. Moscow city merchants were also prominent in the fabric trade, and dominated the markets for dresses, imported woolen goods from England and Berlin, silks, grocery items, optical and precision goods, and, along with St. Petersburg merchants, the lucrative commerce in jewelry made of gold, silver, and precious stones. Russian peasants from Kineshma District in Kostroma Province supplied most of the linen items, while traders from rural Moscow Province sold great amounts of tableware and china in that highly competitive market. Armenians, Tatars, and Circassians from Tiflis and Nakhichevan in the Caucasus brought knotted carpets, Persian silks, and other objects from Central Asia and the Near East. Warsaw merchants were noted for their silver-plated, bronze, and lacquered metal items; shoes, boots, and leather goods came from Minsk; crystal glassware from Roslavlsky District in Smolensk Province; and steel and copper products from Tula.

Berdychiv Jews, in addition to their importance as sellers, bought great quantities of merchandise for resale in the surrounding region. Ethnic Ukrainians, however, did little business at the fair. For example, virtually no sellers came from Kharkiv, Chernihiv, Poltava, or Podil Provinces. Indeed, the groups of merchants from Moscow and Kiev Provinces each accounted for nearly one-third of the fair's salable goods. Traders from St. Petersburg brought about 11 percent, while the Polish provinces accounted for 7 percent and the Caucasus 3 percent. Foreigners accounted for less than 2 percent of the trade volume, and traders from Ukraine outside of Kiev Province probably accounted for no more than 5 percent of the volume.[33] Thus, although Russian merchants were slow to settle in Kiev, they exercised great economic influence in the city through the Contract Fair. Ukrainian merchants and traders were noticeably absent.

Imperial officials had long viewed Kiev as a "Russian" outpost amid a sea of Jewish traders and Polish landlords. Writing in 1868, historian Nikolai Zakrevsky reflected this siege mentality, complaining that while few Russian merchants had settled in Kiev, Jews took advantage of every opportunity, legal or illegal, to pour into the city.[34] As a result of the liberal policies of Alexander II, Jews quickly came to dominate the ranks of Kiev's merchantry (see chapter 5). In 1884 there were only four Chris-

tian first-guild merchants (again, data indicate religion but not nationality), compared with 117 Jews. By 1889 Jewish first-guild merchants numbered 181. Between 1892 and 1894 the number of Christian first-guild
merchants rose dramatically from 10 to 90, but the number of Jews increased from 259 to 301. Christians dominated the somewhat less prosperous second guild, averaging about 240 per year in the 1880s, compared with about a dozen Jews. In 1894 there were 288 Christian and 39
Jewish second-guild merchants.[35]

Whatever their religion or national origin, it is likely that from midcentury onward Kiev's merchants used Russian as the primary language of
commercial intercourse. Of the 4,835 merchants recorded in the 1897
census, about half were categorized as Russian by language, and the other
half were Jews. The prominence of Jewish merchants contributed to the
Russification of Kiev's commercial culture, for more than any other
group Jews had to accommodate to survive. They adapted to their masters, and their masters were Great Russians.[36] In 1897 Ukrainian-speakers were virtually absent from the ranks of society most likely to have
economic influence, constituting only 1 percent of Kiev's merchants and
only 6 percent of its noblemen and civil servants. Great Russians accounted for almost three-quarters of the 30,410 residents registered as
members of the nobility or the civil service. Of the rest, most were Poles.[37]

On the other hand, Kiev was a cosmopolitan city in language and culture. The Pole Ciechowcki recalls that many shops had street signs in
Russian and French, and that inside the shop someone could speak
French or German (an indication of frequent commercial contact with
Europeans).[38] If merchants and their employees could use European languages, it stands to reason that they could also use Ukrainian when commercial circumstances dictated. Commercially, Kiev had become a "Russian" city, but it is doubtful that Ukrainian completely disappeared from
the city's commerce.

THE UKRAINIAN MOVEMENT IN KIEV

Claiming a nationality was a difficult task for many midcentury intellectuals. Many saw themselves simply as Slavs. Pan-Slavic sentiments were
much in vogue. "I was born in Zhitomir to a Ukrainian father and a
Polish mother. To what nationality do I belong?" queried one St. Vladimir student. Said another: "Above all, I am a Slav, more Little Russian
than Pole since I was born, raised, and nurtured in the western region,
and for the most part lived among Russians [Little Russians]."[39] At this
time the Ukrainian national movement was very small, but Kiev was its
recognized center in the Russian Empire. Increasingly, the city attracted

those who were Ukrainophile in sentiment. Upon graduating from the Poltava *gymnasium* in 1884, for example, the writer Volodymyr Samiilenko chose St. Vladimir over the academically more prestigious university in St. Petersburg for precisely this reason.[40]

With good reason, Russian authorities worried that Polish revolutionaries were stirring up Ukrainian activism. Szymon Konarski had tried to recruit Ukrainians in the 1830s, and a few, most notably Oleksandr Cherny, were active in his Kiev circle. Polish political and cultural activity helped stimulate similar activities among Ukrainian students, and the underground Polish library of the 1830s exposed them to illegal Polish and foreign literature. After his arrest, Cherny told investigators that he was attracted to Konarski's movement because of its democratic nature and because of his interest in Polish literature and his admiration for everything Slavic. The writer and ethnographer Panteleimon Kulish (1819–1897) was one Ukrainian intellectual who was influenced by Polish aspirations, in particular those of Michał Grabowski, who tried unsuccessfully to publish a newspaper called *Słowianin* (Slav) in Kiev designed to encourage Polish-Ukrainian unity.[41]

In March 1847 authorities discovered the existence of the Brotherhood of Saints Cyril and Methodius, organized by Kulish, St. Vladimir historian Mykola Kostomarov, poet-artist Taras Shevchenko, and others. With about ninety members or sympathizers, it became a significant outlet for Ukrainian intellectuals to express their views on questions of social justice. Orest Subtelny calls it "the first Ukrainian ideological organization in modern times."[42] Not surprisingly, Ukrainian intellectuals tended to call for the abolition of serfdom and social rank. They envisioned a Ukraine capable of uniting Slavs into a grand, democratic federation whose capital was to be at Kiev. Kulish stressed the development of Ukrainian culture, Kostomarov stressed Slavic unity, and the more radical Shevchenko argued for national emancipation. Shortly after the betrayal of the group in March 1847, its key members were arrested. Kostomarov was exiled to Saratov. Shevchenko, whose paintings of Kiev were confiscated by the secret police (most have therefore been lost), was arrested in the city allegedly with three pistols and forbidden literature. He received the stiffest sentence, ten years in a Siberian labor battalion.[43] Poles called these Ukrainian organizers "Italians from beyond the Dnipro,"[44] an apparent reference to midcentury conspiratorial movements within the still-to-be-unified Italian states. According to Subtelny, the Brotherhood

> represented the first, albeit unsuccessful, attempt of the intelligentsia to move from the cultural to the political phase of national development; it alerted the tsarist government (which until this time had tried to play

Ukrainophilism off against Polish cultural influences in Ukraine) to the potential dangers of growing Ukrainian national consciousness; it signaled the onset of an anti-Ukrainian policy and marked the beginning of a long, unceasing struggle between the Ukrainian intelligentsia and the imperial Russian authorities.[45]

Having survived their punishments, Kostomarov, Kulish, and others convened the first *hromada* (society) in St. Petersburg after the death of Nicholas I in 1855. *Hromady* were formed throughout Ukraine to improve the lot of the peasantry. Kostomarov and Kulish focused on cultural and educational objectives in order to avoid provoking the authorities. For twenty-two months beginning in 1861, the group published *Osnova* (Foundation), "the first Ukrainian periodical in the Russian Empire,"[46] and Ukrainophiles went from village to village distributing popular Ukrainian-language brochures. Shevchenko, more political than the others, was extremely popular with Russian and Ukrainian audiences, and often appeared publicly with Dostoevsky, Turgenev, and other literary giants. He died on March 10, 1861. He had loved Kiev, and his popularity in the city was evidenced by the large crowd that turned out on June 6 to honor him as the boat carrying his body passed by on the way to its final resting place at Kaniv. While the Polish historian Tabiś argues that Kiev's *hromada*, founded in 1859, was not very significant in the St. Vladimir student body as a whole, others note that it became "the most active and enduring *hromada*" in the Russian Ukraine. "It was not only the chief cultural, and to some extent political, society of Ukrainian intelligentsia in Kiev but also, through its contacts with similar societies in other cities, the most important catalyst of the Ukrainian national revival of the second half of the nineteenth century."[47]

Among the early members of *hromada* were the so-called *khlopomany* ("peasant-lovers," from the Polish word for peasant, *chłop*). These activists were predominantly concerned with emancipating the Ukrainian peasantry from the burdens of serfdom. *Khlopomany* lived among the Ukrainian peasants, adopting their speech, dress, and customs. Easiest to reach were the children of the peasants who worked in the homes of Polish magnates. Poles or Polonized Ukrainians, usually from the landowning class, were prominent in the ranks of both the *khlopomany* and *hromady*, and one Pole stated that "the Ukrainian *hromada* [was] without Ukrainians."[48]

Volodymyr Antonovych was the leader of the *khlopomany*. A firm believer in maintaining strong ties with the Polish student undergrounds from St. Petersburg to Cracow, he bitterly opposed the exploitation of Ukrainian serfs by Polish landlords and Polish territorial claims on the Ukraine. At St. Vladimir he lobbied to get certain courses taught in Ukrainian.[49] Less well known than Antonovych, but important to Kiev's

Ukrainian movement, were Paulin Swięcicki and Antoni Kocipiński. Swięcicki, a student at St. Vladimir, believed in a democratic union of Poles and Ukrainians and, upon the death of Shevchenko in 1861, established a three-class Sunday school in Kiev in which instruction was to be carried on in Ukrainian. Kocipiński (1816–1866), born near Cracow to a musical Polish family, was educated in Lviv. He became interested in musical ethnography and came to the Right Bank in 1845. Exiled by Bibikov, he returned from Vienna to Kiev in 1852 or 1853 and opened a music shop on the Khreshchatyk. Popular in the student underground, Kocipiński collected Ukrainian songs and put them on paper. A second edition was printed in Latin (Polish) script so that it could be sold in Europe. Although he was under police surveillance, Kocipiński hosted weekly musical evenings for lovers of Polish and Ukrainian songs. *Kievlianin* attacked him because he printed Cossack songs in the Latin script (which was specifically prohibited by Alexander II in 1862). Alfred fon Iunk, editor of the city newspaper *Kievskii telegraf*, defended him, but Kiev authorities subsequently banned sales of his music books. Hounded, he died in 1866, and authorities confiscated his collection. His works were not republished for another twenty-five years.[50]

The first clash between liberals and more radical democrats may have come in the fall of 1859 over the direction and character of instruction in the Sunday schools (described in chapter 3). Shevchenko, a proponent of strong Polish-Ukrainian ties against the tsar, donated books and money to the Kiev Sunday schools. A "Temporary Pedagogical School," which trained Sunday school teachers, opened in Kiev, as did the Society for the Friends of the People, whose members conversed only in Ukrainian. St. Vladimir student Mykhailo Drahomanov (1841–1895), who would later found the Ukrainian socialist movement, was a member of Friends of the People.[51]

The *hromada* movement spread throughout the Ukraine, producing such contributors to the Ukrainian cause as Pavlo Zhytetsky and Borys Poznansky. But despite their moderation, these Ukrainophiles were attacked in the aftermath of the Polish Insurrection of 1863. There is some irony here, since the refusal of the great majority of Ukrainian peasants to aid the Polish insurgents contributed greatly to this insurrection's failure. Marakhov contends that in Kiev Province an estimated 120,000 peasants took part in government (anti-Polish) patrols, and that overall, 300,000 participated in patrols on the Right Bank.[52] Yet in 1863 Minister of the Interior Petr Valuev secretly banned the publication of all materials in Ukrainian except for belles lettres, and the movement was disbanded until the 1870s.

At least in the countryside, the language question continued to be a hot topic, according to Kiev's newspaper *Zaria*. The Chernihiv provincial zemstvo actively campaigned to replace Russian with Ukrainian in its

schools. In 1881 the Kremenchuk Zemstvo Assembly unanimously petitioned to allow Ukrainian in elementary schools in the hope that it would
gradually become "a language of state." Others argued that it was more
practical to strengthen existing Russian-language schools and keep
Ukrainian as a second language. Pragmatists also noted that discrimination against the Ukrainian language was self-defeating. A. M. Dondukov-
Korsakov, Kiev's governor-general from 1869 until 1878, saw correctly
that it provided a cause for Ukrainian political activism and argued that
the Ukrainian language should be phased in first in the elementary
schools and then in the secondary schools.[53]

LANGUAGE AND PUBLICATION IN KIEV

The founding of St. Vladimir University in 1834 and a growing interest in
Kiev's storied past were the two most important factors that stimulated
the growth of a publishing industry in the city. The statistical and historical compilations of Governor Ivan Funduklei were particularly important
in this regard. In 1851 a commission was established to supervise publication on the region's flora, fauna, geology, and economy, and a university committee gathered materials on area history and archaeology. Summaries of faculty research were also published, and a university bulletin
(*Universitetskie izvestiia*) began to appear in 1861. Before midcentury,
efforts to found newspapers and journals were largely unsuccessful, however. One such effort, *Kievskie novosti* (Kiev news), which was to be published two or three times a week on current events and literary matters,
got only a handful of subscriptions, for it was too expensive. *Kievskie
gubernskie vedomosti* (News of Kiev Province) began publication in
1838. It ran information about prominent visitors, the fairs, weather, and
epidemics, and from 1845 included a section on local history, ethnography, and news. The Kiev Academy began to publish *Voskresnoe chtenie*
(Sunday reading) in the 1830s for the purpose of moral edification.[54]

In 1846 the Austrian Valner opened a printing and lithography shop.
His success encouraged others, notably F. Gliuksberg, who specialized in
Polish books, and the German Hammerschmidt, who opened a shop in
1852. By the mid-1850s, Kiev had come to rival Moscow and St. Petersburg as a center of publication. In 1856 the city had five bookshops, two
specializing in foreign books, and a reading room called "The Pharmacy
for the Soul." Founded initially in Podil, it moved to the Khreshchatyk in
the 1860s and offered newspapers, journals, and fiction, but no scholarly
works. St. Vladimir professors published books in Russian, Ukrainian,
French, and German (although censorship was rigorous). In 1852
Kievskii al'bom (Kiev album), which described noteworthy regional sites
and antiquities, was published in the city. German romanticism was

much in vogue, and prose, poetry, and collections of folktales and songs were published in both Russian and Ukrainian.[55]

The assault on the Ukrainian language restricted but did not eliminate the ability to publish in that language. In 1871 *Kievskii telegraf* noted that of 420 periodicals published in the empire (excepting Finland and the Caucasus), 327 were printed in Russian; 33 were written in German, 31 in Polish, 7 in French, 5 in Estonian, 4 in Latvian, 3 in "Jewish languages" (Hebrew or Yiddish), and 1 each in Finnish and Latin. There were no Ukrainian-language periodicals at all (unless the data simply subsumed Ukrainian titles under the heading of Russian). As a center of publication, Kiev ranked a distant sixth with 13 periodicals (behind St. Petersburg's 131, Moscow's 39, Warsaw's 33, Odessa's 16, and Riga's 14). The list mentioned all cities with at least 5 periodical publications. Notable was the absence of Kharkiv from the list. Evidently, by 1871 fewer than 5 periodicals were published there. Of the other towns with universities, Derpt (Dorpat) had 12 periodicals and Kazan 6. The remote Russian provincial town of Voronezh, which did not even have a university, had 7![56]

By the mid-1870s, however, Kiev had apparently resurfaced as a major center of Ukrainian-language publication. Editions of Shevchenko, Ivan Kotliarevsky (1769–1838), Ivan Nechui-Levytsky (1838–1918), and other popular Ukrainian authors appeared, as did translations of Russian and foreign classics. An estimated one-quarter of the product of Kiev's ten print shops was published in Ukrainian at this time.[57] The *hromada* movement began to function again. But on May 18, 1876, Alexander II issued the Ems Manifesto, which prohibited the use of Ukrainian in the printing of any text, original or translated, except for belles lettres and historical records. Importing Ukrainian books from abroad was prohibited; so was any public recitation or performance in the language. Ukrainian was not to be used in the schools, nor could school libraries hold Ukrainian-language materials. In 1881 publication of Ukrainian dictionaries was permitted if the Russian alphabet was used, and Ukrainian theater could be staged as long as troupes were not composed exclusively of Ukrainian actors. Each performance had to be approved by local authorities.

In 1883–1884 *Rada* (Council), an almanac of Ukrainian literary works and biographical sketches of their authors, was published, but the Ems Manifesto threatened to drive what was left of the Ukrainian language from Kiev, further dividing those activists who restricted themselves to cultural pursuits from those who sought a more overtly political course. Kostomarov saw no alternative but to accept the 1876 restrictions. Antonovych and Zhytetsky continued to work to foster Ukrainian cultural distinctiveness, while emphasizing "that it should not lead to the separation of the Ukrainians from the salutary impact of Russian culture and empire."[58] Meanwhile, Mykhailo Drahomanov chose a more confrontational course. He rejected Pushkin's belief that "all Slavic rivers should flow into a Russian sea," and argued that "on balance Ukrainians lost more than they gained under Russian rule."[59] Needless to say, there was no room in Russia for the likes of Drahomanov, and the center of the fledgling Ukrainian national movement moved to Geneva and then to the Austrian province of Galicia where it centered in Lviv, then called Lemberg.

Thus, while Kiev's *hromada* continued to be the main center of the Ukrainian movement in the Russian Empire, its adherents contented themselves with small deeds and advantages. Shevchenko's *Kobzar* was published in Kiev during a liberal respite under Minister of the Interior Mikhail Loris-Melikov. Ukrainophiles wrote for the Russian-language newspaper *Kievskii telegraf* and for the journal *Kievskaia starina* (Kievan antiquity). An unofficial Ukrainian Club met at the Hall of Mineral Waters, where Mykola Lysenko (1842–1912) rehearsed his popular Ukrainian choir. Restricted to purely cultural work, and unable to attract younger people, the city's *hromada* membership fell from about one hundred to perhaps a dozen. In 1873 the Russian Geographical Society opened its southwestern branch in Kiev. Led by ethnographer Pavlo Chubynsky (1839–1884), it conducted the city census of 1874 and served as the general staff for what was left of Kiev's Ukrainian movement. In the 1880s the progressive city paper *Zaria* published articles, in Russian, that were sometimes sympathetic to the plight of Ukrainians as well as Poles and Jews, and a Ukrainophile thrice-weekly *Trud* (Labor), published by G. T. Korchak-Novitsky, also appeared for a brief period.

Interestingly, in 1883 the eminent Ukrainophile Professor Antonovych served as managing editor of the Russian nationalist *Kievlianin* (Kievan) when its owner Maria Pikhno (the daughter of the paper's founder Vitaly Shulgin) went abroad for reasons of illness. This arrangement lasted only briefly, and Antonovych soon became editor of *Kievskoe slovo* (The word of Kiev), started up by Sergei Witte, then the director of the Southwestern Railroad. Rail freight rates, and not national issues, dominated the news at this time, and these lucrative journalistic endeavors helped Antonovych build a five-story house on fashionable Vladimir Street.[60]

KIEV: A RUSSIAN CITY?

What conclusions can be drawn about the extent to which Kiev had become "a Russian city" by the latter decades of the nineteenth century? By and large, Russian authorities had succeeded in driving the Ukrainian language from public life. Already in 1844, during a visit to Kiev's Polish-language Institute for Noble Girls, Nicholas I remarked on how well local students spoke Russian in comparison with the Ukrainian spoken in Poltava.[61] Farther east, in Kharkiv I. A. Ustynov wrote in 1881 that the city had

> completely lost its character as a Little Russian city, even in the speech of its inhabitants. It is much unlike the district cities of Khar'kov Province and even Poltava. In Khar'kov even among the simple people it is rare to hear Little Russian speech. In the lowest classes Russian is used almost entirely with some mixing of Little Russian words and figures of speech; in the middle classes Russian is used almost exclusively; and in the upper classes remnants of Little Russian have completely disappeared, although the Russian letter *g* among certain Khar'kovites reveals their Little Russian origin.[62]

Among the educated in Kiev, it was difficult to find Ukrainian-speakers. Kiev's Mariinsko-Blagoveshchensk Street unofficially came to be called "Ukrainian Street," for some of the more prominent Ukrainophiles such as Lysenko lived there. But in the 1880s even here it was said to be difficult to find a family in which Ukrainian prevailed over Russian. Even in homes where some Ukrainian was spoken, schoolchildren did their homework in Russian. They were taught to think in Russian, for this was the language of instruction and learning. Denied the chance to develop, literary Ukrainian could not keep pace with the terminological demands of fast-changing scholarly and scientific fields, and some Ukrainian intellectuals feared the language would die out. Antonovych took consolation in the fact that the Irish had not lost their intense national feelings despite linguistic Anglification.[63]

When Kiev's Second *Gymnasium* was founded in 1836, Russian, and not Polish, became the language of instruction. Education and culture, in fact, quickly became associated with speaking Russian. Even though Poles predominated in St. Vladimir's student body until 1863, the university had been founded to provide a Russian alternative to Polish-dominated education, and it carried out its function. In the latter decades of the century, Professor Florinsky of the Philology Department recognized the independence of all Slavic languages *except* Ukrainian.[64] The other higher educational institutions, such as the Commercial Institute and the Polytechnical Institute, also were Russian in content and instruction. Prominent Ukrainian scholars such as Pavlo Zhytetsky taught in the secondary schools because they were excluded from the university, but overall, the more schools that were built, the more the population became Russified. Now more than ever, Ukrainian was seen as a peasant language. Chykalenko remembers that in Kiev Ukrainian boys were ashamed to use their language, the language of the *khlop*.[65]

Politics also helped Russify the city, since the official business of local and imperial administration was conducted in Russian. Migrants from the Russian provinces did not necessarily control city affairs, however.

Russian-speaking Ukrainians were prominent, as was true in Kharkiv
where the son of A. A. Skrynnikov, "a simple *Maloros*" who had supplied regional fairs with *svyty* (coarse, homespun cloaks), became mayor
of the city.[66] In Kiev's city council, at least seventeen of the sixty-eight
individuals who served in 1886–1887, for example, were identifiably
Ukrainian in background.[67]

In the early 1890s one could still meet "pure Ukrainians" at the Cave
Monastery, although they expressed surprise upon meeting "a gentleman" who could speak the language of the peasant. These Ukrainian
speakers were probably clergymen who had frequent contact with
Ukrainian pilgrims from the villages and continued to use the peasant
tongue.[68] However, Kiev's Orthodox clergy probably stood with the state
on political matters, or tried to avoid "politics" altogether. (Their passive
role during the October pogrom in 1905 would testify to that.) Even by
1800 Kohut concludes that "the church in the provinces of the former
Hetmanate had become a pliable servant of the empire."[69] During the
fuss in 1914 over efforts to celebrate the hundredth anniversary of
Shevchenko's birth, one newspaper noted that in Kiev, excepting the Russian nationalist organization called Two-Headed Eagle, it was the clergy
who stood most opposed to honoring Shevchenko.[70]

The church did get involved in an interesting controversy over efforts
to erect a monument on St. Sophia Square honoring Bohdan Khmelnytsky, seen as a great national emancipator by politically conscious
Ukrainians, but as a unifier of Russia and Ukraine by supporters of a
Russian-dominated empire. Commissioned in 1869 by Alexander II, the
original model, brought to Kiev in 1872, had Khmelnytsky on a horse
trampling the corpses of a Jesuit, a Polish nobleman, and a Jewish lease-
holder. After some debate, it was deemed inappropriate. Alternative
models encountered a variety of technical and financial problems, and in
1881 the church objected because the planned monument threatened to
block the view between the St. Sophia Cathedral and the Mykhailiv Monastery, and because the rear end of the horse faced the cathedral. The
statue was finally finished in 1888 because the city fathers were embar-
rassed by the prospect that an unfinished monument might mar the forthcoming celebration marking the nine hundredth anniversary of Russia's
Christianization. Its inscription read "To Bogdan Khmelnitskii, a united
indivisible Russia, 1654–1888."[71]

In the 1890s one young visitor was disappointed to find that Kiev was
"not Ukrainian in character, but rather, Muscovite. Russian script and
Russian words appeared on street signs, storefronts, restaurants, and taverns. And when we said that we neither spoke nor understood Russian,
people tried to speak to us in Polish. Here and there a villager spoke

Ukrainian, as did a few from the working poor, all of which left a disagreeable impression."[72] Arriving in Kiev in 1904, the Ukrainian student Sadovsky was surprised by "the complete absence of outward signs of Ukrainian life" in the city. Only "now and then" did he hear "isolated Ukrainian phrases and jargon," but never the pure language. No wonder a contemporary historian of Ukraine has said, "Ukrainians remained a rural people attached to the soil, and although urbanization took place in Ukraine it did so 'without substantial participation by Ukrainians.'"[73]

Yet it is easy to overstate the depth of Russification in Kiev. The census of March 2, 1874, taken by the Southwestern Branch of the Russian Geographical Society, revealed a population of 127,251 people. By primary language, 98,205 (80 percent) spoke "Russian," 12,917 spoke "Jewish" (Yiddish, 11 percent), 7,863 (6 percent) spoke Polish, and 2,583 (2 percent) spoke German. Of the 98,205 "Russian"-speakers, 38,553 (39 percent) were listed as speakers of Little Russian (Ukrainian), meaning that about 30 percent of the entire city population was considered Ukrainian-speaking. Of the remaining "Russian"-speakers, only 9,736 (10 percent) were considered "Great Russians," and only 1,479 (2 percent) were considered Belarusians by speech. The remaining 48,437 (49 percent) were listed as speaking *Obshcherusskoe narechie*, or "generally Russian speech," which probably meant that they were Ukrainians, and to a lesser extent Belarusians and Poles, who could speak enough Russian to be counted as Russian-speakers in the census. By place of origin, only 16,872 Kievans (13 percent) came from Great Russian provinces, and many of them were in the city temporarily. Sixty percent of the Russians came from Orel, Kaluga, and Kursk Provinces. (Kursk had a mixed Russian and Ukrainian population.) By contrast, 26 percent of Kievans were natives of the city or of Kiev Province; another 14 percent came from adjacent Chernihiv, Podil, and Volyn Provinces.[74]

The official state census taken in 1897 reveals that while the population in Kiev District (Kievskii *uezd*), the farmland and villages just outside the city, was overwhelmingly Ukrainian, "Russians" predominated within the city limits (table 4.2). The census also reveals that while some Russians, particularly men, had migrated to Kiev, primarily from Orel and Kursk Provinces, most migrants had come from the adjacent Ukrainian provinces, and half of Kiev's 247,723 residents had been born in Kiev or in Kiev Province. As in 1874, there were comparatively few Great Russian migrants in Kiev at this time (table 4.3).

Furthermore, even after 1876 enforcement of the ban on Ukrainian was haphazard. The library at the comparatively liberal Second *Gymnasium* maintained an outstanding collection of Ukrainian literary works, beginning with the poet and playwright Kotliarevsky, as well as scholarly works by Ukrainians in Ukrainian, Russian, and Polish.[75] George

TABLE 4.2
Major Ethnic Groups of Kiev and Kiev District by Language, 1897

	Kiev		Kiev District	
	Male	*Female*	*Male*	*Female*
Great Russians	71,722	62,556	5,114	4,528
Ukrainians	31,721	23,343	122,416	126,720
Jews	15,798	14,139	14,289	15,643
Poles	8,571	8,008	939	938
Belarusians	1,709	1,088	1,012	300

SOURCE: *Pervaia vseobshchaia perepis' naseleniia Rossiiskoi imperii, 1897 g.* (St. Petersburg, 1904), 16:88–90.

TABLE 4.3
Province of Birth of Kievans in 1897, Excluding Kiev Province

Males		Females	
Chernihiv	10,689	Chernihiv	8,703
Orel	6,467	Poltava	4,054
Podil	6,357	Volyn	3,608
Kursk	5,417	Orel	3,231
Poltava	4,717	Mogilev	3,013
Volyn	4,564	Minsk	2,796
Mogilev	3,481	Kursk	2,772
Minsk	2,962	Podil	2,656
Kaluga	2,855	Kherson	1,657
Kherson	1,469	Kaluga	1,476

SOURCE: *Pervaia vseobshchaia perepis'*, 16:40.

Shevelov notes that Ukrainian "did not completely lose its function as a literary language," and that Ukrainian theater, despite "senseless and arbitrary restrictions, continued . . . to enjoy great success, even in St. Petersburg and with Russian critics."[76] In 1872 playwright Mykhailo Starytsky (1850–1904) and composer Mykola Lysenko (1842–1912) helped organize a circle for the production of Ukrainian plays in Kiev. Actor-director Panas Saksahansky (1859–1940), who would live in Kiev from 1912 until 1940, first performed in the city with the Starytsky troupe in 1883. Strangely, it was required at times that Ukrainian and Russian plays be performed back-to-back on the same evening. The journalist Iaron remembers the good-natured hisses and catcalls from the Ukrainian audiences during the Russian performances and the rowdy behavior afterward.

In 1884 Kievan youths, spurred by teachers, staged a noisy demonstration at a Ukrainian play. Governor-General Drenteln consequently banned Ukrainian theater from Kiev and the surrounding provinces for nearly a decade. But from 1893 Mykola Sadovsky (1856–1933) brought his troupe to Kiev almost yearly, and Saksahansky did the same beginning in 1895. Marko Kropyvnytsky (1840–1910), famous as an actor, director, and playwright, also performed. It appears that Ukrainian performances were expected to avoid political commentary and featured mostly *hopak* (a folk dance) and vaudeville song, dance, and comedy routines which often portrayed drunkenness. Nevertheless, they were received enthusiastically, especially by young people, and they played an important role in keeping the Ukrainian language and culture alive. In 1906 Sadovsky founded the first permanent Ukrainian theater, in Poltava, and in 1907 moved it to Kiev's Troitsky People's Club.[77]

In their daily routines, Kievans continued to eat the same borshch and cheese dumplings and entertain themselves with the same songs as did the surrounding Ukrainian villagers. Young girls commonly made the traditional embroidered shirts for young men as signs of friendship (and not necessarily romance), not in an effort to make a political statement, but simply because it was an old Ukrainian custom. While some officials found this irritating, and some Ukrainian nationalists would later scorn "embroidered patriotism," in the 1880s even policemen wore these traditional shirts. At Christmas carolers strolled about carrying stars as they had done earlier in the century, and Christmas and Easter festivities appear to have been celebrated much as they were in the villages. *Paska* (Easter bread) and painted eggs were a part of Easter in Kiev, and the sometimes week-long festivities were said to amaze "the Muscovites." There were small differences; young boys were not allowed to ring the church bells as they were in the villages, for example. Perhaps with a touch of nationalistic nostalgia, Slavinsky even recalls that people did not shout as much on Kiev's streets as they did in Moscow; nor was profanity used as commonly on its streets as in the capitals. (He does concede that some Ukrainian profanities were heard on the streets because the local population had trouble mastering Russian obscenities.) When he traveled from Kiev to Moscow and other Russian cities, it was as if these cities "were in a remote and barely known land."[78]

Linguistically, on the Khreshchatyk and in Lypky and Pechersk, full of officials, the affluent, and the upwardly mobile, Russian was heard almost without exception. But in the city as a whole, linguistic Russification was less complete, for many Kievans spoke blends of Russian and Ukrainian that were said to offend the ears of Great Russians accustomed to the "pure" Russian of Moscow or St. Petersburg. The Great Russian language was "weakly spoken" in Kiev in comparison with the fine Russian heard on the streets of St. Petersburg.[79] And if Kievans spoke in linguistic blends, their culture was a blend of the Russian and Ukrainian as well. In customs, celebrations, and social etiquette, they retained much from the surrounding Ukrainian countryside. This blending of language and custom was what Governor Muratov had in mind when he remarked that by the end of the reign of Nicholas I Kharkiv's residents had become "a special cross between Great Russians and Little Russians."[80]

Similarly, it was difficult to find pure Polish spoken in Kiev in the latter decades of the nineteenth century. The writer Konstantin Paustovsky recalls from his boyhood "that frightful Polish-Russian-Ukrainian jargon which we in Kiev used to think was the Polish language."[81] In sum, even today Kievans commonly speak blends of Russian-Ukrainian called *surzhyk*. Perhaps represented by the category *Obshcherusskoe narechie* in the 1874 census, *surzhyk* must have been even more common in the nineteenth century. Antonovych was said to have joked: "Kievans speak neither Russian nor Little Russian. They speak a little in Russian."[82] Kiev had a Russian face, but linguistically and culturally, Kiev was not Moscow, as Muscovites were quick to point out.

THE UKRAINIAN MOVEMENT IN
LATE-IMPERIAL KIEV

In the late 1870s and early 1880s, students boldly and noisily argued their views on the streets, and some of Kiev's Ukrainophiles, lacking legal channels to pursue their goals, joined the radical movements such as "Land and Freedom."[83] One antidote to all of this was an infamous prosecutor who terrorized the radicals, once grabbing a fifty-two-year-old worker by the throat and threatening to strangle him. When police turned up the heat, radical circles met on boats on the Dnipro. Gun battles with police were not unknown in the city, and costumed assassins once nearly killed a suspected double agent at a masquerade ball at the Merchants' Club. One who was arrested at this time was Ivan Saranchov, a socialite and law graduate of St. Vladimir whose sister was married to one of the Tereshchenko sugar barons. For four years he ran an illegal press out of the fashionable Lypky home of his father, a lieutenant-general. The trial set Kiev society astir, and, in a defense not unlike that of American heiress Patty Hearst decades later, it was argued that Saranchov, a gullible victim, had succumbed to extortion. While incarcerated, Saranchov was given furniture, servants, and meals from home. Soon pardoned, he ultimately became the chairman of a provincial court in Tobolsk.[84]

As the political repression of the 1880s settled in, the Ukrainian movement continued to be divided between "culturalists" and the more politicized *Drahomantsy*, inspired by Mykhailo Drahomanov and other activists in Galicia. Osyp Hermaize recalls that in the 1890s *hromada* experienced a "renaissance" fueled by contraband literature from Galicia and supplemented by "the Russian Ukrainian diet of Shevchenko, nationalist poetry, populist novels and the cult of the Cossacks."[85] In the 1890s the language restrictions of the 1876 Ems Manifesto tended to be ignored, and cheap Ukrainian books were again published, many of them popular scientific and "how-to" booklets. One organizer of Kiev's Ukrainian movement at this time was St. Vladimir Russian-language professor Volodymyr Peretts. His followers were few in number, however, and most were students, many of them women, who were interested in Ukrainian history and culture. They were of little concern to local police.[86]

In Galicia the first Ukrainian political party was formed in 1890. In 1898 the Kiev student *hromada* began to publish under the name of Vik, and Kiev, especially St. Vladimir University, became the center of the Brotherhood of Taras, a small organization founded in Kharkiv for the purpose of rejuvenating the Ukrainian movement. Absorbed into the so-called General Ukrainian Organization by 1897, these activists carried out "a more militant form of cultural work within the Ukrainian movement." Although they were not a political party, Boshyk calls them the "first organized expression of modern Ukrainian nationalism" in the Russian Empire.[87]

As socialism became the dominant oppositional political current in the 1890s, Ukrainian activists cooperated more easily with the Polish Social Democrats than with the Russian socialist organizations because the latter were less tolerant of the Ukrainian movement. A Ukrainian Social Democratic Party was formed in 1897, but it never became an important political force. "The popular conception that one could be either a Marxist or a Ukrainian but not both was still prevalent at this time," Boshyk notes.[88]

Spurred by ongoing cooperation with Ukrainian activists in Lviv, in January 1900 the Revolutionary Ukrainian Party (RUP) was founded in Kharkiv, and in 1900 the Ukrainian Socialist Party was founded in Kiev by Polish students sympathetic to the Ukrainian cause. The RUP became the more significant of the two. Initially hostile to Marxism, it sought to work primarily among the peasants, and it called for an independent Ukraine from Galicia to the Caucasus. The RUP won some support from the city's *gymnasium* students and gained control of the local *hromada*, which at this time was said to have no more than twenty-five members. Kiev became the organizational center of the RUP.[89]

By 1902 the RUP was attempting to win converts among workers, concentrating on small workshops, where employees tended to be less Russified, and on the Ukrainian-speaking areas on the outskirts of Kiev. Peasants were sometimes brought to Kiev for political education, and a good

working relationship was forged with the Jewish Bund. Kiev's massive
strike of July 1903 (see chapter 7) further encouraged the RUP to look to
the working classes for support, and by the end of that year, the RUP had
become essentially a social democratic party. The poet Lesia Ukrainka
(1871–1913), the niece of Drahomanov, was one influential Kievan who
translated some of Karl Marx's works into Russian and Ukrainian. The
student Sadovsky recalls the popularity of Lenin's ideas in 1904 and
notes that for politically active Ukrainians there was really no alternative
in Kiev. Hermaize recalls as well that the RUP had little success in competing against the much larger Russian social democratic movement in
the city.[90]

The revolutionary upheavals of 1905, discussed in detail in chapters 7–9,
showed that the injustices of the workplace and a desire to abolish political authoritarianism were far more potent sources of discord in Kiev than
were national aspirations and conflicts at this time. Nevertheless, during
the "Banquet Campaign" at the end of 1904, Ukrainian activists used a
celebration in Kiev honoring the writer Ivan Nechui-Levytsky to pass a
series of resolutions seeking an end to restrictions against the Ukrainian
language. These activists came from throughout the Ukraine, and similar
resolutions were sent from Kharkiv, Odessa, and elsewhere. The Literacy
Societies in Kiev and Kharkiv, the Kiev Pedagogical Society, and the
Odessa City Council supported these resolutions, and on January 21,
1905, two weeks after Bloody Sunday, the Council of Ministers authorized a review of language restrictions.

  In mid-February Prime Minister Sergei Witte assured a Ukrainian delegation that restrictions would be lifted, but the opposite seems to have
occurred. In Vinnytsia (Vinnitsa), for example, it was reported in March
that "the Little Russian language is being driven out of the public reading
rooms by force. The attempts of the Vinnytsia People's Club to permit a
brochure in Little Russian were rejected, and the building itself has been
occupied by troops."[91] Demands for language rights continued. In
Poltava the Ukrainian Circle of the Union of Equal Rights for Women
petitioned that St. Vladimir University be opened immediately to women
and teach Ukrainian subjects in Ukrainian whenever possible.[92] Activist
Serhii Efremov observed that the question of Ukrainian language rights
really masked the more central question of "poverty, ignorance, and
darkness." At the top, the Ukrainian intelligentsia was small in number;
at the bottom, even literate Ukrainian peasants could not read the pamphlets on public health or protection from cholera, for they were published in Russian.[93] A letter to Zhytomyr's newspaper *Volyn'* in 1905
claimed that Ukrainians would remain culturally "primitive" without
Ukrainian schools, model farms, and special training in modern farming

methods. As for the Poles and the Russians, its author warned, they forget that they are only "guests" in Ukraine.[94]

Although the fledgling Ukrainian movement remained a sideshow in 1905, contributing only sporadic challenges to local authority, the upheavals that followed Bloody Sunday split the weak RUP. One faction, headed by Mykola Porsh (1879–1944), tried to direct the movement more toward the urban worker and away from the peasant. Porsh objected, however, to the use of Russian in agitational work among Ukrainian workers. The Ukrainian Social Democrats, headed by Marian Melenevsky (1879–1938) and more commonly called "Spilka," accused Porsh of concentrating too much on appeals to Ukrainian nationalism. The pragmatic Spilka above all sought to overthrow the tsar. It stressed trade unionism and cooperation with Russian oppositional movements, and it became the dominant Ukrainian party, with membership estimates ranging from three thousand to seven thousand before it was decimated in the repression that followed 1905.[95]

With headquarters in Kiev, Spilka functioned as an autonomous Ukrainian group within the broader Russian Social Democratic movement. It had many Russian and Jewish members and published commonly, though not exclusively, in Russian, even in its agitational work among peasants. Observes Boshyk: "Not without irony can it be said that the more successful Spilka was, the less 'Ukrainian' it became, both in terms of membership and the language used in propaganda and agitation."[96] Sadovsky recalls that interest in Ukrainian nationalism among Kiev's students was not very great, and, in fact, "our knowledge of the Ukrainian language was not even very good."[97] Yet the very existence of a separate Spilka organization reflected the fact that at least some local socialists felt a sense of Ukrainian patriotism.

THE AFTERMATH OF UPHEAVAL

The new liberal order promised by Nicholas II in October 1905 had immediate consequences for the Ukrainians. The first Ukrainian newspaper, *Ridnii krai* (Native land), appeared in Poltava in December 1905, followed shortly by Kiev's *Hromads'ka dumka* (Hromada opinion). But of thirty-four Ukrainian publications that appeared in the first half of 1906, only nine survived in some form by mid-1910, and most were out of business by 1907. Many folded after their first or second issue. In 1910 Kiev's Ukrainian press consisted only of the daily paper *Rada*, which succeeded *Hromads'ka dumka*; two monthlies; two weeklies; a publication devoted to practical information; and the scholarly journal *Zapysky Ukrain'skoho naukovoho tovarysta* (Notes of the Ukrainian Scholarly

Society). The publishing house Chas had published a popular biography of Shevchenko. The Poltava zemstvo bought thirty thousand copies for distribution before the right-wing *Kievlianin* and Kiev's Russian Nationalist Club exerted enough pressure to bring this practice to a halt. St. Vladimir students had taken the lead in asking that Ukrainian history and literature be taught in Ukrainian at the universities in Kiev, Kharkiv, and Odessa. But these efforts had come to nothing. The Ukrainian press was fined for referring to Ukrainian festivals or to the bleak conditions in the countryside, although similar references were permitted in the Russian-language press. Readers of the Ukrainian press were accused of being Austrian spies. Efforts to use Ukrainian in regional elementary schools were generally quashed, as was the attempt of the Kozlenko private secondary school in Kiev to introduce Ukrainian literature, language, and history into its curriculum. Concluded Serhii Efremov: "It is like 1863 or 1876."[98]

Evhen Chykalenko recalls the problems inherent in beginning the newspaper *Hromads'ka dumka*, first published in Kiev on December 31, 1905. Heady egos and difficult personalities, particularly that of the ethnographer and linguist Borys Hrinchenko (1863–1910), compounded ideological differences. A resident of Kiev since 1902, Hrinchenko had worked on a dictionary of the Ukrainian language. In 1905 he helped found the liberal Ukrainian Radical Party, which sought mainly to end restrictions against that language. After the October Manifesto it joined the Ukrainian Democratic Party to form the Ukrainian Democratic Radical Party, but like their socialist counterparts, the Ukrainian liberal movement had little influence at this time. The party soon dissolved into the Society of Ukrainian Progressives, and many of its members joined the Russian Constitutional Democratic (or Kadet) Party. Some wanted to emulate the moderate *Osnova* of the early 1860s; others sought to build a revolutionary movement with mass appeal. The decision was made to publish a newspaper four times a week, as well as a magazine, but even these modest efforts would have to rely on donations for years: there were not enough potential subscribers to enable the group to approach breaking even.

Then too the governor and other local officials balked, and the group had to appeal to the Senate. On December 28, 1905, Efremov, Kiev's leading Ukrainian journalist, was arrested amid a wave of political reaction. Nevertheless, about a thousand subscribers had been lined up, and on December 31, five thousand copies of the first edition rolled off the press, only to be confiscated by police. Uncertain whether a single edition had been confiscated or the entire operation closed down, the editors went to the censors and were told to soften the paper's "sharp tone." *Hromads'ka dumka* thus continued, albeit more cautiously, until police ransacked its office on August 18, 1906. Bitter editorial feuding continued, and when its successor *Rada* appeared on September 15, the financially strapped editors were forced to resort to the local custom (pioneered by the Russian papers, with the exception of *Kievlianin*) of paying fifty rubles per month in bribes to the censors and special bribes of one hundred rubles on New Year's and Easter. Left-leaning Russian-language newspapers such as *Kievskaia pochta* (Kievan post) and *Kievskaia mysl'* (Kievan thought) carried on the political fight and supported rights for Ukrainians, Jews, and Poles.[99]

In 1906 the number of subscriptions reached 4,093 but fell to 1,509 later in the year. Some readers had subscribed only for a month or two. Others had been scared off. Police continued to confiscate issues. One zemstvo worker acknowledged that subscribing to the paper cost him four times the official four-ruble subscription price, for he would have been fired had he not also subscribed to *Kievlianin* for an additional twelve rubles. With expenses of about six thousand rubles each month, the editors debated about whether to cut back from four issues per week to two.[100] Ultimately *Rada* received a subsidy from a wealthy Kherson benefactor.

Other problems beset the paper as well. Hrinchenko complained that it lost subscribers because it was really "a Russian paper written in Ukrainian." Editor-in-chief Matushevsky countered that no more than a thousand subscribers were interested specifically in Ukrainian issues; many simply wanted the news. With its limited staff, resources, and publication schedule, *Hromads'ka dumka* could not really compete with *Kievskaia mysl'*, which had better and more famous journalists and correspondents elsewhere in the empire and abroad. Nor could it compete outside of Kiev against comparable local papers. Some were put off by the paper's literary Ukrainian, either because of differences in dialect or because they were used to *surzhyk*, the more familiar Russified Ukrainian. Frequently hostile to the clergy and the affluent, the newspaper directed its message to the masses who could not buy it because they lacked the money or because they could not read it. Such were the entrepreneurial and editorial problems that Ukrainian publicists faced in the hostile environment created by decades of Russification and the political reaction that followed 1905.

Ukrainian activism had surfaced in several cities in 1905. For example, the famous historian-publicist Mykhailo Hrushevsky (1866–1934) joined Ivan Steshenko to issue sharp challenges in *Iuzhnykh zapiskakh* (Notes from the south), published in Odessa, and *Syn otechestva* (Son of the fatherland), published in St. Petersburg. But in those final years spanning the 1905 revolution and the collapse of the imperial order in 1917,

Kiev was clearly the main center of the empire's small Ukrainian movement. The most influential members of the Ukrainian intelligentsia resided in the city. Bureaucratic oversight, while burdensome, was at least more consistent in Kiev and less likely to fluctuate in accordance with personal whims. By 1912 Russia's *entire* Ukrainian periodical press consisted of five journals and seven daily or weekly newspapers. All but two of these periodicals were published in Kiev.[101] *Rada*, which supported Ukrainian schools and rights for Jews and Poles, had the greatest circulation. It ran 3,000 copies in its initial printing on September 15, 1906, and it continued to print between 2,100 and 4,000 copies per issue. A second paper began as *Slovo* (The word) in 1907–1908; it was changed to *Selo* (The village) in 1909, and *Zasiv* (Sowing time) in 1911. Hrushevsky was involved with this Social Democratic weekly, which averaged about 2,000 copies per issue. The democratic *Svitova zirnytsia* (Morning star) was first published by Polish landowners in Mogilev in 1906. It came to Kiev in March 1911 from a small town in Podil Province. It printed about 500 copies per issue. *Ridnii krai*, a purveyor of nonpolitical, cultural Ukrainianism, moved to Kiev 1912. It had become a weekly with a run of about 800 copies per issue.

Of the monthly journals, *Literaturno-naukovyi vistnyk* (The literary-scholarly herald), begun in Lviv in 1898, moved to Kiev in 1907. It was edited by Hrushevsky and became, after *Rada*, the most important Ukrainian organ in the Russian Empire. Its 1907 printing run of 2,000 copies increased slightly to 2,200 by 1912, but only 56 Kievans subscribed. Half of the copies were sent to Habsburg Lviv, while 714 subscribers lived elsewhere in the Russian Empire. *Ukrains'ka khata* (The Ukrainian hut), begun in 1909, printed runs of 500–600 and remained in chronic financial difficulties. It focused on literary modernism. *Svitlo* (The light), begun by the teacher G. P. Sherstiuk in September 1910, stressed educational and cultural themes. Its second issue was confiscated for advocating the creation of secret Ukrainian schools with Ukrainian textbooks. *Moloda Ukraina* (Young Ukraine) was intended to get children used to reading Ukrainian instead of Russian. Begun in 1908, it was often distributed free. The tenth Ukrainian publication in Kiev was the *Zapysky* (Notes) of the Ukrainian Scientific Society. The only Ukrainian-language organs in the Russian Empire published outside of Kiev were *Dniprovi khvyli* (Dnipro waves) in Katerynoslav and *Snip* (Sheath), a weekly paper "for intelligentsia" which began on January 1, 1912 in Kharkiv.

Kiev's importance to the Ukrainian movement was further underscored by the fact that thirteen of the seventeen Ukrainian publishing houses that existed in Russian Ukraine in 1909 operated out of the city. The oldest was Vik, which had ties with *Rada* and often published articles from the Ukrainian press. In 1912 newer firms included Chas, Lan, Ranok, Khvyli, Krynytsa, Zoria, Teatral'na Byblioteka, Zhyttia i Mystetstvo (associated with *Ukrains'ka khata)*, Ukr.-Rus'ka Vydavnycha Spilka, I. I. Samonenka, and E. P. Cherepovsky. In 1908, 220 Ukrainian books and booklets were published in the Russian Empire; in 1909, 191; in 1910, 196; in 1911, 242 (some in connection with the Shevchenko Jubilee). Many of these publications were translations from Russian and other languages; some, like Lviv Professor Stepan Rudnytsky's short geography of Ukraine, published by Lan, were originals. Because of the small number of Ukrainian readers, the buying public was limited, and editions of 500–600 copies were typical.[102]

Kiev *Prosvita* (Enlightenment), which formed shortly after 1905, "set the tone for the Ukrainian movement in Russia" in the view of local censor S. N. Shchegolev, who kept close tabs on Ukrainian activists. Its six hundred active members included Lesia Ukrainka, Serhii Efremov, Mykola Lysenko, and the son and daughter of Mykhailo Drahomanov. In four years it sponsored more than 150 lectures and literary or musical gatherings and published 34 popular booklets and brochures in 164,000 copies, many on social and historical themes intended to raise political and national consciousness. It campaigned for basic rights and dreamed ultimately of an independent Ukraine within a free federation of Slavic republics.[103]

The scope of the Ukrainian movement continued to be limited by decades of discrimination against the Ukrainian language, however. According to the 1897 census, in Kiev only 56 percent of the 17,485 "Ukrainian" men and only 28 percent of the 6,382 "Ukrainian" women were considered literate. It is not clear whether these "Ukrainians" could read Russian or Ukrainian, or both. The number of literate Russian-speakers in Kiev who could read both languages is also unknown. It is clear, however, that the Ukrainian-speaking countryside was mostly illiterate. For example, in rural Kiev District, just outside the city, there were 249,136 recorded Ukrainians. Only 26,586 (11 percent) were deemed literate, almost all of them men, and this pattern was replicated throughout rural Ukraine. In 1914 a zemstvo survey indicated that the effort to combat illiteracy in rural Kiev Province was making little or no progress. Only about one-third of the eligible rural students were attending school.[104]

Although the goals of most Ukrainian activists were modest, Russian authorities, fearing even "ethnographic separatism," reacted sharply against the small Ukrainian movement, closing down Kiev *Prosvita* in 1910. Among the authorities' targets of censure were the exhibit of Ukrainian artists in Kiev, which ran from mid-December 1910 until mid-January 1911 (such exhibits had begun in Poltava in 1903); claims (rather premature, it appears) that a Ukrainian architectural style was emerging (Poltava's provincial zemstvo building designed by Vasyl Krychevsky [1873–1952] was an early example); Ukrainian theater productions (*Rada* saw theater as a school that improved and ennobled Ukrainian speech); the "cult of the *kobzar*" spawned by the musical evenings featuring Ukrainian folk music and instruments; the Ukrainian Scholarly Society of Kiev, founded late in 1906, which sponsored lectures and printed materials in Ukrainian on science and medicine; and the Ukrainian Society for the Assistance of Science, Literature, and Art in Kiev, whose secretive activities were said to be "hushed up by the Ukrainian press."[105]

Of the fourteen *prosvity* that had existed in 1908 (including groups in Baku and Vladivostok), only seven were still operating in 1911. *Prosvity* in Kiev and Odessa had been shut down by authorities, but several others had closed for lack of interest or because of fear. In the schools Ukrainian subjects were also under attack. At Kiev's church-supported Girls' Secondary School Number 1, where many of the students were training to teach in village schools, evening programs that had been entirely devoted to Ukrainian culture between 1906 and 1909 reverted to Russian themes and the Russian language in 1910.[106]

SHEVCHENKO RETURNS TO KIEV

When in 1906 a series of nice warm days had suddenly turned to snow, the wry Samiilenko, noting the importance of politics in just about everything, assumed "that spring had been confiscated." He stopped by the offices of *Kievlianin*, where editor Pikhno assured him that Kiev indeed had a very Russian climate. Samiilenko wondered if the new Duma might fill up with "foreigners." "Said Mr. Pikhno, all of our troubles stem from the fact that in Kiev we have so many foreigners."[107] For the Pikhnos, Savenkos, and Shulgins, who dominated Kiev politically from the time of Bibikov, Jews and Poles had long been the "foreigners." "Little Russians" who saw themselves as Ukrainians were not as threatening, but they too now qualified.

As the world war that would destroy tsarist Russia drew nearer, Ukrainian-Russian politics in Kiev came to focus on the legacy of Taras Shevchenko. In February 1911, on the fiftieth anniversary of his death, a Ukrainian choir sang at a requiem mass at St. Sophia to an overflow crowd, most of whom were students. Kiev's city museum exhibited Shevchenko's manuscripts and memorabilia. However, the Nationalist Club protested, and authorities confiscated many of his works, including *Kobzar*, published in censored form in 1906, and an edition of verse for children. Also confiscated was a Jubilee cantata by Mykola Lysenko and

Samiilenko's *Death of a Poet*. Even many conservatives found these measures to be foolish and excessive. State Duma member Count Kapnist II, for example, noted that Ukrainian pride in their region did not make them separatists, and *Rada* noted that Shevchenko had not been a separatist in the political sense.[108] In Lviv blue and yellow Ukrainian national flags and banners appeared during the celebration. In Kiev no such banners were reported, but *Rada* noted that some students donned national costumes or pinned blue and yellow ribbons to their chests. Kharkiv's leading Ukrainian activist, Professor Mykola Sumtsov, used the occasion to call for programs in Shevchenko studies at regional universities and a new Ukrainian theater in Kiev. The implications of donating to the campaign to build a monument in Shevchenko's memory became a matter of public debate. Kiev's *Literaturno-naukovoho vistnyk* stated that such contributions implied sympathy for Ukrainian national goals, but Kharkiv's progressive Russian-language paper *Utro* (Morning) argued that while "nationalist romanticism" was not altogether absent, interest in Shevchenko was more the result of his struggle against social injustice.[109]

Ukrainian city councils inevitably became involved in the ferment. Kharkiv's council approved Sumtsov's requests to fund a portrait of Shevchenko for the city museum and a yearly prize for student projects on Ukrainian history, literature, and ethnography; to increase funding for the Ukrainian collection in the public library; and to rename a street after Shevchenko. Kiev's provincial zemstvo board was strongly Ukrainophile, but the Kiev city council remained indifferent. In 1910 Ukrainian voters tried to form an electoral bloc, but very few were elected. A 1911 petition mainly by Polish councilmen for a special Ukrainian section in the Kiev Public Library was ignored. The council did designate separate Ukrainian and Russian theater seasons at the People's Club and leased the theater to the popular Ukrainian director Sadovsky.

In 1914, however, even the staid Kiev city council got caught up in the ferment over efforts to celebrate the hundredth anniversary of Shevchenko's birth on February 25. It decided unanimously to honor Shevchenko, agreed to rename a school and theater after Ukrainian historian Mykhailo Hrushevsky, and pledged (by a 23–20 vote) to contribute five thousand rubles to the forthcoming festival. It further resolved to rename Bul'varno-Kudriavska Street Shevchenko Street, pending approval from the Ministry of the Interior. State and church officials, meanwhile, vetoed the idea of a festival. Bishop Nikodim said that requiem services could be held, if no more than five people were permitted to attend and if choirs were banned. The "older generation" of Ukrainophiles were also said to oppose the demonstration, fearing the disappearance of what was left of the freedoms won in 1905.[110]

The festival was held anyway and drew crowds said to number up to eight hundred. Two-Headed Eagle, a group of Russian nationalist extremists, tore up portraits and smashed busts of Shevchenko, claiming the festival was an Austrian-inspired move to spur Ukrainian separatism. (These nationalists hated nearly all of the great writers of the times, including the Russians Tolstoy and Gorky.) Other than the violence committed by these thugs, the demonstration was peaceful. A few small workshops and the South Russian Machine Works did strike, but many false reports appeared in the rightist press: that the demonstration had been led by a Jew on a white horse, that half of the demonstrators were Jews, that banners calling for Ukrainian separatism and support for Austria had been unfurled, and that the crowd marched to the Austrian Consulate shouting "Down with Russia, Long Live Austria." Widely reprinted, these accusations seem part of an effort by Two-Headed Eagle to use the demonstration to incite a pogrom. Thomas Prymak observes that "these were the first mass demonstrations ever staged by the Ukrainian movement in Russia." "No longer could the Ukrainian movement be ignored, no longer could it be explained away as just so much foreign intrigue."[111] On the other hand, Shevchenko was a symbol of revolutionary zeal, a fighter against social injustice, and not simply a symbol of protest against persecution of Ukrainians. Even though Russian Social Democrats had not been active in the planning of the demonstration, many saw it as a rallying point for the city's underclass, regardless of nationality, and a broad protest against autocracy.[112] Socialism and class-generated appeals still carried more clout than did militant Ukrainian nationalism in Kiev in 1914; but opportunities for a new social, political, *and* national order were by now less than three years away.

Jewish Kiev

RECORDS of Jewish settlement in Kiev date back at least to 1018, when it was reported that local soldiers attacked Jewish homes during the Polish occupation of the city.[1] The city wall had a "Jewish Gate," later renamed Lviv Gate, and then Zhytomyr Gate. However, the size of medieval Kiev's Jewish community is not known.

The Polish-Lithuanian state, which extended its authority over Kiev, had one of the largest concentrations of Jews in Europe. With no regular means of raising revenue, Polish kings relied on tolls exacted from merchants on roads and at bridges and river crossings. Jews commonly paid the treasury a fixed sum for the privilege of collecting local toll revenues and may have settled in Kiev for this purpose.[2] The fact that the famous linguist and scholar Rabbi Moses Ben Jacob lived in Kiev for a time indicates that the city had a Jewish community of some significance in the early sixteenth century, as does the fact that in 1522 Sigismund I (1506–1548) authorized the creation of a Jewish cemetery beyond the Lviv Gate near the settlement of Kudriavets.[3] The tolerant Sigismund Augustus (1548–1572), an enlightened patron of the Renaissance who defended Jews against accusations of ritual murder, granted equal rights to Kiev's Jews on the grounds that they paid the same taxes as Podil's burghers.[4]

Polish sponsorship of Jewish settlement in Kiev added fuel to the conflict that already existed between the Orthodox and Catholic churches. At least twice during the reign of Sigismund Augustus, in 1557 and again in 1565, Jews were prohibited, presumably by local burghers, from trading in the city without special permission. Thus, it appears that despite protection from the Polish kings, Jewish trade and settlement rights remained precarious in Kiev, and the city's Jewish community almost certainly remained small.

In 1618, at a time when Kiev was in turmoil over conflicts between Uniates and Orthodox, Sigismund III (1587–1632) gave itinerant Jewish and Christian merchants the right to trade in Kiev's private homes, but not in its main trade row. On February 18, 1619, probably in an effort to mitigate local anti-Polish opposition, Sigismund issued an edict prohibiting Jews from holding real estate in Kiev and allowing them the right to trade in the city only for brief periods during the fairs. Although a few Jews remained in Kiev under the protection of officials who saw them as important sources of revenue, after 1619 local burghers relied on this edict as legal grounds for keeping Jews out.[5]

As the Polish state weakened, conditions for Jews deteriorated. Horrible pogroms accompanied the Khmelnytsky-led Cossack uprising in 1648–1649. Townsmen reasserted their privileges, and Jews lost their political and legal autonomy. Expelled from Kiev in 1654, Jews probably were not able to settle in the city again until the early 1790s. Throughout the eighteenth century, attacks on Jews continued in the surrounding region. One massacre took place in 1768 in nearby Uman, then a private city belonging to the Potocki estate. One Cossack practice was to hang a Pole, a Jew, and a dog from a tree with the inscription, "*Lakh* (Pole), *zhid*, and hound—all to the same faith bound."[6]

It was sometimes said that because of the trade caravans coming to Kiev, silk from the East was cheaper in the city than linen in Vilnius, imported pepper cheaper than salt. The extent to which Jews contributed to the city's prosperity, and the impact of banning them from the city, were controversial subjects. Jews commonly went to the great European fairs such as Leipzig's to trade furs and other products from the Russian and Polish lands in return for high-quality, low-cost dry goods, which were otherwise scarce or unavailable. Furthermore, the competition they provided kept prices down. But this same competition was also blamed for severely hampering the entrepreneurial activities of the city's burghers and for retarding the city's economic growth.[7]

The successive partitions of Poland brought large numbers of Jews into the Russian Empire. The first partition in 1772 brought in an estimated 100,000 Jews, and over the next fifteen years, in certain provinces, Catherine the Great allowed them to practice their religion, maintain their communal self-government, own property, and trade in alcoholic beverages. The second and third partitions in 1793 and 1795 brought an additional half-million Jews into the empire, and on June 23, 1794, Catherine delineated the Pale of Settlement, consisting of territories, including Kiev Province, that were open to Jewish residence. Data for 1792 indicate that there were already 73 Jews in Kiev, 61 of them Polish, 12 Belarusian. There were 4 tailors, 2 lace makers, 2 contractors, a silversmith, a bootmaker, a tavern owner, and an engraver. The rest were apparently dependents.[8] By 1795 there were 94 Jews in Kiev, and by 1797 the number had risen to 566, 3 classified as merchants, the rest as burghers. Counting dependents, the figure for 1797 may have exceeded 1,400.[9] The sudden increase in numbers resulted from the arrival of the Contract Fair in 1797. Jews worked the fair as trade brokers and suppliers of credit, and bought large quantities of goods in order to peddle them in the towns and villages throughout the region. Traditionally, even where Jews had been banned from permanent residence, as in Warsaw, they had been allowed to trade when the Polish diets were in session, which usually coincided with the great fairs. According to the Polish Constitution of 1768, this was done in the interest of "the common welfare and the necessity of reducing the high cost of merchandise."[10]

Invoking the 1619 edict, Kiev's burghers fought back, and in 1801 Jewish settlement rights in Kiev were temporarily suspended, but by 1810 70 Jewish homes could be found in the city, 65 of them in the Esplanade along the Pechersk fortress.[11] A synagogue was built in 1815 in a section of Podil near the Florivsky Monastery called Black Dirt (*Chernyi griaz*). Its ground floor had a stone exterior, while its second story was made of wood. There were also two prayer halls, the summer hall (which burned in 1829) and the winter hall.[12] Local officials accused Jews of disrespectful behavior, in one instance for allegedly singing and celebrating during the consecration of a church, and other petitions blamed Jews for bringing "disorders, suits, and disputes" to the city. The main objective was to drive Jews out of Podil, Kiev's commercial hub where Magdeburg privileges still existed. Pechersk and Old Kiev had never been given self-governing privileges, and newcomers to the city had traditionally located there. Wary of burgher pretensions, state officials took the position that whatever the local tradition, regulations regarding Jews were to be maintained only as long as they conformed to the laws of the state.[13]

On December 2, 1827, Nicholas I expelled Kiev's seven hundred Jews. Those with real estate were given two years to resettle; others were given six months to a year. Initially, resettlement plans were stalled for a number of years because of a cholera epidemic and because some burghers and local officials argued that expulsion would hurt Kiev's economy. Nevertheless, this edict signaled the beginning of new efforts to reduce the urban area where Jews could live, and similar expulsions soon occurred in Sevastopol, Mykolaiv (Nikolaev), and the Baltic region. A series of policies designed to assimilate Jews followed, including the abolition of the *kahal*, or self-governing Jewish community, in 1844, and the taxing of Jews who wore traditional attire.

Expulsion was justified on the grounds that Jews were exploiters and agents of Polish control. Jews controlled the rural inn and tavern trades, and local peasants frequently fell into arrears, ultimately having to surrender foodstuffs and livestock to pay off their debts. "The increase of *zhidy* and the terrible consequences of their dominion always and everywhere is the consequence of Polish rule," it was argued. Jews drive "the simple people to drunkenness, into debt, and away from their accustomed way of life and from honest trade and labor."[14] Heavily Jewish towns such as Berdychiv had indeed become important financial centers, if only because of the absence of banks and alternative credit facilities in the region.

Defending their "moderation and simple lifestyle" and noting their economic importance to the city, Governor-General Lewaszew was one proponent of a Jewish presence in Kiev. However, in 1836, Kiev was excluded from the Pale of Settlement, which meant that Jews could live in Kiev Province but not in the city itself.[15]

Thus, at midcentury first- and second-guild Jewish merchants who came to the fairs could stay in Kiev for up to six months. Other Jews could stay for three days if they brought provisions or purchased or transported goods, and if they slept at either of two inns designated specifically for them, one in Lybid, the other in Podil. (The proprietress who paid the city four thousand rubles per year for the right to operate the inns complained that other inns were housing Jews illegally.) After months of petitioning, Iosif Zeiberling, a censor of Jewish books and an important supplier of canvas to the army during the Crimean War, was allowed to open an office in the city, but such exemptions were rare.[16] Nevertheless, strong Jewish commercial ties with the city continued. In 1845, *in addition* to those who came to the Contract Fair, some forty thousand Jews visited Kiev.[17]

In 1804 the tsarist government had decreed that Jews must be classified in one of four categories: landowner, factory owner (*fabrikant*), merchant, or burgher (*meshchane*). Data for 1845 indicate that Kiev Province had 158,283 Jews: 84 percent were listed as *meshchane*, which covered virtually every occupation imaginable. There were only 6,383 merchants (4 percent), and 776 landowners (less than 1 percent). Twelve percent of the Jews still remained outside these categories. The merchants of Berdychiv, whose 1840 population of 41,000 was almost entirely Jewish, dominated much of the region's trade and commerce. They had strong ties with Moscow's manufacturers and with the great fairs at Kharkiv and Sumy. In the 1840s most of the capital at the Contract Fair was supplied by Berdychiv and Odessa lenders. Kulisher argued that at midcentury, Kiev was economically vital during the fair, Berdychiv for the entire year.[18]

Jewish control of trade in the smaller towns of Kiev Province differed from place to place. In Cherkasy (pop. 9,400) the merchantry was evenly divided between Jews and Christians. In Radomyshl (Radomysl, pop. 5,120), Skvyra (Skvir, 6,045), and Zvenyhorodka (Zvenigorodka, 7,501), the great majority of merchants were Jews, but in the latter two towns Christian burghers (most likely Ukrainian) outnumbered Jews, in Zvenyhorodka by a five-to-one majority. Nevertheless, Jews were roundly condemned for their economic dominance. Claiming that "almost all of the local working capital is in the hands of Jews," Funduklei estimated at midcentury that Jews in Kiev Province were involved in some capacity in 60 percent of the local grain trade, and were heavily involved as well in the wood, alcoholic beverage, and sugar trades, particularly as middlemen.[19] Writing in 1868, historian Nikolai Zakrevsky wrote that Kievans typically blamed Jews for rising prices of basic goods.[20]

A particular target of the policies of assimilation were the Hasidic Jews. Hasidism had become a powerful force in the towns around Kiev in the eighteenth century, especially Berdychiv and the small Kiev Province community of Chornobyl (Chernobyl), then noted for its fishing lakes, now notorious for its nuclear accident. In the 1840s Chornobyl was inhabited by 1,485 Jews and 772 Orthodox peasants, most of them serfs. A "dynasty" of teachers and miracle-workers called *tzaddikim* had been established there by the itinerant preacher Nahum. His son Mordecai, known affectionately as Rabbi Motele, attracted large numbers of pilgrims who brought *pidyons* (contributions believed to have the power to stave off impending death or misfortune). Rabbi Motele died in 1837, and the dynasty divided into bitter feuds among his eight sons, who staked out territories for themselves in Kiev and Volyn Provinces. The Jewish scholar S. M. Dubnow argued that Hasidism's "strange emotionalism," "unintelligible religious ceremonies," and zealous commitment to the idea of a Chosen People made reconciliation between Jews and Christians more difficult.[21]

Although Hasidic Jews must have been common in Kiev, nineteenth-century sources did not distinguish them from the more secular Jews. I found no indication, for example, that Hasidic Jews were special targets of the pogrom mobs in 1881 or 1905. Hasidism did become an issue during the notorious Beilis Affair in 1911. When the body of thirteen-year-old Andrusha Iushchinsky was discovered in a cave, the anti-Semitic press from St. Petersburg and Moscow and Kiev's Two-Headed Eagle "patriots" accused Hasidic Jews of ritually murdering the boy.[22]

THE EMERGENCE OF JEWISH KIEV

During the comparatively liberal reign of Tsar Alexander II (1855–1881), Kiev was opened to Jewish settlement, and its Jewish community grew very rapidly. In 1858 the special inns in Lybid and Ploskaia were abolished, and within several months Jewish merchants meeting certain guild requirements were allowed to settle as long as they did not bring more than one office worker and four servants. In 1861 the rules for Jewish settlement were liberalized further, and Jews who had been first-guild merchants for five years were allowed to settle anywhere in Kiev, including the fashionable Khreshchatyk and Lypky Districts. The wealthy Brodskys, Ginzburgs, and Zaitsevs took up residence in Lypky.[23]

Responding to local opposition, police announced in 1863 that Jews were to leave within seven days and that apartment owners were responsible for enforcing their departure. Efforts at expulsion proved ineffective, however, and in 1865 *Kievlianin* contended that 8,000 Jews were already living in Kiev.[24] By the census year 1874, Kiev's 14,000 Jews could be found in almost all professions. The largest employment category was the apparel trade (629 worked as tailors, 187 of whom owned their own shops). About 100 were employed in the manufacturing of cigarettes, 69 were involved in the hotel or tavern trade, 67 were joiners or furniture makers (including 32 who owned their own shops), 66 were bakers or confectioners, and 27 were involved in distilling or wine making. There were 6 Jewish physicians and 28 midwives.[25]

Jews constituted fewer than 3 percent of the residents of Lypky, Old Kiev, and Pechersk in 1874, but they already made up 29 percent of Ploskaia, 15 percent of Podil, and 9 percent of Lybid District, which would soon become the center of Jewish life in Kiev. Outlying Demievka also had a substantial Jewish community. Jews had begun to settle there in the 1830s, and Jewish entrepreneurs such as Gorenshtein, who operated a brickyard, and Iankel Markon, who ran a vinegar distillery, located there. Izrail Brodsky founded the Alexander sugar beet refinery in Demievka. By the 1880s it had become Imperial Russia's largest sugar refinery.[26] "A new Jewish ghetto" had emerged in Lybid and Ploskaia. Writing in 1871, *Kievskii telegraf* described neighborhoods overflowing with cold and hungry craftsmen who had come "to a city strange to them" to escape the poverty of the *shtetlach*. Jews "poke about anywhere they can, from house to house, just in case someone might have some work, but they find things little better here than where they came from."[27] An inexpensive cafeteria for indigent Jews was built with proceeds from a bakery run by Eugenia Brodsky.

Charges that Jews were unproductive and parasitic continued. They were accused of controlling trade in Chernihiv Province "almost without exception."[28] Forty-eight of 78 distilleries and wineries and 120 of 146 wholesale alcohol warehouses in Poltava Province were said to be run by Jews. The Jewish *kabak* (tavern) continued to be identified as the place where cunning Jews dealt in contraband and milked simple peasants of their bread in return for vodka. The peasant does the work, but the Jew ends up with much of the harvest, it was argued. The claim was also made, probably with exaggeration, that Jews bought up one-third of the land in the southwest region abandoned by exiled Poles after the 1863

17. Kiev's synagogue. Located on Malo-Vasilkovskaia Street, Lybid District. Photo from the early 1900s.

insurrection. That Jews worked as *faktory*, *maklery*, and *kommissionery*, as brokers handling transactions in everything from grain to prostitution, was often cited as evidence that Jews were parasites.[29]

Kiev's mayor added his voice to the outcry, complaining that the growth of Jewish competition had driven down prices and hence tax revenues for the city. (Such complaints gave unintended support to the argument that Jewish competition was good for consumers.) Wealthy Jewish merchants were supplying capital and credit to other Jews, he warned, making it tough on Russian traders. Furthermore, "Russians" who could not get loans from banks and credit establishments (at 6 to 9 percent) had to borrow from Jews at 18 to 24 percent. Bibikov's efforts to free Russian merchants from the Berdychiv banks, he concluded, were being undone.[30]

POGROM

On April 16, 1881, a pogrom began in the Ukrainian garrison town of Elysavethrad (Elizavetgrad, pop. 40,000), located between Kiev and the Black Sea. The pogrom grew out of a dispute, which turned into a brawl, eventually destroying more than seven hundred local Jewish homes and shops. The local paper, *Elizavetgradskii vestnik* (Elizavetgrad herald),

contended that a powerful bloc of Jews in the city council had not addressed the needs of the city's "Russian" population. Jews also controlled
local trade, the banks, and the taverns. (Nearby Rovnoe [pop. 11,000]
had thirty-eight taverns and no school.) "Let the Jew deny a drink to a
drunken or penniless peasant and the hatred begins," the paper noted.[31]
The violence in Elysavethrad set off a wave of pogroms that swept
through Ukraine.

Accounts indicate that initially Kiev's Jews did not feel threatened by
reports of pogroms elsewhere. After all, Kiev was "the mother of Russian
cities," and imperial troops were posted in its garrison. But on April 23,
as a crowd watched a young girl do acrobatic acts on the street, a Jew was
struck and a fight broke out. Some Jews escaped by jumping into the
Dnipro, but others fought back. Gangs formed, demanding free vodka
from Jewish tavern keepers and smashing up Jewish taverns. Jews were
warned that a pogrom would begin "with the arrival of a gang of Muscovites who were expected at any time."

The pogrom began on Sunday noon, April 26. The initial crowd, estimated variously at fifty to five hundred, apparently grew to four thousand by Monday, though many were simply onlookers or individuals
who sought to profit from disorder by picking up looted items. Some Jews
hung crosses and icons on their doors and windows, hoping to hide their
identities. Others vandalized their own property in an effort to convince
the mob that they had already been victimized. After the shops were ravaged, the mob turned to Jewish homes, especially in Podil and in outlying
Demievka and Solomenka. On the next day, a brawl involving some six
hundred people occurred near the railway station. The synagogue was
destroyed, and damage was widespread. Most property in affluent Lypky
and the Khreshchatyk was protected, while the poorer neighborhoods
were ravaged. The plight of the poor Jewish artisans and soldiers who
had settled in Ploskaia was said to be "especially tragic." Many were
veterans of the recent war with the Ottoman Empire, and they had lost
everything.

Peace was restored by Tuesday, but by then 6 had been killed (3 of
them Jews), 187 had been injured (the number of injured who were Jews
was not reported), and 4,000 Jews had been left without shelter or belongings. About 1,800 Jews crowded into makeshift shelters at Pechersk
where they were protected by the governor. In contrast to Elysavethrad,
where the pogromists were said to be sober, Kiev's mob was described as
drunks, ruffians, and mindless rabble. It was easy for the mob to stay
drunk in Kiev, for it looted a large vodka warehouse owned by the
Brodsky family.[32]

Kiev's *Zaria* reported that hatred was most pronounced among the
trading classes because of economic competition; the paper urged that

opportunity be expanded for Jews so that they could pursue other tasks than "usury and running taverns." *Zaria* spotted "well-known members of Kiev's barefoot brigade" in the mob. (Barefoot boys in rags, common around the Dnipro port, had come to Kiev on freight barges, often from Mogilev and Smolensk Provinces.) But the paper also noted that Kiev's pogrom crowd included Great Russian artel workers. "You saw them all over the city with their visor caps, greatcoats, swords, and high boots. Never before was this element so visible in Kiev." These *katsapy* had disappeared, but rumors circulated that they would return, reinforced "by Moscow," to lead pogroms on the holidays of May 1 and May 9 so that "not a *zhid* would remain in Kiev, the mother of Russian cities." Pogroms did not recur, and on May 9 *Zaria* reported that 1,783 had been detained in Kiev, "the overwhelming majority of them Great Russian." Not surprisingly, Kiev's prosecutor stated that the city's pogrom had been incited mainly by people from the north.[33] Apparently, only 379 were actually arrested and charged. Some had come from Russia, particularly from Kaluga Province, and from Belarus, but official data indicate that the majority came from Kiev and Chernihiv Provinces.[34]

Such reports fueled the arguments of those who believed that the 1881 pogroms resulted from a Judeophobic conspiracy. Dubnow blamed the pogroms of 1881 on hordes of Great Russian tramps, arguing that Kiev's pogrom "was carefully prepared by a secret organization which spread the rumor that the new Tzar [Alexander III] had given orders to exterminate the Jews, who had murdered his father, and that civil and military authorities would render assistance to the people, whilst those who would fail to comply with the will of the Tzar would meet with punishment."[35] Omeljan Pritsak assigns responsibility for the violence to merchants from Moscow and St. Petersburg and believes that artels of railroad workers spread the pogroms from town to town.[36] The theory that tsarist officials conspired to organize the pogroms has never been proven and appears unlikely. Although he was a notorious anti-Semite, Kiev's governor-general Alexander Drenteln warned publicly that "God commands not to do evil to anyone, and the tsar does not permit plunder and pillage." During the pogrom Drenteln rode through the streets calling for order, and he issued an appeal on May 3 that property stolen from Jews be returned. The more perplexing question is why Kiev's troops failed to prevent the pogrom, or to stop it once it had begun. During the early hours of the pogrom, troops apparently were not authorized to use force. Initially, authorities feared that mobs would attack non-Jewish targets as well, and troops were deployed to protect key installations such as the Arsenal. The army had no experience in quelling urban disorder, it is argued, and the number of troops available was insufficient to disperse the mob.[37]

These arguments are plausible, but not entirely convincing. It is unlikely that there were too few troops in the city to control the mobs, for
example. Frequently the violence was committed by groups numbering
only fifty to one hundred individuals. Reportedly, mobs were sometimes
led by women and young children. Small groups of students, workers,
and doormen were able to turn mobs away at certain locations. In
Kharkiv rumors of impending pogroms began to circulate in the taverns
and bazaars even before the news of the Elysavethrad pogrom had
reached the city. But in contrast to Kiev, it was said that Kharkiv's "administration made sure that disorders would not occur." In Berdychiv
local police and civilian groups (allegedly bribed by Jews) kept tabs on
strangers in the city and patrolled the bazaars day and night to ensure
against violence. At the station a Jewish militia apparently kept *katsapy*
from leaving the train. In Cherkasy local officials and priests maintained
order. Kremenchuk also avoided disorders. Two-thirds Jewish, it was reported to be "full of soldiers." At the trial in late May, army officers
reported that they had been warned that disorders might break out in
Kiev two weeks before April 26. Where they were deployed, there was
little plunder.[38] Thus, while there is no evidence that Kiev officials were
part of a conspiracy, more could have been done to prevent the pogrom
or at least reduce the damage once it had begun.

Extremists at both ends of the political spectrum saw some merit in the
pogrom. Some Jewish students at St. Vladimir, who were sympathetic to
the revolutionary movement, saw themselves "as 'men,' not as 'Jews.'
Jewish concerns had no appeal to us. There was one cure for all the ills of
the world—socialism."[39] Kiev's revolutionary South Russian Workers'
Union wrote to its "Brother workers" during the pogrom that "one
should not beat the Jew [*zhid*] because he is a Jew . . . , one should beat
him because he is robbing the people, he is sucking the blood of the working man."[40] On the Right, *Kievlianin*, which had long criticized Jews for
"insolence, impertinence, and exploitation," blamed the pogrom on retired soldiers and a young railway telegrapher who had been fired for
drunkenness and brawling. The telegrapher, it alleged, ran a protection
racket for Solomenka residents who could ensure their property against
destruction for a thousand-ruble fee. The semiofficial *Kievskie gubernskie
vedomosti* (News of Kiev Province) stated that Jews had made the situation worse by spreading rumors and reproaching peasants who meant
them no harm. Jews must be careful "to treat the native population with
sensitivity," it warned. Everyone could agree that public indifference
aided the pogrom mob. Concluded one onlooker: "It was a calm and
sunny Sunday holiday. Christians were strolling about. I don't know
what astonished me more, the boldness of the plunderers or the shocking

indifference of the public."[41] Indifference apparently spilled over into the ensuing trial. Of the nearly 1,800 arrested, only 123 were tried, and only 89 were convicted.[42]

KIEV'S JEWISH COMMUNITY:
A LATE-IMPERIAL PROFILE

Of 762 heads of Jewish families who remained under the protection of the Pechersk garrison after the 1881 pogrom, 134 were listed as tailors, 84 as merchants or clerks, 65 as owners of small enterprises such as grocery stores, 46 as haulers, 35 as teachers, cantors, or religious officials, 28 as bootmakers, and 27 as carpenters or wood turners. Only 43 were listed as speculators, profiteers, or dealers in second-hand merchandise, while 28 were said to be tavern owners, and 22 were listed as bazaar and street peddlers. Widows headed 43 of the families.[43] This sampling suggests that Kiev's Jews were heavily involved in trade, that many produced goods, and that few were involved in activities that could be considered "parasitic." Later, in 1914, a sampling of the 1,184 heads of Jewish families in Demievka indicated similarly that a majority of 655 (55 percent) had trades of some kind.[44] The accuracy of such data is questioned, however, by Kiev's journalist Iaron, who asserted that while many Jews had come from the Pale as artisans or *prikazchiki* (clerks and office personnel), and were officially categorized as such, many actually lived by moneylending and deal making. Those who worked the streets aggressively wooed potential customers (it required a "special heroism" to walk down Alexander Street in Podil, he recalled). Jews themselves were victimized by cutthroat competition, and some were forced out of business and into street hawking, deal making, and usury; even Jews sometimes asked authorities to check the papers of arrivals pouring in from the Pale.[45]

Residence in Kiev continued to be determined by decrees and by the whims of the local police. For example, in 1861 Jews and their families were allowed to come to Kiev for mineral baths and other treatments, and for education and apprentice training. In 1890 this decree was amended to apply only to state-supported schools, apparently to prevent Jews from coming in to study at privately established boarding schools. In 1865 certain kinds of artisans were allowed to settle, in 1867 retired Jewish soldiers, in 1879 Jews with higher education. These decrees were often challenged. In 1889, after a long fight against considerable opposition, the right of Jews to own real estate anywhere in the city was upheld. In 1891 the number of office workers that a Jewish businessman could hire from the Pale was left to the governor-general on a case-by-case basis.

Officials varied in their attitude toward Jews. For example, it was well known that Drenteln, who served from 1881 until 1888, disliked Jews, but Iaron contends that he was nevertheless a fair and honest administrator. Likewise, some of Kiev's police officials enforced the morass of changing state regulations, while others did not. Not every policeman took bribes, but it appears that payoffs were common. Sometimes they were brazen. In the 1880s police captain Mikhailov extracted money and goods from Jews *and* gentiles alike until his wagon was full. Egalitarianism earned him a conviction in court.[46]

Following the pogrom, Kiev's Jewish population dropped to an estimated 3,200. Some emigrated, mostly to America, and emissaries were sent to Palestine to look into opportunities for resettlement there. In May 1881 police began to round up and expel "illegal" Jews. Further expulsions followed; some 2,000 families were expelled in 1886. During the remaining years of the Russian Empire, even Jews who had been in the city for years continued to face expulsion, and Kiev became infamous for its roundups (*oblavy*). On March 24, 1905, *Kievskoe slovo* complained editorially that it could find no statutory authority giving Kiev's police the right to enforce regulations intended for the Pale. Ironically, local police salaries were drawn partly from special taxes on kosher foods.

However, roundups and expulsions did not change the fact that a substantial Jewish community had taken root in Kiev. In the 1880s Jews even opened their own postal service in the city. It quickly established a reputation for efficiency, and *Zaria* used Jewish postal couriers to get papers to its subscribers in Berdychiv and Zhytomyr, preferring them to the government postal service.[47] Apparently threatened by efficiency, authorities closed the Jewish postal service.

By 1887 Kiev's Jewish population had grown to an estimated 16,000, by the census year 1897, to 32,093. Hundreds came to study, to cut and sew in the city's sweatshops, to hawk and peddle on its streets. In 1910 police records listed a Jewish population of 58,387, about 12 percent of the city's nearly one-half million people.[48] Schools continued to be major avenues of entry. In 1911 as many as 4,000 Jews were studying (or said to be studying) in Kiev's higher educational institutions.[49] *Kievskaia mysl'* estimated that 2,000 Jewish families were living in Kiev on education permits.[50] Private Jewish schools were again operating on the eve of the First World War. The number of private Jewish schools in Kiev, although unknown, must have been substantial. Of the sixty-nine elementary schools in Poltava in 1913, only fifteen were funded by the city; by contrast, twenty-one were run by Jews.[51] Private schools became a particular target of authorities. In April 1914, for example, three private girls' schools in Kiev were closed, enabling the expulsion of several hundred Jewish families.

One portrait of a typical Jewish student in Kiev appeared in *Kievskoe slovo*. "She is young and full of hope, and she has managed to survive," it began.

Her story isn't long or new, but it deserves attention. Her life has been stormy, punctuated by whistles. A Jew from a remote corner of the south-western region, she has known hunger and cold but never gaiety or joy. At eighteen she came to Kiev, getting lost in its bustle, without a kopeck or the notorious residence permit. She came to study, and fate smiled on her. She got instruction in her native tongue [Yiddish] and managed to earn six rubles a month. . . .

"And you lived on this?"

"Well, two rubles went for a corner in a doss house, the rest for necessities."

She became acquainted with a poor Russian boy and learned some Russian. A year passed. She took an exam and got admitted to a class on midwifery. "I began to earn twelve or fifteen rubles a month, so my brother came, and I tried to get him ready for school. My brother and sister got into school. We lived wonderfully and even got a bit spoiled. Once in a while we ate meat or went to the gallery in the opera or the theater. I'm still trying for the medical course in Paris."

"Why not St. Petersburg?"

"The quotas are too strict, and the fight to keep my residency is wearing me out. I'd rather go abroad. There at least I'll have the same opportunity as others."[52]

In September 1917, after the fall of the tsarist regime, 87,246 Jews were recorded in Kiev's census, 19 percent of the city's population. At this time Ukrainian-speakers were said to account for less than 17 percent.[53]

KIEV'S JEWISH ELITE

While many Kiev Jews endured great personal insecurity because of the persistent threat of expulsion, some did very well for themselves. Particularly notable was the Brodsky family. Meir Schor came to Russia at the beginning of the nineteenth century from Brody in Austrian Galicia. Settling in Zlatopil (Zlatopol), in Kiev Province, he changed his name to Mark Brodsky. His five sons all became prominent. One of them, Izrail Brodsky (1823–1888), came to Kiev in the 1870s and founded the Alexander sugar refinery in Demievka. His network of refineries stretched as far as Odessa, and the Brodsky sugar empire came to control about one-quarter of Imperial Russia's sugar production.

All of this passed to his sons, Lazar (1848–1904), Lev (1852–1923), and Solomon. Lazar expanded his father's sugar empire and got into milling and boat building on the Dnipro as well. The counterpart to St. Petersburg's Kenig, "the sugar king of the north," Lazar Brodsky became "the sugar king of the south." He owned three homes in Kiev (in Podil, Lybid, and Lypky), and he had major financial interests in Kiev's tram network, gasworks, and sewage facility. His factory barracks always had good housing and tearooms to discourage drunkenness among workers. He served on the city council until Jews were excluded by the 1892 "counterreform," and for a time chaired the local stock exchange. On September 20, 1904, Lazar Brodsky died in Basel, ironically of the "sugar disease" (diabetes). By then in Kiev he had founded the Bacteriological Institute, a tuberculosis sanitorium, a clinic for midwives, the Kiev Society for the Struggle against Contagious Diseases, and a trade school for Jewish boys. He expanded the city's Jewish Hospital, built by his father, making it one of the best medical facilities in the city, and helped finance the new synagogue, built in 1898. He helped found the Polytechnical Institute in 1898, gave generously to the Literacy Society, the People's Club (whose reading room bore his name), the Kiev Red Cross, and a host of other charities. He left five hundred thousand rubles to Kiev for the purpose of building a modern covered market at Bessarabka so that meat, fish, and vegetables could be kept fresher. The income from the market was to go to Jewish charities.[54]

Affluence did not fully protect the Brodsky family from the wrath of the pogrom mob. "To Brodsky's" had been a battle cry of the mob in 1881, which in drunken stupor looted a family factory and a vodka warehouse. On Bolshaia Vladimir Street one Brodsky home was plundered, its belongings hurled to the street from a second-floor balcony. Another Brodsky home on Theater Square was ringed by troops and protected. After the pogrom, rumors circulated that bread and flour sold by Lazar Brodsky were responsible for poisoning several children. Police Chief Mastitsky denied the rumor, stating that Brodsky flour had been chemically analyzed and found to be safe.[55]

In September 1904 a large crowd assembled at the railway station when Brodsky's body arrived from Switzerland. Among the 150 wreaths and sprays came one from Mayor Protsenko and the city council, thanking him for his largess and wishing him eternal peace. A year later the epithet "Black Hundred hooligans" would be hurled at Protsenko and the council for their inactivity during a pogrom that decimated Kiev's Jewish community. Two Brodsky family homes were plundered in that pogrom, and a younger member of the Brodsky family, Grigory, was severely beaten after killing two members of the mob.[56]

TABLE 5.1

Income-Producing Property Ownership in Kiev, 1913

	Total	Orthodox	Polish	Jewish	German
Below 1,500 rubles	4,372	4,022 (92%)	209 (5%)	69 (2%)	48 (1%)
1,500–10,000 rubles	3,003	2,452 (82%)	273 (9%)	205 (7%)	61 (2%)
Above 10,000 rubles	1,913	1,278 (67%)	201 (11%)	316 (17%)	96 (5%)
Totals	9,288	7,752 (84%)	683 (7%)	590 (6%)	205 (2%)

SOURCE: TsGIA, *fond* 1288, *opis'* 5, *delo* 170 (1914), p. 130. The category "Orthodox" was not broken down by nationality.

Milling was one Kiev industry in which Jews became prominent. In the 1890s, of the eight largest flour mills in the city, at least four were owned by Jews.[57] Jews were also prominent in banking circles, and in 1902, 414 of Kiev's 432 first-guild merchants were Jews, although this figure had less significance than earlier figures, for in 1898 the government allowed nonmerchants to purchase business certificates, and many Russian merchants dropped this estate identity.[58] Table 5.1 reveals the extent of Jewish ownership of income-producing real estate by 1913.

It should be noted that the great majority of Kiev's Jews were too poor to appear on the tax rolls. One indication of this came after the pogrom of 1905, one of the most destructive of property in the empire, when about 1,800 Jewish tradespeople petitioned for financial restitution. More than half requested only one hundred rubles or less, and most of the rest only one hundred to five hundred rubles. Similarly, of the 3,472 artisans petitioning for restitution, 3,328 asked for less than one hundred rubles.[59] The fact that about one-quarter of Kiev's Jews had to apply for Passover alms is another indication of the poverty of its Jewish community.[60] What is striking in table 5.1, however, is that 316 Jews numbered among the most affluent owners of taxable property, while only 69 Jews numbered among the least affluent. There were many poor Jews in Kiev, and a substantial number of affluent Jews, but a lower-middle class of Jewish property owners apparently did not exist.

THE BOY WHO KNEW TOO MUCH

In Kiev, nighttime roundups and expulsions of Jews dominated the local news as events in the Balkans plunged the country toward war in 1914. Crime was also in the news, for gangs of thieves worked the city with great brazenness. One of the most notorious gangs was run by Vera Cheberiaka. It targeted even the riches of St. Sophia Cathedral. Thirteen-year-old Andrusha Iushchinsky, a friend of one of Cheberiaka's sons, was a frequent visitor at her apartment, where plots were hatched and stolen loot was stashed. On March 20, 1911, Andrusha's body was discovered in a cave. Pogrom agitation intensified, as leaflets alleging that dozens of Christian boys were ritually murdered at Easter circulated at his funeral. The Beilis Affair had begun.

In fairness to Kiev, the Beilis Affair was more a national than a local crusade. On April 9 the anti-Semitic St. Petersburg paper *Zemshchina* claimed that "without a doubt" Andrusha had been ritually murdered by Hasidic Jews. Other rightist newspapers around the country picked up the story. The State Duma in St. Petersburg had begun to discuss abolishing restrictions against Jews, including the Pale of Settlement itself, and an outraged anti-Semitic Right had mobilized in response. On April 29 it demanded that the duma investigate the "ritual murder" of Andrusha. Spurred by these allegations and by a hostile public mood, Kiev's Two-Headed Eagle, led by Vladimir Golubev and a priest, Fedor Sinkevich, demanded that all Jews be expelled from the city and openly agitated for a pogrom. But with Nicholas II coming in the fall to unveil a statue of Alexander II, neither city nor state officials wanted disorders, and Golubev was dissuaded out of fear that a pogrom would force Nicholas to cancel his visit.[61]

Convinced that Andrusha had been victimized by Hasidic ritual, Golubev nevertheless "identified" the ritual murderer as a certain "Mendel" who worked for the wealthy Jewish entrepreneur Zaitsev near the spot where the body was found. Various Kievans joined the charade; they included a mentally unbalanced Jewish "informer" and a university professor who stated in the name of science that the "race" of the murderer could be determined through an examination of the victim's corpse. Kiev police detectives fingered Cheberiaka's gang, deducing that a gang member had killed Andrusha because he knew too much. Cheberiaka herself was active in the campaign to "unmask" Jewish ritual murder. On June 9 she was arrested, at least in part to defuse local agitation, as flyers urging that Jews be beaten to avenge Andrusha's death continued to circulate. Later in the summer two of her children died, officially of dysentery. Racist groups blamed Jews, but police investigators suspected that both had been killed by their mother's henchmen as part of the cover-up.[62]

The anti-Semitic Muscovite lawyer and city councilman A. S. Shmakov, who had defended Kiev's 1905 pogrom leaders at their trial in 1907, returned to assist in the prosecution of Mendel Beilis, but despite the best efforts of the imperial government to convict him, Beilis was acquitted in October 1913. A month earlier, on September 4, while Nicholas II was in Kiev, Prime Minister Stolypin was assassinated, and hundreds of Jews had fled the city, fearing a massacre. Although a pogrom was averted—thanks to the efforts of Stolypin's successor, V. M. Kokovtsev—Dubnow contended that the Beilis Affair amounted to "a bloodless pogrom" which extended over two years.[63]

Hard times did not cease with the acquittal. On June 28, 1914, the day Archduke Franz Ferdinand was assassinated in Sarajevo, *Kievskaia mysl'* carried a report that authorities were going to expel up to five thousand Jewish families (or thirty thousand people). Two days later it reported that ten thousand families might be expelled, depending upon whether the Ministry of the Interior would wait for the Senate to rule on a petition filed on behalf of the prospective victims. Real estate owners in Lybid and Ploskaia complained to the city council that an expulsion of this magnitude would destroy the rental market. Others worried that prices would rise if hundreds of Jewish artisans were expelled.[64] Dubnow asserted that "no place in the empire could vie as regards hostility to the Jews with the city of Kiev—this inferno of Russian Israel."[65] Kiev officials were doing their best to prove him right. As the imperial order neared collapse, the Beilis Affair kept Kiev in the news inside the empire and throughout the world.

JEWISH KIEV: SOME CONCLUSIONS

Excluded for about a century and a half from residence and continuous trade, Jews again began to settle in Kiev in the 1790s. After much local opposition, the Russian government expelled the city's Jews in 1827. At this time Kiev and nearby Berdychiv, also in Kiev Province, had approximately the same populations, and Berdychiv had the stronger economy. From the 1830s, however, Kiev was favored with tax breaks and other commercial advantages, the founding of the university, and advantageous rail lines. Heavily Jewish Berdychiv was allowed to stagnate. By 1913 Kiev had grown to 574,356 inhabitants. Berdychiv had only 82,848.[66]

Alexander II changed the rules, and in the 1860s Jews began to pour into Kiev. The rapid growth of the Jewish community constituted the single most dramatic change in the composition of the city's population during the ensuing decades. Although most Jews were poor, several hundred amassed enough wealth to rank among the city's most affluent property owners. Among owners of property generating ten thousand or more rubles of income annually in 1913, one in ten was a Pole, and nearly one in five was a Jew. These figures may be somewhat inflated, for assessors could levy high taxes on Jewish real estate (or understate property values of gentiles), but they are nevertheless an impressive testament to Jewish entrepreneurial initiative and skill.

Because the Jewish community lacked deep roots, and because few Jews could feel certain that continuous residence was secure, Jewish political, self-defense, and cultural organizations seem to have been weakly developed in Kiev. The writer Shalom Aleichem (1859–1916), living in Kiev, founded a literary journal, *Di Yidishe Folksbibliotek*, in 1888. "The first volume created a great stir in the Jewish literary world and was a turning point in the history of modern Jewish literature."[67] The second volume was of similar quality, but in 1890 the project stopped when Aleichem went bankrupt. In general, however, Odessa and Vilnius were more notable as centers of Jewish culture than was Kiev. Educated Jews, outwardly Russified, were said to be indifferent to Jewish culture, and Kiev had only a few establishments, mostly in the outskirts, where Jewish music, storytellers, or theater could be enjoyed. In 1911 one Jewish commentator described these establishments as "the only oases in the enormous cultural desert that is Kiev Jewry."[68]

In the city council the obstructionist Right sometimes practiced racial politics, attacking progressive councilmen who supported developmental projects in poorer neighborhoods as Jew-lovers, for example. Prior to the 1910 election, the Nationalist Club tried to disenfranchise voters representing any property in the city that had Jews among its owners or even stockholders. There is no way of knowing the extent to which ethnic hatreds influenced voters, but the ugly politics of race baiting deflected attention from important issues such as the need to municipalize services and utilities, and no doubt convinced many civic-minded and progressive individuals to steer clear of local politics altogether.[69]

Dubnow observed that in earlier times Jews had been looked upon "as transient foreigners, who, by pursuing any line of endeavor, could only do so at the expense of the [native population]."[70] The belief that the Jew was an injurious alien never completely disappeared from the culture of late-imperial Kiev. From the 1870s until the collapse of tsarism in 1917, controlling the size and character of the Jewish community preoccupied Kiev officials, and the rapid growth of that community produced many more tensions and conflicts in the city than did demands by Poles and Ukrainians for national rights.

· CHAPTER VI ·

Recreation, the Arts, and Popular
Culture in Kiev

BY VIRTUE of its history, its churches, its beauty, and its climate, frontier Kiev had always been a mecca for troops, pilgrims, landowners, and for "simple people who came south as a diversion much as one might visit a foreign land." In the merry minds of Kiev journalists, imaginary rubes from Tarakanovka (Cockroachville) came to the Contract Fair ostensibly to buy their wives Turkish shawls and Kazan soap, but really because in Kiev one could "do some hard drinking." Kiev had amenities not found in smaller communities, and one person's amenity is another's diversion. After all, even after learning that its aerator was not an oil gusher brought to the fair by "two Armenians from Baku," these innocents still found a certain amazement in Kiev's sewage treatment plant. More conventional amusements surely existed.

Researching the popular culture of Kiev is a challenge, for there are no political platforms or secret police reports to rely on, no great revolts, pogroms, or strikes to spur outpourings of description and analysis. There is no study of Kiev as richly detailed as Dmytro Bahalii's history of Kharkiv, although V. S. Ikonnikov and others published a variety of often-colorful materials in *Kievskaia starina*. Memoir accounts, particularly the journalist Sergei Iaron's recollections of the 1880s, are helpful, and data published by Ivan Pantiukhov in 1877 provide some information on marriage customs. The annual provincial surveys also supply useful data of various kinds, but they did not begin to appear until late in the nineteenth century. The best sources for the urban historian, particularly from the 1870s, are the newspapers. In addition to running local news stories, by the turn of the century most had "all-over-town" columnists who filled the back pages with rich commentary about the local scene. However scattered and anecdotal this information may be, at least a partial picture of custom and lifestyle in Kiev can be reconstructed.

LIFE AT THE TOP: THE BEAU MONDE

For much, if not all, of the nineteenth century, great balls and masquerades dominated the social calendar of Kiev's beau monde. Late January
was the high season for these social extravaganzas, for the Contract Fair
provided the assemblage of wealthy landowners and merchants with the
opportunity to strut and display. The balls reflected the Polish-Russian-
Ukrainian blend of the city. Noblemen mixed with one another in high
society regardless of nationality, conversing in French in the early decades
of the century. To the orchestral sounds of flutes, banduras, clavichords,
and guitars, Kievans danced the Ukrainian *metelytsia* and *kozachok*, as
well as Polish mazurkas, and sang Ukrainian *dumy* (sentimental ballads)
as well as French, German, and Italian romantic songs.[1]

At least until the 1860s, Poles were particularly prominent on the social scale, for they owned the great estates of the surrounding countryside. At midcentury they still predominated at the *soirées littéraires*,
where literature, some of it in manuscript form, was read and discussed.
Ideas were exchanged in French, German, and even Italian. Great Russians rose on the social register as the city became Russified. Anecdotal
evidence suggests that well-to-do "Little Russians" also participated fully
in the city's high culture. The home of the Ukrainian Iiulia Veselytska, for
example, was a center of the city's social whirl early in the century.

Polish gentlemen considered Kiev a bit backward at this time. Count
Tadeusz Bobrowski complained that to live well one had to bring his own
furniture, coaches, and servants. Kiev, he alleged, had only one good
shop (Finke's, apparently from Nuremberg); one book shop; only two
real hotels (one of which, the Mineral Waters, was mainly for Polish noblemen); and two good restaurants (one run by a Frenchman, the other by
an Italian). In frontier Kiev, "luxury in home furnishings and luxurious
carriages did not exist. Women dressed tastefully but simply. Only at the
great balls during the Contract Fair did the sumptuous jewelry and toilet-
ries appear."[2] Great balls seemed to play a more important role in the
social life of early-century Kharkiv than they did in Moscow or St. Petersburg.[3] The same could be said of Kiev.

By the twentieth century, however, these events had become shadows
of their flamboyant past. Kiev's main annual ball, held every January 6,
had become "boring and banal," a columnist for *Kievskaia gazeta* complained. "There was a time when behind the masks people hatched plots
and revealed the secrets of the heart"; now "the masks are stupid, and the
dirty costumes are rented from hairdressers who in turn get them at the
flea markets. . . . They even smell bad. . . . I know in advance who'll be
there, what they'll say to me and I to them. . . . Let's take the masks off

the masquerades!" In a follow-up piece written after the ball, the columnist wrote that he had sensed boredom in the hall, but he acknowledged that a large crowd had attended and, true to tradition, many stayed until two o'clock in the morning before moving on to restaurants.[4] No longer the gala extravaganzas of earlier times, masquerades were still important enough as social events to warrant comment in the press, but their decline in stature and originality seems to have echoed the decline of the gentry itself.

Every resident of Kiev belonged to a *soslovie* (estate), a legal category that traditionally determined privileges and obligations. While much social activity centered on the home, the estate organizations contributed greatly to the city's social life. The Nobleman's (*dvoriantstvo*) Club, built in 1838, and the Merchants' Club, located in the Contract Hall, sponsored many of the great balls and masquerades. Sometimes these events drew five hundred people, and they often served as fund-raisers for collective needs and for charity. Although there is little solid evidence upon which to build generalizations about long-term change in the social habits of affluent Kievans, my impression is that wealth, and not estate designation, became increasingly important in determining one's social circle as the city grew into a large and diverse metropolis. Kharkiv provides a clue. Bahalii recalls that there was little social mixing among the classes in Kharkiv early in the century, but when the city's Commercial Club opened in 1858, it sponsored six balls and fourteen masquerades during the winter season, not to mention countless evenings of dining and billiards. Generally these events were open to all who could pay.[5]

References to the lifestyles of Kiev's merchants are rare, but again it is possible to look to Kharkiv for clues, for Great Russians dominated the merchant ranks in both cities (in Kiev's case until the emergence of a powerful Jewish merchantry late in the century). Midcentury Kharkiv's great merchants were easily recognized by their long frock coats and distinctive fox-fur outer coats. Their "powdered and rouged" wives liked to "flit about the city on splendid thoroughbred trotters, frequenting the fashionable shops . . . , feeding their corpulent bodies." While their sons learned the business, the world of their daughters revolved about the piano, lessons in French, fancy gowns, and teas. Such luxury was alien to the more typical merchant, whose values reflected simplicity, moderation, and hard work.[6] Kiev merchants even had a reputation of being humorless; they were accused in the press of being "great enemies of merriment." "We seem to think merriment is the mother of vice," complained a columnist for *Kievskoe slovo* in 1903.[7]

In 1898 imperial regulations were changed so that anyone could obtain a business permit without enrolling in the merchant estate. "Apparently, by the end of the century merchant status was largely irrelevant as a mark of social standing," Daniel Brower writes, for in 1899 the great majority of Russian merchants abandoned their membership in the merchant estate when the opportunity to do so arose.[8] By this time most of Kiev's powerful merchants were Jews, which further diminished the social value of merchant status for the rest of Kiev society.

By the twentieth century, the *soslovie* called *meshchane* numbered 80,000 members, who had long since ceased to be drawn exclusively from Podil's burgher class. They included tradespeople from skilled icon painters to prostitutes from throughout the city. Most Jews carried this designation. Little is known about the *meshchane* organization. In 1905 it cost two rubles per year to join in Kiev, but only one person in seven could afford the fee. Particularly after the 1905 revolution, new associations formed around trade or skill. For example, the Society for the Mutual Assistance of Clerks and Office Workers (*prikazchiki*) provided libraries, labor exchanges, and modest benefits for widows and children of former members. It is likely that these organizations also took over many of the social and fund-raising functions of the older estate organizations.[9]

CONVEYANCE AND STATUS

In midcentury Kharkiv, although the dirt and plank streets were congested and often barely passable, great noblemen "considered it their duty to ride about the city in carriages pulled by six horses."[10] Horsemanship was also important to Kiev's gentry, for they retained strong ties with the countryside. At midcentury they too rode about the city in showy carriages. Though few in number, they owned enough property for stables and hay to maintain half of the 4,300 horses in the city. Conveyance in Kiev often reflected rank. In 1845, of the 712 carriages ranking above *drozhky* in size and status, 591 (83 percent) were owned by noblemen or civil servants. Clergy owned 57, merchants owned 45, and burghers only 19 (almost all of them cabriolets). Of the 219 fanciest carriages (*karety*), 201 were owned by noblemen and civil servants. Of the 393 *koliaski* (prams), 318 were owned by noblemen and civil servants, the rest by clergy or merchants. Noblemen also owned 72 of the 100 cabriolets, another rung down in carriage size and status, while burghers owned 17, and merchants 11. By contrast, of the 646 simple *drozhky* (a one-horse, two-wheeled covered cab called a hansom in England), 389 were owned by nobility, 136 by merchants, 54 by burghers, and the remainder by assorted peasants, clergy, and others.

There were also 1,918 work carts in the city. Functional but completely devoid of status, they were distributed fairly evenly among burghers, noblemen, and merchants. Animals were abundant in the city, and ownership of livestock other than horses generally was associated with the burgher class. They owned 75 percent of Kiev's 430 oxen, indicating wide use of ox-carts. Burghers owned about half of the 3,900 cows that grazed in the city, and almost all of the sheep, pigs, and goats. Some of these animals were owned by butchers, but many Kievans had a cow or two or some pigs to supplement their incomes. Pigs commonly wandered about the city, and in the 1880s the city council ordered that unfenced pigs be confiscated and given to charity.[11]

HOLIDAYS AND FESTIVALS

Among the most important holidays in early nineteenth-century Kiev were the public events held to celebrate special occasions: for example, Alexander I's affirmation of the Magdeburg Rights in 1802, and the hundredth anniversary of the Battle of Poltava in 1809. (At Poltava Peter the Great had ended Swedish attempts to dominate northern Europe, as well as Ukrainian attempts to break away from Russia.) The opening of the first *gymnasium* in 1812 and the funeral of Mayor Rybalsky in 1813 were also marked with great flair and fanfare. The burgher militia performed with great pride at these events, and the guilds, carrying golden gonfalons emblazoned with pictures of their patron saints, marched in processions throughout Podil. To celebrate the collapse of the Turkish fortress of Silistra during the Russo-Turkish War of 1828–1829, Nicholas I gave three new banners and the key to the fortress to Kiev's burghers, whose ancient privileges he would soon terminate. The city militia paraded these objects around town before placing them in St. Sophia Cathedral.[12]

Otherwise, Christmas, Easter, the guild holidays, visits from important dignitaries, and the Feasts of the Epiphany and Maccabeus were important holidays in the city. Some of the festivals were specific to certain guilds. For example, fishermen marked the end of the prolific spring fishing season with a festival on May 9. The Feast of the Epiphany, held on January 6, and the Feast of Maccabeus, held on August 1, both featured the consecration of water. Epiphany began with a solemn service at Podil's Bratsky Monastery; this was followed by a procession of clergy and guildsmen to a special place on the Dnipro, which was usually frozen. The consecration took place a week or two before the Contract Fair, but visitors sometimes came early to observe it. "Clergy came from every church, and the guildsmen came, and eight squadrons of city militia stood around the hole in the ice." The metropolitan blessed the water and sprinkled it in all directions, "because Kiev is the capital for all the Slavs."[13]

The Epiphany festival was part of a wider Ukrainian tradition often called the "Jordan-Blessing of the Waters." Crowds of people "went to the local stream or river where the men had carved a large cross from the river's ice, often stained red with beet juice. There, the cross and the waters were blessed by the priest" as a way of celebrating Christ's baptism while at the same time seeking protection from the spring floods.[14] The festival was also celebrated in Russia. Descriptions from sixteenth-century Moscow indicate that high church officials and monks led the procession to the frozen Moscow River, and that the tsar himself sometimes participated. Prayers were said to exorcise the devil from the water. Salt was thrown into the river and incense was cast about. Crosses were hung on doors and windows in homes throughout the city so that the devil, having been driven from the river, could not resettle in a private residence. Muscovites then gathered water from the purified river and allowed their horses to drink. Some Muscovites jumped in fully clothed; others jumped in naked.[15] Kiev's Epiphany festival reflected the importance of religious festivals in popular and high culture everywhere in the empire, but it also denoted the Dnipro's importance to the city and Kiev's special place in Slavic history.

Even in the early decades of the nineteenth century, it was common for most of the city to turn out on August 1, Maccabeus Day, to consecrate the Dnipro, which was believed to have magical powers on this day. Men dressed in Cossack attire, and those with fevers swam in the river. Maccabeus also marked a holiday for all the guilds. Guildsmen assembled at the Samson Fountain, built in Podil in 1808 on the site of the old city well. Sitting high in their Cossack-type saddles, the burgher cavalry assembled at the Assumption Cathedral. Dressed in their traditional green ceremonial cloaks (*kuntushy*) decorated with golden cord, red long coats (*zhupany*) and tall golden-tasseled, crimson Astrakhan velvet hats, they awaited the procession, sabers hanging from their silk sashes, a pair of pistols from their saddles. Guildmasters drew their sabers as the procession, led by the magistracy's brass band, moved toward the Florivsky (Florovsky) Monastery. After concluding the church service, clergy blessed the waters in the Samson Fountain. Then, amid the brass fanfares and pounding of drums, the procession fanned out to appointed spots, and a meal was shared by prominent clergy and burghers at the Contract Hall. The festival ended with a great roar: a cannonade set off by the barbers' guild; the firing of weapons of all kinds; the collective cheer of Podil's inhabitants, many bearing jars of blessed water; the ringing of church bells; loud music; and the neighing of frightened horses. For all the chaos, it was said to be a solemn moment. For the remainder of the night burghers were allowed to fire their guns from their yards. Although they could be fined for failing to participate in these festivals, enjoyment—not compulsion—drew burghers to these celebrations. Recalled one: "When

I'd sit on my horse, my blood began to flow, and I could scarcely recognize myself." "I'd be a son of a bitch, almost like a general; even the *moskali* [Russian soldiers] were afraid of me. Yes, the tradition was alive!"[16]

In older times parish fair days (*khramovye prazdniki*), honoring the saint for whom the church had been named, had commonly evolved into fairs for specific tradesmen, for individuals pursuing those trades tended to cluster into certain neighborhoods and parishes. For example, churches built in blacksmiths' neighborhoods were often named for Saints Cosmas and Damian, the patron saints of blacksmiths, and November 1 came to be known as Saints Cosmas and Damian Day in many towns and villages. Although some trades waned in importance, and the dominance of neighborhoods by specific trades or crafts disappeared, parish fairs continued to be held. In the 1880s, for example, the fair at the wall of the Mykhailiv Monastery was still celebrated on November 8. In the seventeenth and eighteenth centuries, it had marked the day when nearby monastic taverns allowed unrestricted purchase of brewed drink (which brought people to Kiev from far and wide).[17]

Orthodox religious festivals continued to be observed throughout the entire period under study, reflecting the importance of religion both to the public and to the ideology of the state. Around 1900 Kiev's trade establishments closed for three days at Easter and for two days at both Christmas and New Year's. On eleven other religious holidays, they opened only between eleven o'clock in the morning and three in the afternoon. During the 1905 upheaval, some strikers demanded time off to observe religious holidays. In Kharkiv workers wanted holidays for the twice-yearly processions honoring the "miracle-working Ozerianska Mother-of-God icon." These processions, originating in 1843, were headed by high church and civil officials and involved carrying the icon between the city and an outlying monastery. Guild representatives with their ancient flags and military choirs participated, and throngs lined the streets. In Kiev some striking workers also asked that factories close on saints' days and holy days, as well as Coronation Day and the days commemorating the emancipation of the serfs.[18]

Easter continued to be celebrated with great pomp. Priests led processions, sprinkling Easter cakes with holy water as they passed. Cakes, sausages, painted eggs, and other items were collected in great boxes, presumably to be distributed to the poor.[19] The celebration of the Assumption of the Virgin on August 15 was a particularly busy day at the Cave Monastery because thousands of pilgrims came to Kiev for the occasion. In 1884 the city council appropriated ten thousand rubles to celebrate the fiftieth anniversary of the founding of St. Vladimir University and asked that the commemoration coincide with religious festivities on this day. On July 15 Kievans celebrated St. Vladimir's Day, which marked the Christianization of Russia. Churches overflowed with people, and there were processions from St. Sophia Cathedral, Podil, and Pechersk to the bronze statue of St. Vladimir, designed by Baron Klodt and unveiled in 1853. Towering over the river, it could be seen by the entire Podil population below and by the villagers on the Left Bank. Strings of electric lights were ultimately wired to the cross, "and the blazing cross hung high in the sky over the slopes of Kiev."[20]

Of the more secular celebrations, the guild festivals and the parades on Epiphany and Maccabeus Days disappeared with the abrogation of the Magdeburg Rights in 1835. The consecration of the Dnipro was filmed in 1907–1908, but this was probably an attempt to capture a fragment of the city's colorful past for commercial purposes. The three-day student holiday in May, which had once been an outdoor festival of singing, dancing, and athletic contests for the entire city, seems to have disappeared with the demise of the Kiev Academy.[21]

Iaron's recollections of the 1880s mention only a few festival days. *Bryksy* (from the Ukrainian *brykaty*, to frolic about) was celebrated on the first day of Petrivka (Petrovka), a period of fasting before the Feast of Saints Peter and Paul. On this day women were pulled by their husbands on sleigh runners, often to taverns, and freed from chores and responsibilities. (Iaron assures us that this was the *only* day of freedom for these women, but that liberation had been firmly secured by the wives of the *intelligenty*.) March 25 (Annunciation Day), said to mark the day when birds began to nest, was celebrated with the release of thousands of songbirds from captivity in Podil's flea market and Poultry Row. This was a traditional Ukrainian folk festival, and the return of the songbirds helped the arrival of spring. In the 1880s Kievans also continued to celebrate the Festival of the Candles on September 1, but only at the Grain Market, the city's oldest market. On this day traders and artisans had traditionally celebrated the decision in 1506 to lift the ban on open fires in their homes, which had been imposed for reasons of public safety. Members of less privileged classes, for whom the ban on fires continued, had been invited in to partake of the warmth and glow of these fires. Before 1700 September 1 had also begun the new year, and the traditional New Year's symbols, trees and thistle wreaths decorated with fruit, nuts, and candles, continued to be used. In the city as a whole, higher taxes and the evolution of larger, more impersonal, shops contributed to the holiday's demise.[22]

How did Kievans greet the new year? According to the early twentieth-century press, many attended prayer services, and families lit the *elka* (the tree used to celebrate Christmas and the arrival of the new year). Depending on taste and income, one could also attend a masquerade ball or orchestra concert, or a performance by "American-style starlets" in a local hotel. Or one could simply enjoy ice-skating or promenading around Christmas trees with electric lights. The "foreign" tradition of dinner at a restaurant had also become popular, at least among the affluent. Kiev's better restaurants were run mostly by foreigners, but meals had "a Russian flavor—plenty of drink."[23] It is difficult to gauge the extent to which holidays had become commercialized. In 1900 newspapers ran few advertisements, but some seemed directed at Christmas or New Year's shoppers: turkeys and geese (presumably for holiday preparation); canaries and talking birds; sleighs; furs; luggage; toys; travel items; tree ornaments; photographic portraits; and bathhouses, some with private rooms. Dementev's Tea Shop, with shops in Kiev, Odessa, "and every Ukrainian city of any size," advertised wooden Japanese tea cannisters.

PERSONAL CELEBRATION

Personal celebration of church sacraments was also important in Kiev's popular culture. New parents sometimes celebrated christenings by giving the midwife wreaths and flowers and taking her to the neighborhood tavern. According to data for 1866 to 1870, Kievans did not marry during March and December because these were months of fasting.[24] October was by far the most popular month for marriage, accounting for 18 percent of all weddings. Almost half (43 percent) of all weddings occurred during the three months that followed the harvest (September through November); 55 percent occurred in those three months plus January (December being a month when weddings were not held). Financially, these were likely to be months when food supplies were secure, and they were months when peasants had leisure time. Comparatively few weddings took place during the five months from April through August, when agricultural work was most intense. It would seem that rural marriage customs continued to be widely observed in Kiev, for it is probable that many Kievans took spouses from the countryside, and many city residents were themselves recent arrivals from the villages.[25]

These same data show that among among Orthodox (Ukrainian and Russian) women, about one-third were under twenty when they married, and a second third were between twenty and twenty-five. Only 6.5 percent of the men who married were under twenty; 27.5 percent were twenty to twenty-five; and 26 percent were twenty-five to thirty. Jews traditionally married young, and this pattern can be seen in Kiev. Of 390 Jewish couples to marry during 1866–1870, 56 percent of the women were under twenty, as were nearly one-third of the men. Jews married commonly in every month of the Christian calendar. Summer was the most popular season, followed by spring. Polish women married younger than Polish men in Kiev. In nearly 40 percent of Catholic (mostly Polish) marriages, women were under twenty, but only 2 percent of the men were that young. In fact, almost two-thirds of the Catholic men who married were between twenty-five and forty, indicating a considerable age differ-ence in a typical Polish marriage. Poles also avoided marrying in the fast-ing months of March and December (only 4 of 184 weddings were held in those months). About one-third of Catholic weddings occurred in the summer, another third in the fall.[26] I have no data for Kiev for other years, but according to one scholar, by the century's end, at least for the upper classes, eighteen to twenty-two was considered a desirable marry-ing age for women, and up to thirty for men. By that age, it was assumed, men "had finished with their youthful follies and had grown wiser."[27]

Anecdotal evidence suggests that evening get-togethers (*vechorki* in Russian, *vechirky* in Ukrainian) continued to bring together marriageable young men and women within the protective framework of the family, although the city afforded many other ways of meeting members of the opposite sex, not the least of which was the promenade, discussed later in this chapter. Matchmakers began to appear in Imperial Russian cities in the nineteenth century, and one can assume that they played at least some role in the betrothal practices of Kiev. Matchmakers looked over pros-pects at promenades, at church, and wherever young people appeared. They developed a lingo of their own. "You've got the goods, I've got a merchant," was one example. Rejection might take the form, "Our goods are not for sale." In the Russian north, a parent might be asked to choose between a fir and a pine, with the pine signifying rejection of the projected match.[28] Successful matches might be sealed with the exchange of the traditional bread and salt. The use of symbolic language and ritual prob-ably eased the pain of rejection. Where matches were made, symbolism and ritual served to bless the prospective couple, while warding off bad luck.

Although the data are limited, it appears that birthrate reflected in-come, with the poorest couples producing the most children. For a thirty-three-year period ending in the 1870s, Pantiukhov notes that the highest birthrates per marriage (6.5 births) occurred in some of the poorest par-ishes, where death rates were also the highest in the city. The richest par-ishes tended to record the fewest births per marriage, often 4, and in one parish, 2.5.[29]

THE ARTS

Traditionally, artistic expression was associated with the city's great monasteries and with the Kiev Academy. The Cave Monastery had long been identified with accomplishment in iconography, fresco painting, and decorative book illustrations. The Bratsky Monastery, known for its instruction in church music, was an important force in the city's musical culture. In the eighteenth century, the Kiev Academy provided the city with theater, an orchestra, and a popular choir. The first and second *gymnasia*, which opened early in the nineteenth century, also had popular choirs. Chamber quartets and ensembles were popular, as were touring serf orchestras, which sometimes featured performers who composed their own music.[30]

The city magistracy also contributed to Kiev's musical culture. Before the great fire of 1811, four trumpeters played on the balcony of the city hall from 10:30 in the morning until 12:30 in the afternoon during the summer. In the evenings, and apparently sometimes during the day, the city orchestra, consisting of sixteen musicians, played on the gallery. The magistracy established a music school in 1768, mostly for children of the burghers, and especially for orphans. Math, history, and other topics were taught as well. Graduates were supposed to commit themselves to the orchestra, which survived until 1852, for the entirety of their professional lives. The musicians were given uniforms for everyday use and special uniforms for ceremonial appearances. A musicians' guild also existed in Kiev at least from 1677. Composed of thirty-five members in 1742, it played at weddings and festivals and in taverns, and it trained performers in various instruments, including the bandura, gusla (a kind of zither), and violin.[31] Some of its graduates performed for various tsars.

During much of the nineteenth century, Poles were culturally prominent in Kiev. Their importance to the musical culture of the city is illustrated by the popularity of mid-nineteenth-century Polish composers J. Witwicki and Michał Zawadzki, who incorporated Ukrainian poems and folk melodies into their music. Witwicki and Zawadzki taught in local schools, and Czech musicians and teachers were also prominent among the city's musicians and music teachers. In 1848 Italian opera came from Odessa. That same year a symphonic society was formed that organized weekly songfests and monthly concerts at the university. In 1867 a Russian opera troupe was founded in Kiev; many of its musicians had formerly performed in serf orchestras. Works by Glinka, Verdi, Rossini, and others were performed, and inexpensive tickets could be purchased. Some of the most popular operas, such as Glinka's *Ruslan and Liudmila*, featured local life and customs from the time of Kievan Rus.[32]

Traditionally, itinerant entertainers were popular nearly everywhere in the Russian Empire. One illustration from the Moscow area in 1636 shows a troupe of minstrel-entertainers consisting of two musicians, a one-man puppet theater, and a dancing bear and his trainer.[33] Professional minstrel-entertainers (*skomorokhi*) performed on the streets of ancient Kiev, and their acts were depicted in frescoes in St. Sophia Cathedral. After the collapse of Kievan Rus, this tradition seems to have been more a part of Russian than of Ukrainian culture. The Ukrainian scholar Mykola Kostomarov suggests that oral traditions left behind by the Cossacks and embodied in the *dumy* supplanted the earlier minstrel tales in the Ukraine.[34]

In the seventeenth century Kiev Academy students performed on the city streets for food or money, celebrating the accomplishments of local notables and entertaining visiting traders in the Grain Bazaar. "Daily, at noon and in the evenings, [the students] banded into small groups and went among the townspeople with panegyrics, psalms, recitations, and short plays," Sydorenko observes, noting that such activities amounted to organized forms of begging and that the practice irritated the local populace.[35] By the nineteenth century organized begging by students had probably disappeared, but wandering minstrels—*kobzari* and *lirnyky*—continued to spin their ballads and heroic tales, especially in the markets and near the churches and monasteries. The *kobzar* plucked a multistringed instrument called a *bandura*, and the *lirnyk* played a crank-driven hurdy-gurdy called a *lira* that produced a bagpipe-like sound. Only the blind were permitted to join these groups of minstrels, who, like beggars, worked specific circuits. Guitar and sitar players also entertained, and around the turn of the twentieth century, harmonica players and accordionists appeared on the streets.[36] Newspaper accounts from 1903 speak of the arrival of "Spaniards" from Berdychiv, "Italian impersonators" from Kishinev, and Serbian singers from Odessa.[37]

Among the most popular forms of entertainment were the puppet shows called *vertepy*. Written accounts speak of *vertep* performances in Lviv in 1666, but the ethnographer Oleksa Voropai believes the tradition may have begun in Kiev during the time of the Cossack hetman Petro Sahaidachny early in the seventeenth century. Prominent burghers, students, and clergymen carried the theater from one location to another, and Kiev Academy students seem to have been influential in developing the specific form and content of the religious plays that were performed. The scripts must have changed over time, for they were passed along among students and clergy by memory and were not written down until the late eighteenth century.[38]

Vertep theaters were often housed inside the amusement carousels that were common in the market squares. The State Museum of Ukrainian Theater, Musical Instruments, and Film Art, currently located on the grounds of the Cave Monastery, exhibits a splendid example of one such theater and carousel from the nineteenth century. The upper tier of the theater is larger, for it was used for religious plays. Secular and comedic plays were performed in the smaller lower tier. The puppets were controlled by strings and wires; one skilled puppeteer could manipulate up to forty puppets in a single performance! Because of their transcendent sounds, violins and lyres were used to accompany the religious plays, while drums, tambourines, and cymbals accompanied the secular performances on the lower tier. *Vertep* theater was especially popular at Christmas and Easter, but in the late nineteenth century, the lower tiers tended to become larger than the upper tiers, indicating that secular performances had become more important. *Vertep* performances were often held at night under streetlights, sometimes as part of street festivals. Masks from these festivals on display in Kiev's theater museum run the gamut from elaborately crafted faces of fierce animals to simple masks made of burlap or tree bark with corncob noses. A person dressed as a goat (or possibly a satyr) was frequently a main character in these festivities. Street theater ultimately found its way to rural schools, churches, military encampments, and even abroad.[39]

"A THEATER CITY"

In the eighteenth century Kievans relied on the Kiev Academy for theater until, late in the century, the school's religious authorities decided to ban theater altogether. During the first half of the nineteenth century, although Kiev had a theater building, a wooden structure seating 740 patrons designed by the Pole Melenski and built on the Khreshchatyk in 1806, it did not have a permanent theater company. Polish troupes came into the city, performing Ukrainian, Russian, Polish, and foreign plays and operas, as did itinerant troupes from Odessa, Kharkiv, Lviv, Moscow, France, and Germany. Serf actors, including a famous troupe from Chernihiv Province, also visited the city. Theater troupes often mixed Ukrainian, Russian, and Polish actors. Plays such as Ivan Kotliarevsky's *Natalka-Poltavka* (Natalya from Poltava), a folk drama about daily life in Ukraine, were popular in Kiev, and troupes sometimes performed Shakespeare, Molière, or Schiller, which appealed to more literate audiences.

At midcentury the Kiev city government subsidized the theater to the tune of three thousand rubles yearly. It was torn down in 1851 to make way for the Hotel Europa, and a new 850-seat city theater was finished in 1856. (It burned down in 1896.) Important to the city's cultural life was the Bergon'e Theater, founded in 1868 by the Frenchman August Bergonier.

During the thaw before the Polish Insurrection of 1863, Polish plays forbidden in Warsaw and Vilnius were performed in the comparatively liberal environment of Kiev, and the city's theater was said to be under the thumb of Tadeusz Borkowski, who saw the theater as an instrument of Polonization. After the insurrection Russian theater prevailed. It remained popular, and Kiev achieved a reputation as "a theater city." In 1903 one performer complained that Kiev audiences were "cold," but a popular columnist wrote that "Kiev's theaters are never empty."[40]

UKRAINIAN THEATER

The freedom to stage plays in Ukrainian was severely restricted by the language decrees of 1863 and 1876. The right to use the Ukrainian language on the stage was regained in 1881, and the troupe of the famous actor-director Marko Kropyvnytsky performed in Kiev in 1882. However, authorities were frightened by the enthusiastic, often raucous, reception that Ukrainian theater received, and they subsequently banned it for another decade. In 1892 itinerant Ukrainian theater returned to Kiev. Frequent travel made it difficult for these troupes to maintain high standards for sets and choral and orchestral music, and social and political themes were discouraged. Nevertheless, from the 1890s the prohibitions against the Ukrainian language were lightly enforced, and it was common to find rave press reviews of performances such as *Natalka-Poltavka*, Kropyvnytsky's *Olesia*, the operetta *Sorochinsky iarmarok* (The Sorochinska fair), and the lively vaudeville annual reviews. A *Kievskaia gazeta* review on January 20, 1902, for example, applauded the young actress Liubov Linytska (1866–1924), who "once again proved the strong aristocratic talents of Ukrainian theater." "Ukrainian evenings," often featuring Shevchenko's poems, were held in Kiev and other towns, with proceeds applied to Ukrainian cultural goals.[41]

Similarly, the choir of Mykola Lysenko, consisting of eighty to ninety student singers, sang Ukrainian songs and carols as well as Ukrainian renditions of Musorgsky, Haydn, Mendelssohn, and others. *Kievlianin* mocked the choir, calling Lysenko the "maestro of the *khokhli*," but the choir was immensely popular in the city, and Lysenko took it to the tearooms of the outskirts to entertain the poor. A distinguished teacher, pianist, conductor, and composer, Lysenko compiled seven collections of Ukrainian folk songs, carols, and festival songs. He also staged musical evenings devoted to Glinka, Tchaikovsky, and the other great Russian composers. Sympathetic to the revolutionary movement, he organized a benefit concert in 1901 for the university students forcibly conscripted into the army, gave benefit concerts for political exiles in 1905–1907, and wrote a cantata for the Shevchenko celebration in 1911.[42]

Outdoor Ukrainian theater was popular during the warm months. In the 1880s local notables gathered at the Château des Fleurs, on the site where the Kiev "Dynamo" soccer stadium is now located. It had a hall with a great buffet and an outdoor garden with an open stage where operetta troupes, folk dancers, cancan girls, storytellers, and satirists en-

18. The Biograph Shooting Gallery and Theater, a popular amusement spot on Vladimir Hill.

tertained the crowds. This simple but tasteful entertainment was said to be appropriate for families. On the eve of the First World War, the Château des Fleurs was still popular, and Sunday performances there concluded with a magnificent fireworks display. Other clubs also opened gardens. Trukhanov Island had an outdoor orchestra of banduras, har-

monicas, and violins. Rowing to the island was popular until a violent
storm in 1883 capsized numerous boats, drowning more than twenty
people. Private boats were consequently banned, but a steamer service to
the island was begun.[43]

The October Manifesto in 1905 brought new opportunities for popular cultural expression. The talents of Marko Kropyvnytsky, Panas
Saksahansky, and others, "who under different circumstances would
have been famous throughout Europe," could now flourish. Kiev's Literacy Society, founded in 1882, built theaters in the Troitsky and Lukianivka People's Clubs. In 1907 Mykola Sadovsky moved his Ukrainian
theater troupe from Poltava to the Troitsky Club. It was inexpensive; one
could get into a matinee performance for as little as five kopecks. Because
it was Ukrainian, some called it a theater for yokels. Hryhory Hryhorev
remembers his teacher telling him that it was nothing but a place "for
weavers, haulers, and other drunkards. Respectable people don't go
there." His interest piqued, Hryhorev became a devotee.[44]

Sadovsky's troupe was particularly popular during Kiev's summer season as the tsarist era drew to a close, but some complained that Ukrainian
theater was "in a state of crisis." Writer-director Mykhailo Starytsky had
died. Marko Kropyvnytsky was aging. (The famous actor-director-play-
wright gave banner performances in Kiev just before his death in 1910,
concealing from his audiences the fact that he was nearly deaf.) Sadovsky
ultimately left Kiev to head the Ukrainian National Theater in Lviv. Female actors were said to excel, but good male performers were hard to
find. Yet at least three dozen Ukrainian troupes, most of them itinerant,
were staging plays in the Russian Empire in 1912. Seeing a Haidamak
troupe rendition of a Kropyvnytsky operetta at the Bergon'e "brightened
these difficult times just a bit for those who love Ukrainian choir and
music." And thanks mostly to Sadovsky (whose actors sometimes performed in two different plays in two different theaters on a single night),
Ukrainian theater was losing its old association with "Little Russian"
peasant theater. No longer limited to frivolous, comic-buffoon vaudeville
demanded by wary state officials, it was engaging serious themes.[45]

Theater was sometimes likened to schools and reading halls in shaping
public morals. One Kharkiv critic wrote in 1898: "We must aspire to the
time when people wait in line not at the doors of the wineshops, but at the
people's theater."[46] For Ukrainian activists, the ability to stage plays in
Ukrainian was a political weapon; at the very least, in the words of Kiev's
leading Ukrainian newspaper, *Rada*, Ukrainian theater was like a school
that was improving and ennobling the Ukrainian language.[47] It is difficult
to gauge the extent to which theater bridged class distinctions in the city.
Cheap seats could be obtained in the galleries, but for many in the outskirts the theater was identified with the alien and "bourgeois" culture of

downtown Kiev. Some workers organized their own cultural activities. Railway workers ran a theater in a warehouse at the main railway terminal; Arsenal workers had a theater and a small orchestra; Greter & Krivanek employees organized a musical group; and a drama company of fourteen operated at a furniture plant.[48]

EARLY FILM IN KIEV

A profound challenge to theater arose with the new art of filmmaking. Russian movie houses began to appear in the mid-1890s, mostly in Moscow and St. Petersburg, which together had 180 movie houses by 1908. The Pathé Brothers, a French firm, opened a shop selling films and projection equipment in Kiev in 1907, and Nikolai Kozlovsky opened a movie theater called Illiuziia (Illusion) in 1908. After it folded, he returned to St. Petersburg where he joined the famous filmmaker Alexander Drankov in the shooting of Russia's first documentary film, *Cossacks of the Don*, which consisted "entirely of trick-riding and scenes of camp life."[49] Early filmmakers often went on tour in the provinces, giving "limited engagements." One such entrepreneur, I. Gutzman, "the first showman to comprehend the future of the business that he had adopted as a temporary show idea," spent time in Kiev making newsreels before moving on to Riga, where his "Crystal" and "Progress" theaters attracted a young boy named Sergei Eisenstein, whose name would later become synonymous with the early Soviet film industry. Eisenstein, it is said, was accompanied not by his parents, "but by his nurse because his nurse's dignity was not at stake."[50]

Kiev was featured in several early films. *Solemn Procession of Pilgrims in Kiev* (1907) is one of the first films to have wide distribution on Russian screens, and around 1907–1908 films were made of the Mykhailiv Monastery's Jubilee and the festival of the Consecration of the Dnipro. Although filmmaking quickly came to emphasize the exotic and the sensational, films of manufacturing processes were also made. One such film featured the making of cigarette wrappers in Kiev. Meanwhile, an American film, *Russia: The Land of Oppression* (1910), also featured Kiev, depicting the persecution of Jews there and in Kishinev.[51] But if movie theaters were initially slow to catch on in Kiev, at least in comparison with the capitals, between 1908 and 1911 thirty movie houses opened in the city, mostly in the central neighborhoods.[52] Films provided news and information. Newsreels were made of the Beilis trial and the burial of Prime Minister Petr Stolypin, who had been assassinated in Kiev in 1911, for example. Movie houses offered travelogues, melodrama, farce, even ballet, and were cheaper than theater. Katerynoslav's D. Sakhnenko, who began with local newsreels and then produced films featuring the beauty of the region's natural environment, pioneered filmmaking in Ukraine. In 1911 Mykola Sadovsky joined Sakhnenko as producer and actor in the filming of popular Ukrainian plays. Their highly successful *Natalka-Poltavka* was shown until 1930. Popular theater actors such as Liubov Linytska and Maria Zankovetska (1854–1934) performed in early films. By 1915 two film studios were operating in Ukraine, one in Kiev, the other in Odessa.[53]

"AND OLD KIEV PLAYS CARDS"

In his study of Soviet urban leisure culture, John Bushnell argues that urban leisure activities derive largely from informal personal interaction among peasant villagers: "leisure preferences of today are determined less by the current condition of society than by the preferences of yesterday." Traditional urban leisure activities have been characterized mainly by *obshchenie* (visiting friends) and by *progulka* (strolling, hanging out, playing cards, and the like).[54] At midcentury Kievans strolled and picnicked, played cards, and hung out.

Gambling remained a popular passion throughout the entire period under study. The high-stakes games run by Polish magnates at fair time in the nineteenth century's early decades have already been described. Card games were a constant at the Noblemen's and Merchants' Clubs, and local officials continued to participate despite an 1879 ban by the Ministry of the Interior on macao and other popular games of chance. Looking back at the 1880s, when the Noblemen's Club celebrated its fiftieth anniversary, Iaron observed that the club had served mainly as a place for the city's elite to gamble at cards. In 1887 proceeds from card games and fines reached fifty thousand rubles, some of which went to charity. (Morals remained "patriarchal" [traditional], but "no one was shocked" when card players or bowlers at the German skittles alley took off their coats, we are told.)[55]

Lotteries reinforced the public's passion for gambling, but they were also an important means of raising money for human needs. At the Merchants' Club lotteries sometimes ran until eleven o'clock at night. They drew huge crowds and helped finance charities such as day-care centers for the poor, which neither Kiev's city council nor the provincial zemstvo had been willing to fund. In 1911 the Merchants' Club raised sixteen thousand rubles in lottery revenue; in 1912, however, lotteries with jackpots of more than fifteen hundred rubles were declared illegal.[56]

Of course, gambling and lotteries have been popular forms of entertainment in many cultures. They helped pay the colonial American soldiers who fought for independence against the British. Gunther Barth has written of nineteenth-century America: "Gambling appealed to some city written of nineteenth-century America: "Gambling appealed to some city people as a mark of gentility, or struck others as an exciting diversion from everyday problems. For some, it also affirmed a deep-seated suspicion about the inclination of heterogenous people to transgress the morality of the lawmakers."[57] This analysis could easily apply to imperial Kiev as well, particularly to the flamboyant Poles. Recalling how hard it was to leave the Contract Fair, one visitor observed: "One could say that Warsaw dances, Cracow prays, Lvov falls in love, Vilna goes hunting, and old Kiev plays cards."[58]

The famous high-stakes card games that accompanied the fair probably disappeared as the fair itself waned in importance, but games of chance continued to be popular well into the twentieth century. Billiards and dominoes for stakes were commonly played in restaurants and cafés. Card games ran constantly in the city's three flea markets, and many a cardsharp made a living fleecing peasants. Unskilled laborers waiting for work whiled away their time gambling. Even children played games of chance. After 1905 the right to authorize the opening of new clubs was transferred from the Ministry of the Interior to provincial officials, and the number of new clubs, with names such as Bicycle Club, Sportsmen's Club, and Artists' Club, proliferated. Many were run by card sharks and soon closed down.[59]

HANGING OUT IN KIEV

For many Kievans recreational life remained centered in the home, and some put red lights in their windows to signal that friends were welcome to drop in. Of the public places, the streets, particularly the great streets such as the Khreshchatyk, the bazaars, the parks and woods, the churches, and the taverns all were important centers of social interaction.

Boating was popular as well. In the mid-1850s two Belgian-built steamers, part of a fleet of twelve Polish-owned steamers on the Dnipro, came regularly to Kiev. The river produced extra income too, as children and adults made baskets from the willow thickets along its banks for sale in local markets, a skill first taught to Kievans by a religious pilgrim in the 1840s. Troops from Kiev's garrison practiced building pontoon bridges across the Dnipro, and this exercise, as well as nighttime artillery practice and the detonation of explosives, often drew big crowds. In winter Kiev had plenty of water and hills for skating and sledding.

As much as anything else, however, strolling dominated Kiev's recreational scene. The writers Nikolai Gogol (1809–1852) and Nikolai Leskov (1831–1895), both of whom lived in the city for a time, were among those who enjoyed strolling among its monuments and vistas. Visiting dignitaries—for example, those who came in 1888 for the great celebration of the Nine Hundredth Anniversary of Russia's Christianization—were taken for strolls along the Dnipro or the canal that cut through Podil. Another favorite spot for strollers was aristocratic Lypky, named for the stately linden trees that surrounded the homes of the affluent who lived there. The Tsar's Garden and Vineyard, the origins of which went back to the seventeenth century, were located in Lypky. Early in the nineteenth century, a military band played almost daily in good weather, attracting great crowds to the garden. Poles promenaded as a way of showing off. "May promenades" were held without fail on the first, fifteenth, and thirtieth of the month. Each *gymnasium* class had its own banner that was unfurled during festival days.[60] Parents took these promenades very seriously, for they were one way of displaying an educated son.

The orderliness of Bibikov's Kiev reinforced the popularity of this diversion, and perhaps the rudeness of the carters and haulers, notorious even at midcentury, helped convince people that walking was enjoyable. Upon visiting the city in 1851, Nicholas I decreed that Lypky should be maintained in the best possible fashion, and a city orangery was created there. Regrettably, a few decades later the city council allowed most of the plants to be sold off by the family in charge of maintaining it.

Strolling was a popular diversion for the entire population and served as a way for groups of young people to look over members of the opposite sex. On summer evenings, Ikonnikov recalls, "the entire beau monde of Kiev" strolled through the Tsar's Garden. Nationalities mixed. One could hear Russian and Polish, French and German, catch a glimpse of the infamous man who had killed the poet Lermontov in a duel, or of the coveted beauties of high society. In the mornings one could enjoy the mineral waters of the garden to the tunes of an outdoor orchestra.[61] The Russian word for strolling (*gulian'e*) and its Ukrainian equivalent (*huliannia*) also can mean merriment or revelry, and particularly on holidays strolling was punctuated with merrymaking and group dancing, usually in a circle and called *khorovod* in Russian, *khorovid* in Ukrainian. Such events enabled young men and women to interact. Sometimes young women sat on benches, strategically placed at yard gates, hoping to be noticed by passersby.[62]

Strollers in Kiev had some complaints. If one got caught in the rain, it was impossible to get a carriage, and, in any case, sedans quickly filled up with water. Moscow, St. Petersburg, Kharkiv, and Riga regulated their carters (*izvozchiki*), it was said, but not Kiev, where horses were driven at breakneck speed and allowed to make sharp right-hand turns without slowing down.[63] Missing in Kiev was the institution of the *pol'za* ("facility"), a place where women could freshen up, make sanitary changes, and even hire a seamstress to sew a torn dress. Noting the appearance of these

19. Street scene from nineteenth-century Kiev showing a well-dressed, upper-class woman (left) and a barefoot milk peddler.

conveniences in such cities as Samara, Saratov, and Ekaterinburg, a "well-traveled woman" suggested in one Kiev newspaper that here was an opportunity awaiting local entrepreneurs. The *pol'za* was undoubtedly intended to assist middle- and upper-class women out on the streets. Poor women, usually on their own and looking for work, often slept in courtyards or open fields and devised their own means of protection "from being dragged off." Rows of women tied themselves together with a long rope that was tied to a post or tree. This custom was said to be especially prominent in the south, where women were "dead tired after working sixteen-hour days."[64]

The Khreshchatyk was admired throughout the south. Kerosene street lamps were added in 1869. (The practice of carrying burning splinters had previously been banned because of the fire hazard.) Gaslights were installed in 1872, electric streetlights around 1900. By 1904 Kiev had about one thousand streetlights.[65] In winter the Khreshchatyk was completely deserted by evening, but in warm weather working-class people in their finest attire assembled in the evenings and on Sundays to stroll along its wide sidewalks. Hryhorev remembers watching the young village girls employed in the city's cigarette factories deny to passersby that they actually worked with tobacco (which was considered a dirty and demeaning job), and describes the soldiers out for a stroll who had to stand at attention when officers appeared.[66] Strolls along the Khreshchatyk afforded

20. Police patrol a square in the center of town, ca. 1900. Note that the sign at the corner advertising the chocolate shop is in Russian and French.

Kievans the chance to window-shop in what had become the city's high-fashion shopping district. As in the capitals, a fashion calendar had evolved in Kiev, its "seasons" no longer dependent upon the fairs.[67] Residents of Kharkiv complained that their city "did not have a single good broad boulevard similar to the Kreshchatik in Kiev, the Esplanade in Helsingfors [Helsinki], Bolshaia dvorianskaia in Voronezh, or the incomparable Ujazdowskie Allei, the best place to stroll in all of Warsaw."[68]

Fittingly, strolling became a metaphor for aimlessness and a lack of public-mindedness. During the bitter month of November 1905, physicians in Kiev were accused "of preferring to stroll in green fields than to take a stand against government arbitrariness."[69]

"DEBAUCHERY AND CRIME OF ALL KINDS"

In contrast to the stately and orderly Khreshchatyk was the scene at Kiev's crowded bazaars. On Sunday afternoons at the Alexander Bazaar, in addition to pickpockets, cardsharps, Gypsies, and charlatans, the market was flooded with chickens and geese, "suspicious-looking" fish by-products, old books, clothing, and consumer items of every kind, even grand pianos. Once a month unclaimed railway freight was sold. Anyone could trade without worrying about a permit or paying taxes on the transactions. The Pole Maria Kozieradzka remembers in particular the cranberries and the contraband goods, the Turks selling halva (sweetened sesame cakes), and the arrival in August of the Tatars on camels and in huge coaches filled with grapes and wine.[70] Halytsky Bazaar, with everything from large stores to countless street vendors, was another popular hangout. With its rows of stands and carts offering a variety of inexpensive foods, it was an especially popular place to eat. It was also called Jewish Bazaar, or Evbaz (from *Evreiskii bazar*) for short. Still today, older Kievans from the neighborhood will say, "Ia Evbazivs'ky" (I'm from the Evbaz).

Strolling and other outdoor activities could flourish only in a safe environment, and nineteenth-century Kiev appears to have been safe, at least in terms of violent crime. Murder, for instance, was uncommon. If official data are to be believed, in the 1840s Kiev averaged only four murders per year (about one per 12,500 inhabitants), compared with an average of about six yearly suicides, seventeen drownings, twenty deaths from "fits" associated with illnesses, and three from "intemperance."[71] In 1901 murder was still uncommon in Kiev (pop. 281,000). That year six murders were recorded, about one per 47,000 inhabitants. From this point the number of murders increased sharply, although the number of murders per inhabitant did not significantly exceed that registered in the "safe" 1840s. Officially, in 1902 Kiev recorded thirteen murders; in 1906 (pop. 340,000), twenty-two, or one per 15,500 residents. In 1913, in the sprawling metropolis of 626,000, there were forty-three murders, or one per 14,500 inhabitants.[72]

In the first decade of the twentieth century, Kiev's press published numerous complaints about street crime, homeless boys, "bazaar ruffians," and the generally bad manners of the public. In 1903 a *Kievskoe slovo* columnist reported that people feared visiting Vladimir Hill and the Tsar's Garden in the evenings because the absence of police and a general lack of care had turned these parks into "sanctuaries for debauchery and crime of all kinds." "Never in Kiev has there been so much shameless, impertinent behavior . . . so many wayward, dissolute people."[73] Angrily, a columnist from *Kievskaia gazeta* contended that Kiev had more "itinerant, tattered street-children" than any other imperial city. Denied educational opportunity, they became thieves and pickpockets.[74]

Similar complaints were registered elsewhere. St. Petersburg newspapers complained of "boundless insolence" and harassment on the streets. *Odesskie novosti* (Odessa news) blamed a pogrom in Yalta on "a small group of vagabonds and rogues who were helped by hundreds of street boys."[75] In Rostov-na-Donu it was said that "nowhere in Russia, except in Odessa, are there as many vagabonds, pimps, and pickpockets. . . . Robbery and violence are normal occurrences there." The Moscow press spoke of nightly assaults and the need to pack a revolver on the back streets of the unruly cities of the south. Kharkiv's press called these tales "a bit exaggerated, but not altogether false." The paper blamed poor housing, homelessness, and the abusive treatment of children as causes.[76]

Arrests for petty crimes in Kiev more than doubled from 3,583 in 1902 to 8,237 in 1904. In 1904, of the 8,237 arrested, 2,114 were adult men, 742 were adult women, 1,298 were boys, and 101 were girls. The large number of arrested boys seems to reinforce the popular view that cities were raising a new generation of young criminals. The great majority of arrests (65 percent) were for theft, and many others were for vagrancy and loitering. That only 702 (9 percent) of these arrests came during the fall may indicate that some of the city's underclass returned to the villages to help with the harvest. Also, religious pilgrims were common targets, and their numbers declined in the fall. On the other hand more than half of the 327 robberies were committed during the fall.[77]

There are many possible explanations for the rising number of arrests. Population continued to grow; the number of police may have increased; data collection may have improved; or officials simply may have cracked down. In her study of St. Petersburg, Joan Neuberger suggests that "hooliganism arose and flourished, so to speak, as part of the process of class self-identification and self-assertion that was taking place at the turn of the twentieth century in connection with rapid urbanization, industrialization, and the spread of education." The growing problem of hooliganism, especially when the targets were people or property in the more affluent central neighborhoods, may have been an expression of defiance, a challenge to "the balance of power on the streets" by an increasingly assertive lower class.[78] Kiev's journalist-memoirist Iaron reflected the popular view that the streets had become increasingly unsafe, contending in 1910 that violent crime, shocking in the 1880s, had become commonplace. "You live from day to day. You really don't live, you vegetate. You take a breath and thank God."[79]

Most of the victims of street crime were themselves residents of the poorer outlying districts where police were few and far between, such as Kiev's Shuliavka and Solomenka and Kharkiv's Cold Hills. Like other large cities, Kiev provided cover and anonymity for criminals. Thieves hid stolen goods in flats called *passazhy* (the same word used to denote the long shopping arcades). Individual clubs and taverns, each with its own *dezhurnyi*, or lookout, acquired reputations for harboring specific types of criminals and specific goods. In the outskirts theft was said to be "so common, it's not even reported, particularly since you know what will happen to you if you do report it." Often located near the railway stations where large crowds provided more victims and cover, these areas were said to be dangerous even by day; at night residents went out only if necessary, and then in groups. Police estimated that half of Kharkiv's petty criminals lived in Cold Hills. Protection money, long a reality for Jews, became a necessity for many shopkeepers. Like the city, crime itself had become anonymous. "In the past the lives and the property of the peaceful Cold Hills residents had been considered inviolable. Such was the thieves' tradition. But in recent years everyone has become fair game, especially the small shopkeepers who are routinely extorted and pay for protection or risk the destruction of their shops."[80]

Thus, while strolling continued to be popular, its time and place became more dependent on lighting and police presence. Strolling had always been a group activity, a means of displaying oneself and interacting with one's peers and members of the opposite sex. Growing concern for personal safety ensured that it would remain a group activity.

STROLLING PROFESSIONALLY IN KIEV

In 1856 a special committee was set up to try to curb the spread of syphilis in Kiev. That year 106 women were known to be prostitutes (in a city of at least 50,000 inhabitants). The 1874 census listed 403 registered prostitutes (396 of whom were women), but this figure taps only those who might be called openly professional.[81] As was true all over Europe, many others survived unofficially as prostitutes. St. Petersburg, with 1,400,000 people at the turn of the twentieth century, had 3,000 registered prostitutes, and perhaps up to 50,000 unregistered. In 1907 Berlin was said to have 50,000 prostitutes, of whom only 4,000 were registered.[82]

Kiev was said to have many brothels, some of them famous. Alexander Kuprin (1870–1938) wrote about prostitution in the city in his novel *Iama* (The Pit). I could find no specific data for the number of brothels in Kiev, but in 1879 Kharkiv, with about 100,000 people, had at least 33 known brothels with 248 female prostitutes. Syphilis was common, and often went untreated or treated by home cures recommended by *baby*. That year police doctors made 9,336 pelvic examinations and sent 120 women to the hospitals with varying stages of venereal disease. Interestingly, 90 of the 120 were *not* registered as "public women."[83] Kiev's Iaron recalls that weekend "orgies" in "houses of pleasure" had been acceptable forms of behavior for civil servants and the like, but that morals tightened in the 1870s and early 1880s. Some prominent brothel owners consequently turned to selling firewood to make a living.[84]

At one point, apparently around the turn of the twentieth century, one of Kiev's governors died of a heart attack while cavorting with a prosti-

tute in one of Kiev's most famous brothels. His successor tried to close
Kiev's brothels down. Although he failed, it appears that he nonetheless
managed to concentrate brothels in certain neighborhoods—for instance,
the even-numbered side of the Khreshchatyk near city hall. Unescorted
women did not enter this area.[85]

On July 3, 1903, a prostitute named Paulina Primakova hanged herself
in a district drunk tank, having been brought there from the Khreshchatyk for fighting and violent behavior. The fact that she died in a
police building fanned many rumors. Led by their pimps, one hundred
prostitutes gathered at Alexander Hospital during the autopsy, demanding to see the corpse. Several times they broke into the autopsy room,
stabbing an orderly with an autopsy knife and beating up a policeman in
the process. It took ten policemen to chase the prostitutes from the hospital and disperse them.[86]

The Society for the Defense of Women, arguing that women's choices
were often limited to complete dependence upon an employer, hunger, or
streetwalking, sought inexpensive cafeterias, job-training workshops,
day-care centers, labor exchanges, and shelters where women could find
a refuge from abuse "and the dangers of the big city." "On the streets
only the blind don't know that we have prostitutes who are eight and ten
years old." Most prostitutes would opt for an honest life if they had the
opportunity, it was argued. An impassioned debate ensued between those
who wanted to help prostitutes protect themselves from abuse and those
who sought to abolish prostitution altogether. Several hundred, including
many university students, attended the first meeting of this organization
in 1904.[87]

Statistics for 1904 recorded 28 arrests for pimping, 170 for adult female prostitution, and 9 for prostitution by girls under fourteen.[88] Many
prostitutes came from the ranks of domestic servants. In 1905 Kiev's
lower domestic servants often lived on three to five rubles per month. In
some households, especially if there were small children, servants worked
all day and ate the leftovers from the family meal. The majority of employers sought to destroy their servants' sense of dignity, one article complained. Servants had no rights; any form of protestation could be
deemed insolence, "a sign that they've been spoiled by the city." Sexual
abuse was said to be common, particularly of twelve- to fifteen-year-old
girls, which "probably accounts for the fact that a significant percentage
of prostitutes come from the ranks of domestic servants."[89] In 1899
Kiev's Literacy Society opened a reading room at the women's prison.
Forty of the 150 inmates enrolled in twice-weekly classes. Most were in
jail for two or three months, suggesting that they had been incarcerated
for prostitution, vagrancy, or theft; most were young (22 of the 40 were
between fifteen and twenty-one), born in Kiev Province, and unmarried;

30 were Orthodox (2 were Catholic, 2 Jewish, the rest unknown); and almost all had been housemaids.[90]

Streetwalking, like outdoor activity in general, was a bit more comfortable in the better climate of the south, but prostitution was probably no more or no less prevalent in Kiev than it was in other Imperial Russian cities. Prostitution did contribute to the venereal disease that afflicted an estimated one-third of all Kievans in the early 1870s.[91] Eye disease and blindness, an unfortunate ramification of advanced syphilis, sparked an interest in eye-related research at the university, and an important eye-disease clinic, sponsored by the merchant E. G. Popov, opened in 1887. In the early twentieth century, Kiev's press began to blame some violent crimes on the ravages of advanced syphilis. One lurid account spoke of a "deranged and degenerate" nobleman, suffering from advanced syphilis, who killed a woman and then himself, "splattering blood and brains all over the apartment." On the same day the paper reported the rape and murder of a woman in the wooded outskirts of the city, and warned that police harassment was rendering Kiev's prostitutes more vulnerable to abuse by pimps and clients.[92]

With regard to the collective effort by prostitutes to defend themselves in the face of alleged police harassment, police brutality was hardly unique to Kiev, and such incidents no doubt occurred in other imperial cities. The incident reflects the misogynist values that were much a part of Ukrainian culture at that time. In the patriarchal Ukrainian villages, Christine Worobec argues, women were viewed as temptresses in need of strict control. "The brutality of men toward women, the sexual double standards, and the vulnerable position of women in a patriarchal society underscore the harshness of Ukrainian peasant life in which the struggle for survival in a precarious agricultural economy was constant."[93] Since Kiev was a city composed mainly of individuals with Ukrainian village backgrounds, it seems likely that misogynist values remained strongly entrenched in its culture.

It should also be noted that economic prospects for women were limited, partly because there were few educational opportunities for them in the city or the countryside. Kiev's Society to Assist the Poor established a school for indigent girls in 1834, and the Institute for Noble Girls was founded in 1838, but in 1845, of the 3,600 students enrolled in all Kiev schools, only 293 were girls.[94] Only after 1905 did significant numbers of women begin to enroll in secondary and higher educational institutions. The number of secondary schools increased from twelve in 1900 to thirty-five in 1913 mainly because schools were opened to women. Interestingly, of the twenty secondary schools established for women, only one was publicly financed. In higher education St. Vladimir University had admitted a few women beginning in 1878, mostly for the purpose of training secondary teachers, but in 1886 rescinded this opportunity, and in 1889 the last female student left the university. In 1905 a university-level Higher Women's Course was opened; by 1910 it was enrolling 2,220 women.[95]

THE TAVERN, THE CROWD, AND THE SUBCULTURE OF VIOLENCE

Brawling had a long history in the towns of Russia and Ukraine. In 1274, not long after the Mongols decimated Kiev, Metropolitan Kirill, concerned about disorderly behavior among the general populace and the clergy, threatened to excommunicate participants in public fistfights and deny a church burial to those who were killed. Brawling nevertheless continued, particularly in winter, often on frozen bodies of water (snow and heavy clothing cushioned one's fall), and at Shrovetide, just before Lent. Banned in 1823 and again in 1832, mid-nineteenth-century winter fights, with all the appeal of organized sport, were still attracting thousands. Fights took three forms: the general free-for-all; the "wall-against-wall" in which teams representing neighborhoods, villages, occupations, or other collective identities went at each other; and the "one-on-one" competition, which often preceded a general melee. Students were notorious brawlers, and men from all classes participated. The poet Alexander Izmailov (1774–1831) wrote about St. Petersburg's legendary Gordei (known as Iron-head), and the feats of Moscow's Semyon Treshchala also appear in verse.

> From his Moscow factory
> Comes the fighter Semyon.
> With his iron fist
> He knocks a tile from the stove
> In a single stroke.
> In battle he is feared
> As he advances against the wall.
> They topple.
> As the battle ends, cries of joy
> As our triumphant hero leads everyone to the tavern
> For refreshment.[96]

In Kharkiv the brawlers Ruban and Kovalev became legends. Representing Kharkiv's lower town, Ruban fought in a red sash, a pipe hanging jauntily from his mouth (for he seldom took a blow to the face). The medical student Kovalev, his opponent and friend, fought in a black velvet hat. Their "one-on-ones" were rituals of skill and finesse, Sunday and holiday exhibitions that brought them gifts and adulation from students and merchants. Of course, sometimes fights got out of hand. Once twenty seminary students beat Ruban unconscious.[97] In Odessa Easter fistfights between Greeks and Jews had also become a ritual, but in 1871, when police lost control, "Russians" joined Greeks in a full-scale pogrom that led to one thousand arrests.[98]

Full of students and divided by geography into distinct neighborhoods, Kiev was ideally suited for the sport of fistfighting. The writer Nikolai Gogol recalled from his youth the great brawls in winter and at Shrovetide. "Thick-necked" theology students usually organized them and usually outfought the philosophy students, noted for their long mustaches, and the rhetoric students. Fights were arranged so that neither side had an advantage in weight or physical stature, and large crowds gathered on the hillsides to watch.[99] Early in the twentieth century, fights were still popular during Easter and other festival days, and police sometimes had difficulty breaking them up. Carters tried to avoid the sites of brawls because police ordered them to transport those arrested to precinct stations free of charge.[100]

Cultured Kievans liked to think of their city as a special place of beauty, order, sophistication, and even tolerance. After all, Kiev was "the mother of Russian cities" and one of the empire's most important educational centers. Kiev journalists sometimes wrote condescending articles about other towns, attacking Kishinev in 1903, for example, as "a city of boredom, ennui, and savagery," and likening its beau monde to a crowd of murderers. Kishinev's winter season of balls, it was said, began with a series of sensational fights and ended in duels "that amount to firing six shots into a tree." Clinging to archaic concepts of chivalry, Kishinev's "ignorant noblemen go to Odessa to raise hell, drink for days on end, then return to Kishinev, get bored, drink more, and play at being knights. . . . Such is the Kishinev beau monde, which reeks of cognac." "We are a wild bunch," Kishinev's residents readily admitted, or so concluded a Kiev journalist.[101]

More than Kiev, late-imperial Kishinev (1900 pop. 110,000) was a big village where rural, archaic, and antimodern values persisted. But Kishinev certainly had no monopoly on drunkenness, for drinking was central to popular culture everywhere in the Russian Empire except for its Moslem regions and Jewish *shtetlach*. In the eighteenth century Kiev had a tavern on every block. In 1874 at least twenty-eight Kiev enterprises made alcoholic drinks from vodka to kvas (a drink made from fermented rye bread), and the city had about eight hundred taverns of various kinds,[102] one for every 112 adults over twenty. Lukianivka District had a tavern for every hundred inhabitants, but only two schools to serve its 7,300 residents.[103] Artels, factory workers, even thieves had their favorite pubs that catered to their respective needs and values. Women drank too. One recorder of Kiev's public morals wrote in 1904: "On Sunday and holiday nights, hundreds of Kievans can be seen returning from parties and get-togethers. Both husband and wife are drunk. . . . They are noisy and sometimes singing." Children of all ages can be seen tagging along. "He berates her for flirting, she screams at him for losing at cards." Sometimes it ends with a slap, or one of the kids gets cuffed. "Such are the morals in our city."[104]

In Kiev the most virulent form of urban disorder was the pogrom, which differed fundamentally from other forms of disorder: it targeted a minority that had been identified and dehumanized by centuries of propaganda as the killers of Christ and the exploiters of the simple peasants. Particularly in 1905, the pogrom occurred with at least the tacit consent of local authorities. Large cities offered anonymity, and pogroms were spawned by their tavern culture. Perpetrators could easily fade into the background of the impersonal, mobile urban population. The victims— the Jewish bread peddlers, chicken sellers, and shopkeepers—having been dehumanized, were also frequently anonymous, and it was therefore easier to commit acts of violence against them. The ubiquitous taverns provided alcohol and places for agitators to mobilize the rabble. (Decades later, the executioners who shot Jews for the Nazis were liberally supplied with alcohol to dull their senses.) In his study of the 1881 pogroms, Aronson has written: "A pogrom had the advantage that it promised, as a bare minimum, a bellyful of vodka. . . . Any adventure, any outlet, was likely to be eagerly seized upon."[105] In 1881 one observer described the pogrom as "the grandiose street disorder—the real fair. Knowing nothing better to do on Sundays and holidays than to get drunk and fight, the ignorant *chern* [rabble] . . . [is] easily swayed by rumor, for it is incapable of thinking critically."[106]

Out of thousands of Kiev residents, only a few hundred ever actively involved themselves in pogroms. Most simply looked on, declining either to participate in the violence or to defend the victims. But however small in number, the *chern* remained powerful, for it could be mobilized into a mob, and the potential of a pogrom continued to lie semidormant in the taverns and bazaars, awaiting only the right agitator and the right moment to rise against the city's most noticeable and hated minority.

ALTERNATIVES TO THE TAVERN: THE TEAROOM
AND THE PEOPLE'S CLUB

No wonder the reformist committees of public care (*popechitel'stva*) tried to compete with the taverns by running tearooms, especially in and around the chaotic bazaars. Here police kept order, and the newcomer could learn where to get medical care or how to get his child into school. "Here the old women [*baby*] can complain about their various misfortunes." Here people could come and "warm up, not only physically but spiritually." Tearooms often had reading areas. Educated people sometimes came and shared ideas, offering impressionable children contact with positive role models.[107]

By 1905 Kiev's committees of public care were serving 2,146 students in twenty-six free evening classes on practical and academic subjects. Half of the enrollees were women; most were young (aged fifteen to twenty-five), and about one-quarter were Jews. In addition, they were running ten tearooms, seven of which had reading rooms, three shelters for drunks, and a small facility for alcoholics. They also sponsored a choir and a series of dances, plays, and other social events. While the tearooms could hardly expect to compete with the tavern culture of Kiev, the fact that they had reading rooms and classes made them attractive in an educationally impoverished culture with an enormous passion for learning. In 1905 striking workers included better access to education among their demands.

Kiev's Literacy Society, founded in 1882, contributed to popular culture in many ways. Between 1882 and 1900 it helped sponsor seven hundred lectures that attracted 160,000 listeners. It helped found the Troitsky People's Club, finished in 1902, which had a thousand-seat auditorium, a center for the free distribution of books to the various literacy programs, a children's museum, an inexpensive tearoom for workers, meeting halls, reading rooms, and a legal aid office. During its first year of operation, its library and reading rooms had 80,000 visitors.[108]

Although the monarchist *Kievlianin* and the liberal *Kievskaia mysl'* were the leading newspapers after 1905, the masses preferred the boulevard or "kopeck" press, above all *Iuzhnaia gazeta* (The southern paper), also called *Iuzhnaia gazeta kopeika*. An evening edition, *Vechernaia gazeta* (Evening paper), and, later, *Gazeta kopeika* (Daily kopeck) also became popular. These tabloids offered rumor, gossip, local color, and serialized mysteries and romances. By this time Kiev also had about eighty small bookshops, two of them Ukrainian (additional Ukrainian bookstores were not permitted), and cheap books could be bought as well in the kiosks of the Evbaz. Detective stories starring Nick Carter, Nat Pinkerton, and Sherlock Holmes were in great demand; they sometimes sold for three kopecks.[109]

One frequent visitor to a Literacy Society reading room was profiled in a city newspaper. "Pale, tired, and with angry eyes," Maria V., age thirty, and her five children were often beaten by her husband, a petty civil servant. Books became "a fantasy world that took her beyond the world of turmoil and gave her the strength to face another day." For some the Literacy Society reading room provided the only access to education. At first some patrons were rowdy. But "they got used to the atmosphere of a library and now there is order," *Kievskaia gazeta* reported in 1904.[110] *Prosvita*, the organization of Ukrainian activists discussed in chapter 4, set up at least fifteen tea- and reading rooms in the outskirts of Kiev to bring Ukrainian culture to the semi-Russified children of the working poor. *Prosvita* was closed down in the political reaction that followed 1905, as were the Literacy Society and its reading rooms, in January 1908. Paranoid officials saw the reading rooms and people's clubs as dens of conspiracy. The Troitsky People's Club was taken over by the city and leased out for office space. The library was reopened after four years, but on a paying basis. With fitting irony, the tearoom was turned into a bar.

ORGANIZED SPORT

Missing from Kiev was anything akin to the immense popularity of baseball in turn-of-the-century America, with its leagues and schedules, its passion for records, its idols, and its emphasis on fair play and competition through rules. A powerful distraction from the conflicts and routines of everyday life, organized baseball provided America's city dwellers with "a socially acceptable outlet for emotions."[111]

While touring America in 1903, one Kievan sent letters back to *Kievskaia gazeta*. Many things impressed him: "the hustle and bustle" of New York; the coffee (and the contrast with Germany, where the service staff said "good morning or good evening a hundred times a day"—in America "you got your morning cup of coffee without a word from the waiter. . . . You come and go and no one pays the slightest attention to you"); the sweet potatoes and fried terrapin; the fact that in New York, "seemingly all the flower sellers are Greek and all the plasterers are Italian"; the quantity and variety of goods for sale; and the absence of beggars. "In America, begging would be fruitless," he concluded.

But baseball fascinated him more than anything else. The sport had its own jargon. Evening newspapers published special sports editions. "Women [fans] chewed gum or candy, and men chewed tobacco or a cigar." "If Spaniards behave frantically at a bullfight, American baseball fans are just as wild." From Chicago the Kiev tourist went to Milwaukee, where "there were churches of fifty different faiths, each with a great organ, choir, and sermons." And in Milwaukee, he found "more baseball."[112]

Although Kiev had no recreational distraction like baseball, organized sports were beginning to catch on. As in Europe and America, there were bicycle rides and races, horse races, and tennis tournaments that included mixed doubles. In 1899 the Kiev Athletic and Gymnastic Society was formed. One of its members was the novelist Alexander Kuprin. In 1901 Czech and Slovak employees of the Greter & Krivanek Machine Works introduced Kievans to soccer, and in 1904 formed the first team, called "South." The Polytechnical Institute also formed a team ("Politekhniki"), and in 1911 a league was formed. That year Kiev soccer players played their first intercity match, against players from Kharkiv, and also played teams from Moscow, St. Petersburg, Gomel, Kursk, and Mykolaiv. Matches drew a few thousand fans. Other sports organizations included the "Russian Falcon" gymnastic society, formed in 1909. Within a year it had 650 members, including 60 women, and began to sponsor gymnastic meets. Kiev boxers won the championship for the southwestern provinces in 1913.[113]

THE AUTOMOBILE AND THE MIRACLE OF FLIGHT

Although trains had become commonplace in the 1870s, in 1905 it still took thirty-eight hours to reach Moscow by rail.[114] The automobile industry took up the challenge, and in 1904 an auto club opened in the city. In 1914 club members managed to drive from Moscow to Kiev in sixteen hours, excluding stops. Drivers noted some hostility in rural areas toward the strange contraption along the way.[115]

Within the city there were still plenty of ox-carts and horses. In 1905 10 percent of the users of a doss house, which provided beds for 25,670 people that year, came on horseback.[116] But motorized transport was transforming the city. Around 1912 the city council purchased several buses, permitted motorized taxis, and required existing carriages to add roofs and rubber tires. Meters were installed with the purpose of ending the age-old practice of haggling over fares. It was argued that rubber tires would reduce wear and tear on the city's bridges, reduce noise said to be harmful to those with nervous disorders, and assuage midwives, who were sure "that a great many female ailments are caused by walking along rutted bridges."[117] The internal combustion engine added new sounds and odors to the city, and automobiles quickly became identified with modernity. Kharkiv's auto club, in fact, called itself "Club Modern." No doubt with cities like Kiev in mind, Ford Motor Company ran ads in the newspapers of the empire, picturing their Ford Runabouts under the slogan, "The only automobile for the worst roads."[118]

Airplanes were in the news too, more as entertainment than anything else, and Kiev became an early center of the flight industry. In 1908 an aviation group was founded at the Polytechnical Institute, and in 1909 it built and flew a biplane. A society of balloonists was also founded at the institute in 1909, and soon a dirigible built by F. F. Anders could occasionally be seen floating above the city. Pioneer-aviator S. I. Utochkin piloted the first airplane flight over Kiev, on April 21, 1910. Between 1909 and 1912 about forty different types of aircraft were built in the

21. The architecture of "downtown" Kiev, ca. 1914. Note the automobile.

city.[119] One of the city's aviation designers was Igor Sikorsky. Born in Kiev in 1889, this 1908 graduate of the Polytechnical Institute designed the first multiengine aircraft in 1913. In 1918 he left the Russian Empire, arriving in America in 1919. Later he was instrumental in pioneering transoceanic aircraft, and in 1939 developed the first successful helicopter.[120] The bold Captain Petr Nesterov (1887–1914) took aerial shots of Kiev for the early film industry and captured the city's imagination. A death-defying flight loop was named after him. In 1914 he managed to fly from Kiev to Odessa in a record three hours and eight minutes. Sometimes pilots took passengers for Sunday rides, drawing crowds of twenty thousand or more. These flights, commented one newspaper, are "miraculous, rare entertainment. The whole public is enraptured."[121] Within a few years their amusement value would be tempered by the realization that they represented a new dimension in weaponry to which cities were especially vulnerable.

SOME FINAL THOUGHTS

Although limited and anecdotal, available evidence provides some insight into the social and recreational lives of Kievans. For the socially advantaged in the early decades of the nineteenth century, the Noblemen's Club and the Merchants' Club were the hubs of social activity. Landowners

22. Gorodetsky House. The ornamentation on this house, built in 1902–1903 for the architect V. Gorodetsky and located at the top of a steep hill, depicts hunting themes and mythological figures. The owner of one of Kiev's first cement plants delivered free cement while the house was being constructed in order to advertise his product.

dominated Kiev's social scene, and the agricultural cycle dictated the social calendar of the city's beau monde. The apogee of Kiev's social whirl came each winter during the Contract Fair. Great balls and gambling marathons provided a stage for the predominantly Polish landowners of the region to strut and display. Just as railroads diminished the economic importance of the fair, industrialization created new sources of wealth and a more complex and varied social structure. Toward the end of the nineteenth century, social rank (*soslovie*) declined in importance, and occupation, education, and income came increasingly to determine status and recreational choices.

Because of their wealth, Poles dominated Kiev's social scene in the early and middle decades of the nineteenth century. In the mid-nineteenth century, a time when "everyone [was] oppressed by the lethal stupidity of contemporary Russian life," Slavophile Ivan Aksakov observed that Kiev's Poles "were generally well educated. They receive and read foreign newspapers."[122] Socially, Poles, Ukrainians, and Russians seemed to mix easily. Kiev had always been a frontier blend of peoples, and the great balls and soirees were blends of Polish, Ukrainian, and Russian culture.

Did political watersheds significantly affect social relationships? After the insurrection of 1863, did Poles and Russians continue to mix socially, or were Poles shunned by Russians? Did nationality make any difference at all in social relationships in a city where many were Russified anyway? The answers are not clear.

Likewise, we cannot ascertain the extent to which bonds forged by wealth and occupation overcame barriers between Jews and Christians in the late nineteenth and early twentieth centuries. Family records indicate that the Brodskys mixed socially with affluent Gentiles, and sometimes married Gentiles, but in general, there is little information on Jewish social life and culture in late-imperial Kiev. One can surmise, however, that Jews were unlikely to call attention to themselves in their social activities in a city where roundups, expulsions, and pogroms punctuated an uneasy coexistence with their Christian neighbors.

The urban environment did provide many sources of empathy and tolerance: the university was one such source, and, quite probably, so was the expanding educational system as a whole. Progressive newspapers taught compassion by publicizing the plight of ethnic and class underdogs. Some political and professional organizations promoted liberal ideals such as universal equality before the law. Socialists preached hostility toward class oppressors, but they often opposed pogroms.

The urban environment also reinforced social and ethnic divisions and prejudices, however. Only a tiny propertied elite was allowed to participate in city governance. After 1892 Jews were completely excluded from the civic polity. The ability to speak good Russian became increasingly important as a determinant of status, and the term *Ukrainian* became more and more associated with the newly arrived peasants who hung around the bazaars, hoping to find work as day laborers or domestic servants. Many spent their days in idleness, passing the time playing cards at one of the three flea markets (on Alexander Square in Podil, at the Haymarket, and at the Troitsky Bazaar). At Troitsky hiring was usually done at ten or eleven o'clock in the morning, at the noisy Haymarket, from two until five in the afternoon. After five o'clock police "invited" the crowds to disperse. Wages were negotiated openly, and those hired as cooks, nannies, and domestic servants were sometimes cursed out of envy by those left behind.

In 1897 nearly one-fifth of the adult "Ukrainian" men in Kiev worked as domestic servants or day workers, and more than one-quarter were soldiers. Sixty percent of the adult "Ukrainian" women worked in domestic service or as day workers.[123] Some expressed concern that Ukrainians would remain a rustic, unproductive urban underclass, speaking the language of the peasant, living in the disadvantaged outskirts.[124]

Others saw the flea markets as devil's playgrounds, warning, as one columnist did in 1904, that people "sit on the street in the blazing sun. There are no facilities at all, not even the most primitive. Many inexperienced country women in particular are in the city for the first time. Dark people poke about all the time, striking up conversations with the women . . . the topics we can only guess." [125]

"Democratic" forms of entertainment were readily available. Advertisements for 1897 make note of the Wax Museum, with its snake charmers and "thousand novelties," and the daily French circus at the Troitsky Bazaar. Inexpensive outdoor theater, *vertep* performances in bazaar carousels, films, soccer and boxing matches, and aerial exhibitions could be enjoyed by all. However, although the evidence is fragmentary, my impression is that there was little mingling among social classes. In the warm weather the beau monde congregated in the garden of the Château des Fleurs, in winter at the Noblemen's Club or at A. P. Diakov's "Northern" Restaurant (later called the "Metropol"). [126] Whatever the weather, the lower classes continued to gather at their favorite taverns. In general, popular forms of entertainment probably did little to bridge the class or ethnic divisions that existed in the city. Nor did they foster a broader sense of urban community. Although most Kievans liked to stroll and promenade, for example, it is doubtful that factory managers and workers strolled *together*, or that prominent merchants linked arms with household servants or Jewish shopkeepers.

Kiev lacked a citywide diversion such as baseball, which could appeal to all regardless of class or nationality. And in a city struggling to provide basic needs such as schools and sewers, little money was spent on recreational facilities. Thus, there were few opportunities for adversarial groups to assemble, recreate, and surmount traditional prejudices.

The machine age was only beginning to reshape Kiev's popular culture by 1914. Film was challenging theater as the hub of the entertainment industry. The internal combustion engine was making the news, but automobiles were still uncommon and airplanes were still exotics to be gawked at. Faster forms of transportation had made the city more accessible to all. By the same token, it became easier than ever to leave the city and its ills. For example, newspapers carried full-page advertising supplements encouraging those with means to leave the city "to take the water cure." One four-page supplement in 1900 invited readers to take the cure with Drs. Divaris and Gordon in Tahanrih (Taganrog). For 100 to 250 rubles per month full-board, or 35 to 75 rubles without board, one could enjoy "high-pressure showers"; dry-heat and steam baths; "electric baths" and electrical massage; mineral, sulphur, and pinewood baths; and mud baths with special "Fango" mud from Italy. Hydrotherapy, it was claimed, was good for neurasthenia, hysteria, insomnia, giddiness, palpitation, migraines, St. Vitus's dance, spinal tabes and consumption, chronic digestive and intestinal ailments from dyspepsia to diarrhea to hemorrhoids, diabetes, heart and blood disorders, rheumatism, excessive perspiration, alcoholism, morphine addiction, advanced syphilis, kidney disease, *polliutsia* (apparently premature ejaculation), impotence, menstrual problems, and other "disorders of the sexual sphere." At lunch one could enjoy six or seven dishes or choose a special diet of kefir (buttermilk) and kumys (fermented mare's milk). Teachers, students, civil servants, and military personnel received discounts.[127]

In a city where water quality was a public scandal, and where the absence of good water posed serious health problems for many, the fact that the advantaged could leave the city to take the water cure reflected, however unintentionally, the reality that rich and poor had little in common in lifestyle or opportunity.

• CHAPTER VII •

The Promise of Change: Kiev in 1905

On Bloody Sunday, January 9, 1905, troops in St. Petersburg fired on a large but peaceful demonstration, killing or wounding several hundred people. In response, Kievans joined angry subjects from throughout the empire, taking to the streets in unprecedented numbers to challenge authority. Initially, demands focused on redressing workplace grievances and creating a more humane economic order. By the fall these grievances had fused with aspirations for broader political changes, and Nicholas II was forced to grant the historic October Manifesto.

Polish and Ukrainian activists vocalized national goals, but as organized groups played a very insignificant role in Kiev's 1905 upheavals. The extent to which Jews challenged authority became a controversy, for opponents of change sought to use alleged aggressive behavior by Jews to justify the backlash of repression. Between October 18 and 20, a horrible pogrom decimated the Jewish community, and rightist forces argued that it was a legitimate and "patriotic" response to Jewish insurrectionism. What occurred in Kiev was hardly exceptional when measured against events elsewhere in the empire that year, however. Kievans followed rather than led in the drama that is collectively called the Revolution of 1905.

"AN ABUNDANCE OF REVOLUTIONARIES"

Kiev provided plenty of inspiration for those who dreamed of radical change. After all, the organizing center of ancient Rus had been the citadel of the new and aggressive ideology of that time, Christianity. And in the previous century, Kiev had nurtured Decembrists and Polish insurrectionaries. During the heyday of Russian populism in the 1870s, it was said that Kiev always had "an abundance of revolutionaries," and that the loss of one was always followed by the quick arrival of another.[1]

Populists from around the empire congregated in the apartment of Olga Ivanova, and in 1873–1874 the Kiev Commune, a "unique apartment-commune" of populists influenced by the anarchist Michael Bakunin (1814–1876), operated in the city. It produced a circle of about thirty radicals, including the well-known Ekaterina Breshkovskaia (1844–1934) and Pavel Akselrod (1850–1928). In 1874 the group went "to the people," trying to stir the peasants especially around Chyhyryn in Kiev Province, where it was hoped that the spirit of a bloody eighteenth-century Cossack uprising could be reawakened. After the movement failed, Iakiv Stefanovych's Kiev-based anarchists fabricated "tsarist manifestos" which claimed that the tsar had ordered peasants to rise against their landlords and local officials. About a thousand peasants in the so-called Chyhyryn Conspiracy were subsequently arrested.[2]

In the late 1870s protest degenerated into random acts of terrorism. In 1878 radicals identified with the Land and Freedom movement killed a Kiev police official and nearly killed a prosecutor. Around 1879 an embryonic labor movement began to develop. Agitators targeted the Arsenal, the Main Railway Shops, and the workshops of Podil, attacking low wages and poor working conditions. Print-shop workers worked fifteen-hour days, railway workers sometimes eighteen or nineteen hours per day at this time. (Their consciousness raised, some railway workers responded by spreading revolutionary materials from town to town along the tracks all the way to Odessa.) New to the city was the weapon of the strike. It was first used in 1879 when a group of workers from the Southwestern Railway's Main Shops—the city's largest enterprise, with one thousand employees—walked out (and were consequently fired). Elizaveta Kovalskaia (1851?–1933) and Nikolai Shchedrin organized a branch of the South Russian Workers Union in 1880, but it was penetrated and destroyed in October 1881, and for several years Kiev remained comparatively quiet on the labor front.

Mykola Ziber (1844–1888), an 1866 graduate of St. Vladimir and a professor of political economy and statistics at the university in 1873–1875, was as influential as anyone in popularizing the ideas of Karl Marx in Kiev. However, the city's first Marxist circle was organized only in 1889, by Emil Abramovich who had come from Minsk a year earlier. It included about thirty print, metal, and railway workers. Abramovich and fellow Jewish agitators Shlemma Berkovich, David Galperin, and Izrail Golomb were arrested in 1889, but Marxism quickly resurfaced with the organization of a group of students in 1891–1892. At least one Polish socialist organization, led by two physicians, also operated in the city at this time. For the next few years, Kiev's most influential leftist agitators were the Pole Edward Pletat, the Jew Boris Eidelman, and the Russian Iuvenaliia Melnikov (1868–1900), who came to Kiev after his arrest in

Kharkiv. Before his arrest in 1896, Melnikov ran a "workshop-school" in his apartment called the Lukianivka Club to train workers and intellectuals in Marxist ideology.

In 1895 Melnikov, Eidelman, Albert Poliak, and others were able to crystallize the movement into a "Worker's Organization," and leaflets began to be published with some regularity. In November 150 tailors and 25 upholsterers, followed by 25 bootmakers, went on strike. Around 1896 the so-called Worker Cause (*Rabochee delo*) came to predominate among Kiev's socialists. It sought to spur workers to act on their own behalf rather than simply school them in revolutionary ideals.[3] In 1897 the Polish Socialist Party joined Worker Cause. Illegal foreign literature poured into Kiev from Vilnius, and couriers went regularly to Moscow, Odessa, and elsewhere to exchange information and leaflets. Small cells spread throughout the city, targeting the railroads, the big plants such as the South Russian Machine Works (Kiev's largest factory, with about five hundred workers in the 1890s) and Greter & Krivanek, as well as the smaller workshops. Women seemed as eager to strike as men. In 1897 women struck the Kogen tobacco enterprise, protesting the fact that money was taken from their wages to compensate the owners for the theft of tobacco by other workers. Women corset makers demanded and won concessions on the issue of fines and deductions from wages because of mistakes. May Day was celebrated for the first time in Kiev in 1897, when five hundred railway workers staged a symbolic walkout after lunch. Other abuses censured by the labor movement were the long workdays and the levying of heavy fines against workers who were a few minutes late.

In March 1898 "an entire army" of ninety-five city and secret police lowered the boom. About one hundred were arrested in Kiev, including most of the radical leaders, and the two underground printing presses were seized. But by the turn of the century, patterns of authority were beginning to break down in the city. In 1900 some twenty bakeries and food-processing shops struck, and in 1901 several hundred tailors struck.[4] Strikes were becoming common.

THE SOLIDARITY STRIKE OF 1903

For all of this, Kiev's organized labor movement remained small, and most of its hard-core activists were intellectuals, and not workers. The underground press run by the Social Democrats could print only one thousand to two thousand copies of flyers, and it often took a day to print a single page. Sympathetic correspondents helped the cause by writing articles for legal newspapers, particularly *Kievskaia gazeta*, on class injustice, government persecution, and the brutality and senselessness of pogroms.

In early July 1903, as strikes that began in the Odessa railway shops and the Baku oil fields spread from city to city, the Jewish schoolteacher Iushuf set Kiev's antigovernment organizational machinery into action. On July 21, led by employees of the Main Railway Shops and the South Russian Machine Works, about four thousand struck. The next day they were joined by workers from the remaining large factories, and from the print shops, bakeries, and other small enterprises. Ten were arrested, but the strike continued to spread, and on July 23 workers from the Arsenal joined. The mood had been festive—at one point the crowd cheered as Trukhanov Island boat builders commandeered a vessel on the Dnipro—but on that day troops fired into the crowd, said to be unarmed, causing many casualties. In response, more enterprises struck and the crowds grew, and by July 24 something close to a general shutdown of commercial activity in the city had occurred. On July 25 another confrontation, this one in Podil, produced more casualties. From this point city life began to return to normal, and the strike ceased altogether by August 1. A Social Democratic leaflet accused Governor-General Dragomirov of saying, "We are more concerned about money and bullets than we are about people." Whether or not he actually said this, the killing of unarmed Kievans left a bitter and unresolved legacy of anger. Kiev had its own martyrs, its own version of what would come to be called Bloody Sunday.

"STUDENTS DID NOT WANT TO BE
TREATED LIKE PEASANTS"

Since the founding of St. Vladimir University in 1834, students had served as the core of the city's protest movements. In the 1870s an estimated five hundred students had taken part in the populist movement.[5] Admission to the universities became less restricted; by the 1880s only half of St. Vladimir's student body came from the nobility. If nothing else, university protest was an embarrassment, for much of it took place in the highly visible environments of Moscow, St. Petersburg, and Kiev, and it reflected the estrangement between the state and the educated classes.[6]

When the government of Alexander III issued the University Statute of 1884, the state assumed virtually complete authority over the universities. The Ministry of Education, displacing the faculty councils, took control of appointments, disbursement of funds, the awarding of scholarship aid, and student discipline. Aside from maintaining order, however, the government did not pursue a coherent educational policy, "only an inconsistent succession of half-measures in alternating periods of reaction and comparative liberalism."[7] From September 1884 until January 1885 the university was closed because of unrest, but the first nationwide student strike did not occur until 1899, and then over a police beating in St. Petersburg. Student drinking and misconduct, and not political causes, were at issue. A public brawl between students and janitors had occurred in 1895, and tensions between students and police remained high. Resentful over being manhandled, St. Petersburg "students did not want to be treated like peasants." For that matter, they did not want to be treated like workers. In Kiev, Samuel Kassow has observed, "although the students did not like the police, they had assumed that, unlike peasants, students enjoyed a certain deference, an immunity against being beaten on the streets."[8]

Friction surfaced again late in 1901 when two St. Vladimir students refused to spend time in the university jail cell. Names were taken of those who had attended a large protest meeting, and authorities forcibly conscripted 183 students into the army and gave more than 200 others lesser penalties. Although students became increasingly active in the various antistate movements, most refused to affiliate with any political organization. Nor were students necessarily ready to join the Social Democrats or any other party in collective antistate actions. Kassow argues that student unrest moved unpredictably, usually in response to university-related issues, and continued to agitate and embarrass authorities. Student protest in 1899 and 1901 was more significant than in 1905 or 1917, he believes, because in the earlier years no one else was battling the autocracy.[9]

In Kiev's underground, 1904 began with a wave of arrests; during the night of January 1, Lenin's mother, his brother Dmitry, and his sister Anna were among those arrested. Toward the end of the year, liberals became increasingly active in the so-called banquet campaign, hoping to press the regime to move toward constitutional reform without encouraging violence from below. Lawyers, members of the Literacy Society, teachers of natural science, and professors from the Polytechnical Institute were among those who staged banquets in Kiev. A banquet on November 20 may have attracted more than one thousand participants. Social Democratic students and agitators, demanding more radical changes, sometimes seized the floor. Mensheviks dominated the Social Democratic organization in Kiev and brought in agitators from St. Petersburg expressly for this purpose.[10]

THE AFTERMATH OF BLOODY SUNDAY

Kiev's first strike in 1905 came at the South Russian Machine Works on January 12, three days after the massacre in St. Petersburg on Bloody Sunday. Workers at other enterprises, large and small, followed. No one group of workers dominated Kiev's strikers or demonstrators, and co-operation among the militant parties seemed tenuous, at least until the opportunities of October forged a broad revolutionary front.

Although much has been written on the 1905 revolution in Kiev, the role of the organized parties is not fully clear. Particularly perplexing is the role of the Jewish Bund. Founded in 1897, the Bund (its formal title was the General Jewish Labor Union in Lithuania, Poland, and Russia) believed that real change could come only through revolution, and that the Jewish proletariat must act as a distinctive Jewish force in realizing that goal. By 1905 it was well entrenched politically among the Jewish working masses, and until the creation of the Socialist Zionist Labor Party (SSRP) in February 1905, it was the only specifically Jewish revolutionary party. Its Kiev supporters were concentrated mainly in Podil, and initially it mounted the quickest and best-organized response to Bloody Sunday in the city, publishing three thousand leaflets urging a general strike. Yet in comparison with Warsaw, Odessa, and many cities in the Pale, Kiev had not become a Bund stronghold, and the organization seemed notoriously absent when it was needed most, during the October pogrom.

Socialist Revolutionaries (SRs) operated in the city, but the extent of their following is unclear. Within the Social Democratic movement, the Bolsheviks, having rejected Menshevik tactics as insufficiently militant, had been steering their own course at least since the fall of 1904. In September the flamboyant Bolshevik agitator and railway worker Alexander Shlikhter (1868–1940) would clearly emerge as the dominant personality and most notorious symbol of the "heroic days" of Kiev's labor movement.

The strikes that followed Bloody Sunday in Kiev were economically motivated. South Russia's workers sought 50 percent wage hikes, an eight-hour workday, and state-provided insurance against illness, among other things. On January 13 Greter & Krivanek's employees came to work, but virtually everyone left after lunch. When they finally returned on January 19, they had won a workday reduction from eleven to ten hours (nine on Saturdays) and the right to have factory medical personnel treat sick workers in their homes, including those who lived at a distance from the factory. Sixty of Młoszewski's Machine Works' ninety-four employees went out on January 14 (spurred by the same agitators who had led the walkout at South Russia two days earlier), as did nearly all of Needl & Ungerman's foundry workers (who were very much influenced by Greter's workers since the plants were close to one another). Needl & Ungerman apparently provided factory barracks, for the demands focused on better housing, food, lighting, and ventilation. Their strike lasted three days; no concessions were granted.

It is worth noting here that even though workers who did not live in factory barracks seldom listed housing problems among their concerns, demands for higher wages were in part a response to the high cost of housing in the city. A Dr. Dukelsky, probably a sanitary doctor, had earlier surveyed 1,380 working-class apartments housing 7,576 people. Of these, 225 were basement apartments, and many were dark and damp. It was estimated that 3.2 percent of Kievans lived in basements, and that the average one-room flat housed 4.6 people. On an average rents consumed 30 percent of a worker's wage, and the cost of living had gone up an estimated 10 to 15 percent over the past few years.[11]

In general, strikes were short-lived. With each day more of South Russia's workers returned: 140 worked on January 13; 424 on January 14; 530 on January 15; 613 on January 17; 700 of the 780-man work force by January 19. Some concessions were apparently won. Workers feared for their jobs, however, and at this point, Kiev's labor force was tentative and divided. Few could be considered hard-core socialist militants. Although the strikes were peaceful, authorities were not reluctant to show force and on January 18 surrounded the factories with troops, arresting some three hundred.[12] The specter of 1903 loomed in the background.

For the Social Democrats "times were tough," Pravdin (V. V. Vakar, 1878–1926) recalls. The police had everyone under surveillance. Unlike the Bund, the party had no printing press at this time. But Bloody Sunday had improved the spirit and the stature of the Bolsheviks, and in early February Shlikhter, Vakar, and Gleb Krzhizhanovsky (1872–1959) formed a new group, numbering twelve to fifteen, called Vpered (Forward), a name taken from Lenin's Geneva publication. Similar organizations formed in Rostov-na-Donu and Kharkiv, giving the Bolsheviks new momentum in the south.[13]

Bloody Sunday also divided the comparatively weak Ukrainian movement. The Ukrainian Socialist Party had all but disappeared in 1904. It had been a small party of Poles and Polonized Ukrainians whose significance lay in its efforts to popularize the idea of a politically independent Ukraine among the revolutionary socialist Ukrainian and Polish intelligentsia.[14] Meanwhile, twenty-six-year-old Mykola Porsh, who had come to Kiev from Poltava in 1904, had moved the focus of the Revolutionary Ukrainian Party (RUP) toward the urban worker and away from the peasant. The son of German and Christianized Jewish parents, Porsh campaigned against the use of Russian in RUP agitational work, however. Influenced by Kiev's July Days of 1903, he sought to build an urban Ukrainian Social Democratic organization that could ally with the Russian Social Democrats in a federation of national parties. Non-Ukrainian RUP members were encouraged to join the Bund or the Russian or Polish SDs.

Since most of Kiev's industrial work force was at least partially Russified, Porsh's opponents, headed by Marian Melenevsky, questioned the wisdom of using the Ukrainian language. Noting that the RUP had been a territorial party dedicated to overthrowing tsarism, and not exclusively a party for ethnic Ukrainians, they argued that emphasizing national differences would only hamper the public movement and reduce the chances of freedom for everyone. On January 12 Melenevsky left the RUP and created the Ukrainian Social Democrats. A few days later they joined the Mensheviks as the Ukrainian Social Democratic Union, better known as Spilka. Given the emotions generated by Bloody Sunday and the growing strength of the workers' movement, it is not surprising that Spilka's adherents would find Porsh's Ukrainian nationalism particularly ill-timed. Although the pragmatic Spilka quickly became the dominant Ukrainian party, these divisions further reduced the political appeal of the Ukrainian movement in Kiev.[15]

Of the major plants, only South Russia struck for a second time during the winter. On February 21 its workers went out with less radical demands, including a nine-hour day and 30 percent wage hikes. Claiming that the plant was in poor shape financially and that it had a year's worth of orders based on fixed payroll expenses, management shut it down and fired many workers. Many were rehired only after agreeing to prestrike conditions. On February 7 Shlikhter helped organize the ferment at the Main Railway Shops, where about one-third of the 2,600 employees were women. Their demands, forty in number, were complex and included paid vacations (two weeks for workers with five years' experience, one month for workers with ten); paid sick leave and the hiring of more medical personnel, including pediatricians and dentists; provisions for widows and children of deceased railway employees; and special preparatory classes for employees' children who were about to enter school. Because of the railway's importance to the war, strikers were threatened with imprisonment, and some began to filter back after a week. A strike was apparently averted when management conceded a nine-hour workday.

Although workplace demands continued to predominate, broader political concerns were beginning to surface. On February 13 calls for political freedom and the creation of a constituent assembly brought stormy applause at a mass meeting. These were perhaps the first public demands in Kiev in 1905 for fundamental political changes, and authorities responded by banning mass meetings after February 13.[16]

The strike movement also spread beyond the big factories and the railroads. On February 18, for example, 110 men and 210 women struck at the state wine warehouses, which contained a huge inventory of alcoholic beverages. Police and troops thenceforth guarded the premises. At the Demievka sugar refinery, which employed 250 to 400 women in its work crew of 1,200–1,300, workers struck on February 28, asking for a raise of ten kopecks per day. At this time Demievka employees were making about twelve rubles per month for twelve-hour shifts (or about three kopecks an hour!) and were not given lunch breaks. Management stated that workers should be grateful for the good housing and hygienic conditions at the plant, but angry employees countered that "in no other industry are wages so low."[17] There is no indication that any specific party led this walkout, but the RUP had been active in organizing the beet plantations throughout the region. Strikes had begun in the Skvyra District in Kiev Province, ultimately spreading and involving as many as 150,000 workers. Plantation owners brought in strikebreakers, and clashes were common. Spilka also played a major role in organizing the predominantly rural beet workers.[18]

In all, a broad spectrum of Kiev laborers had joined the struggle. Claiming they earned "a beggar's wage," three hundred employees of twenty-seven pharmacies struck from February 8 through February 25. Medicines became difficult to obtain, and some therefore returned to work on a limited basis. All pharmacies agreed to grant two days off a week (workers had wanted three). Wage demands and the issue of "polite treatment" remained unresolved. Various print shops closed briefly at this time. Cooks, maids, and household servants shut down one hiring hall. Hairdressers seeking reductions of sixteen-hour to twelve-hour workdays and two days off per week met at the Khreshchatyk's Monaco Restaurant to air their grievances. At a second meeting, they "nearly came to blows" with representatives of the shop owners. Also in February, clerk and office-worker (*prikazchiki*) representatives, speaking for 3,500 employees throughout Kiev's economy, made demands that included a citywide closing of all shops at eight o'clock. On the Khreshchatyk "first-class food and fancy-goods shops" sometimes forced their employees to work from seven in the morning until after midnight, *Kievskaia gazeta* reported on February 22.

Arsenal workers, one thousand strong, declined to strike, but even they presented a list of demands. Between March 13 and March 25, about five hundred tailors of women's clothing struck. Initially, they sought monthly wages instead of piecework rates, but they quickly added political demands: creation of a constituent assembly, and freedom to strike, speak, assemble, and publish. Many of the tailors were probably Jewish, and the influence of the Social Democrats and Bund seems apparent here.[19]

Some secondary-school students also struck. "The Kiev Committee of the Kiev Student Social Democratic Hromada of the RUP" had formed in November 1904 for the purpose of organizing secondary-school students, especially at the Kiev Art School. Porsh had worked hard to win the support of Ukrainian students, but reports by "patriots" in the press identified these young "internal enemies of the state" only as Jews, Poles, and Armenians.[20] That Ukrainian-speaking students were not mentioned may reflect the fact that the Ukrainian movement was lightly regarded by the Right, which focused its wrath on Poles and Jews.

University students were on vacation when the news of Bloody Sunday arrived. After vacillating, the government decided to allow institutions of higher education to open. After reassembling, students nearly everywhere passed similar resolutions, including the decision to strike until September 1. Kassow points out that most students had resisted the efforts of party activists to organize the student movement; there is no evidence to suggest either interuniversity cooperation or any party influence in these decisions. Yet, "by 1905, the student movement, for all its spontaneity, amorphousness, and resistance to direction and control," had moved beyond its earlier "political ambivalence." Students were now responding to events outside the universities, and at most of their meetings calls rang out for a constituent assembly.[21]

Nevertheless, the fact that the university and Polytechnical Institute remained closed for virtually the entire year meant that Kiev students would play an insignificant role in the events of 1905.

THE MIDDLE MONTHS: "DECENTRALIZED TERRORISM"

The breadth of the public movement encouraged some militants to act more boldly. The Bund tried to organize an "armed demonstration" and general strike on May Day, to be held actually on April 18 to coincide with May Day celebrations in cities on the European calendar. However, the Kiev Bund seemed more effective in organizing Jewish workers in the smaller towns outside of Kiev than it did in Kiev itself. In Radomyshl in February it had organized a one-day strike demanding political change that the town's entire Jewish proletariat (about 350 workers) and a few gentile workers supported. Although it continued to have difficulty attracting workers in Kiev, the RUP cooperated successfully with the Bund in smaller communities such as Bila Tserkva (Belaia Tserkov), where some 600 workers and salesclerks waged a two-day strike in mid-April. The Bund reportedly turned out the entire Jewish work force for strikes in Berdychiv and Cherkasy on April 18. Plans for self-defense were set up in at least ten towns, each of which was linked to Kiev's Bund by a designated agitator.[22]

In Kiev it was reported that only 20 to 40 supporters attended the Bund's agitational meetings, compared with estimates of 500 in Kishinev, 2,000 in Minsk, 3,500 in Dvinsk, and up to 5,000 in Warsaw! Warsaw Bundists published 30,000 leaflets, two-thirds in "Jewish languages," one-third in Polish; in Kiev the Bund published only 1,500.[23] The fact that the Bund joined forces with the city's comparatively weak RUP probably reflects the fact that both groups had decided to target workers in the smaller towns, and that considerable friction existed between the Bund and the more influential Russian Social Democratic Party in Kiev. In April both the SDs and the SRs suffered from arrests, and the Bund may have lost experienced agitators as well. It should be noted too that Kiev's most influential Jewish radical, attorney Mark Ratner, was not a Bundist, but rather was a former populist and member of the SRs who had made Jewish causes his top priority as a result of the Kishinev pogrom. Ratner was active in the oldest Jewish cultural organization in Russia, the Society for the Dissemination of Enlightenment, or OPE, which stood for the democratization of Russian and Jewish life and the use of Yiddish, rather than Russian or Hebrew, as the main pedagogical language.[24]

As the May Day strike drew near, Kiev remained calm on the surface. The planned demonstration was to begin at South Russia and Greter & Krivanek, and a battle unit was to be formed. Such plans proved to be as divisive as they were premature. According to some Soviet accounts, the fact that the Menshevik-dominated SD executive committee backed away from the plan evoked "the strongest possible dissatisfaction among the masses."[25] Caution also seemed expedient because authorities let it be known that they might retaliate by unleashing pogroms. The SRs divided, at least partly over the issue of the timeliness of an armed uprising. Workers struck and demonstrated in many cities on May Day, but not in Kiev. Shortly after May Day, bakers struck, if only to show they had the solidarity to do so, and the Bund led a successful twelve-day strike of 150 *zagotovshchiki* (suppliers). Otherwise the city remained quiet.

May Day demonstrated that tactical disunity still prevailed among Kiev's revolutionary parties and that the state had a powerful potential weapon in the retaliatory pogrom. It also seemed to show that workers in the smaller workshops, many of them probably Jews, were at least as committed to bold forms of activism at this point as were the workers in

Kiev's large factories and railway shops, where the Bolsheviks seemed to be strongest.[26] The great majority of workers, however, still declined to affiliate with any one party.

During the summer the labor movement remained quiet. There were few strikes, but beneath the surface agitators had already made significant gains in organizing a "Western Branch" of the railway union among Kiev's rail workers, a process that had begun in February. On the streets periodic clashes punctuated the calm. Angry that a vodka shop had been closed, youths from the outskirts and army reservists smashed in its door on June 20 and began stealing vodka. A crowd of several thousand gathered and, when police made an appearance, became unruly. Shots were fired from the crowd, wounding one policeman. Podil merchants began to panic and close down their shops. Arrests were made and the crowd dispersed, but another crowd of reservists formed, and again shots were exchanged.[27] The celebrated mutiny on the battleship *Potemkin* near Odessa harbor kept tensions high, and leftist agitators found army reservists receptive to their propaganda. Social Democratic agitators—most likely Bolsheviks—continued to plot an "armed demonstration," but on June 24 a meeting was interrupted by police who proceeded to arrest nineteen participants, including "Sonya" and "Olga," the two women who had organized the meeting. Undaunted, the RUP apparently organized a mass meeting on June 27, but police were comparatively unconcerned about the activities of the Ukrainian group.[28]

Many of the summer confrontations appear to have involved Jews. On July 2 demonstrating Jews in Demievka fired off weapons as they moved toward the city. Bund-influenced strikes occurred in the small carpentry workshops in Podil and Ploskaia. Attempts to demonstrate led to clashes with police and beatings. When Podil policemen detained two agitators, angry crowds tried to knock down the jail door. Rocks were thrown, injuring two policemen. More than one thousand dressmakers and shoemakers (crafts dominated by Jews) struck in July, but the atmosphere in the city tended more to acts of "decentralized terrorism" that could easily turn into ugly confrontations. "Beat the police" became a battle cry for the crowds, and the SRs capitalized on this tension by committing individual terrorist acts that the SDs and Bund opposed.[29] Strangely, in its survey of 254 pogroms beginning with the Kishinev pogrom of 1903, *The American Jewish Yearbook* states that a July pogrom in Kiev left 100 dead, 406 wounded, and 100 homes looted.[30] No such pogrom occurred.

Politically, the summer was "hotter" elsewhere in Kiev Province. There were 811 peasant disturbances during 1905 in the province,[31] and reports about them frequently filtered into the city. In Berdychiv the Bund organized a one-day general strike on July 25. Youths shut down the shops and bazaars, and at night a large crowd called for an end to autocracy. Police and troops opened fire on the crowd, wounding many. In Kiev, emboldened by the absence of coordinated, large-scale, organized activism, employers continued to counterattack. About 650 print workers were locked out of various shops for ten weeks,[32] a tactic that had greater intimidation value than anything the police might do, for it dramatized how easily most workers could be replaced.

August and September continued to be quiet, at least in terms of strikes, but there were tense moments. On August 7 a crowd of two thousand assembled at the labor exchange on Bolshaia Vasilkov Street. On August 18, after hairdressers refused to close their shops at eight o'clock in the evening, employees went along Bolshaia Vasilkov, closing them by force. Bolshaia Vasilkov was the heart of Lybid's Jewish neighborhood, and one can surmise that Jews were heavily involved in these confrontations. Early September brought concessions to employees of the sign-painting workshops that included guarantees of polite treatment, 15 percent wage hikes and payment of weekly wages, an end to beatings, greater educational opportunities for youths, and early quitting times on Christian and Jewish holidays. On September 10 thirty-nine were arrested for trying to demonstrate in Podil. Jewish youths led demonstrations in nearby settlements such as Dashevka and Fastiv (Fastovo). Crowds formed more or less continuously in Kiev's Jewish neighborhoods, Hermaize recalls, and police and army reinforcements were brought in.[33] Although the workers of the city's big factories had been quiet since February, discontentment in the Jewish neighborhoods and workshops kept tensions high. *Kievlianin* saw in each discovered bomb and demonstration "proof" that Jews were behind the public movement. No wonder police and provocateurs tried to counter labor unrest with anti-Semitism, the "socialism of fools."[34]

THE PEOPLE'S MEETINGS

On August 27 the imperial government returned much of the responsibility for running the universities to the faculties, including that of maintaining order. St. Vladimir and the Polytechnical Institute suddenly became havens from police harassment and took center stage. The first "people's meeting," held at St. Vladimir on September 7, drew a crowd of about three thousand. Kievans donned the double-breasted jackets worn by students in order to get into university buildings, and subsequent meetings grew in size. As word spread quickly about the openness of these meetings, they became focal points for activism in St. Petersburg and Moscow as well. Kassow notes that "the workers had little patience for hearing arguments between the various revolutionary parties, but they showed avid interest in using the meetings for education and self-expression. It was not unusual for workers to ask for the floor in order to read their own poetry. Soon whole factories would turn up at the university without notice."[35] In a confidential memo, Prime Minister Witte was told that workers had undergone "profound psychological changes" at these meetings. "By day rudely treated and deprived of respect, the Russian workers became, as soon as they crossed the threshold of the university, people who were treated with consideration and even deference."[36] "After the end of the meeting, after having sung the 'Marseillaise' and the 'Varshavianka' . . . the throng is in a holiday mood. It leaves in small groups, agitatedly discussing what it heard and promising to call new comrades to the next meeting." Observed Trotsky: "Here the orators of the revolution reigned unchallenged."[37]

On September 8 and 11 disturbances occurred at the Second Congress of Russian Psychiatrists, meeting in Kiev, and on September 14 a "bloody battle" with police broke out at a meeting of the Literary-Artistic Society. *Okhranka* reports contend that the main contingent of those who gathered were young Jews of both sexes, and that tensions between Jews and "the simple people" began to mount.[38]

During the first week of October, crowds of five thousand assembled at the university. On October 1, after the burial of the popular attorney Kopernik turned into a demonstration, shots were exchanged (authorities claim someone in the crowd fired first), and a Jewish woman was killed. Rhetoric on the "imminence" of revolution escalated. On October 4 a political address at the Polytechnical Institute was given in Yiddish, "surely the first time that had occurred at a Russian institution of higher education."[39] At these meetings Polish speakers called openly for an independent Poland, and some Ukrainian orators demanded an independent Ukraine "from Lviv to Kharkiv."[40]

Although there were no major strikes in Kiev in September, the labor movement was heating up elsewhere. In St. Petersburg forty thousand workers walked out in 260 separate strikes, while in Moscow, which was rapidly becoming the center of unrest in the empire, the Sytin & Co. print shop walkout quickly spread among other printers, tobacco workers, bakers, carpenters, and metalworkers. Toward the end of the month the strike movement in Moscow began to ebb, but violent clashes—including an October 3 Cossack attack on a spontaneous demonstration occasioned by the funeral of the popular liberal and former university rector Prince Trubetskoi—left the city tense. Despite the reluctance of the Bolshevik-led Moscow Social Democratic Committee, the Central Bureau of the Railroad Union called for a national railroad strike to begin on October 4. Henry Reichman, who has studied the role of the railwaymen in 1905, believes that no one in Moscow was really in control of the situation at this time. When a handful of individuals on the Moscow-Kazan line walked out, the Central Bureau decided to back them. "Far from being well planned by the Central Bureau, the October railroad strike began as something of a last gasp effort to salvage a situation that for several days had been confused and even deteriorating." Nor can the Bolsheviks be given credit for initiating or planning the strike. They too were "prisoners of events"; backing the strike only after the Kazan employees walked out, they were "skeptical about extending the movement into a national or even a citywide general strike."[41] Once begun, however, the strike spread rapidly throughout the empire, plunging the government into its deepest crisis yet.

On October 8 Kiev students decided to boycott the parliament that had been proposed, the so-called Bulygin Duma, which was to have only consultative powers, and obstruct elections to it. On October 9 Alexander Shlikhter, the Bolshevik leader of the railway workers, responding to the railway strike that was spreading across the empire, became the first in Kiev to call openly for a general strike. An *okhranka* agent contends that a majority of railway workers (who indeed had been very quiet in Kiev throughout the tumultuous year) opposed the strike. Agitators from Moscow appeared on October 10, and on October 11 railway workers began to strike in Kiev. The stoppage of trains at Kiev Station II forced the closure of railways whose workers opposed the strike. Southwestern Railway workers began to walk out as early as October 11 or as late as October 13 (accounts differ). One of their demands was for a parliament elected by universal and direct suffrage.[42]

On October 13 a crowd estimated at ten thousand turned out at the university. It included more than a dozen military officers. SR and Bund orators were said to predominate, but the Bolshevik Shlikhter chaired the assembly and allegedly told the crowd that a constituent assembly was already sitting in St. Petersburg and that troops had sided with the revolutionaries. On the previous evening orders had been received (apparently from St. Petersburg) to close down the city's higher educational institutions and arrest the revolutionary leaders. Kiev's governor-general apparently did not act upon these orders, fearing, perhaps, that a bloody insurrection would result if Shlikhter, a flamboyant symbol of these heady days, was arrested. The sheer size of the crowd, or the fact that a broad cross section of the population was represented in it, may have intimidated him.

Workers from the South Russian Machine Works struck on October 13, and workers from the other large plants followed a day later. A general strike was declared, and revolutionaries vowed to force schools, shops, and factories to close if necessary. Martial law was declared on the evening of October 14, and public assembly was banned, but commercial and industrial Kiev continued to close down. Arsenal workers joined on October 15. Authorities angrily argued that force, or the threat of force, had shut the city down. The deputy-governor wrote that only the workers at the South Russian Machine Works and the Main Railway Shops had struck voluntarily.[43] While this interpretation is probably exaggerated, the exact mix of force and genuine antigovernment ardor will never be known. Shopkeepers were not likely to stay open if property damage or a beating might result. On the other hand, the discontent which had surfaced in fits and starts had crystallized at the university meetings, and the rail strike added a sense that the rest of the country was with them. Driven by this turn of events, without objection and "without much wavering or discussion," the revolutionary parties formed a joint committee with equal representation for Bolsheviks, Mensheviks, SRs, Bundists, Polish Social Democrats, and the leaders of Spilka.[44]

Except for *Kievlianin*, the city's press closed down from October 14 until October 23, forcing historians to rely primarily on police and governmental sources. Official accounts note that the military meant business. A special unit had been formed in August to deal with disorders, and many arrests were made. Martial law failed to prevent large crowds from assembling, however. Sporadic clashes with troops occurred, but in general Kiev remained calm, and, with the exception of the Khreshchatyk, where shopkeepers could afford to stay closed, most shops began to re-open on October 15. The trams, always the target of militants because they were so easily overturned, began to run again.

When publishing resumed on October 23, the press (except for *Kievlianin*) spoke of the great sense of anticipation that had pervaded the city during these heroic days. The decisive moment had come. "In the crowds members of all classes literally stood together, including army officers with red ribbons in the buttonholes of their coats."[45] On October 18 Kievans heard the news of the October Manifesto, Nicholas II's dramatic promise to institute civil liberties and a lawful parliamentary order. The university and Polytechnical Institute reopened. Many of those who had been arrested were released, including Mark Ratner. Alexander Shlikhter, who had gone into hiding to avoid arrest, reappeared. Red flags hung everywhere. Even Senator Turau, who strongly sympathized with the beleaguered tsar, acknowledged that the manifesto had produced "a joyous mood everywhere in the city."[46]

• CHAPTER VIII •

The Promise Shattered: The October Pogrom

THE JOYOUS MOOD of celebration that had spread through Kiev lasted only until the late afternoon of October 18, 1905, when a bloody confrontation in front of city hall left more than one hundred casualties. A few hours later, attacks against Jews and their property began. Kiev's October pogrom would continue for three days.

On October 18 Kievans assembled at the usual spots, St. Vladimir University, the Polytechnical Institute, and the Main Railway Shops, before breaking into two main groups. One group moved along Bolshaia Vasilkov Street; the other, led by the Bolshevik Shlikhter on horseback, waving red streamers from his left hand, moved along the Khreshchatyk. By afternoon a throng estimated at fifteen to twenty thousand had gathered in front of city hall to listen to political speeches and celebrate the news of the October Manifesto. Absurdly, some government witnesses later testified that Jews constituted 85 percent of the crowd. Because they would argue that the October pogrom was a "patriotic Russian" response to Jewish insolence and insurrectionism, local authorities, including the *okhranka*, had a vested interest in exaggerating the Jewish presence. Although the composition of the crowd on October 18 will never be known with certainty, it is unlikely that Jews predominated, and the estimate of conservative law professor and city council member Otto Eikhelman (1854–1943) that Jews constituted "no more than one in five" is probably close to the truth.[1] Interestingly, the lengthy report of the deputy-governor on the October days in Kiev makes no mention of Jews at all.[2]

Acting mayor Plakhov allowed the leaders of the crowd to go inside city hall, and from that point accounts differ greatly as to what actually happened. Authorities accused Shlikhter and others of inciting the crowd by demanding the creation of a fully democratic republic. They claimed that a portrait and insignia of the tsar and the monument to Nicholas I had been damaged. Jews were accused of trying to pull the monument down, of knocking down a priest, and of taunting Christians with such cries as: "We gave you God, we gave you freedom, and we will give you a tsar." Similar accusations were hurled in other towns where demonstrations had also occurred. In Odessa, for example, Jews denied that they had tied portraits of the tsar to the tails of dogs and set them loose in the city.[3]

Accounts from inside city hall indicate that Shlikhter, Porsh, Ratner, and the other leftist leaders vacillated over what to do next. One Social Democrat, searching for "a way out of the dead end the demonstration had become," recommended dispatching the crowd to local prisons to demand the release of the remaining political prisoners. Some believed that the opportunity had come to incite an armed uprising and advocated seizing government buildings, but Shlikhter wavered. Suddenly, outside city hall, shots rang out, and some in the huge crowd panicked and fled. Along the streets the *pogromshchiki* were already assembling, cursing those who fled by them.[4]

Kiev's deputy-governor would later write that revolutionaries threw rocks and fired on the troops, and that the infantry fired on the crowd only after it was shot at from city hall and nearby residences. In the ensuing panic, between 7 and 12 were killed (one of them an artillery soldier), 110 to 130 were injured, including 10 soldiers (at least 22 severely), and 124 were arrested. Except for *Kievlianin*, Kiev's press described the scene differently, claiming that at four-thirty in the afternoon troops suddenly surrounded a peaceful crowd, firing on it without warning, and that many of those killed or seriously injured were women who had been trapped in alleys and beaten with clubs by Black Hundred thugs.[5]

At seven o'clock in the evening a "patriotic crowd" appeared on Alexander Square, bearing portraits of the tsar. Fights with Jews broke out. "As if on signal," the pogrom began simultaneously in Podil and at the Troitsky Bazaar. A delegation of fifteen professors and city councilmen demanded that the Cossacks be removed and that the remaining troops be instructed to protect property. Governor-General Karass and Deputy-Governor Rafalsky refused them audience, so they telegrammed Prime Minister Sergei Witte in St. Petersburg. Witte's response, urging Karass to stop the pogrom, was received on October 19, but the pogrom was allowed to continue through that day.[6] It was finally stopped on October 20 after three days of savage violence.

Although there were plenty of troops in the city, hooligans were allowed to reign for three days "with cruelty unheard of even in the Middle Ages," *Kievskie otkliki* wrote. "Children plunder, sensing it is permitted. Troops are demoralized." Police and soldiers at times joined in the loot-

23. City hall, built on the Khreshchatyk, 1874–1876. On October 18, 1905, a huge crowd listened to speeches celebrating the October Manifesto in the square in front of this building. Troops fired on the crowd, and a pogrom began that evening. Note the shops on the main floor.

ing; others fired at those who tried to defend themselves. The long-awaited "rising sun of civic freedom" had brought to Kiev "the horrors of Baku and Kishinev, Gomel and Zhitomir, the bloody business of black reaction that has plagued Russia in a dark cloud of endless shame." The pogrom "was planned long ago and was carefully directed," the paper concluded, echoing the views of *Kievskoe slovo* and *Kievskaia gazeta*. "It was the final convulsion of a dying organism."[7]

Kiev's October pogrom claimed between 47 and 100 lives (again, accounts differ); another 300 to 400 were hurt. Approximately 1,800 homes and shops were plundered, and 3,000 Jews were left without a place to work. There were fewer casualties in Kiev than in Odessa, but Kiev probably suffered more material destruction, estimated at 10 to 40 million rubles, than any other city.[8] Some of the vandalized property was owned by Christians, several of whom sat on the city council. Once the authorities decided to restore control, 650 were arrested.

Kiev did not stand alone in savagery. Pogroms occurred in at least 17 settlements in Kiev District alone (in Demievka, for instance, 109 apartments and 54 shops were sacked), in nearby towns such as Uman and Zhmerynka, in Odessa (where an estimated 1,110 were killed and 3,000 wounded and where a "permanent pogrom, uninterrupted terror against Jews" was said to exist),[9] and throughout the empire, even in distant Saratov and Rostov-na-Donu, far from the tense and wretched Pale.

"WE WERE CAUGHT UNAWARE..."

Kiev's press reported that a prominent and well-connected Jewish family had been warned two weeks earlier by police officials that a pogrom was coming and that no protection would be provided. Pogrom rumors had been circulating, in fact, "for a long time." Nevertheless, Kiev's Jewish community seems to have been caught largely by surprise. A young Jew named Kernes lamented: "[On October 19] I searched for self-defense units that I could join, but there were none to be found. It was as if the pogrom had fallen out of the sky. No one foresaw it. Its perpetrators were very silent. We were caught unaware and could only run through the streets seeking, but not finding, each other."[10]

The absence of effective self-defense in Kiev is perplexing, for after the Kishinev pogrom of 1903, many Jews had become convinced that self-defense units were essential. There were fewer casualties in the Gomel pogrom, which followed Kishinev's, because Jews fought back. Armenians, Tatars, and Greeks also fought back, and they were left alone. In the spring of 1905, it was said that Zhytomyr's self-defense could have "easily" beaten back the mob, had not troops interfered.[11] Senator Turau stated that in Kiev shots were fired "from many buildings," mostly by individuals involved in self-defense, but the many detailed and uncensored accounts that found their way into the city's press indicate that only a few residences were defended. At 36 Malo-Vasilkov Street resisters held off six attacks on October 18 and 19. On October 20 soldiers opened fire against the house. Two were killed, one of them a seventeen-year-old Jew, the other a member of the mob, and two were wounded. But the mob could penetrate only a ground-floor bakery, which it ravaged. Of the thirty-six apartments in the house at 15 Marinsko-Blagoveshchensk Street, thirty were occupied by Jewish craftsmen. With five revolvers, residents and students drove off the hooligans until troops opened a barrage of fire that continued for five minutes. The hooligans then entered the house and looted it for more than five hours, murdering one Jew in the process.[12] It is not clear whether these were isolated acts of individuals simply protecting their property or of small, organized resistance units. In general, the account by the young Jew Kernes, who searched for organized self-defense units but found none, seems an accurate depiction of those nights of horror in Kiev.

Frightened Jews, refugees from homes only blocks away, huddled together in hotels and at the Troitsky People's Club and *planned* a defense. But by then it was too late. What seems to have been missing was carefully organized preparation *in advance* of the pogrom. *Kievskaia gazeta* concluded as much, noting that "self-defense was generally caught by surprise and did not put up proper resistance."[13] Organizing armed resistance under any circumstances was extremely risky and appealed mainly to militant youths. But, despite the threat of a pogrom in May, Kiev's Jewish community seemed complacent. Some had apparently concluded that pogroms were relics of the past; ethnic peace, after all, had reigned for decades, and the city did have "a twentieth-century culture."[14] Jewish leaders could not have foreseen the sudden issuance of the October Manifesto. Police and right-wing elements could arm the hooligans quickly; it was more difficult for revolutionaries or Jews to keep caches of weapons hidden from the police, and arrests of Jewish militants during the general strike may also have disorganized resistance units.

One lengthy survey of the Bund and the Jewish workers' movement in 1905 barely mentions Kiev, reinforcing my own impression that Jewish political organizations were much weaker in the city than they were in Vilnius or Warsaw.[15] And the city's Russian Social Democratic Party, while speaking out against anti-Semitism, appears not to have put much effort into organizing self-defense groups. Shlikhter, who fled the city during the pogrom, is said to have been shocked by the violence.[16] By contrast, in Kharkiv, where the Jewish community was comparatively small, militant workers, mostly gentiles, led an assault against the Black Hundreds. An initial defense unit of sixty or seventy quickly swelled to three hundred and drove off a pogrom mob in mid-October. Units of fifteen to twenty-five men left the barricades to battle hooligans in the dark alleys of the city whenever violence seemed imminent. One revolutionary recalls "arresting" hooligans in their "dens," hauling them off to the Gelferikh-Sade factory, where they were photographed, and warning them that they would be shot if they misbehaved. Workers reported finding loot from the pogrom in Katerynoslav, but Kharkiv itself experienced no major pogrom.[17]

Whatever the case, encountering little resistance from their victims and protected from individual resisters by the rifles and even the artillery of troops, the boozy mobs ravaged Kiev almost at will; each shattered pane of glass, each orange-red inferno, each round of cheers when another battered door gave way, must have intoxicated the perpetrators with power and excitement. They were in control of the city.

KIEV'S POGROM CROWD

Who were the *pogromshchiki*? The 1903 pogrom in Kishinev, in which thirteen hundred shops and apartments were plundered and forty-five Jews killed, had been blamed on "drunken *bur'ian* ["weeds"], teenagers, and young boys" by a local newspaper, though "there were cases of policemen, civil servants, and other such people plundering apartments."[18] In Yalta "small groups of vagabonds and rogues with the help of hundreds of street boys" were said to have carried out the March 1905 pogrom.[19] A more perplexing picture came from Melitopil (Melitopol, near the Crimea, pop. 16,000), where "men behaved like wild animals during the holy days of Easter." Here the crowd was said to consist of "about a thousand craftsmen, workers, and sons of prosperous families. Why would a sixteen-year-old bootmaker, self-employed and making money, willingly fight and die? Why would building contractors incite their workers to violence? Why would the prosperous foundry owner, Glassen, a member of the city council, appear on the streets in front of city hall to incite the mob? Or five of his six workers, all of them secure?"[20] A pogrom had been expected in Melitopil for a long time; that so great a cross section of society participated in it illustrates a frightening breadth and depth of hatred.

In the Russian Empire Ukraine was "the crucible of [Jewish] suffering."[21] Some in Kiev's mobs saw themselves as patriots justifiably enraged by the general strike, the October Manifesto, and the vandalism of government symbols, all of which had humiliated their tsar. The deputy-governor said he was infuriated by the fact that portraits of the tsar had been torn up at city hall. *Kievlianin* saw the pogrom as a natural and spontaneous outburst of patriotic Russians who simply rose up to defend their tsar and his government, and averred that darkness had made it impossible for police and troops to control the crowd.[22] One St. Vladimir student, a native of Moscow, wrote that while cultured people protest verbally, "the uncultured protest with pogroms, with the murder of Jews. If the attacks were organized, why did so many break out at the same time? I protest the name 'Black Hundreds,' for 90 percent of the Russian people share their views. If you want to call them Black Hundreds, call them the 'Black Hundred Million.'"[23]

To be sure, there were identifiable agitators, but they were not identified as Great Russian outsiders (*katsapy*) as had been the case in 1881. Eyewitnesses spoke of the mysterious "Velikan" ("Giant"), who had contacts in Kiev's community of artists. Another instigator was the "well-known local hooligan" Vaska Grigorev, 27, son of a prominent bootmaker. After an argument with a doorman over whether or not Jews lived in a particular building, Grigorev stabbed the doorman to death. Arrested along with "another thug from Rostov," Grigorev was later accused of vandalizing the insignia on the city hall's balcony on October 18. The implications are clear: the damage may have been caused by provocateurs looking for a pretext to attack.

Some prominent Kievans also involved themselves in the violence in various ways. On October 19 a crowd of "patriots" was addressed by the assistant editor of the anti-Semitic *Kievlianin*, by the son of the police chief, and by several civil servants and students. *Kievlianin* editor Pikhno also made an appearance. In Demievka the sugar refinery manager B. P. Vasilev was accused of leading the mob and of permitting refinery workers to take time off with pay to plunder and loot. Others were similarly identified, including a certain I. Shirokov, 36, who held honored citizen status and who was said to be instrumental in pointing out Jewish shops.[24] Senator Turau's investigation revealed that Police Chief Tsikhotsky and Major-General Bezsonov, one of the officers in charge of maintaining order, were seen on the streets encouraging the mob.[25]

However, Kiev's October pogrom was not a mass upheaval. It was not at all like the antigovernment movement, with its massive strikes and huge but peaceful public meetings. There was nothing popular or patriotic about it. The antigovernment press insisted that the mobs were fueled by provocateurs and by "anyone willing to sell his soul," and that the pogrom was not supported by "productive people." *Kievskaia gazeta* called the mob "a band of plunderers organized by police and provocateurs," and Zhytomyr's *Volyn'* noted that initially the pogrom mob in Podil may have numbered no more than twenty.[26] In Solomenka young boys often did much of the plundering, egged on, no doubt, by their elders. St. Vladimir professor Ivanov kept a diary in which he identified looters as mainly "women of the servant type" and men "of the lower clerk, tram conductor, and hauler type." According to one letter in *Kievskie otkliki*, most in the mob were drunk. On the final day of the pogrom, the crowd numbered no more than fifty or sixty, but soldiers continued to fire at Jews who attempted to defend their property. "My impression is that one home was taken jointly by the mob and the soldiers," Ivanov reported.[27]

Hatred of Jews in Kiev ran deep enough to produce shocking atrocities. On Kostel (Catholic church) Street butchers wielding axes and wearing blood-spattered white overalls went after six Jewish women with children in their arms. Such atrocities should not overshadow the fact that few Kievans actively participated in Kiev's October pogrom, however. The picture is rather of small bands of thugs incited by agitators, protected by police and soldiers, and supported morally and verbally by "patriotic demonstrators," at times perhaps a thousand strong. Except for *Kievlia-*

nin, Kiev's press agreed that a mob of no more than 100 to 120 people terrorized all of Podil, and that similar bands terrorized other parts of the city. One letter claimed that on Blagoveshchenie (Annunciation) Street, a crowd of no more than 25 plundered at will under the protection of at least 25 soldiers. Later in the year, when Lev Brodsky headed a drive to help pogrom victims, hundreds of Kievans gave what they could, even if it was only 25 or 50 kopecks.[28]

RUMOR: FUEL FOR DISORDER

As is often true in times of disorder, rumors helped inflame the pogrom crowds. In the villages near Zhytomyr, old women (*baby*) ran through the fields swearing that Christians were being massacred. They produced such terror "that women and children one and all fled into the forests."[29] In Kishinev the 1903 pogrom had been triggered by reports that Jews had ritually murdered Christian youths.[30] Wild stories that swept through Rostov-na-Donu were said to be spread by provocateurs and by the ubiquitous *baby*, "who zealously swear to the truth of such occurrences."[31] In 1905 in Uman, Jews accused of having demanded their own tsar were instructed to organize a patriotic march. Most of them did, displaying large portraits of the emperor along with their Torahs.

In Kiev several rumors fanned the pogrom: that Jews had sacked the Holosivka (Goloseev) Monastery in the outskirts of the city; that as many as seventeen thousand Jews were "cutting up" Christians near the monastery; and that Jews numbering ten thousand strong were organizing retaliatory forces in Demievka in order to pillage monasteries and slay monks. Meanwhile, in the outskirts, rumors circulated, in this case correctly, that the authorities in Kiev were permitting the crowds to plunder Jews. In Hostomel (Gostomel, in Kiev District), a pogrom was begun when agitators carrying portraits of the tsar were joined by peasants from nearby villages who believed that in Kiev Jews had killed two hundred monks.[32]

These descriptions are not unlike those of the cholera riots in Saratov and Astrakhan, where old women kept the rumor mills alive with fantastic tales, while supplying kerosene for arson. Rumors preceded the outbreaks of violence and spurred the mob on once violence had begun. Amid Saratov's 1892 cholera epidemic, stories spread that live people were being put into coffins and that the epidemic itself was a fabrication of physicians. Hospitals were attacked and burned, cholera patients "liberated" from them and treated with folk cures. Physicians were attacked, and their homes were ravaged. As was the case during pogroms, agitators appeared periodically like breezes fanning a smouldering fire. In Saratov a man clad only in a sheet ran through the berry market claiming he had "escaped" from a cholera hospital; a mob then proceeded to sack a precinct police headquarters. When a priest left a local hospital, someone in the mob shouted, "There's the priest who buried me. You buried me, but I escaped from the coffin." The priest replied, "If you just got out of the coffin, why are you drunk?" Voices from the mob demanded that the priest be beaten with stones, and the priest was seized but then rescued by a soldier.[33]

Rumor added to the excitement of the moment, encouraging the large crowds that followed the mobs picking up clothing and other items that had been strewn about by the looters. "Prominent women" openly purchased looted goods on the streets. At the Haymarket day workers joined the hooligans in carrying off huge slabs of meat. The pace of the looting was often leisurely, and not just in Kiev. Saratov's pogrom crowd moved "everywhere in the same way. In front there were teenagers with clubs, behind them the Tatars and hooligans with bags and boxes for loot, and finally the *baby* with sacks picking up what was left." Surrounding villagers soon joined the crowd.[34] Sometimes looting occurred for the sake of sheer destruction rather than for material gain. In Rostov-na-Donu pogromists sold stolen gold and silver items for a few kopecks. One employee of a clothing and fur shop followed the mob and bought back two thousand rubles worth of looted items for six rubles! "Hunger didn't produce the pogrom," *Donskaia rech'* argued, "for the hungriest didn't participate."[35] And in Kiev's Halytsky Bazaar, one looter walked off with eighty pairs of shoes, none of which were matching pairs.

LOCAL AUTHORITY IN KIEV

Who defended Kiev's Jews? Certainly not the police, although, ironically, special taxes on kosher products raised about fifteen thousand rubles annually for police salaries. Police served the interests of the state officials to whom they were responsible. They determined which Jews could live in Kiev, and for how long, and periodically they carried out nighttime roundups of Jews for the purpose of expelling them from the city. (In 1905 roundups were banned on the grounds that they were a "barbaric measure for a cultured city," but they began again once officials were able to restore order.) Eyewitnesses told the press that after the violence began on October 18, the crowd broke into small bands which took instructions from neighborhood police. One wrote: "Yesterday in your paper you asked us to turn all our plundered goods over to the police. We ask you to advise the police to turn over all the goods they plundered to us. They took more than we did."[36] As in 1881, some Jews locked their shops with crosses, or displayed icons or portraits of the tsar, hoping to convince the mob that these were Christian shops. It seldom worked, for agitators often had lists of which shops were Jewish, and police also pointed out Jewish shops and apartments.

The fact that police could not be relied upon to keep order in situations where authorities seemed to sympathize with those committing disorder had to concern all property owners. In Solomenka after the pogrom, irate residents, bitter at police refusal to protect lives and property (and possibly at police participation in the disorders), petitioned for the removal of the entire Solomenka police force.[37] Zhytomyr's *Volyn'* accused Kiev's civilian and military officials of "organizing the bloodbath brazenly and without precedent in modern times" and of simply turning the pogrom over to a small group of hooligans. Given the absence of a reliable police force, it too called for the creation of an urban militia.[38] Odessa's police distinguished themselves by firing mainly at Jews who defended themselves, while in Rostov-na-Donu an angry city council resolved to institute a city militia of one hundred men to keep order and allocated ten thousand rubles for it. The militia was to be paid for by a special tax on business.[39]

Some soldiers and a few policemen did protect individual pieces of property, either out of compassion or because they had been bribed. Kiev Chief of Police Detectives Rudoi personally defended his house, in which Jews lived, and later testified that a single soldier on horseback or the appearance of two or three Cossacks commonly sufficed to disperse the mob. Lukianivka Bazaar was defended by two or three patrolmen acting on instructions from a precinct police captain who feared that the mob might break into a nearby prison. The mob loudly accused the patrolmen of having been bought off by Jews, but left without committing serious damage. Throughout the city homeowners paid off roving bands to defend their property. A single paid-off soldier successfully defended one five-story home. Said *Kievskoe slovo*: "The main culprit is the inactivity of the authorities who simply wink their eyes. The banner of a free Russia flies in St. Petersburg, but in Kiev and other provincial towns an oblivious government sanctifies pogroms and anarchy."[40]

While the number of Kiev's police who actually participated in the pogrom can never be known, it is possible that the force was under instructions not to interfere with the pogrom. Commonly, police told desperate victims, "this is a military, not a police, matter." Just as commonly, soldiers responded that the police were responsible for protection.

The local press openly blamed Chief of Police Tsikhotsky, Lieutenant-General Drake (who was in charge of maintaining order), and Governor-General Karass and Deputy-Governor Rafalsky, who gave orders to police. Turau argues that the military was ready for disorder (although it expected disorder from leftist revolutionaries) and had a plan in place to deal with it. Drake tried to get local officials to act decisively, he contends, but Tsikhotsky and Major-General Bezsonov, who had been put in charge of the troops assigned to protect Podil and Old Kiev, were especially sympathethic to the pogromists. Tsikhotsky had been in hot water before, particularly over alleged violations and abuse of the rules governing Jewish residence in the city. He had rapidly grown rich as police chief and had purchased property in Poltava Province valued at one hundred thousand rubles—a hefty sum at a time when sugar beet refinery workers were making twelve rubles per month! His daughter and her husband had also purchased expensive properties in Kiev and Poltava Provinces. Major-General Trepov was among those who sought to press criminal charges and remove Tsikhotsky from office because of irregularities found in an audit. In May 1905 the police department had filed complaints, setting another investigation in motion. Both investigations were apparently in progress in October, but Tsikhotsky had a powerful protector in Governor-General Kleigels. The knightly Kleigels was a personal favorite of the tsar, but Witte characterizes him as "dull-witted" and "totally unfit" to occupy his position. Kleigels had become inactive, Witte claims, and simply abandoned his post.[41] On October 18, the first day of the pogrom, Kleigels was replaced by Lieutenant-General Karass. With Kleigels gone, Turau reasons, the anti-Semitic Tsikhotsky knew he would soon lose his position and thus had little incentive to uphold his duty and protect victimized Jews.[42]

At the very least, Tsikhotsky's refusal to instruct his patrolmen to protect property contributed to general confusion in police ranks. Numerous witnesses saw the chief stroll about the city as it was being plundered. Tsikhotsky even took part "in certain patriotic demonstrations," and stood accused of praising the mob during the sacking of Lev Brodsky's home. Bezsonov, meanwhile, gave approving smiles to the cry "Beat the Jews" and at one point is said to have told the mob, "You can smash things up, but you can't plunder." When Director of the Governor-General's Chancellery Molchanovsky demanded to know why measures were not being taken to quell the pogrom, Bezsonov replied, "What pogrom? This is a demonstration." Police Detective Rudoi heard Bezsonov tell the mob, "You know how to stand up for your tsar," to which the mob yelled, "Hurrah," stepping up its ravenous pace in the belief that violence "would be tolerated until eight o'clock the next morning."[43]

The inexperienced Rafalsky, appointed deputy-governor on August 20, 1905, tried without success to get police and soldiers to intervene, Turau argues. But other sources indicate that Rafalsky had also signed an order enabling police to arrest an undetermined number of potential resisters on October 15, three days before the pogrom began. Once the mob had begun its assault, he was said to have walked through the streets, "lending an official air to the pogrom." Military officers, even generals, were often seen on the streets. "We're not allowed to interfere," they said.[44] A group of city councilmen, professors, and public figures approached Rafalsky and Karass, urging them to stop the pogrom, but they were denied an audience. The group then telegraphed Minister of the Interior Witte in St. Petersburg asking him to remove authority from the hands of the military. On October 19 Karass read a telegram from Witte urging that the violence be stopped, but it does not appear that he energetically tried to implement effective measures. Kiev's mayor, V. N. Protsenko, allegedly a member of the Black Hundreds, conveniently left the city during the pogrom. While it is uncertain who gave what order to whom, it was widely believed by soldiers and civilians that the hooligans could run rampant for three days, the traditional length of pogroms in Imperial Russia. No wonder that when one patrolman pulled a revolver, the mob convinced him to back off, arguing that "the governor had approved" the pogrom and that the tsar himself approved because his portrait had been defaced. Noted city councilman Iassirsky, "Even the *izvozchiki* [carters] said that the governor would permit only three days of plunder."[45]

In his official report, Turau tried to discredit the widely held belief that the pogrom was sanctioned by higher officials, noting that on October 12 and 13, the Ministry of the Interior issued orders to quell public disturbances, and that on October 14 martial law was declared in Kiev. Although it has never been proven that instructions to organize or permit pogroms came from high up in the government, perplexing questions remain. Why was General Kleigels removed as the pogrom began? Why did Lieutenant-General Drake wait until October 20, the third day of the pogrom, to put an end to the plundering? (When troops did act decisively on that day, the pogrom quickly stopped.) As in Odessa, where Robert Weinberg has written that "it is questionable . . . whether the pogrom was purely spontaneous,"[46] the bigotry of some Kiev officials certainly contributed to the permissive attitude toward the violence. Turau's efforts to place much of the blame on administrative confusion, inexperience, and ineptitude also are probably on the mark. If nothing else, pogroms underscore a fundamental irony in tsarist Russia: for all of the authoritarianism of the imperial system, its cities and its provinces were sorely undergoverned. In times of crisis, few bold and decisive leaders surfaced who were willing or able to take charge and ensure the maintenance of order. In 1905, from the mayor to the governor-general, Kiev seemingly had no such official at all.

"THE BLACK HUNDRED COUNCIL AND
THE HOOLIGAN MAYOR"

It had taken a long time in January 1902 to elect the city council that would govern Kiev during the next four years. Voters had to vote yes or no on each candidate, and many candidates were turned down. Some fifty-eight councilmen gained seats in daily voting that ran from January 21 through January 30. The remainder could not win enough votes until supplementary elections were held during the week of February 7.

The election was largely a referendum by the tiny propertied elite on the performance of the 1898 council—a council that stood accused even by the conservative professor Eikhelman of poor management, of favoritism toward concessionaires, and of making no real progress on providing public services. This council had chosen not to build a municipal electric streetlight network; it had failed to take even the most elementary sanitary measure, that of covering the sewage ditch; it had not extended the horse-tram network; nor had it taken "any measure to improve the cultural level of the masses."[47] The new council had thirty-four members who had served in the ranks of the 1898 council; it included twenty-three merchants, thirteen lawyers, eight physicians, six engineers, seven professors, seven military officials, and four teachers. Thirty-six had some higher education. Eikhelman was one of those reelected from the 1898 duma. The son of a well-known St. Petersburg landowner, he was a graduate of the German classical *gymnasium* in Revel (now Tallinn) and the juridical faculty at Derpt (Dorpat) University, and had come to St. Vladimir in 1880 as a specialist in international law. He wrote numerous articles for the local press, chaired five of the council's twenty-six committees, and was notably active in the city's orphanage and in the Kiev Society for the Protection of Animals. Eikhelman ran for mayor but lost to Podil physician Protsenko. Ironically, both Eikhelman and Protsenko would become major figures of controversy in 1905.[48]

There were councilmen in Kiev who sympathized with the public movement in 1905. In February Kiev councilmen joined representatives from Kharkiv and Nizhnyi Novgorod to select a bureau chaired by Moscow mayor V. M. Golitsyn, which in turn would organize an all-Russian congress of city leaders. But Mayor Protsenko refused to participate in a May 22 meeting of city mayors in Moscow, and he and his clique were accused of acting as if "Kiev didn't belong to the Russian state and couldn't benefit from the improvements sought in other towns."[49] The October Days seemed to frighten many in the council, and, aside from A. K. Rzhepetsky, no one spoke out in favor of protecting the public from the police and Cossacks. Finally, on October 17, the council created a twelve-man committee to mediate between public and government. It asked further that preliminary censorship of the press be lifted and that the public be allowed to air its grievances. While noting that censorship matters were beyond his control, the governor-general expressed support for these initiatives.

From that point Kiev's city council sank to appalling depths. When the pogrom began, it held a closed emergency meeting but apparently took no action. Only on October 21, *after* the pogrom had ended, did the council call for calm; on that same day, the council voted 31–19 to *thank* the troops for their assistance during the pogrom! The issue was then removed from the agenda and the city fathers proceeded quickly to the next order of business, the opening of a new performance at the city theater. No doubt in a voice heavy with sarcasm, Councilman Iassirsky "justified" thanking the troops by noting that "not every Jewish shop had been plundered."[50]

From there the situation further deteriorated. Citing the "hopelessness" of trying to get the council to do anything, many progressives apparently resigned, leaving fewer than fifty councilmen (many of whom seldom came to meetings) to deal with the moral, political, and financial crises of the times. The resignations perhaps fulfilled the suggestion offered two years earlier that "the good half of our councilmen ought to resign on the grounds of incompetence, and the other half long ago should have refused the honor of sitting with the first half."[51]

Mayor Protsenko simply disappeared during or just before the pogrom, returning only on November 1. Supposedly, he went abroad, but it is possible that he had been warned of the impending pogrom and had chosen to leave the city. Ironically, Protsenko had been a popular physician among Podil's Jews, many of whom preferred him to the district's Jewish doctors. Many had supported him because they assumed he would take drastic steps to rid the city of its "Asiatic guest" (cholera). Protsenko failed on all counts, and his anti-Semitism was sensed before the pogrom. Wrote columnist "Starik" (Old-timer) in April: "Perhaps our popular Podol doctor is an anti-Semite, though when he took our rubles, he sure didn't show it. . . . Maybe he's from Odessa."[52]

In early November the rump council voted 42–1 against sending delegates to the "sharply political" Congress of Zemstvo and City Officials meeting in Moscow, making it clear that Prince E. N. Trubetskoi and other local councilmen who were already there had no authority to speak for Kiev. In contrast, the Kharkiv city council sent a telegram to the congress asking it to help bring a democratic constitution into existence. Kiev's council also voted 21–14 against a committee recommendation to grant a paltry five thousand rubles to the pogrom victims. By contrast,

Rostov-na-Donu's council donated ten thousand rubles to pogrom victims in that city.[53] The Kiev Merchant Association asked the banks for two hundred thousand rubles of credit to help victimized merchants rebuild. Credit was to run through 1912, and fifty thousand rubles were to be raised by a self-imposed merchant tax that was to be nonobligatory for Jews. The Merchant Society probably included many powerful Jews, but gentile merchants also must have been uneasy over the tolerant attitude toward massive property destruction displayed by local authorities.

Some city councils had taken bold initiatives to help bring about changes in 1905. Saratov's council called for the release of political prisoners and telegrammed Witte requesting a formal amnesty.[54] Moscow city councilmen walked out when fellow councilman and lawyer A. S. Shmakov (a notorious Judeophobe who would defend Kiev's pogromists at their trial in 1907) took the floor for an anti-Semitic tirade. (Shmakov at one point was challenged to a duel, but a Kiev paper reported that duels were passé and that Moscow public opinion opposed the likes of Shmakov anyway.)[55] By contrast, Kiev's council seemed ill-prepared to meet the challenges of that year, and while it played no apparent role in the pogrom, its actions seemed to sanction it. Kiev's councilmen must have been reluctant sanctioners, for they were property owners who surely blanched at the sight of rabble run wild, but the council seemed paralyzed, as it had often seemed before. "Popular for its scandals and utter inactivity," it simply outdid itself; it has immortalized itself as "the hooligan council," wrote *Kievskaia gazeta* on November 8. It is "a Black Hundred council with a hooligan mayor," it concluded on December 9. On the next day, with political reaction rapidly setting in, the newspaper was shut down.

THE ROLE OF THE CHURCH

Some church officials had acquired reputations for tolerance and goodwill toward Jews. One late nineteenth-century example was Kiev's popular Orthodox metropolitan Platon, and Jews participated in an 1887 celebration marking sixty years of Platon's service to the church. In 1903 the synod urged priests to speak out against pogroms, to let people know that pogroms were insults to Christianity and that Jews were creatures of God and subjects protected by the tsar's laws.[56] The extent to which such pronouncements influenced the parish clergy can never be known.

Icon in hand, one Kiev priest from the Borys and Hlib Church, Mikhail Edlinsky, personally defended a house full of poor Jews from the mob in 1905; he was subsequently honored at a prayer service led by Rabbi Zuckerman. But aside from Edlinsky, very few clergymen were identified as having actively and publicly opposed the pogrom in Kiev. On October 19, Turau notes, Metropolitan Flavian blessed a crowd of about one thousand "patriotic demonstrators." Flavian asked the crowd not to commit excesses, but some priests joined the demonstration, which, to the accompaniment of a military marching band, paraded through the city carrying portraits of the tsar and pieces of mirror glass allegedly broken during the demonstration at city hall the day before. Jews were forced to kiss these objects or face a beating.[57]

Some priests had become socially and politically active in Russia; the most notable example was Grigory Gapon, who had led the St. Petersburg demonstration on Bloody Sunday. Numerous village priests had sympathized with the antistate disorders in the countryside in 1905, and at least eighty were consequently stripped of their authority. But the predominant image of the church was that of a conservative, state-supported institution which opposed change, and rumors abounded that the clergy had a role in the pogrom in Kiev and in other cities. According to Saratov's *Privolzhskii krai* (Along the Volga), "it was no secret" that Bishop Germogen of Saratov and Tsaritsyn inspired the publication of literature which was "of prime importance in agitating the restless in the bazaars."[58] Aside from an isolated instance or two, however, I found no evidence to indicate that clergy were active participants in Kiev's pogrom. Rather, most of the criticism directed at them resulted from their utter passivity in the face of mob violence. Their sermons call for moral perfection but say little about real-life situations, *Kievskaia gazeta* asserted. "The sermonizers of peace live huddled in their cozy apartments observing from a distance the exploits of their flock."[59] Wrote another critic: "With lifeless eyes they looked upon the ravaged city with their usual silence and banal phrases. . . . Their lifeless eyes did not cry out."[60]

The influence that individual priests could have exerted should not be exaggerated. During Kiev's 1881 pogrom, a priest had confronted a mob ready to break into a warehouse, noting that it was a Russian and not a Jewish warehouse. "Down with the priest," the mob responded. "This priest's been bribed by the *zhidy* for three rubles. Break it apart."[61] In 1905 Turau contends that during the destruction of Brodsky's property, High Priest Platon, rector of the Spiritual Academy, and Bishop Chigirinsky implored the mob to stop, but some in its ranks shouted back, "You're a Jew-lover."[62]

Sadly, the prestigious Cave Monastery was accused of helping prepare the 1905 pogrom. On November 3, 1905, *Kievskie otkliki* published an open letter from Privat-dotsent (Assistant Professor) V. Chagovets claiming that on September 11 and 12 he had personally witnessed tables full of pamphlets entitled *To the Russian People* in the monastery's print shop. This pamphlet encouraged Russians to "defend the fatherland to the last drop of blood." Chagovets claimed that it called Russians to arms against revolutionaries, and that it was written to imply that God sanctioned the beating up of Jews. Judging from its style, he guessed it had been written by monks.

On November 5, Viceregent (*Namestnik*) Arkhimandrit Antony acknowledged that the monastery's print shop had published the tract, but said it had been composed by the Kiev Patriotic Circle of Workers. The monks did not compose any Black Hundred literature, he argued, claiming also that the pamphlet in question was nothing more than a "sincere, Christian, patriotic publication" which did not specifically call for an uprising against the Jews. "I should sue for slander, but in the interest of Christian reconciliation, I shall leave it to Mr. Chagovets to repent his sins and avoid similar acts in the future." Chagovets replied by letter on the same day that "where there is fact there can be no slander. . . . The words of the pamphlet speak for themselves." Christianity should be "love and peace." Since the full text of the inflammatory pamphlet is not available, it is impossible to decide what it said or implied.

Rightists liked to argue that pogroms were a kind of religious crusade. *Kievlianin*, for example, called the pogrom "an elemental outburst of rage of the holy people turned against the Jews," and argued that the mob had killed only Jewish resisters, and not defenseless people. Even when enraged, the crowd "kept its conscience" and "acted with God in its heart."[63] Clearly, the church did not stoop to that level, but the Cave Monastery's written reply to Chagovets's accusations does appear callous, for while denying that the monastery had composed that pamphlet or any other Black Hundred literature, Antony did not condemn the pogrom itself. Belatedly, in November, at least one Kiev monastery, the Holy Trinity Monastery, publicly condemned pogroms,[64] but in general the church had failed to speak out when it counted, which could scarcely be comforting to the genuinely spiritual in the troubled city.

THE POGROM IN ITS 1905 SETTING

"It is difficult to describe the panic that seized the entire Pale of Settlement when the shocking news from Kiev, Odessa, and Kishinev reached them," wrote one correspondent from Podil Province. "Let them plunder. We're used to that. But why do they shoot, why do they blow us apart, where is their Christian God, this Christ about whom we are always being reproached?" For the young, there was self-defense; for the older, "we've nothing to defend ourselves with. We've learned only to suffer . . . and pay. We'll give gold to save our blood." The fact that there had been no pogrom in Poltava left that city's Jews to wonder, "Is this the day? Will

I be alive by evening?"[65] Jews left Poltava for Kiev and Odessa; pogroms, they reasoned, would not be permitted in the same place twice. Some left Russia permanently. The Yiddish writer Shalom Aleichem, "materially helpless and spiritually broken" by the Kiev pogrom, left for America a few weeks later.[66]

In 1881 Jews had been blamed for exploiting an impoverished native population. Jewish tavern owners stood accused of "plundering" the peasantry, Jewish moneylenders of charging extortionate interest rates. By 1905 a new set of images mixed with these ancient charges. Jews had become identified with sudden and fundamental political change. "I've known this province for twenty-five years," said Mogilev's governor. In the 1880s there had been "Jewish oppression." Now "the Bund and the Social Democrats are all Jews. There are others, but the instigators are Jews." Jews "are no longer submissive, no longer respect authority, no longer even acknowledge the police. Jewish parents have lost control over their children." "Jews even run into my wife on their bicycles."[67]

Jews were active in the oppositional movement that resulted in the October Manifesto, which promised to bring to Russia some of the greatest political changes in its history. Fundamental change is often misunderstood or feared, for it brings new responsibilities, new insecurities. It was easy to identify that which was feared or poorly understood with those who were different. The ignorant dockworker on the Kiev pier saw little personal gain from abstractions such as "constituent assembly." If intelligible at all, such concepts must have seemed irrelevant to his needs. The haulers, day workers, and petty craftsmen were not likely to welcome changes that gave rights to their Jewish competitors. They would not welcome changes that appeared to cave in to the demands of well-organized railway and factory workers who had already made impressive gains in wages and benefits. Nor would they welcome changes that met the demands of already-prosperous professional groups and arrogant students. Seen from a modern American perspective, the great political changes of 1905 seem a rare opportunity in Russian history for civil liberties to take root. But for many subjects of the tsar in 1905, concessions forced by military defeat and national humiliation must have been threatening, alien, poorly understood intrusions brought by Jews, socialists, and others from beyond the closed and primitive world of native tradition.

Thus, for some, "Beat the Jews and the democrats" gave the pogrom a noble cause; fear and resentment took on the form of a patriotic and religious crusade. Pogromists beat Jews while crying, "Here is your freedom." "You're not one of those who wants his freedom, are you," snarled a carter to Kernes, unsure whether Kernes was a Jew. After all, local authorities tolerated, even encouraged, the pogrom, and—by implication and rumor—so did higher authorities, possibly even the tsar. In

Rostov-na-Donu one city councilman witnessed the distribution of "whole cartloads of vodka" to the pogrom crowd on orders of the police."[68] Such incidents only reinforced what was sensed anyway, that public authority winked at disorder as long as it targeted Jews. When local police left their posts, the final symbol of authority, the final bulwark of social restraint, was removed.

The year 1905 began with the killing of peaceful demonstrators by government troops. These troops had responded to orderliness with lawlessness; this, in turn, encouraged the undercurrent of anarchy that had long existed in Russian society. In 1905 incident after incident fostered the growth of mob rule. In St. Petersburg the Austrian ambassador complained that "mobs regularly attacked well-dressed people and anyone who appeared to be educated. On a single day in July, between 70 and 80 people were injured. 'The police were invisible; only in the evening of that day did the Governor issue a statement to calm the population.' "[69] All over the empire various groups, from merchants to workers, organized their own self-defense.

Traditional defenders of order played ambivalent roles. In Kiev the Cave Monastery denied accusations that it had encouraged the mob to beat up *intelligenty* "in the name of the Father, Son, and Holy Ghost," but with apparent pride also stated that it took "no initiative in public affairs and exist[ed] only to satisfy the spiritual needs of pilgrims and serve as an example of 'the pious and virtuous life.' "[70] Given the tensions of the times, reinforced by an unpopular and unsuccessful war, by lawlessness from above and below, by some authorities' sanctioning of selective disorder, it is surprising that in a city the size of Kiev the pogrom crowd was not substantially larger.

· CHAPTER IX ·

The Final Years of Romanov Kiev

FOR A FEW WEEKS after the bloody days of October 18–20, Kievans continued to win redress of job-related grievances. For example, on October 24 the first eight-hour day in the milling industry was introduced at the Brodsky steam mill.[1] However, the great triumph of 1905 had been the October Manifesto, for it promised freedom of conscience, speech, and assembly, and the establishment of a law-based state. Regrettably, in Kiev as in the empire as a whole the promise of the manifesto would diminish sharply within a month.

On October 13, a few days before the October Manifesto was issued, the first workers' soviet was created in St. Petersburg. With six thousand members and an arsenal of revolvers, hunting guns, and garden spades, it quickly became a shadow government in the capital. In Kiev militant socialists followed their lead. Demanding that the discredited city council be disbanded, at a mass meeting on October 21 they created a local soviet.

THE KIEV SOVIET

The Kiev Soviet met for the first time on October 30, more than two weeks before a soviet was organized in Moscow. Its first chairman (and chief organizer) was the Greter & Krivanek worker and Bolshevik sympathizer F. P. Alekseev. Initially, its delegates came from Kiev's nine major industrial plants (South Russia, Greter, the Main Railway Shops, the Arsenal, the First Mechanical Artel, AUTO, Szymanski, Bertram, and Młoszewski). Some two hundred additional delegates, mostly workers in smaller establishments, were given less significant authority in the form of a "consultative voice" (*soveshchatelnyi golos*) in the soviet's proceedings.

Kievskaia gazeta stated that the Social Democrats were the predominant group in the Kiev Soviet,[2] but no one party seemed able to command Kiev's proletariat. The Socialist Revolutionaries continued to be influential, working, for example, with Shlikhter and the Bolsheviks among the railway workers. *Kievlianin*, "always well-informed about *okhranka* business," according to *Kievskaia gazeta*, carried reports of one roundup of SRs in Kiev.[3] A month later *Kievskie otkliki* reported that an SR speaker found an enthusiastic audience of four hundred Greter & Krivanek workers who refused to allow police to approach the speaker and arrest him.[4]

The Kiev Soviet's first act was to express its solidarity with the St. Petersburg Soviet. It then debated whether to cooperate with the liberal Union of Unions, called by one delegate "a bourgeois mixture of all shades." Having "hidden under the bed before October," liberals now were surfacing to enjoy the fruits of victory, one delegate argued. Mensheviks apparently supported the creation of independent unions allied with the Union of Unions, while Bolsheviks favored party-led unions and no alliance. Rejecting the warning by a railroad delegate that "disunity now is criminal," the soviet decided not to affiliate with the liberal association.[5]

On local issues the Kiev Soviet took a cautious stance, resolving only to boycott *Kievlianin* and its print shop; blacklist *Kievlianin*'s workers; provide financial assistance to workers who had been fired from Baron Shteingel's nailery for attempting to negotiate with management; and, through the emerging unions, attract delegates from Kiev's entire work force. Representatives from the Brodsky mill, the Kogen tobacco works, and other enterprises joined, and on November 27, the Kiev Soviet resolved to recruit one delegate for every one hundred workers. The ratio in Moscow was said to be 1:300; in St. Petersburg, 1:500.[6]

In mid-November some seven hundred local employees joined the empirewide postal-telegraph strike, adding another element of tension and confusion to the city. But ominous signs for the soviets were already apparent. In St. Petersburg a late-October campaign to introduce an eight-hour workday fizzled, resulting in a lockout of one hundred thousand workers. The St. Petersburg Soviet's call for a general strike also failed, and few joined the walkout of the postal workers. Sensing that anti-government unity had peaked, Nicholas II grew bolder. In Kiev, as elsewhere, unemployment, fueled by pogroms, disorder, and the end of the war late in the summer, loomed as a constant threat, and there were many arrests. On November 5 St. Vladimir's faculty council voted 30–28 to close the university because students were boycotting the classes of Professor Eikhelman, who had voted in the city council to thank the troops for their role in the pogrom. This same council had agreed to open the university only six days earlier, and its decision did not augur well for the new era of freedom. In December students would be further punished by the vindictive remnants of the city council, who seemed to identify education with upheaval. The council voted unanimously not to grant stipends to students and refused to give even a small subsidy to the Literacy Society.[7]

UNION FEVER

In November many trade unions and other forms of collective association began to form. For example, tailors met on November 8 at the Literacy Society, debating whether to form an artel, a union, or a consumer society. Jewish tailors were not invited to join. Carpenters and joiners also met, agreeing to leave the self-employed, who constituted the majority in their professions, out of their union. Organizing physicians decided not to invite other medical and dental personnel to join their union. A letter to *Kievskoe slovo* on November 25 criticized doctors for preferring "debauchery with each others' wives to working for civic freedom." Its author accused some doctors of continuing to call for pogroms against Jews and Social Democrats and of driving away patients with revolvers. The progressive Union of Kiev Physicians decided to boycott *Kievlianin* and the Filipovich pharmacy for their role in the pogroms, but at least 115 physicians, some of them members of St. Vladimir's medical faculty, refused to join or support either the boycotts or the progressive professional association.

In general, the new unions did not affiliate with any political party or movement. Physicians decided to support anyone "not to the right of the Kadets." Strongly influenced by the Social Democrats, bakers included a statement on the importance of defending "the interests of the entire working class" as one of their forty organizational goals, and they called unanimously for a democratic constituent assembly and the transfer of land to the peasants who worked it. Watchmakers, jewelers, and engravers also stated that socialism was the ultimate goal of their unions, but these assertions seemed to be statements of principle rather than calls for alliance with a specific socialist party. Union organizers warned that 90 percent of the print workers would join a union with purely economic goals, but only 20 percent would adhere to a specific political platform. Print workers proved them right, rejecting a political platform in favor of a bland statement calling for the defense of "the economic and political interests of print workers and their moral and intellectual development."[8]

About sixty teachers came to the initial meeting of the progressive Kiev Teachers' Association on November 23, and even teachers at church schools began to organize. Teachers were deeply divided, however. One spoke passionately against strikes (citing Tolstoy's statement that they were "harmful and untimely"), attacked the West ("which Russia had saved from the Mongols"), and warned of the "psycho-satanic" nature of the times. Probably in protest against teachers' political activism, a Father Troitsky produced a cartoon depicting a turkey dressed in a teacher's frock. As if to underscore the uncertainties of the times, Professor Florinsky admonished that "children no longer know what is permissible and what is not."[9]

During the last week of December, waiters held their first meeting, deciding to follow the lead of waiters in the capitals. Their main demands included ten rubles per month minimum income; "decent" accommodations and meals or an increased food allowance; two days off per week; an end to the requirement that they clean rooms, beat furniture or rugs, or perform tasks other than waiting on tables; an end to the obligation to compensate owners when patrons left without paying; an end to interference by employers in their personal lives; mediation boards in cases of dismissal; and polite treatment, including the use of *vy* (the polite form for "you") when they were addressed by employers and patrons. "Union fever" continued into 1906. Construction workers, said to be "barely conscious peasants," began to organize, having previously been indifferent to the idea. On January 10, 1906, representatives of the twelve largest bootmaking shops met to discuss creating a union; they too warned that organizational efforts would succeed only if political affiliation was avoided. This group made a special effort to show its sensitivity to the plight of the peasantry, for peasants supplied their leather and constituted a major market for boots.

Although eighteen unions formed in the city, Kievans were never permitted the freedom to organize that existed in the capitals. Even in November it was impossible for any group to hold a general meeting. Social Democratic and Bund members often were the most enthusiastic union activists, but none of the unions formally affiliated with a political party, and none excluded individuals because of political views.[10]

ARTELS

In addition to fending off police agents, unions had to compete with established artels, which also had formed around common skills or geographical origins. For example, St. Petersburg's famous bootmakers' artel was composed of craftsmen who had migrated from Tver Province. Until its business began to decline late in the century, this artel took up an entire street.[11] Construction artels from clusters of Russian villages were common in Kiev at midcentury, and almost certainly beyond. One of Kiev's most prominent artels, the so-called vagabond (*bosiaki*) artel, was described by *Kievskaia gazeta* in 1904. Consisting of forty-eight army veterans, aged twenty-four to fifty-six, who carried great bags of grain, groats, lime, and flour to and from the boats at the Dnipro port, the artel was known for its honesty and hard work. Its members worked from six in the morning until seven at night. Their boss (*starosta*) Kasatkin negotiated their wages, usually from 1.5 to 2.25 rubles per day. Wages were given to sick or drunk workers as long as the drinking bouts did not last for more than two or three days. The artel paid for hospital costs and, collecting fines for violations, created a fund to help the wounded in the war with Japan. It hired women to mend bags for sixty or eighty kopecks a day. In winter, when navigation ceased, Kasatkin went to work at the Brodsky mill, and most of the other members joined the ice cutters on the river. The *bosiaki* enjoyed credit at nearly all of the taverns and small shops around the docks, but they had a favorite hangout, a tavern where they drank, sang, and danced. Card games were popular in the barges or along the riverbanks; sometimes several days' wages were won or lost.[12]

Artels were communities unto themselves. It was said that among the *bosiaki* there were former *intelligenty*, merchants, noblemen, princes, and counts, but Kasatkin contended that such distinctions had disappeared. In 1903 the *bosiaki* began to write down their rules, but they never finished, for written codes were unnecessary among these honest and hardworking men. Disputes were resolved by the *starosta* or by majority vote; they never got as far as the police or the courts. In general, artel members did not associate with other workers except in rare cases when they could not find enough work. Sometimes artels fought each other, as in the brawl at Chicken Row in the Seed Bazaar in September 1903. This brawl turned into an ugly confrontation with police when the latter tried to interfere.[13] Sometimes artels helped defuse ethnoreligious conflicts, as in 1881 when some spoke out against the pogroms.[14]

Although the number of artels in Kiev is not known, they appeared to be common in the city.[15] Russians, or Russified workers, may have been more likely to join them than Ukrainian-speaking workers. In the 1870s Pantiukhov noted that the "Little Russian is little inclined to join associations or artels, and has an aversion to compulsory labor."[16] It is doubtful that Jews and Christians mixed within artels, but otherwise I found no evidence that artel membership was restricted to individuals of specific nationalities. These tightly knit, self-governing artels resembled the guilds of earlier times, and their social bonds seem to have been just as strong or stronger than the bonds that were coalescing around ethnic identities or loyalties to political parties or ideologies. In Odessa Robert Weinberg has discovered that craft associations inhibited socialist attempts to form broader worker associations during and after 1905.[17] In Kiev artels and specialized craft associations also provided considerable competition for the trade union movement.

THE KIEV SOLDIERS' *BUNT*

More troublesome to the government than the formation of new labor associations was the sudden increase in the number of military mutinies. Between mid-October and mid-December 1905, there were 211 mutinies in the Russian army and navy. On October 26–27 Kronshtadt soldiers and sailors plundered local businesses, and on October 30 sailors plundered Vladivostok. Otherwise, few of these mutinies involved serious violence. According to Abraham Ascher, "The soldiers and sailors evinced little interest in the political arrangements of the civilian sector. Indeed, they generally adopted political demands only to humor civilians, and the radical agitation often turned them into opponents of the revolution."[18] Of primary importance to soldiers were bread-and-butter issues in the military itself.

After troops had fired at unarmed Kiev workers in July 1903, the city's Social Democrats created a special organization to try to increase their influence within the army. Spreading literature critical of war and military service, and harping on the poor living conditions and harsh discipline in the army, the SDs hoped to convince their targets that good soldiers did not fire at unarmed countrymen. Soldiers were hard to get at, however. They lived in closed barracks and were subjected to frequent searches and constant military propaganda. Efforts to win their sympathies went badly until the Russo-Japanese War deepened discontentment. During the summer of 1904, in the area behind the Jewish Bazaar, groups of as many as one hundred soldiers secretly met on Sundays with revolutionary activists, many of whom were women. These soldiers smuggled Lenin's *Iskra* (The spark) and other materials into their barracks.

The infantrymen posted in Kiev came predominantly from peasant backgrounds and remained unreceptive to socialist propaganda. More than half of the sappers, however, came from the urban working class, and they became the primary targets of the militants. One breakthrough came in 1904 when the Third, Fourth, and Fifth Sapper Pontoon Battalions demanded better food and rations of tea and sugar. But arrests disrupted these agitational efforts, shutting down the *iavki*, the secret apartments where soldiers could make contacts and get literature.[19] That soldiers had not been won over was evident in October 1905. Only a few soldiers could be found among the celebrants of the October Manifesto, and troops fired on the crowd in front of city hall. During the pogrom, they stood idly by, passively observing the destruction and sometimes firing into the homes of "Jewish insurrectionaries."

In November 1905 "Andrei Vasilevich," actually the nobleman and graduate of the Moscow Kadet Corps Alexander Vannovsky, took over

Kiev's Social Democratic military organization. The SRs cooperated in establishing a joint committee called the Kiev Military Collective. After the October Manifesto was issued, contacts became easier. Secret apartments were reestablished, and meetings occurred almost daily. Soldiers were told about the Kronshtadt and Vladivostok disorders and the Sevastopol mutiny of November 14–15. Tensions mounted when sappers were told to take over jobs vacated by striking postal-telegraph workers. During this strike, hundreds of Cossacks were deployed throughout the city.

On November 16, angered by the fact that their barracks had no kitchen, dining area, or even places to sit, the Third and Fifth Pontoon Battalions voted to strike, citing the bad food, scarcities of tea and sugar, and poor-quality uniforms as additional grievances. The more highly politicized soldiers demanded the creation of soldiers' courts to try unfit officers and the immediate election of a soldiers' soviet. That evening fifty or sixty soldiers met with agitators (Manilov calls them Social Democrats) to work out a plan of action. Almost all were sappers, and only one was an infantryman. The group divided bitterly between those who favored insurrection and those who cautioned that it would be futile until the support of the infantry could be assured. The decision was made to stage an "armed demonstration" at the Arsenal in the hope that this would trigger an armed rising.[20]

On the following day, led by Andrei Vasilevich, the insurgents assembled at the Nicholas Barracks next to the Arsenal and proceeded down Moscow Street toward the Pechersk Bazaar. Their thirty-one demands included improvement in the various living conditions described above; issuance annually of two complete uniforms or a stipend of thirteen rubles; daily access to the *bania* (steam bath); more liberal rules regarding leaving the barracks and writing letters; free access to books, literature, theater, and public events; unrestricted use of the tram; the right to publish soldiers' newspapers and journals; and election of committees to look after soldiers' interests. Soon the insurgents confronted other sappers. One colonel cried out: "Whoever loves the tsar and the fatherland, join us." About thirty-five responded, and a scuffle broke out, but spirits were buoyed when government troops refused to obey orders to attack the insurgents.

The procession moved on toward the barracks where the 126th Kursk Regiment was quartered. A musical unit (led by Jews, *Kievlianin* insisted) joined the insurgents, but only three infantrymen were drawn in. Moving behind the military orchestra, the number of rebels grew to about 750, and loyal troops still refused to move against the demonstration. The insurgent sappers moved through Pechersk uncontested.

As the insurgents left Pechersk, they were joined by a small number of soldiers from the Third and Fourteenth Sapper Battalions posted at the railway station, and by workers and youths from Demievka and the Bol-shaia Vasilkov neighborhood. Asserting that the soldiers did not really know what they were doing and that they presented no demands, *Kievli-anin* reported a bizarre scene. A woman dressed in a soldier's cap ap-proached Lieutenant-General Drake with hands outstretched, asking for bread "for the poor, hungry soldiers." Said Drake to the troops, "Broth-ers, doesn't the tsar feed you? Do you need to beg?" "No, we have every-thing we need," the soldiers responded, after which the woman was sent off with a strong warning.[21]

Tension peaked when six Cossack units, with rifles poised, surrounded the crowd. The rebels cheered when they were allowed to proceed, not realizing that they were being surrounded. When the crowd reached the barracks of the Thirty-third Artillery Brigade near the South Russian Ma-chine Works on Zhilianskaia Street, they found that most of the troops quartered there had been removed and that those who remained had been disarmed. Caught by surprise, South Russian workers joined the crowd, increasing its size to about three thousand, but they were mostly un-armed. Greter & Krivanek's workers were also unprepared for the mu-tiny. They were particularly incensed at this time because management had reduced wages for their unskilled employees from seventy to forty-nine kopecks per day, ostensibly because orders had declined. Greter had also gone to seven-hour work shifts, a further sign of hard times. Manilov argues that the most militant segments of Kiev's proletariat could offer little help to the soldiers at this critical moment because the Menshevik-dominated Social Democrats had failed to organize armed worker units.[22]

The end quickly came when troops from the largely peasant Mirgorod Regiment opened fire on the trapped crowd near the Halytsky Bazaar. Some chose to fight it out; others were trapped as Cossacks and dragoons sealed off potential escape routes. Another confrontation occurred near the People's Club where two hundred unarmed soldiers tried unsuccess-fully to win over infantrymen. Estimates of the casualties ranged from one hundred to two hundred.

With the declaration of martial law on November 19, Kiev's days of com-parative freedom ended. Officially, they had lasted one month. On that day, Zhilianskaia Street was blocked at both ends, isolating the South Russian factory, and the Main Railway Shops were closed. The press was shut down on November 19 and 20. When the newspapers reopened on November 21, they were occupied by troops and could say little about the bloodbath. They reported only that clashes had occurred between work-ers and notorious "hooligan" gangs, some of which had begun because of hooligan efforts to start another pogrom. Somehow *Kievskie otkliki* managed a brief report on the confrontation in its December 1 edition, noting that when word of a soldiers' *bunt* (mutiny) spread, many reservists were put on active duty and sent out of the city.

At about this time, a committee headed by future mayor Ivan Diakov recommended modest financial assistance for pogrom victims, but the city council rejected the recommendation by a 21–14 vote. At the council meeting on November 16, *Kievlianin*'s correspondent was permitted to sit at a special table close to the podium; the reporters from the other papers had to sit behind him. Underscoring its irrelevancy, the council discussed F. N. Iasnogursky's request to have the "houses of pleasure" on Iamskaia Street moved somewhere else. Someone gleefully suggested adorning houses on the Khreshchatyk with camelias and making the neighborhood over to look like Tokyo. The council decided to move the houses of ill-repute away from the city center. Said one paper: "Our city council has suddenly turned red. But the Black Hundreds shouldn't worry. The red has nothing to do with the flags unfurled before it on October 18. It is the red of embarrassment for not having done a single constructive thing in four years."[23]

Meanwhile, on November 19 as many as six thousand people attended an all-day meeting and discussed the possibility of a general strike to protest the killings of November 18. Boycotting the city council and helping the families of those killed or injured were also considered. Meeting at the Polytechnic Institute, the soviet called for a general strike, but on November 20 only small demonstrations took place, and the school was closed. Rumors that pogroms were about to occur in Kiev and Odessa flew about the city. Troops had already gunned down their brothers-in-uniform; they would not hesitate to kill civilians, and they were said to be "especially hostile" to Jews. Police prevented the plundering of at least one Podil shop. At least one monastery, the Holy Trinity, publicly opposed pogroms against Jews or *intelligenty*. On November 23 the Kiev Soviet called off a general strike that was clearly not going to occur.

THE SHULIAVKA REPUBLIC

In the view of Soviet historians, at the end of 1905 the Kiev Soviet established a "strict revolutionary order" in Shuliavka, Kiev's infamous factory district.[24] The "Shuliavka Republic," they claim, constituted the final heroic episode in Kiev during that tumultuous year. In retrospect, however, these final weeks seem anticlimactic. On December 4 *Kievskaia gazeta* reported, for example, that the printers' union, now seven hundred members strong, was not allowed to hold a general meeting. On December 5 it editorialized that despite martial law, orderly people were afraid to walk the streets. In Podil, "people are afraid even to go to church." "On the streets of Kiev there is a wild orgy of prostitutes and hooligans." (The breakdown of law and order had opened the streets everywhere to gangs; the Odessa newspaper *Odesskie novosti* even began to run a newspaper column entitled "Hooligans.") Predictably, *Kievlianin* blamed the crime and disorder on Jews, and Kiev Black Hundreds—now led by music professor Nikolai Ikonnikov, a member of the French Academy of the Arts and the Society against Cruelty to Animals—distributed street leaflets entitled "The Truth about Jews and the Talmud." On December 9 *Kievskaia gazeta*'s reporters were barred from city council meetings. "Long ago we stopped viewing council sessions as serious business and councilmen as representatives of the city," the paper responded. "What can the honest, independent press expect from a hooligan mayor and a Black Hundred council?" On December 10 *Kievskaia gazeta* was closed down.

If a "Shuliavka Republic" existed, its main task was self-defense, for police had virtually disappeared from the factory district. Street justice now prevailed. On November 16 about 50 workers and "boys" went into Podil's flea market looking for hooligans, chasing them out, beating them up as they fled. Once reinforced, the hooligans attacked a group of boat workers, savagely beating them. With police absent, a gunfight erupted at the White Elephant restaurant, and several were killed. Three worker self-defense units (*obkhody*) of about 150 men then moved through Shuliavka to rid the streets of dangerous and unsavory elements. When an *obkhod* found hooligan "sinners," an ultimatum was given to "return to an honest working life or face proletarian wrath." Some repented on the spot, even begging forgiveness for their role in the pogrom.

On November 28 police detectives went to Shuliavka looking for pogrom loot. A well-known hooligan named Kuksa opened fire. Workers from Greter & Krivanek came to the assistance of the detectives and beat Kuksa severely. However, after learning that the detectives had helped Kuksa during and after the pogrom, workers turned on them and beat them viciously. Police then retaliated by arresting about fifty members of the self-defense unit. Enraged, workers at Greter & Krivanek and the Main Railway Shops again debated going out on strike. City council member Iasnogursky asked why the city bothered to spend 260,000 rubles per year on police salaries. In the outskirts police simply disappeared as street attacks increased. "[The hooligans] are worse than the revolutionaries," he noted; "at least the revolutionaries don't plunder."[25]

Given the collapse of the revolutionary movement throughout the country, the Shuliavka Republic stood little chance of surviving, even as an organ of self-defense. The most prominent of the militant organizations, the St. Petersburg Soviet, in the words of Abraham Ascher, "had succumbed to hubris. Instead of consolidating its achievements, it became increasingly militant, and even reckless."[26] On November 26, convinced that people were tired of disorder, the government moved against it, arresting its leaders. On November 29 Nicholas II gave local governors the authority to take decisive action against any disruption of rail, postal, or telegraph services. Sergei Witte grew increasingly isolated politically. A broken man, he could not sleep and became depressed and unpredictable. Fearing assassination, and on December 5 publicly confessing that the whole revolution had been a "nightmare for him,"[27] he too came to support repression.

On December 11 the government published a decree weighting the promised State Duma heavily in favor of the gentry and the middle class. (Even this law would produce a radical duma that would meet during the savage repression of 1906.) On December 12 prison sentences were prescribed for strikers at any enterprise "of public or state importance." The use of military force accompanied these decrees. In Moscow, where the soviet's militia had been poorly prepared, more than one thousand were killed in the December crackdown, most of them civilians who had not been involved in the upheaval. In Kharkiv about sixty were killed or wounded on December 12 when cannons were turned on the Gelferikh-Sade factory, that city's last citadel of revolution.

Prior to the government crackdown, on December 6 the Moscow Soviet had called for a general strike, and rumors quickly surfaced in Kiev that Shuliavka would respond. On December 12, with Shuliavka residents again upset by the murder of two well-dressed men, apparently civil servants, by unknown assailants, Kiev's Main Railway Shops and major factories struck.[28] Some secondary schools joined, and Podil workers tried to forcibly close down local establishments. The soviet tried to regulate hours for shops to open and close, but most shops and bazaars stayed open. Except for the Shuliavka and Sviatoshino lines, the trams continued to run. An effort to blow up the electrical supply for the tram network failed.

On December 16 shop owners on the Khreshchatyk, Bolshaia Vasilkov, and the Bessarabka panicked when agitators appeared and demanded closure, but Cossacks quickly came to the rescue. In most of the city life continued normally. Aside from the Main Railway Shops, most railway employees continued to work through the strike, perhaps because arrests of their co-workers had begun on December 9, before the strike's onset. Bolshevik leaders Shlikhter, who had returned to Kiev on some unknown date, and Krzhizhanovsky fled the city. Kharkiv's *Iuzhnyi krai* reported that "cruel fights" had broken out among Kiev's railway workers over whether to support the walkout; *Kievskie otkliki* denied the report. The Kharkiv paper also reported that Kiev was without water on

December 17 because of the strike, but this is unlikely since the soviet had insisted that critical services and groceries remain open.[29]

On December 15 and 16 troops surrounded Shuliavka and police began to move through its neighborhoods, "missing hardly a house," confiscating weapons, and arresting at least seventy-eight. More than one hundred secondary students were arrested and reportedly beaten by police. Decimated by arrest, the Kiev Soviet held its last meeting on December 22. In a final gesture of futility, it voted to continue what was left of the strike until December 25.[30]

The year ended with frightened workers turning on one another. At least 192 Southwestern Railway employees were fired, and the Main Railway Shops remained closed until December 28. At Greter, called by *Kievlianin* "Kiev's nest of revolutionary terrorists and murderers," 350 of its 900 workers were fired, and the plant remained closed until January 17, 1906. The remnants of the Shuliavka Republic were left to blame each other for the inglorious end to a glorious year. Writing after 1917, Manilov blamed Kiev's Mensheviks, dominant among the city's Social Democrats, for using the soviet, not as an instrument to lead an armed uprising, but as an organ of government to mediate local disputes. In a city sealed off by the postal-telegraph strike, if the sapper insurrectionists had occupied key government buildings in Pechersk, if they had spread out and not allowed themselves to be surrounded, and if the Menshevik-dominated SDs had organized armed worker units, things might have turned out differently, he argued.[31] Given the reality of events elsewhere in the country, Manilov's view seems implausible.

Symbolically, 1905 ended with a whimper when wives of the lower ranks of army reservists created a disturbance on December 21 and 22. "We are hungry and our children have nothing to eat," they cried. Cossacks restored order.

THE END OF THE PUBLIC MOVEMENT

The collapse of the sappers' mutiny, the Kiev Soviet, and the Shuliavka Republic clearly put the imperial government back in charge, and repression quickly followed. The university was allowed to reopen in September 1906, but in November, the 26 members of its Council of Student Representatives were arrested after Kiev's Union of Russian People charged them with planning to commemorate a 1902 political execution. When students began to disrupt classes, the faculty closed the university for a week. Prime Minister Stolypin was furious, for this action raised doubts about the government's ability to maintain control, and the university was reopened. Police took down the names of those who attended a subsequent meeting, and the professors' court then suspended 719 students for a year.[32] An abortive soldiers' *bunt* occurred in Kiev on June 4–5, 1907. It was quickly suppressed, and repression intensified.[33] Agitators who managed to avoid arrest left the city. Efforts by moderate Polish and Ukrainian organizations to achieve even cultural goals were thwarted. The Ukrainian organization *Prosvita*, discussed in chapter 4, was finally disbanded in 1910. Harassed by the government and disadvantaged by the small number of individuals who could read Ukrainian, by 1912 the entire Ukrainian periodical press in the Russian Empire consisted of five journals and seven daily or weekly newspapers.

Labor walkouts occurred on May Day in 1908 and 1909, but between June 1907 and June 1910 Kiev workers managed only twenty-two strikes.[34] A report for 1911–1912 indicates that the city's Social Democratic movement consisted of only some twenty circles, each with about seven or eight active members, but that this network was regarded as one of the most significant in the empire at this time. Members and sympathizers donated 1 percent of their wages "for needy families." The party did not have a printing press, and nearly all of its publications had to be printed surreptitiously in legal print shops. Newspapers published abroad by Lenin, Trotsky, and others were hard to get, single copies arriving by mail in envelopes. Ties were maintained with Spilka, which had cells in Berdychiv, Zhytomyr, and other regional centers. Bakers, who labored under some of the worst working conditions in the city, were among the most active SD supporters, and the Shuliavka factory district continued "to have a special significance."[35]

Bolsheviks and Mensheviks continued to do battle in what was left of the trade unions and in workers' clubs. In 1911–1912 the club named "Arts and Scholars" had six hundred members. In the evenings it was always crowded. It was a "neutral spot" where workers could gather and exchange news. "There the cheery atmosphere could always raise your mood."[36] Such clubs were closed by officials but reopened under new names.

A resurgence of labor militancy occurred in Kiev and elsewhere after the massacre of the Lena Goldfield workers in April 1912. Led by the workers at the South Russian Machine Works, twenty-eight strikes and a two-day protest at the university occurred in the city between April 9 and 17. On April 18 Kiev's Bolshevik leaders were arrested. Chief among them was Evgeniia Bogdanovna Bosh (1879–1925), the mother of two daughters, thirteen and twelve, who had come to Kiev four years earlier after separating from her husband, a carriage maker in Kherson Province. These arrests allowed the Mensheviks to further strengthen their control of the city's Social Democratic movement. As in other cities, Kiev's workers continued to be assertive until war intervened in 1914. On May Day 1912, employees at fourteen Kiev enterprises struck. Between January and July, 1914, the city experienced fifty-four strikes involving forty-five hundred workers.[37]

THE FIRST WORLD WAR

The First World War punctuated an exceptionally pleasant summer in Kiev. Ukrainian memoirist Hryhory Hryhorev recalls the leisurely pace of the summer of 1914, the boat trips, merry-go-rounds, swings in the parks, balls, and masquerades. Prices in the markets had dropped to 1880 levels. News that the Russian army had mobilized brought some arguments about the merits of the cause that St. Petersburg had joined, but almost everyone rallied behind the government. The government showed little faith in its subjects, however, declaring martial law on July 18, 1914. The Ukrainian newspaper *Rada* was closed down even though it supported the war effort. Speculators surfaced immediately, and five- and ten-ruble notes quickly disappeared. Operas and concerts continued, but the brass band that played in the Summer Garden of the Merchants' Club went to the front. Such German composers as Wagner, Beethoven, and Schubert were banned; Goethe's *Faust* was performed, but only the operatic version by the Frenchman Gounod. Kiev filled with AWOL troops, all claiming they were trying to catch up with their units. Monks were not subject to the draft; the number of brothers in Kiev's monasteries consequently increased.[38]

Early in the war, Kiev seemed vulnerable, and in 1914 plans were made to move the university to Saratov. When the military threat failed to materialize, some industrial enterprises were moved to Kiev from exposed cities such as Riga. Local industries converted to wartime production. The Main Railway Shops, for example, manufactured three trains for use on the narrow-gauge Austrian railways. Women, refugees, and prisoners of war assumed many production roles on factory floors. Greter & Krivanek employed 750 prisoners of war in 1916. That year, of 225 enterprises in Kiev, women constituted 30 percent of the work force, boys under 17 and men over 45 another 12 percent.[39] The liberal newspaper *Kievskaia mysl'* continued to act as the city's conscience, criticizing, for example, ongoing reliance on child labor. Even before the war, in 1913, it contended, about 11 percent of the workers had been between the ages of 12 and 17.

Strikes became rare once the war began. Many of the more politically conscious workers were drafted. On July 25, 1914, practically all Bolsheviks in the city were arrested. From mid-1914 until the February Revolution in 1917, there were only twenty-three strikes, virtually all over economic grievances.[40]

Beneath this comparative calm, the deficiencies of Nicholas II and his government and the economic weaknesses of the country became more apparent. So too did the weaknesses of the tsarist system of municipal governance. Kievans were slow to organize to meet the changing circumstances created by the war. Although inflation was a serious problem, in February 1915 *Kievskaia mysl'* reported that not a single consumer society existed in the city. There were five hundred such societies, which bought products in large volumes at lower prices, in the surrounding towns and villages of Kiev Province, but not one in the city itself.[41] By the spring of 1916 Kiev's castelike city government had developed a plan for rationing firewood and had opened a bakery and several bread shops to help ease the burden of rising food costs, but in general, when forced to confront wartime problems, it refused to recruit individuals who were not part of the narrow electorate. Suspicious of anyone outside its ranks, Kiev's government drew particular criticism in the national publication *Gorodskoe delo* (Urban affairs) for its ineffectiveness in mobilizing local human and material resources. Many Kievans signed a petition to the State Duma, pleading for a democratic system of local governance that could mobilize and organize resources efficiently, but the imperial government ignored such warnings as it continued to slide toward collapse.[42]

• CONCLUSION •

As if to underscore the importance of the steppe to the early history of Kiev, a graffito in St. Sophia Cathedral, possibly from the eleventh century, refers to Kiev's ruler as a "kagan," the title of the rulers of the Turkic nomads.[1] Its rise occasioned by the interaction of Varangian warrior-merchants and Eastern Slavs, and its culture greatly enriched by Vladimir's decision in 988 to convert his subjects to Byzantine Christianity, medieval Kiev became the ruling center of the largest political entity in Europe and one of the largest cities in Eurasia.

A prime target of nomadic raiders, Kiev was destroyed by Mongols in 1240 and sacked again in 1416 and 1482. Although the city did not recover its earlier size or significance for centuries, burgeoning regional empires claimed succession to its cultural and political legacy. Lithuanians, Poles, Jews, Armenians, Tatars, and Western Europeans migrated to Kiev, mixing with the native Eastern Slavic peoples who would eventually become the Ukrainian, Russian, and Belarusian nations. In 1800 Kiev was "Ukrainian" in the sense that its burghers spoke the language of adjacent Chernihiv and Poltava Provinces, but it had always been a frontier town with a frontier blend of peoples and cultures, and in physical appearance these same burghers bore no similarity even to the peasants who lived just beyond the city.

Although Kievans identified strongly with religious faiths and occupational groups, they also saw themselves as Kievans, and their history is characterized by unceasing efforts to protect the self-rule they had won when the Lithuanian prince extended the Magdeburg Rights to Podil's burghers around the turn of the sixteenth century. In 1835 those rights were revoked once and for all by Nicholas I, and during the nineteenth century, as the ideals of the European Enlightenment swept into the city, the struggle to protect medieval privileges gave way to broader demands for natural rights, political, economic, and national.

In response, the authoritarian Russian state applied powerful pressures in an effort to create a uniform "Russian" population. Beneath its Russified veneer, however, Kiev remained a rich blend of peoples. After municipal self-government was established in 1870, the Russianized German Gustav Eisman, Ivan Tolli, a descendant of Greeks who had settled in Odessa, and the Pole Józef Zawadzki were among its first mayors, and the Brodsky clan, descendants of the Jew Meir Schor who had come to Kiev Province from Brody in Austrian Galicia earlier in the century, stood out among its industrialists and philanthropists. Balkan balladeers and Turks selling sweet sesame cakes called halva could still be found on Kiev streets in the early 1900s, and camel caravans of Crimean Tatars continued to come in August, bringing wine and grapes to its bazaars.[2] Itinerant Chinese peddlers, about two hundred in number, sold shawls, silks, and canvas from their flats or from street corners. They spoke little Russian, it was said, but they had "a great respect for Russian vodka."[3] An endless stream of pilgrims—"God's workers"—continued to arrive from Bessarabia and the Austro-Hungarian lands, from distant Perm, Astrakhan, and Irkutsk. "Everywhere you see them trudging along, slowly, covered with dust, burned by the sun, country folk with sacks on their shoulders, staffs in their hands." From the crack of dawn they "proceed silently, gawking at the city's crowded trams, its tall buildings and fountains." In mid-August as many as thirty-five thousand were in the city, nine thousand in the Cave Monastery hotel alone.[4]

Owning much of the land in Right-Bank Ukraine, Poles were a powerful economic force in Kiev, especially during the winter Contract Fair. Although it is doubtful that Poles constituted more than 10 percent of Kiev's population at any time during the nineteenth or early twentieth centuries, they contributed mightily to the city's cultural life. Until the 1830s, Polish was Kiev's language of education, and at midcentury Poles still played important roles in the city's musical and literary circles and its theater.

Although efforts by Poles to win their independence from Russia were centered elsewhere, Polish national goals became the dominant political concern of Kiev's authorities by the 1820s. The Contract Fair served as the perfect cover for political intrigue, for Poles from Warsaw to Berdychiv had an excuse to be in Kiev during that time. Russian officials came to view the fair as a convention spot for revolutionaries and Kiev itself as a den of Polish insurrectionism.

After the unsuccessful insurrection of 1830–1831, Polish influence in Kiev and the surrounding region began to decline. Nicholas I, who loved the city, decided that it should become the center for the dissemination of Russian culture and influence for the entire region. Russian became the language of education and administration, and in 1834 St. Vladimir University was founded. Although Nicholas I intended it to be a *Russian* university in language, spirit, and curriculum, Poles continued to predominate in its student body. Under the governor-generalship of the one-armed army veteran Dmitry Bibikov, epicurean values were encouraged as a means of deflecting youthful energy away from political concerns, and, in the 1840s, St. Vladimir students were said "to be more interested in psychology and billiards than in politics."

Neither Bibikov nor Nicholas could permanently subjugate Polish nationalism, however, and defeat in the Crimean War rekindled interest in political and economic issues. The Purist Society formed in 1856, its very name symbolizing its challenge to the reign of hedonism, and within a year St. Vladimir was riddled with political activism. Kiev students created an organizational network for rebellion on the Right Bank. When insurrection began in Warsaw in 1863, it took three months to spread to Kiev, and order was apparently never violated in the city itself. However, an estimated 600 of St. Vladimir's 900 students joined the rebels. Of 1,336 people convicted in Kiev for their role in the affair, 400 were students.

After 1863 Polish enrollment at St. Vladimir was restricted, and Polish nationalism ceased to be the central concern of authorities in the city. Kiev continued to attract Polish migrants, and Poles retained considerable economic power in the city, although much less so than in Minsk or Vilnius where they owned most of the income-producing real estate and controlled the city councils. Poles remained prominent in Kiev's social and intellectual elite, but they had little political influence for they made up only about one-quarter of the city's voters. Right-wing politicians continued to attack Polish nationalism in city elections right up until the First World War, but overall, after 1863 in Kiev the Polish question became a sideshow on a stage dominated by heightened Judeophobia and the emergence of a powerful labor movement. In the 1890s Polish socialists joined the broader Russian-dominated socialist movement, and Polish organizations played a very small role in the upheavals of 1905 in the city.

In the aftermath of the first Polish insurrection, Nicholas I terminated the medieval privileges of Kiev's burghers and concentrated more authority in the hands of Russian administrators appointed in St. Petersburg. The collective identity of Podil's burghers, forged by three centuries of autonomy, disappeared. Russian became the language of administration, education, and upward mobility. Although artels of skilled construction workers were imported from Russia and Russian merchants were encouraged to relocate in Kiev, Russians did not migrate to the city in large numbers. Russian merchants, especially from in and around Moscow, controlled much of the lucrative trade at the Contract Fair, however. Ukrainian merchants were virtually unknown at the fair, and Dmytro Bahalii's assertion that Ukrainians were generally uninterested in trade, although written with reference to Kharkiv, seems equally applicable to Kiev.

Around the middle of the nineteenth century, Kiev became the center of the Russian Empire's small Ukrainian national movement. The Cyril and Methodius Society, called by Orest Subtelny "the first Ukrainian ideological organization in modern times," surfaced at St. Vladimir University. Authorities suppressed it, signaling the beginning of a struggle with Ukrainian intellectuals that did not fully cease. Although few Ukrainian peasants joined the Polish rebels in 1863, the government of Alexander II declared war on the Ukrainian language, issuing decrees in 1863 and 1876 that threatened to drive it from the city. Schoolboys, already ashamed to use the language of the peasant, now found Ukrainian to be politically taboo as well. The term *Ukrainian* came more and more to conjure up the image of a rustic and unproductive urban underclass, of marginal denizens who lived in disadvantaged outskirts or hung about the city's bazaars. Because the Ukrainian language was increasingly ignored by the urban skilled and educated, some feared it could not keep pace with the fast-changing demands of the modern industrial era. Others took solace in the fact that the Irish had not lost their sense of national identity despite linguistic Anglification.

On the surface, efforts to mold cultural and political uniformity had succeeded, and Kiev became "a Russian city." This very success, however, heightened concern for preserving the Ukrainian identity. In the 1870s and 1880s, Kiev's small *hromada* struggled for cultural pluralism, and especially for an end to the restrictions against the Ukrainian language. Unwilling to accept small cultural concessions, and rejecting the poet Pushkin's assertion that "all Slavic rivers should flow into a Russian sea," Mykhailo Drahomanov and the more politically assertive Ukrainophiles fled to the more permissive confines of Austrian Lviv.

Around the turn of the twentieth century, the Ukrainian movement became increasingly politicized, and emerging Ukrainian parties such as RUP located their headquarters in Kiev. The most influential of these parties, Spilka, used Russian in its propaganda but insisted on Ukrainian autonomy within the broader, Russian-dominated Social Democratic movement. These organizations, like those of the Poles, remained on the periphery of the city's political life, however, and played very small roles amid the challenges hurled against the imperial order in 1905. In city elections, Russian nationalists were much more likely to attack Poles and Jews than Ukrainians, fearing "Polish dominance" and "Jewish exploitation" more than Ukrainian national goals.

After 1905 Kiev continued to be the recognized center of the Ukrainian movement in the Russian Empire, although political repression stifled any chance to win mass allegiance. Persecuted by state authorities and restricted by the small number of Ukrainian readers, by 1912 the empire's entire Ukrainian periodical press had dwindled to a dozen newspapers and journals. Ten of the twelve were published in Kiev, and thirteen of the seventeen Ukrainian publishing houses operating in the empire were also located in the city. Summarizing the frustrations of these years, Kiev's leading Ukrainian journalist, Serhii Efremov, observed: "It is like 1863 or 1876."

Thus, in late-imperial Kiev the Ukrainian national movement was easily controlled by local authorities and failed to develop a broad base of support. During the revolution and civil war, Kievans contributed little to the Ukrainian national movement even though the Central Rada, its organizing center, sat in Kiev. One Ukrainian leader lamented that in general, cities "gave us no help whatsoever during the revolution."[5]

Nevertheless, the extent to which late-imperial Kiev had fully become "a Russian city" should not be exaggerated. Most Kievans had come from the adjacent Ukrainian lands, and anecdotal evidence suggests that they retained much of the Ukrainian culture. As in Kharkiv, where the governor described the inhabitants in the 1850s as "a special cross between Great Russians and Little Russians," Kievans also blended cultures and languages. Although the 1897 census reported that Russian had become the language of the majority of Kiev's residents, many spoke *surzhyk* blends of Russian, Ukrainian, and in some cases Polish, and the "Russian" spoken in the city was said to offend the ears of those accustomed to the language of Moscow or St. Petersburg. "Kievans speak neither Russian nor Little Russian," it was said. "They speak a little in Russian."

The fact that Russia's tsars did not offer an ideology or a social and political order which had genuine popular appeal also limited the potential for successful Russification. Ultimately, communist rule became even more coercive, and the desire of Kievans and Ukrainians to rid themselves of Russian control remained a potent political force, awaiting the right historical moment to blossom.

In the final decades of Romanov Kiev, the deepest and most volatile conflict involved neither Polish nor Ukrainian national goals, however, but centered instead on efforts by Jews to establish themselves in a city that had long excluded them. Despite stiff resistance, under Catherine the Great a small Jewish community gained a foothold in Kiev. A Jewish neighborhood emerged near the Pechersk fortress, and Jews also managed to penetrate the burgher stronghold of Podil. In 1827 Nicholas I expelled the Jews from Kiev, and in 1835 the city was declared to be outside of the Jewish Pale of Settlement. Subsequently, Jews could stay in the city only for short periods of time, but large numbers continued to come. In 1845, excluding those who came for the Contract Fair, 40,000 Jews visited Kiev.

While his government was persecuting Poles and overreacting to the potential threat of Ukrainian nationalism, Alexander II allowed Jews to reestablish a community in Kiev. By 1874 there were 14,000 Jews officially living in the city, most of them crowded into new ghettos in Lybid and Ploskaia Districts. Many found conditions and opportunities in Kiev to be little better than those in the surrounding Pale. In 1897, 32,000 Jews lived in Kiev, and many more lived there unofficially. In September 1917, a census reported that more Jews lived in Kiev (87,246, or 19 percent) than did Ukrainian-speakers (76,792, or 17 percent).

In the late nineteenth century, Jews came quickly to dominate Kiev's merchantry. In 1905 it was estimated that they controlled two-thirds of the city's trade.[6] Although many of Kiev's Jews were poor, and many were students, Jews also owned about one-fifth of its most lucrative pieces of real estate, according to 1913 tax rolls. The rapid increase in the number of Jews in Kiev and the rapid growth of Jewish economic influence in the city rekindled tensions, reinforcing the image popular among Russian nationalists that Kiev was a city under siege, an outpost of Russian culture and rule in a sea of Jewish traders and Polish landowners.

Bribery and extortion characterized relations between Jews and local police, and nighttime roundups and periodic expulsions branded the city with a notoriety equaled in the Russian Empire only by Odessa. Pogroms occurred in 1881 and 1905, rivaling in their intensity the mid-seventeenth-century conflicts between Orthodox and Catholics. Pogroms were products of the deeply entrenched anti-Semitism of Ukraine. For some members of the urban underclass, they had also become the "grandiose street disorder—the real fair." From the 1860s the potential for pogroms lay semidormant in the taverns and bazaars of Kiev, awaiting only the right agitator and the right moment to mobilize against the city's most noticeable and hated minority. Very few Kievans actively participated in pogroms, but very few defended Jews either.

The extent to which Kiev authorities encouraged the outbreak of pogroms is unclear, but particularly in 1905, they clearly tolerated mob violence once it had begun. Kiev had a large garrison, but troops stood by, allowing the mob to destroy more property than in any other imperial city. As in Odessa, they were more inclined to fire at Jews who tried to defend themselves than at the mob itself. Few from Kiev's religious establishment openly opposed the destructive wrath. Kiev's police chief sympathized with the mob; its anti-Semitic mayor left the city; and its city council earned the epithet "hooligan council" after thanking the troops and police for their efforts during the pogrom and refusing to allocate even a small amount of compensation to its victims.

The view that Jews were injurious aliens never fully disappeared from the culture of late-imperial Kiev, and their right to live in the city was never fully accepted. On June 28, 1914, the day the Austrian archduke Franz Ferdinand was assassinated in Sarajevo, rumors that up to thirty thousand Jews would be expelled circulated in Kiev. "No place in the empire could vie as regards hostility to the Jews with the city of Kiev—this inferno of Russian Israel," it was said. While this statement exaggerates the city's singularity, tensions between Jews and Christians far overshadowed conflicts generated by Polish and Ukrainian goals in late-imperial Kiev. Only the hatred spawned by anti-Semitism could bring to the city "the cruelty unheard of even in the Middle Ages."[7]

At the end of the 1870s, a fledgling labor movement emerged in Kiev as it did elsewhere in the Russian Empire. Kiev's first strike occurred in 1879, and about a decade later the first Social Democratic circle appeared in the city. Reflecting its ethnic diversity, Kiev's most important socialist agitators in the 1890s included the Pole Edward Pletat, the Jew Boris Eidelman, and the Russian Iuvenaliia Melnikov. By 1900 traditional patterns of authority were breaking down in the workplace, and strikes were common. Students also challenged authority; in one celebrated event in 1901, 183 St. Vladimir students were forcibly conscripted into the army for their role in a demonstration. In July 1903 troops provided martyrs for the local labor movement by killing unarmed demonstrators during a massive strike.

Kievans did not initiate the revolutionary challenges of 1905 but rather reacted to events in St. Petersburg and Moscow. The first strike occurred at the South Russian Machine Works three days after the infamous Bloody Sunday massacre in the capital. During January and February, most of the walkouts occurred where the labor movement was strong and aggressive, at the South Russian plant, at Greter & Krivanek, and among the railway workers. Strikers demanded that workplace grievances be addressed and that a more humane economic order be created. During the spring and summer months, most of the city's strikes took place in the small enterprises and sweatshops. Tensions were particularly visible in Jewish neighborhoods, and the summer was punctuated by confrontations between Jews and police. Students played a very small role in Kiev's disturbances in 1905, if only because St. Vladimir University and the Polytechnic Institute were closed for most of the year. The Mensheviks controlled the local Social Democratic organization, but no one party seemed capable of commanding the city's proletariat.

By September two individuals emerged who could incite public passions and mobilize the oppositional movement: the Jewish leader Mark Ratner and the Poltava railway worker turned Bolshevik agitator, Alexander Shlikhter. In early September huge "people's meetings" began to occur almost daily at the university and the Polytechnical Institute. These gatherings brought together liberal, socialist, feminist,[8] and nationalist activists. Amid throngs of onlookers, they forged a more aggressive and politicized public movement, which demanded, in essence, the full spectrum of basic human rights. In mid-October a general strike brought commercial activity in Kiev and other cities nearly to a halt, forcing Nicholas II to issue the historic October Manifesto. Kievans turned out in record numbers to celebrate when news of the manifesto reached the city on October 18.

The sense of triumph ended quickly, as troops fired on the crowd in front of city hall and a pogrom began. Both supporters and opponents saw the pogrom as retaliation for the concessions forced from Nicholas II. To those who believed in the principles of the October Manifesto, the pogrom was "the final convulsion of a dying organism," but for opponents of those principles, participation in the pogrom was a noble and patriotic act. Revolt in 1905 had begun when troops killed peaceful demonstrators in St. Petersburg. It culminated with a historic manifesto that promised a lawful order with guarantees of freedom of conscience, assembly, and speech. That order was never fully implemented in Kiev, and on November 19, after a military mutiny, martial law was declared in the city. In December the complete suppression of the antigovernment movement set the tone for the final decade of Romanov Kiev.

KIEV TRANSFORMED

In 1800 one visitor described Kiev as three barely connected settlements, "each village-like in appearance." Kiev, he said, "could barely be called a city at all." To another visitor, the city was distinguished by the "terrible multitudes of the strange" on its streets, by its beggars and pilgrims. Polish gentlemen brought their own carriages and amenities, expecting to find few creature comforts in the frontier outpost.

Beginning in the 1830s, the "barely connected settlements" of Podil, Pechersk, and Old Kiev began to fuse together into a single city. With the coming of the railroad in 1869–1870, which initially linked Kiev with Moscow and Odessa, the city began to grow much faster. In 1870 Kiev had about 70,000 residents; by 1874, 127,000; by 1897, 247,000; and by January 1, 1914, 626,000. The industrial and bacteriological revolutions, pioneered in Europe and America, swept into the city. Streets were planned and paved, and buildings were put up "with American speed." Electricity brought further advances in economic productivity. Internal-combustion engines began to alter the pace of city life, and in 1910 Kiev itself was at the cutting edge of the new aviation industry.

For centuries Podil had been synonymous with Kiev. However, its guilds declined and its burghers lost their cherished autonomy. Fire and flood drove Podil residents to higher, less congested ground. After 1797 the Contract Fair had kept Podil prosperous, but it too declined in importance. As the city expanded far beyond the river port, Podil lost its commercial advantages. Lacking a spur to the main rail line, the new economic lifeblood of the city, Podil became just another city district.

In historic Old Kiev, the open land and ravines around the medieval ruins began to fill in, especially after the university was founded in 1834. Pechersk changed too. Expansion of its fortress in the 1830s forced many residents to relocate. Shops moved away from Pechersk's main thoroughfare, Moscow Street, known for its Siberian furs and gems and considered to be a prime midcentury shopping area. With the decline of Podil and Pechersk, the Khreshchatyk, built along a wooded ravine and creek once favored by hunters, trappers, and anyone who could put up a distilling shack, became Kiev's commercial center and one of Imperial Russia's most famous main streets. City hall, corporate offices, the great banks and hotels, and the best stores located there. Along with the great churches and monasteries, the Khreshchatyk became Kiev's premier attraction. Unlike the monasteries, however, it proudly symbolized change and modernity.

At the turn of the twentieth century, it was said that those who had known Kiev even thirty years previously would not know her now. The developmental gap between city and countryside had widened considerably. Symbolic of this gap was a Kiev journalist's fictional creation, the bumpkin from Tarakanovka (Cockroachville), who stood in awe of Kiev's sewage aerator. At the same time, elements of continuity held fast. During the 1870s and 1880s, a few large industrial enterprises appeared in the city, but Kiev never became a major industrial center like St. Petersburg or Moscow. The Main Railway Shops reflected the advent of the rail age, but agriculture, and particularly the beet sugar industry, continued to drive the city's economy, and large factories such as Greter & Krivanek and the South Russian Machine Works served its needs. Home to 117 sugar enterprises, which had holdings in thirteen provinces,[9] Kiev in fact became a hub of what today would be called agrobusiness. Factories and large stores did not eliminate older forms of enterprise. Around 1900, 3,700 permanent retail stalls and kiosks were operating in the city's nine major bazaars, constituting another element of continuity.

The importance of educational facilities to the city was another constant. In the eighteenth century, the Kiev Academy had served as a conduit for Western learning. Comparable in stature to the universities in Prague and Cracow, for a time it was "the foremost intellectual center of the Eastern Slavic world." By the advent of the First World War, there were ten institutions of higher learning in Kiev, with a total enrollment of more than 15,000. The number of students at St. Vladimir increased from 2,300 in 1895 to 5,300 in 1915. About 4,000 studied at the Commercial Institute, and about 2,300 at the Polytechnical Institute. At the end of the imperial era, some forty institutions, most of them private, taught everything from stenography and accounting to foreign languages and midwifery.[10] The educational sector continued to bring prestige to the city and purchasing power to its economy, as it had in earlier times. In 1806 not a single periodical was published in Kiev; in 1906 some thirty periodicals were published in the city, underscoring its role as an agent of knowledge and change.[11]

Politically, the "introduction" of municipal self-government in 1870 was more a partial restoration than an innovation, for Kievans had a long tradition of self-government. Although Russian officials had attacked the burgher magistracy earlier in the nineteenth century, calling it a narrow, self-seeking aristocracy, the same could be said of the municipal institutions they created in 1870 and even more so in 1892. In 1870, 3,222 of Kiev's 70,000 inhabitants were given the vote and the right to participate in municipal affairs; by 1910 Kiev's population had surpassed 500,000, but the tiny electorate had increased only to 3,757.

The new city councils supervised considerable progress in street paving and lighting, public health, and education, but they failed to fully meet the challenges of rapid population growth, and they failed to take full advantage of new opportunities afforded by science and technology. Periodic cholera epidemics, the result of inadequate water and sewage treatment, continued to ravage the city. On a per capita basis, the number of cases dropped sharply, from one per 40 Kievans in 1872, to one per 115 in 1892, and one per 423 in 1907,[12] but the number of victims remained significant and, since many were poor, highlighted the inequities of a system of governance in which only the advantaged were represented. Excoriating the council for not building a sanitorium, one newspaper columnist asked: "Is there a single person in Kiev who does not have tuberculosis in one stage or another?"[13] In addition to cholera and tuberculosis, typhus, diphtheria, scarlet fever, and syphilis were scourges of urban life, reflecting the poverty and congestion that characterized many neighborhoods, and the underfunding of medical and sanitary needs.[14] Infants were still greatly at risk. In 1911 nearly one-quarter of all deaths were infants under one year of age, and another one-fifth were children between one and ten.[15]

By maintaining a laissez-faire attitude toward public welfare, and by increasing taxes on bazaar trade and maintaining very low tax rates on the property of the affluent, Kiev's city council contributed to the high cost of living for the poor. Decent, inexpensive housing, hard to find when the city began to grow rapidly in the 1870s, continued to be scarce. Between 1900 and 1908 the number of cheap apartments (renting for less than 225 rubles per year) actually declined by 12 percent.[16] For the sake of perspective, it should be pointed out that such problems were not confined to Kiev or to the cities of the Russian Empire. Although often cited as models of civic virtue and progress, German municipal governments were also slow to place the public good above private gain. As in Russia, municipalization of services and utilities came late in Germany, and "the conviction that nothing ought to be undertaken that might hamper private building activity, combined with the political power of the property owners, created a formidable resistance to municipal housing programs."[17]

Whatever its specific successes, municipal politics in late-imperial Kiev left a legacy that was on balance negative. In a city already divided by class, religion, and nationality, the disenfranchisement of virtually the entire population further inhibited the growth of a sense of community. Local authority broke down during times of crisis and sanctioned mob rule and violence against specific segments of the population. Liberal values, including respect for law and for the idea of public service, could not grow easily in a system where power was monopolized by a tiny elite and often exercised in discriminatory and unjust ways. The elitist nature of the tsarist political order did not make revolution inevitable, but it did give additional credibility to socialists who stressed the centrality of class oppression. It also meant that many Kievans had little reason to take pride in their community or rally behind moderate or conservative forces during the revolutionary upheavals of 1917–1920.

The study of late-imperial Kiev underscores the fact that a political system which denies the great majority of its subjects the opportunity to make and carry out public policy cannot effectively govern a large, complex city. In its narrow representation, indifference, and limited effectiveness, the late-imperial municipal order reflected the weaknesses of tsarist polity as a whole, for a system with such limited public participation cannot effectively govern a country either. The ultimate collapse of both the tsarist and communist orders attests to that.

For all of the inequities, injustices, and problems cited in this study, however, the nineteenth and early twentieth centuries were in many ways a grand period in Kiev's history, for they were years of tremendous growth

24. The Mykhailivsky (St. Michael's of the Golden Domes) Monastery. Originally built in 1108–1113, it was torn down in the 1930s.

and startling renascence. For the first time in centuries, Kiev resumed its position as one of Eurasia's largest cities. Sadly, after 1917 history would not be kind to Kiev. During the civil war, Ukraine was reduced to anarchy, and in 1919, as one army replaced another, five different governments rose and fell. Brutal pogroms again swept the city. In 1920 Kharkiv, more a center of Bolshevik support, was made the capital of Soviet Ukraine. Kiev became Ukraine's capital in 1934, at a time when communist fanatics were beginning to destroy many of the city's priceless architectural treasures. The Florivsky Monastery, whose baroque buildings had been redesigned by Andrej Melenski after the fire of 1811, was converted into a campus for metalworkers. Podil's Epiphany (Bohoiavlennia) Church (built in the 1690s), the Zolotoverkhy Mykhailiv Church (St. Michael of the Golden Domes, built in 1108–1113, renovated and enlarged in the seventeenth and eighteenth centuries), the Desiatynna Church (Church of the Tithes, built in 1828–1842), and the Borys and Hlib Church (built 1642) are examples of the many landmark buildings that were torn down as Stalin and his Ukrainian henchman Pavel Postyshev sought to stamp out Ukrainian national distinctiveness and pride.[18] Between 1936 and the arrival of the Nazi armies in 1941, Stalin's political police (NKVD) regularly murdered people in the basement of its Kiev headquarters and at Lukianivka Prison. A secret, fenced-off mass grave was established in a forest in nearby Bykivnia. Perhaps 120,000 victims were buried there; another estimate puts the figure as high as 225,000. Another 100,000 unmarked sites may exist throughout the territories of what was then the Soviet Union, a country "built on bones."[19]

On September 28, 1941, Nazi invaders posted two thousand notices throughout the city, ordering all Jews to appear at a certain intersection the following morning. Stories were circulated that Kiev's Jews were to be resettled. Instead, on September 29–30 more than 33,000 were shot in the ravine called Babi Yar, "a greater killing rate than that of the gas chambers at Auschwitz at their murderous peak."[20] On November 8, 1943, Moscow radio reported that only one Jew had been found alive in Kiev, which had a prewar Jewish population of 140,000.[21]

By the time of Kiev's liberation from the Nazi occupation in November 1943, some six thousand buildings had been destroyed, the Khreshchatyk and the central neighborhoods lay in ruins, and 200,000 people had lost their homes. After the war, rebuilt neighborhoods took on a uniform drabness. The Khreshchatyk is still Kiev's main street and its most notable symbol, but its architecture, from the 1950s, has been aptly called "Mussolini modern."[22]

Taking advantage of the profound changes initiated by Mikhail Gorbachev, Ukrainians declared themselves sovereign on July 16, 1990. In the spring of 1991, the Ukrainian parliament approved laws on freedom of conscience and religion, and work was begun on a new constitution. On August 24, 1991, after an abortive coup against Gorbachev and the reformers, Ukraine declared its independence and banned the Communist party. Ukrainians ratified their declaration of independence by an overwhelming margin in a referendum on December 1, 1991. A few weeks earlier, Ukraine's parliament adopted a nondiscriminatory citizenship law that gave full rights to all residents of the country.

Today Kiev (pop. 2,600,000) is the capital of the largest state in Europe after Russia. Although the economic hardships brought about by the transformation of the totalitarian communist order are severe, Kievans may be on the threshold of realizing the promise of the October Manifesto. For Kiev, better days seem to lie ahead.

NOTES

The following abbreviations are used throughout the Notes:

HUS   *Harvard Ukrainian Studies*
KES   *Kiev. Entsiklopedicheskii spravochnik* (Kiev: Ukrainskaia Sovet-
           skaia Entsiklopediia, 1986)
KS   *Kievskaia starina*
LR   *Letopis' revoliutsii*
OIKGOPO   *Ocherki istorii Kievskikh gorodskoi i oblastnoi partiinykh organ-
           izatsii* (Kiev: Politicheskaia literatura, 1981)
OPD   *Obshchestvenno-politicheskoe dvizhenie na Ukraine v 1863–64
           g.g.* (Kiev: Naukova dumka, 1964)
TsGIA   Tsentral'nyi gosudarstvennyi istoricheskii arkhiv
UCE   *Ukraine: A Concise Encyclopedia* (Clifton, N.J.: Ukrainian Ortho-
           dox Church of the USA, 1987)

CHAPTER I. THE EARLY HISTORY OF KIEV

1. The best estimates of Kiev's population come from Soviet archaeologists such as P. P. Tolochko. See his *Drevnii Kiev* (Kiev: Naukova dumka, 1983), 184–88, for example. For a good discussion of recent research on medieval Kiev, see David B. Miller, "The Kievan Principality in the Century before the Mongol Invasion: An Inquiry into Recent Research and Interpretation," *HUS* 10 (June 1986): 215–40. The estimates for Paris and London are on p. 222.

2. Iu. V. Belichko and V. P. Pidgora, *Kriz' viky. Kyiv v obrazotvorchomu mystetstvi XII–XX stolit'* (Kiev: Mystetstvo, 1982), 261–62 and illustrations 1–3. The earliest known representation of these legendary figures can be found in the Radziwill Chronicle, a fifteenth-century miniature copied from a twelfth- or thirteenth-century manuscript.

3. Omeljan Pritsak, "Kiev and All of Rus': The Fate of a Sacral Idea," *HUS* 10 (December 1986): 279. Working in Podil, a team from the Ukrainian Academy of Sciences' Institute of Archaeology, headed by Mykhailo Sahajdak, has unearthed the remnants of more than thirty log buildings, dating them back as far as the end of the ninth century. See Volodymyr I. Mezentsev, "The Emergence of the Podil and the Genesis of the City of Kiev: Problems of Dating," *HUS* 10 (June 1986): 52–61, for summaries of Soviet archaeological findings. Dendrochronological analysis, he notes on p. 55, is accurate to within one year.

4. Another interesting sketch of early Kiev is provided by John Callmer, "The Archaeology of Kiev to the End of the Earliest Urban Phase," *HUS* 11 (December 1987): 323–53. Older ceramic fragments, Roman coins from the second century, and Byzantine coins from the sixth century have been found, but may have washed down from earlier settlements on the Dnipro or from settlements in the surrounding hills.

5. Orest Subtelny, *Ukraine: A History* (Toronto: University of Toronto Press, 1988), 25.

6. Ibid., 29.

7. Ibid., 34. A. Storozhenko, "Kiev trista let nazad," *KS* 3 (1894): 404 is one source that estimates ancient Kiev's churches at five hundred.

8. According to Miller, "The Kievan Principality," 217–23, despite the political problems, archaeological evidence indicates that the city of Kiev continued to grow in population and enjoy an ascendancy of prosperity until it was destroyed in 1240.

9. *Kyiv. Vchora, s'ogodni, zavtra* (Kiev: Mystetstvo, 1982), 28.

10. Subtelny, *Ukraine*, 106.

11. Ibid., 84, 87.

12. V. S. Ikonnikov, *Kiev v 1654–1855 gg. Istoricheskii ocherk'* (Kiev: Imperatorskii Universitet Sv. Vladimira, 1904), 5.

13. Ivan Pantiukhov, *Opyt sanitarnoi topografii i statistiki Kieva* (Kiev: Kievskii gubernskii statisticheskii komitet, 1877), 114. See also Ivan Funduklei, *Statisticheskoe opisanie Kievskoi gubernii* (St. Petersburg, 1852), pt. 1, 320.

14. Charles J. Halperin, "Kiev and Moscow: An Aspect of Early Muscovite Thought," *Russian History/Histoire Russe* 7 (1980): 312–13.

15. Ibid., 314–20.

16. V. Antonovich, "Kiev, ego sud'ba i znachenie s XIV po XVI stoletie (1362–1569)," *KS* 1 (1882): 35–37. See also Ikonnikov, *Kiev*, 4–5.

17. "Kievskoe predstavitel'stvo prezhniago vremeni," *KS* 5 (1882): 178–82. The magistracy generally consisted of twelve officials. For a discussion of the conflicts surrounding the granting of the Magdeburg Rights, see Iu. Iu. Kondufor, ed., *Istoriia Kieva. Drevnii srednevekovyi Kiev* (Kiev: Naukova dumka, 1982), 229–30. The rights were apparently extended in a series of decrees in 1494–1497, 1499, 1503, and 1514.

18. For example, conflicts over jurisdiction led to their affirmation in 1518 and in 1544. In *The Kievan Academy in the Seventeenth Century* (Ottawa: University of Ottawa Press, 1977), 3, Alexander Sydorenko argues that under Polish rule, Kiev's burghers lost authority because, as semiautonomous jurisdictions, they were not entitled to participate in the Polish diets.

19. It is uncertain when the Magdeburg Rights were translated from Polish into Russian, but according to Ikonnikov, *Kiev*, 150–51, a copy translated between 1732 and 1735 was discovered early in the nineteenth century.

20. Frank E. Sysyn, *Between Poland and the Ukraine: The Dilemma of Adam Kysil, 1600–1653* (Cambridge: Harvard University Press, 1985), 24.

21. Subtelny, *Ukraine*, 108.

22. Nikolai Zakrevskii, *Letopis' i opisanie goroda Kieva* (Moscow: Universitetskaia tipografiia, 1858), 24. At least one Orthodox church was nevertheless rebuilt in the ensuing decades.

23. Subtelny, *Ukraine*, 94–95. See also Antonovich, "Kiev, ego sud'ba," 40–41.

24. Subtelny, *Ukraine*, 95–96. See also Zenon Kohut, *Russian Centralism and Ukrainian Autonomy: Imperial Absorption of the Hetmanate, 1760s–1830s* (Cambridge: Harvard Ukrainian Research Institute, 1988), chap. 2.

25. Sydorenko, *Kievan Academy*, 14. The Orthodox brotherhoods probably originated in medieval times for the purpose of maintaining churches and supplying them with icons, candles, and books.

26. Iu. Iu. Kondufor, ed., *Istoriia Kieva. Kiev perioda pozdnego feodalizma i kapitalizma* (Kiev: Naukova dumka, 1983), 97–98. Part of a four-volume set, this volume was written under the editorship of B. G. Sarbei. Hereafter cited as *Kiev perioda pozdnego feodalizma i kapitalizma*. See also Ikonnikov, *Kiev*, 15.

27. Sydorenko, *Kievan Academy*, 1. By 1817, when it became a theological seminary, Kiev Academy may have produced more than twenty thousand graduates. See Viktor Domanyts'kyi, "Akademichnyi tradytsii Kyievo-Mohyllians'ko-Mazepyns'koi Akademii," *Naukovi zapysky Ukrains'koho tekhinichnoho instytutu*, 5 (1964): 3.

28. V. B. Antonovich, *Monografiia po istorii zapadnoi i iugo-zapadnoi Rossii* (Kiev: E. Ia. Fedorov, 1885), 198–220.

29. M. F. Berlyns'kyi, *Istoriia mista Kyeva* (Kiev: Naukova dumka, 1991), 167. This is a reprint of a work written in 1798–1799.

30. See the surveys in Mezentsev, "Emergence of the Podil," and Callmer, "Archaeology of Kiev." Details may be found in Tolochko, *Drevnii Kiev*; and K. N. Gupalo, *Podol v drevnem Kieve* (Kiev: Naukova dumka, 1982).

31. Belichko and Pidgora, *Kriz' viky*, 262. There are several mock-ups in Kiev museums that re-create medieval Kiev and provide an indication of its splendor. One such mock-up, at the Ukrainian History Museum, was created by Oleksandr Kazanskii. In the nineteenth century Merchant Square was called Contract Square.

32. Ivan Funduklei, *Obozrenie Kieva v otnoshenii k drevnostiam* (Kiev, 1847), ix. See also Zakrevskii, *Letopis' i opisanie*, 24–28.

33. Belichko and Pidgora, *Kriz' viky*, 264–65 and illustrations 17–22. The Golden Gate was restored in 1981–1982 to commemorate Kiev's fifteen hundredth anniversary.

34. Pantiukhov, *Opyt*, 101.

35. Linda Gordon, *Cossack Rebellions* (Albany: State University of New York Press, 1983), 75.

36. Kohut, *Russian Centralism*, 24. See also Sysyn, *Between Poland and the Ukraine*, 22–23.

37. Subtelny, *Ukraine*, 116.

38. Ibid., 125.

39. Ibid., 129. See also I. Kamanin, "Kievliane i Bogdan Khmel'nitskii v ikh vzaimnykh otnosheniiakh," *KS* 2 (1888): 72–73.

40. Funduklei, *Statisticheskoe*, pt, 1, 320–21; Zakrevskii, *Letopis' i opisanie*, 26–27.

41. Ikonnikov, *Kiev*, 72. See also pp. 28–30, 47.

42. Ibid., 68.

43. "Kievskoe predstavitel'stvo prezhniago vremeni," 182. I. Kamanin, "Poslednie gody samoupravleniia Kieva po Magdeburgskomu pravu," *KS* 9 (1888): 603–5. See also Antonovich, *Monografiia*, 253–54.

44. "Kievskoe predstavitel'stvo prezhniago vremeni," 184–85.

45. *Kiev perioda pozdnego feodalizma i kapitalizma*, 87.

46. Ikonnikov, *Kiev*, 33. The Moldavian hussars required 1,489 "apartments," about 60 percent of the total number available in the city.

47. A. Andrievskii, "Kievskie smuty srediny proshlago stoletiia," *KS* 12 (1886): 667.

48. Orest Subtelny, *The Mazepists: Ukrainian Separatism in the Early Eighteenth Century* (New York: Columbia University Press, 1981), 100.

49. John Bushnell, *Moscow Graffiti: Language and Subculture* (Boston: Unwin Hyman, 1990), 5.

50. Pantiukhov, *Opyt*, 109.

51. Institut istorii Akademii nauk USSR, *Istoriia Kieva* (Kiev: Akademiia nauk Ukrainskoi SSR, 1963), 1:192.

52. Andrievskii, "Kievskie smuty," 685–89.

53. I. Luchitskii, "Kiev v 1766 godu," *KS* 1–3 (1888): 73.

54. Ikonnikov, *Kiev*, 67.

55. Luchitskii, "Kiev v 1766 godu," 74. Interestingly, bands of outlaws known as *haidamaky*, often composed of runaway serfs, operated from Podil, raiding the rich estates of the surrounding landowners. Sometimes these bandits attacked monasteries that were allied with the Russian state or the Hetmanate, and both authorities sought to suppress the *haidamak* movement.

56. Kohut, *Russian Centralism*, 159.

57. For example, see *Kiev perioda pozdnego feodalizma i kapitalizma*, 66–67. The anonymous author of "Kievskoe predstavitel'stvo prezhniago vremeni" comes to a similar conclusion (179–81).

58. Kohut, *Russian Centralism*, 288. Ikonnikov, *Kiev*, 40, takes a similar view.

CHAPTER II. THE GROWTH OF METROPOLITAN KIEV

1. Ikonnikov, *Kiev*, 58–59.

2. Funduklei, *Statisticheskoe*, pt. 1, 323–24. Billington is quoted from *The Icon and the Axe*, in Albert J. Schmidt, *The Architecture and Planning of Classical Moscow: A Cultural History* (Philadelphia: American Philosophical Society, 1989), 4. See also p. 41 for Catherine's fears of Moscow.

3. Cited in Ikonnikov, *Kiev*, 90–93.

4. For descriptions of the fair, see ibid., 347–48; Leszek Podhorodecki, *Dzieje Kijowa* (Warsaw: Książka i Wiedza, 1982), 187; and *Kontraktovyi ukazatel' v pamiat o stoletii kontraktov 1797–1897* (Kiev: I. I. Chokolov, 1897).

5. From the poet V. Izmailov, cited in V. Gorlenko, "Kiev v 1799 godu," *KS* 3 (1885): 586.

6. Cited in Podhorodecki, *Dzieje Kijowa*, 183.

7. Ikonnikov, *Kiev*, 151. See pp. 79 and 124 for the population figures.

8. Kamanin, "Poslednie gody samoupravleniia," *KS* 5 (1888): 140–42.

9. Cited in Ikonnikov, *Kiev*, 126.

10. Sydorenko, *Kievan Academy*, 99.

11. *KS* 11 (1903): 60; Ikonnikov, *Kiev*, 190–91.

12. Ikonnikov, *Kiev*, 162, 324.

13. V. P. Teplyts'kyi, *Reforma 1861 roku i agrarny vidnosyny na Ukraini* (Kiev: Akademiia nauk Ukrainskoi SSR, 1959), 38. Twenty-eight percent came from Kharkiv, 23 percent from Bessarabia (now Moldova), and 9 percent from Poltava and Katerynoslav (Ekaterinoslav) Provinces.

14. Ikonnikov, *Kiev*, 204; Funduklei, *Statisticheskoe*, pt. 3, 13–15. Smila (Smela) became the center of the industry in Kiev Province. The first steam-powered refinery was apparently built in 1843 by former Ukrainian serfs, Barons Iakhnenko and Simirenko.

15. See R. Livshits, *Razmeshchenie promyshlennosti v dorevoliutsionnoi Rossii* (Moscow: Akademiia nauk SSSR, 1955), esp. 42, 118–21, 212.

16. A. M. Anfimov, *Krupnoe pomeshchich'e khoziaistvo evropeiskoi Rossii (konets XIX–nachalo XX veka)* (Moscow: Nauka, 1969), 169, 267. For information on monuments see P. Alabin and P. Konovalov, *Sbornik svedeniia nastoiashchem o sostoianii gorodskago khoziaistva v glavneishikh gorodakh Rossii* (Samara: I. P. Novikov, 1889), pt. 2, 903. Bobrinskoi was only the second person to be so honored in the century. Monuments to St. Vladimir, celebrating the Christianization of Russia and of Kiev, were constructed in 1802 and 1853 respectively. A monument to the Cossack leader Bohdan Khmelnytsky was finished in 1888, one to Nicholas I begun in 1887.

17. Teplyts'kyi, *Reforma 1861*, 33–36. The estimate of the number of wagons for the Khreshchenska Fair was made by Ivan Aksakov and reprinted in Teplyts'kyi, 33. In the early 1860s, of 392 Ukrainian town fairs and 2,008 rural fairs, half were in Kharkiv or Poltava Provinces. For Kiev Province's trade figures, see N. N. Leshchenko, *Krest'ianskoe dvizhenie na Ukraine v sviazi s provedeniem reformy 1861 g.* (Kiev: Akademiia nauk Ukrainskoi SSR, 1959), 46–47.

18. Funduklei, *Statisticheskoe*, pt. 1, 349–56.

19. Leshchenko, *Krest'ianskoe dvizhenie*, 34, 38.

20. Teplyts'kyi, *Reforma 1861*, 190.

21. *Kiev perioda pozdnego feodalizma i kapitalizma*, 126, 195. In discussing the municipal reform of 1870 and the size of the city electorates, V. A. Nardova, *Gorodskoe samoupravlenie v Rossii v 60-kh—nachale 90-kh godov XIX v.* (Leningrad: Nauka, 1984), 61, table 1, lists an 1870 population of 70,591.

22. Nikolai Zakrevskii, *Opisanie Kieva* (Moscow: V. Grachev, 1868), 131.

23. *Dvadtsatipiatiletie Kievskoi birzhi, 1869–94 g.* (Kiev, 1895), 130.

24. Pantiukhov, *Opyt*, 287. See also Funduklei, *Statisticheskoe*, pt. 1, 334.

25. "Kiev v sorokovykh godakh," *KS* 5 (1899): 66–68.

26. Belichko and Pidgora, *Kriz' viki*, 290.

27. For the founding of the financial institutions, see *Dvadtsatipiatiletie Kievskoi birzhi*, 139. For descriptions of the avenue, see Podhorodecki, *Dzieje Kijowa*, 176–77; M. L. Shul'kevich and T. D. Dmitrenko, *Kiev* (Kiev: Budivel'nyk, 1978), 92; Starozhil, *Kiev v vos'midesiatykh godakh* (Kiev: Petr Barskii, 1910), 3, 88; and Michael F. Hamm, "Continuity and Change in Late Imperial

Kiev," in Michael F. Hamm, ed., *The City in Late Imperial Russia* (Bloomington: Indiana University Press, 1986), 84, 88. *Kontraktovyi ukazatel'*, 31, published in 1897, notes that the Khreshchatyk alone had electric lights at that time.

28. *Kiev perioda pozdnego feodalizma i kapitalizma*, 120–22. For the Arsenal, see Belichko and Pidgora, *Kriz' viky*, 301 and illustration 161.

29. *Dvadtsatipiatiletie Kievskoi birzhi*, 151–52. Industrialization continued to be fueled by the sugar industry throughout the region. Examples include Count Branicki's facility in Bila Tserkva (Belaia Tserkov), built in 1855 and expanded in 1875, and another enterprise owned by Poles, the Plahecky & Tyszkewicz mill, built in Berdychiv in 1878. See also Podhorodecki, *Dzieje Kijowa*, 178–79. *Istoriia Kieva*, 340, gives a population figure of 154,586 for 1884.

30. P. G. Ryndziunskii, *Krest'iane i gorod v kapitalisticheskoi Rossii vtoroi poloviny XIX veka* (Moscow, Nauka, 1983), 158–59.

31. "Kievskaia pochta v 1731 g.," *KS* 1 (1898): 11; Zakrevskii, *Opisanie*, 127, 129.

32. Ikonnikov, *Kiev*, 199; *Dvadtsatipiatiletie Kievskoi birzhi*, 142–43.

33. *Dvadtsatipiatiletie Kievskoi birzhi*, 144–49.

34. Patricia Herlihy, *Odessa: A History, 1794–1914* (Cambridge: Harvard Ukrainian Research Institute, 1986), 216–17. Tariffs and the fact that Königsberg was close to northern European markets also may have contributed to this fact.

35. *Dvadtsatipiatiletie Kievskoi birzhi*, 149–50, 152; Podhorodecki, *Dzieje Kijowa*, 179; and *Gorodskoe delo* (St. Petersburg) 13–14 (1915): 729–30.

36. Nardova, *Gorodskoe samoupravlenie*, 14–29.

37. Ibid., 61, table 1.

38. See ibid., 53–56; and *Kievskii telegraf* (Kiev), Jan. 8, 11, 22, and 27, 1871.

39. Nardova, *Gorodskoe samoupravlenie*, 84–88; for Eisman, see Starozhil, *Kiev*, 70–72, and Hamm, "Continuity," 100–101; for Diakov, see *Gorodskoe delo* 6 (1911): 656–66. A street was named for the popular Diakov.

40. *Kievskii telegraf*, Jan. 8 and 27, 1871, provides a rough breakdown of each curia by occupation. In its Jan. 11 editorial, the paper noted that no Jews had been elected in the first two curiae. On Jan. 27 the paper published a list of those elected to the third curia. Judging from the names, no Jews were elected.

41. Podhorodecki, *Dzieje Kijowa*, 183.

42. "Dnevnik kontraktovicha," *Kievskaia gazeta* (Kiev), Feb. 13, 1905.

43. *Kievskoe slovo* (Kiev), Feb. 13, 1902.

44. Professor O. O. Eikhelman wrote frequently on city politics for the paper *Kievskoe slovo*. See his Jan. 21, 1902, editorial, for example. There were many additional articles over the following weeks. *Kievskaia gazeta*, Jan. 4, 1902, carried the story on the New York election.

45. "Otdykh," *Kievskoe slovo*, Aug. 31, 1903.

46. Data are from the City Statistical Bureau and were published in *Kievskaia gazeta*, Sept. 14 and 26, 1905.

47. *Obzor' deiatel'nosti Kievskoi gorodskoi dumy za chetyrekhletie 1906–10 gg.* (Kiev, 1910), 81.

48. Tsen. statis. kom. MVD, *Goroda Rossii v 1910 godu* (St. Petersburg, 1914), passim.

49. *Izvestiia Kievskoi gorodskoi dumy* (Kiev) 1 (1915): 153.

50. *Gorodskoe delo* 11–12 (1910): 750; 19 (1910): 1347; 20 (1910): 1410.

51. *Utro Rossii* (Moscow), Sept. 21, 1913. See the Sept. 18 issue for the parody. See also *Rech'* (St. Petersburg), Sept. 18, 19, 1913.

52. *Kievskaia mysl'* (Kiev), Sept. 7, 10, 1912.

53. Robert W. Thurston, *Liberal City, Conservative State: Moscow and Russia's Urban Crisis, 1906–1914* (New York: Oxford University Press, 1987), 47. See also Joseph Bradley, *Muzhik and Muscovite: Urbanization in Late Imperial Russia* (Berkeley and Los Angeles: University of California Press, 1985) 36–40.

54. *Bessarabskaia zhizn'* (Kishinev), May 30, 1913. Kharkiv's income from enterprises was 2,112,444 rubles, Kiev's 484,110 rubles. Income from property taxes in Kharkiv was 944,632 rubles, in Kiev 1,096,300 rubles.

55. These views are found in correspondence pertaining to two loan applications from Kiev in TsGIA, *fond* 1288, *opis'* 7, *delo* 184 (1913), p. 64.

56. Storozhenko, "Kiev trista," *KS* 3 (1894): 409; Pantiukhov, *Opyt*, 427; Starozhil, *Kiev*, 10, 13. The 1874 figure is from *Kiev perioda pozdnego feodalizma i kapitalizma*, 205.

57. A. N. Gusev, *Khar'kov. Ego proshloe i nastoiashchee* (Khar'kov, 1902), 69–70; *Iuzhnyi krai* (Khar'kov), June 23, 1905.

58. *Kievskoe slovo*, May 1, 1905. See also *Otchet' sanitarnago otdeleniia Kievskoi gorodskoi upravy. Kholernaia epidemiia 1907 goda v g. Kieve* (Kiev, 1908), 10, 24–31.

59. *Izvestiia Moskovskoi gorodskoi dumy* (Moscow) 2 (1912): 41–42. See also *Kievskaia mysl'*, May 6, 1914; and Hamm, "Continuity," 89.

60. Pantiukhov, *Opyt*, 107–8.

61. Ikonnikov, *Kiev*, 45–46.

62. Ibid., 42–44; *KES*, 385; and Pantiukhov, *Opyt*, 314. John T. Alexander, "Reconsiderations of Plague in Early Modern Russia, 1500–1800," *Jahrbucher für Geschichte Ost Europas*, 34, no. 2 (1986): 253, makes reference to the near-riot in Kiev. According to Schmidt, *Architecture*, 41, in Moscow an estimated sixty thousand may have died, one-quarter of its inhabitants.

63. Pantiukhov, *Opyt*, 173.

64. Ibid., 142, 232.

65. For the first seven decades of the nineteenth century, Pantiukhov's study (ibid.), based largely on the registry books kept by the Orthodox church parishes (some of which went back to 1769) and on Catholic and Lutheran parish registries, is the best source for public health data. See p. 168 for 1848 and pp. 129–30 for 1831. About 7 percent of the entire population died in 1831, but from all causes. On p. 325 Pantiukhov writes, ambiguously: "In all of the cholera epidemics more than 5 percent of the inhabitants of the guberniia died and up to 15 of the inhabitants of Kiev." The absence of a word after "15" implies that Pantiukhov is referring to a percentage.

66. "Mery protiv kholery 1831 g.," *KS* 11 (1903): 72–73; Hamm, "Continuity," 89–90.

67. Pantiukhov, *Opyt*, 324–25.

68. Ibid., 327, 333.

69. Zakrevskii, *Opisanie*, 126–27; Ikonnikov, *Kiev*, 200. For the 1872 data, compiled by the statistician Iu. Giubner, see Pantiukhov, *Opyt*, 418.

70. *Kievskie vesti* (Kiev), Dec. 10, 1907.

71. Vladimir Porai-Koshchits, "Obshchestvenno-gigienicheskiia bani i kupal'-ni v Khar'kove," *Khar'kovskie gubernskie vedomosti* (Khar'kov), June 26, 27, 1881.

72. "Malenkii feleton," *Kievskie vesti*, Nov. 28, 1907.

73. *Kievskoe slovo*, Apr. 2, 1905, editorial.

74. *Kievskaia mysl'*, Jan. 26, 1914. For the reference to bathing, see Starozhil, *Kiev*, 9–10.

75. Ikonnikov, *Kiev*, 201–2.

76. Pantiukhov, *Opyt*, 292–93.

77. *Kievskoe slovo*, Feb. 19, 1902. The council had the following committees: general auditing, water supply, sewers, legality of actions, sanitation, slaughterhouse, city theater, woods and fields, quartering of troops, bazaar supervision, city gardens, port construction, city hospital, fire brigade, streets, schools, tram, property assessment, and circus construction.

78. See *Kievskaia gazeta*, June 28, 1903, and Jan. 5, 1905, editorial. The fact that there was no city pawnshop also hurt the poor; private pawnshops charged interest of 24 percent.

79. *Kievskaia gazeta*, Nov. 1, 1904, editorial.

80. *Deiatel'nost' obshchestva dnevnykh priiutov dlia detei rabochego klassa za 1875–1911 g.* (Kiev, 1913), 51. This lottery had raised sixteen thousand rubles for the shelters in 1911. See also *Kievskoe slovo*, Mar. 12, 1905.

81. "Memuary," *Kievskaia gazeta*, Nov. 3, 1904.

82. *Kievskaia gazeta*, May 5, 1904, editorial.

83. *Obzor' deiatel'nosti*, 14, 29–31.

84. Count Tarnowski, cited in Podhorodecki, *Dzieje Kijowa*, 174–75.

85. *Kiev perioda pozdnego feodalizma i kapitalizma*, 193.

86. "Russkaia zhizn," *Kievskaia mysl'*, June 6, 1914. The paper listed thirty-one church parish schools. *Kiev perioda pozdnego feodalizma i kapitalizma*, 385, gives the figure of seventy parish schools for 1911. See also *Gorodskoe delo* 13–14 (1913): 891. In 1913 about 15 percent of the city budget was being funneled into education.

87. *Kiev perioda pozdnego feodalizma i kapitalizma*, 260, 390.

88. Starozhil, *Kiev*, 6–10; and "Plod gorodskoi reformy 1892 g.," *Kievskaia gazeta*, Oct 22, 1904.

89. Tsen. statis. kom. MVD, *Goroda Rossii v 1904* (St. Petersburg, 1906), passim.

90. For one columnist's view on Kiev hospitals, see "Obo vsem, *Kievskoe slovo*, Aug. 26, 1903. Hospital-bed data are found in *Istoriia Kieva*, 356, 481; and *Kiev perioda pozdnego feodalizma i kapitalizma*, 205.

91. Daniel R. Brower, *The Russian City between Tradition and Modernity, 1850–1900* (Berkeley and Los Angeles: University of California Press, 1990), 125–26.

92. *KS* 10 (1900): 23–24.

93. *Kievskaia gazeta*, June 15, 1903.

94. "Memuary," *Kievskaia gazeta*, Nov. 13, 1904.

95. For Solomenka, see *Izvestiia Moskovskoi gorodskoi dumy* 1 (1913): 27–28; and Hamm, "Continuity," 91. For Demievka, see *Kievskaia gazeta*, Dec. 13, 1904. The reasons for the petition's rejection were not stated.

96. *Istoriia Kieva*, 540.

CHAPTER III. POLISH KIEV

1. Storozhenko, "Kiev trista," *KS* 2 (1894): 220–24; Ikonnikov, *Kiev*, 98–99. The category of Russians would have included "Little Russians" (Ukrainians) at this time.

2. Podhorodecki, *Dzieje Kijowa*, 158–59.

3. Ikonnikov, *Kiev*, 92–93.

4. K. Glinka, cited in Podhorodecki, *Dzieje Kijowa*, 187.

5. Ikonnikov, *Kiev*, 100–101.

6. O. Levitskii, "Trevozhnye gody. Ocherk' iz obshchestvennoi i politicheskoi zhizni g. Kieva i Iugo. zapad. kraia v 1811–12 g.g.," *KS* 10 (1891): 5.

7. Ibid., 9–10.

8. Ibid., 19; pt. 2, *KS* 11 (1891): 170–75.

9. For general accounts of Kiev's role in the preparation of the Decembrist uprising, see *Kiev perioda pozdnego feodalizma i kapitalizma*, 135–41; and "Kiev v istorii dekabristov," *Kievskie otkliki* (Kiev), Dec. 18, 1905. See also Podhorodecki, *Dzieje Kijowa*, 148–51; M. Hrushevskyi, *Ocherk' istorii Ukrainskogo naroda* (St. Petersburg: Obshchestvennaia pol'za, 1911), 430; and R. F. Leslie, *Polish Politics and the Revolution of November 1830* (London: Athlone Press, 1956), 113–14.

10. Podhorodecki, *Dzieje Kijowa*, 140. For one nationalist attack, see V. Ia. Shul'gin, "Iugo-zapadnyi krai pod upravleniem D. G. Bibikova (1838–1853)," *Drevniaia i novaia Rossiia* 5 (1879): 5–32 and 6 (1879): 89–131. Shul'gin called the Contract Fair and the fairs at Berdychiv and Iarmolyntsi "convention spots" for Polish insurrectionaries.

11. *Kiev perioda pozdnego feodalizma i kapitalizma*, 94; Berlyns'kyi, *Istoriia mista Kyeva*, 164.

12. *Kiev perioda pozdnego feodalizma i kapitalizma*, 101. At this time, the Cave Monastery took a special interest in publishing anti-Catholic tracts in Polish.

13. Ikonnikov, *Kiev*, 110–113.

14. Podhorodecki, *Dzieje Kijowa*, 162; "Zapiski Ivana Matveicha Sbitneva," *KS* 17 (1887): 460, 651–53. V. S. Shandra, "Pochatkova ta serednia osvita u Kyevi v pershii polovyni XIX st.," *Arkhivy Ukrainy* 5 (1980): 63–67, discusses educational opportunity in Kiev in the first half of the nineteenth century. Based largely on *fond* 707 of the Central State Historical Archive in Kiev, the article does not discuss national issues as they pertained to education, however.

15. Norman Davies, *God's Playground: A History of Poland in Two Volumes* (New York: Columbia University Press, 1982), vol. 2, *1795 to the Present*, 320.

16. Podhorodecki, *Dzieje Kijowa*, 151.

17. Jan Tabiś, *Polacy na uniwersytecie Kijowskim, 1834–1863* (Cracow: Wydawnictwo Literackie Kraków, n.d.), 5.

18. Cited in Ikonnikov, *Kiev*, 167. See also Podhorodecki, *Dzieje Kijowa*, 151; and I. Kamanin, "Posledniaia samozashchita g. Kieva," *KS* 7 (1882): 186–88, for the few details we have for Kiev during the 1830–1831 insurrection.

19. Ikonnikov, *Kiev*, 132–34.

20. "Zapiski Ivana Matveicha Sbitneva," 655–57; Shul'gin, "Iugo-zapadnyi," 5 (1879): 11–13.

21. Podhorodecki, *Dzieje Kijowa*, 162; Tabiś, *Polacy*, 10. Shandra, "Pochatkova," 65–67, notes that at midcentury the Podil district school had 148 students, the second district school (in Pechersk) had 71, while the Second *Gymnasium* had 518 students.

22. Tabiś, *Polacy*, 9.

23. Ibid., 27–28. For a general discussion of Count Uvarov and Russian attitudes toward higher education at this time, see James T. Flynn, *The University Reform of Tsar Alexander I, 1802–1835* (Washington: Catholic University Press of America, 1988), esp. chap. 6.

24. Tabiś, *Polacy*, 21–22. Professors were poorly paid, many held second jobs, and turnover was frequent.

25. Ikonnikov, *Kiev*, 207, 217–19.

26. G. I. Marakhov, *Kievskii universitet v revoliutsionno-demokraticheskom dvizhenii* (Kiev: Vishcha shkola, 1984), 18–22. See also Ikonnikov, *Kiev*, 224; Tabiś, *Polacy*, 49–57; Podhorodecki, *Dzieje Kijowa*, 155–56.

27. Tabiś, *Polacy*, 50–53, 56–62. Tabiś points out that there is little evidence that Kiev's professors were involved in the conspiracy.

28. Cited in Podhorodecki, *Dzieje Kijowa*, 162.

29. Leonid Grossman, "Bal'zak v Rossii," *Literaturnoe nasledstvo* (Moscow) 31–32 (1937): 226. See also Ikonnikov, *Kiev*, 189.

30. Funduklei, *Statisticheskoe*, pt. 1, 203.

31. Cited in Ikonnikov, *Kiev*, 190.

32. Ibid., 232–33; G. I. Marakhov, *Sotsial'no-politicheskaia bor'ba na Ukraine v 50–60-e godakh XIX veka* (Kiev: Vishcha shkola, 1981), 59–61.

33. *Stoletie Kievskago universiteta Sv. Vladimira* (Belgrade: Komitet Kievskikh professorov v Liubliane, 1935), 80–81. This picture of student life was originally published in *Kievlianin* in 1876. See also Hamm, "Continuity," 107.

34. Shul'gin, "Iugo-zapadnyi," 5 (1879): 23–24.

35. *Stoletie Kievskago universiteta*, 81. This reference is to the 1850s. Students sought to emulate behavior at Derpt University at this time. See also Hamm, "Continuity," 106.

36. A. Z. Baraboi, "Pravoberezhnaia Ukraina v 1848 g.," *Istoricheskie zapiski* 34 (1950): 97, 104; See Tabiś, *Polacy*, 66–73, for Polish activity in Kiev in the 1840s.

37. Ikonnikov, *Kiev*, 228.

38. Tabiś, *Polacy*, 72–73.

39. Ikonnikov, *Kiev*, 238, 249.

40. Agaton Giller, cited in Podhorodecki, *Dzieje Kijowa*, 168. See also Tabiś, *Polacy*, 75–83; For Herzen's influence, see G. I. Marakhov, "Iz istorii Pol'sko-

Ukrainskikh revoliutsionnykh sviazei v 50-kh—60-kh godakh XIX veka," in *Revoliutsionnaia Rossiia i revoliutsionnaia Pol'sha* (Moscow: Nauka, 1967): 442.

41. Tabiś, *Polacy*, 85–86.

42. The memoirs of both Włodzimierz Milowicz and Wacław Lasocki state that Kiev and Kharkiv students organized a joint conspiracy, but it is more likely that the two movements organized separately from one another. See G. I. Marakhov, *Pol'skoe vosstanie 1863 g. na pravoberezhnoi Ukraine* (Kiev: Kievskii universitet, 1967), 20, 38. See also *OPD*, 136–37. A. Z. Baraboi, "Khar'kovsko-Kievskoe revoliutsionnoe tainoe obshchestvo, 1856–60," *Istoricheskie zapiski* 52 (1955): 235–66, also tends to see a jointly organized conspiracy at the two Ukrainian universities.

43. For a discussion of Antonovych, see Tadeusz Bobrowski, *Pamietnik mojego żyćia* (Warsaw: Panstwowy Institut Wydawniczy, 1979), 2:235–44.

44. V. Miiakovskii, "'Kievskaia Gromada' (Iz istorii Ukrainskogo obshchestvennogo dvizheniia 60-kh godov)," *LR* 4 (1924): 130–31. Tabiś, *Polacy*, 95–96.

45. Marakhov, *Pol'skoe*, 38; idem, *Sotsialno-politicheskaia bor'ba*, 102. Tabiś, *Polacy*, 90–91, notes the absence of archival information on Trojnicki.

46. *OPD*, 454–55.

47. Ibid. See also Bobrowski, *Pamietnik*, 1:213; Tabiś, *Polacy*, 98–105; Marakhov, *Sotsial'no-politicheskaia bor'ba*, 61–65.

48. Marakhov, *Pol'skoe vosstanie*, 75–80, 143.

49. Marakhov, *Sotsial'no-politicheskaia bor'ba*, 140–50; *OPD*, 136–37; Tabiś, *Polacy*, 107–110, 133–34. The architect Beretti died in 1842. His son, a professor of architecture at St. Vladimir, apparently lived in the Beretti home at this time.

50. Podhorodecki, *Dzieje Kijowa*, 159; Marakhov, *Pol'skoe vosstanie*, 75–97; idem, *Kievskii universitet*, 68.

51. Tabiś, *Polacy*, 135. Many of these students applied for readmission after the insurrection.

52. From testimony of May 28, 1863, in *OPD*, 138–39. For Gesse's warnings, see *OPD*, 62–63.

53. Podhorodecki, *Dzieje Kijowa*, 172. See A. Merder', "Gorodskoe opolchenie v Kieve, 1863 g.," *KS* 1 (1900): 2, for the reference to the militia. Annenkov's telegram may be found in *OPD*, 85. R. F. Leslie's study of the insurrection says almost nothing about Kiev, thereby implying that the city played an insignificant role. See *Reform and Insurrection in Russian Poland 1856–1865* (London: Athlone Press, 1963), esp. 160, 222.

54. See Marakhov, *Pol'skoe vosstanie*, 170–85, and idem, *Sotsial'no-politicheskaia bor'ba*, 149–51. The witchcraft charge, later overturned by a higher court, and the allegations against the Jews are mentioned in A. Merder, "Dokumenty, izvestiia, i zametki," *KS* 1 (1900): 1–2. See also *Kiev perioda pozdnego feodalizma i kapitalizma*, 214, 300.

55. Marakhov, *Pol'skoe vosstanie*, 210. For the revolt's failure to get started in Podil Province, see 191–92.

56. Podhorodecki, *Dzieje Kijowa*, 172–73.

57. Marakhov, *Pol'skoe vosstanie*, 242. The letters were torn up and thrown into the Dnipro.

58. For the composition of the student body by religion, gender, and place of secondary schooling, see *Spisok studentov Imperatorskago universiteta Sv. Vladimira* . . . appended to *Universitetskie izvestiia* (Kiev) 18, no. 1 (1878): passim. Marakhov, *Kievskii universitet*, 83–84, supplies data on student participation in the insurrection.

59. Cited in Ikonnikov, *Kiev*, 318, 331.

60. Ibid., 325, 337.

61. Ibid., 329–30 n. 4.

62. Pantiukhov, *Opyt*, 238, 405–6.

63. *Kiev po perepisi 2 Marta 1874* (Kiev: Universitetskaia tipografiia, 1875), 138–53, 244–45.

64. N. V. Iukhneva, *Etnicheskii sostav i etnosotsial'naia struktura naseleniia Peterburga. Vtoraia polovina XIX—nachalo XX veka* (Leningrad: Nauka, 1984), 130, 204.

65. Starozhil, *Kiev*, 112; T. G. Snytko, "K voprosu o vzaimootnosheniiakh i sviazakh narodnichestva s pol'skim sotsial'no-revoliutsionnym dvizheniem v kontse 70kh—nachale 80kh godov XIX v.," in AN SSSR, *Revoliutsionnaia Rossiia i revoliutsionnaia Pol'sha* (Moscow: Nauka, 1967), esp. 222, 230–32, 244, 265, 281, 293.

66. Pavel Tuchapskii, *Iz perezhitogo. Devianostye gody* (Odessa: Gosudarstvennoe izdatel'stvo Ukrainy, 1923), 56–58. See also Podhorodecki, *Dzieje Kijowa*, 195.

67. R. F. Leslie, ed., *The History of Poland since 1863* (Cambridge: Cambridge University Press, 1980), 42. Leslie notes that the Polish population of St. Petersburg increased from 11,157 in 1864 to 70,000 in 1914 (p. 43). For 1897 see *Pervaia vseobshchaia perepis' naseleniia Rossiiskoi imperii, 1897 g.* (St. Petersburg: Tsentral'nyi statisticheskii komitet Ministerstva vnutrennikh del, 1904), 16:260–62.

68. TsGIA, *fond* 1288, *opis'* 5, *delo* 170 (1914), p. 130.

69. Podhorodecki, *Dzieje Kijowa*, 178, 193–94; "Iz Kieva," *Gorodskoe delo* 1 (1910). For Polish dominance of the Minsk electorate, see *Severo-zapadnaia zhizn'* (Minsk), Mar. 19, Apr. 2, Apr. 6, 1913.

70. Iukhneva, *Etnicheskii sostav*, 204. One study of a sugar refinery near Kiev in 1904 shows that of 647 workers, 420 were from Belarus, 355 (85 percent) of whom were illiterate. Those who were literate had generally learned to read in church schools. When questioned, even skilled workers at times did not know the name of the language they spoke, or referred to their language as "Orthodox" or some other faith. The study was made by the South Russian Technical Society. See *Kievskaia gazeta*, Nov. 15, 1904.

71. *Kievskaia gazeta*, Oct. 11 and 17, 1904. In a good year a Belarusian peasant might make eighty rubles per summer working in the south. In the summer of 1904, they apparently averaged only twenty-five rubles.

72. Abraham Ascher, *The Revolution of 1905: Russia in Disarray* (Stanford: Stanford University Press, 1988), 134.

73. *Kievskoe slovo*, Nov. 17, 1905.

74. "Poliaki ob Ukrainskom voprose," *Kievskie otkliki*, Nov. 17, 1905. See also its Nov. 10 and Dec. 1, 1905, editions, and *Kievlianin*, Feb. 3, 1906.

75. *Kievskaia mysl'*, Nov. 2, 1910. See also S. N. Shchegolev, *Ukrainskoe dvizhenie kak sovremennyi etap iuzhnorusskago separatizma* (Kiev, 1912), 464–66.

76. TsGIA, *fond* 1276, *opis'* 17, *delo* 183 (1911), p. 76.

CHAPTER IV. UKRAINIANS IN RUSSIAN KIEV

1. A. Andrievskii, "Arkhivnaia spravka o sostave Kievskago 'obshchestva' v 1782–1797 godakh," *KS* 2 (1894): 193, 202.

2. Kohut, *Russian Centralism*, 267, 276.

3. Andrievskii, "Arkhivnaia spravka," 193–97.

4. Subtelny, *Ukraine*, 226–27.

5. I. Sirii (Tyshchenko), cited in George Yury Boshyk, "The Rise of Ukrainian Political Parties in Russia, 1900–07: With Special Reference to Social Democracy" (Ph.D. diss., Oxford University, 1981), 26.

6. Ikonnikov, *Kiev*, 107–8; Andrievskii, "Arkhivnaia spravka," 194.

7. A. P. Ohloblyn, *Ocherki istorii ukrainskoi fabriki. Predkapitalisticheskaia fabrika* (Kiev: Gosudarstvennoe izdatel'stvo Ukrainy, 1925), 148–59. For reasons that are not clear, Kiev officials refused to allow them to build a refinery in the city.

8. Anfimov, *Krupnoe pomeshchich'e*, 169; Podhorodecki, *Dzieje Kijowa*, 179, 189. The Tereshchenko estates were spread among Kiev, Kharkiv, Orel, Kursk, Podil, Volyn, Chernihiv, and Katerynoslav Provinces.

9. Pantiukhov, *Opyt*, 100.

10. Kateryna Lazarevs'ka, "Kyivs'kyi tsekhy v druhii polovyni XVIII ta na pochatku XIX viku, *Zapysky Istorychnoi sektsii Ukrains'koho naukovoho tovarystva* 22 (1926): 280.

11. Ibid., 295–99.

12. A special storage pond for fish was built in 1791. According to *Kiev perioda pozdnego feodalizma i kapitalizma*, 68, this guild structure was unique to Kiev.

13. Vyacheslav Prokopovych (S. Cherepyn), *Pid zolotoiu korohvoiu* (Paris: U Paryzhi, 1943), 48, 51–53.

14. Lazarevs'ka, "Tsekhy," 282–88, 295; *KES*, 143.

15. Lazarevs'ka, "Tsekhy," 285.

16. Prokopovych, *Pid zolotoiu*, 63–64.

17. Lazarevs'ka, "Tsekhy," 285.

18. Pantiukhov, *Opyt*, 94.

19. Kohut, *Russian Centralism*, 291. See also V. Shcherbyna, "Borot'ba Kyiva za avtonomiiu," *Kyiv ta ioho okolytsia v istorii i pam'iatkakh. Zapysky Istorychnoi sektsii Ukrains'koi akademii nauk* 22 (1926): 210–15. Certainly one of the premier emblems of independence had disappeared when the great fire of 1811

destroyed the symbol of secular Kiev, its famous clock tower. From its second-floor balcony the results of mayoral elections and other important announcements had been given to the crowds below.

20. *Kiev perioda pozdnego feodalizma i kapitalizma*, 122.

21. Prokopovych, *Pid zolotoiu*, 63–69. See also M. I. Kulisher, "Evrei v Kieve. Istoricheskii ocherk," *Evreiskaia starina* 3 (1913): 359–62.

22. Funduklei, *Statisticheskoe*, pt. 1, 229, 380.

23. Iukhneva, *Etnicheskii sostav*, 155–56.

24. See "Egorenko," "Kanun i nachalo 1905 goda," in S. Kramer, *1905 v Khar'kove* (Khar'kov: Proletarii, 1925), 107.

25. Funduklei, *Statisticheskoe*, pt. 1, 381.

26. Ibid., pt. 3, 261–64. Typically, 875 rubles went to carpenters, 200 rubles to haulers of wood and other materials to the site, 170 to metalworkers who installed the roof, 160 to plasterers, 120 to day-worker handymen, 100 to stove tilers and setters, and so forth.

27. Ibid., 273–80. With regard to the bridge, labor needs changed in accordance with its stage of construction and the season, but about 2,100 workers were employed more or less continuously until it was finished. See p. 232. See also Pantiukhov, *Opyt*, 153, 305–7, 391–92.

28. Funduklei, *Statisticheskoe*, pt. 1, 229.

29. *Kievskaia mysl'*, Nov. 11, 1910; Starozhil, *Kiev*, 181–87; and Shcherbyna, "Borot'ba Kyiva," 216. For a reference to alleged Old Believer drinking habits, see Pantiukhov, *Opyt*, 391–92. The Barsky store advertised in *Kontraktovyi ukazatel'* in 1897.

30. D. I. Bagalei, *Istoriia Khar'kova za 250 let* (Khar'kov: Khar'kovskoe gorodskoe obshchestvennoe upravlenie, 1905), 2:240–42. Bagalei is speaking mostly of Left-Bank Ukraine but notes its similarity here to the Kiev region. See also p. 131. According to a study cited in Kohut, *Russian Centralism*, 287, in Chernihiv Province in the 1780s, there were more Russian than Ukrainian merchants, possibly because Ukrainian merchants in the Hetmanate lacked significant amounts of capital.

31. Bagalei, *Istoriia Khar'kova*, 2:169–73, surveys some of Kharkiv's great merchant families, Russian and Ukrainian.

32. Funduklei, *Statisticheskoe*, pt. 3, 544–45, 557–58.

33. Ibid., 533–42, contains a complete breakdown of the origins (but not the nationalities) of the fair's sellers for 1845–1849. See p. 558 for a breakdown of product by place of origin.

34. Zakrevskii, *Opisanie*, 318.

35. See *Dvadtsatipiatiletie Kievskoi birzhi*, 153. Christians predominated among those who held provisional merchant status. In 1886, a typical year, there were 67 provisional Christian and 15 provisional Jewish merchants in the first guild, 487 Christian and 31 Jewish merchants in the second guild. By 1893–1894, there were 647 provisional Christian merchants and 60 Jewish merchants in the two guilds combined.

36. Prokopovych, *Pid zolotoiu*, 64–72.

37. *Pervaia vseobshchaia perepis'*, 16:260–62.

38. Cited in Podhorodecki, *Dzieje Kijowa*, 184.

39. Marakhov, *Pol'skoe vosstanie*, 42.

40. Volodymyr Samiilenko, *Tvory v dvokh tomakh* (Kiev: Khudozhestvennaia literatura, 1958), 2:390.

41. Tabiś, *Polacy*, 60–61; Shchegolev, *Ukrainskoe dvizhenie*, 35.

42. Subtelny, *Ukraine*, 235. According to Ikonnikov, *Kiev*, 228, this was apparently the only secret organization at St. Vladimir at this time. Marakhov, *Kievskii universitet*, 26–29, provides information on its membership.

43. Jaromyr Marko Bojcun, "The Working Class and the National Question in Ukraine, 1880–1920" (Ph.D. diss., York University, 1985), 171–72, discusses the Brotherhood of Cyril and Methodius and Shevchenko's arrest. He notes that there is some difference of opinion as to whether Shevchenko was actually a member of the brotherhood. See also Belichko and Pidgora, *Kriz' viky*, 291 and illustration 120.

44. Tabiś, *Polacy*, 70.

45. Subtelny, *Ukraine*, 237.

46. Ibid., 280. Kostomarov was exiled to Saratov.

47. *Encyclopedia of Ukraine* (Toronto: University of Toronto Press, 1988), 2:244; Tabiś, *Polacy*, 130–31; Podhorodecki, *Dzieje Kijowa*, 170. For the reference to Dostoevsky and Turgenev, see Subtelny, *Ukraine*, 281.

48. F. Rawita-Gawroński, *Włodzimierz Antonowicz* (Lwow, 1912), 58.

49. Miiakovskii, " 'Kievskaia Gromada,' " 130–33; Tabiś, *Polacy*, 121–33. For a short summary of these matters in English, see Subtelny, *Ukraine*, 280–81. In 1878 Antonovych became a professor of history at St. Vladimir.

50. Marakhov, "Iz istorii," 447–49; Marakhov, *Kievskii universitet*, 58–60.

51. Marakhov, *Kievskii universitet*, 124, 128; idem, "Iz istorii," 443; Shchegolev, *Ukrainskoe dvizhenie*, 57–58.

52. Marakhov, *Pol'skoe vosstanie*, esp. 207, 211, 255.

53. "Khronika," *Zaria* (Kiev), June 11, 1881. For Dondukov-Korsakov, see Marakhov, *Sotsial'no-politicheskaia bor'ba*, 137–38.

54. Ikonnikov, *Kiev*, 297–99.

55. Ibid., 301–8, 313–14.

56. *Kievskii telegraf*, Apr. 2, 1871.

57. *Kiev perioda pozdnego feodalizma i kapitalizma*, 281.

58. Subtelny, *Ukraine*, 284. Volodymyr Samiilenko remembers coming to Kiev around this time and joining the "Chytanka" group, which tried to write popular booklets for the masses. "Our work was not very valuable in terms of Ukrainian scholarship," he recalls, but the group did gain a new appreciation for the older generation of Ukrainian intellectuals and the purity of their language. See Samiilenko, *Tvory*, 391–93.

59. Subtelny, *Ukraine*, 285.

60. Samiilenko, *Tvory*, 405–7; Starozhil, *Kiev*, 52–56.

61. Ikonnikov, *Kiev*, 261.

62. I. A. Ustynov, *Putevoditel' po g. Khar'kovu* (Khar'kov, 1881), 75.

63. Maksym Slavins'kyi, "Spomyny," *Ameryka* (Philadelphia) 109, 150 (1960); Evhen Chykalenko, *Spohady (1861–1907)* (New York: The Free Ukrainian Academy of Sciences in the U.S.A., 1955), 291, 296–97. At this time some of the Kiev *hromada*'s most active members were not Ukrainians at all, as in the case

of the Jewish sympathizer Viliam Berenshtam (1839–1904), an exile from St. Petersburg.

64. Samiilenko, *Tvory*, 407–8.

65. Chykalenko, *Spohady*, 86.

66. "Mestnaia khronika," *Khar'kovskie gubernskie vedomosti*, July 22, 1879.

67. The list of councilmen may be found in Alabin and Konovalov, *Sbornik svedenii*, 227–28. Serhii Bilokin, a historian and member of the Ukrainian Academy of Sciences in Kiev, analyzed the list for me, relying both on his extensive knowledge of the city's history and, in some cases, on surnames. Of the remainder, perhaps twenty-eight were Russians, six to eight were Jews, four were Poles, two were Germans, and the background of a dozen or so others is uncertain.

68. Evhen Olesnyts'kyi, *Storinky z moho zhyttia* (Lviv: Dilo, 1935), 70. Slavins'kyi, "Spomyny," 109 (1960), mentions these clergymen from the Cave Monastery, some of whom regarded themselves as "true Ukrainians."

69. Kohut, *Russian Centralism*, 233.

70. *Utro* (Khar'kov), Feb. 2, 13, 1914. While some clergymen may have disliked Shevchenko because of his association with Ukrainian nationalism, many churchmen also viewed his writing as "blasphemous and antichurch."

71. Starozhil, *Kiev*, 133–35.

72. Olesnyts'kyi, *Storinky*, 69.

73. Patricia Herlihy, cited in Boshyk, "The Rise of Ukrainian Political Parties," 14.

74. These data are discussed in Pantiukhov, *Opyt*, 276–78, 389–92. He observes on p. 392 that "the influence of the purely Great Russian population on the contemporary character of Kiev's population is insignificant."

75. Slavins'kyi, "Spomyny," 125 (1960).

76. George Y. Shevelov, "The Language Question in the Ukraine in the Twentieth Century (1900–1941)," *HUS* 10 (June 1986): 76–77.

77. *KES*, 492–94, 544; Starozhil, *Kiev*, 197–98; Shchegolev, *Ukrainskoe dvizhenie*, 67–70.

78. Slavins'kyi, "Spomyny," 106, 108, 144 (1960).

79. Valentyn Sadovs'kyi, "Students'ke zhyttia u Kyivi v 1904–1909 rokakh," *Z mynuloho. Zbirnyk*, vol. 2, *Pratsi Ukrains'koho naukovoho instytutu* (Warsaw, 1939), 49:5–6.

80. Bagalei, *Istoriia Khar'kova*, 2:131.

81. Konstantin Paustovsky, *The Story of a Life*, trans. Joseph Barnes (New York: Pantheon Books, 1982), 307.

82. Slavins'kyi, "Spomyny," 108 (1960).

83. A. Vychkov, "Delo o revoliutsionnykh kruzhakh v Kieve v 1879, 1880, i 1881 g.g.," *LR* 2 (1924): 53.

84. Ibid., 2 (1924): 42–53; 3 (1924): 164–65.

85. Osyp Hermaize, *Narysy z istorii revoliutsiinoho rukhu na Ukraini* (Kiev: Knyhospilka, 1926), 42; Boshyk, "The Rise of Ukrainian Political Parties," 31; Tuchapskii, *Iz perezhitogo*, 13–14, 25–34.

86. Dmytro Doroshenko, "Ukrains'kyi rukh 1890-ykh rokiv v osvitlenni Avstriis'koho konsula v Kyevi," *Z mynuloho. Zbirnyk. Pratsi Ukrains'koho nau-*

kovoho instytutu (Warsaw, 1938), 48:68–69. Kiev's Ukrainophiles were said to be less radical in their ideas than many priests trained at the Orthodox seminary in Kremianets.

87. Boshyk, "The Rise of Ukrainian Political Parties," 41. See also Shchegolev, *Ukrainskoe dvizhenie*, 444.

88. Boshyk, "The Rise of Ukrainian Political Parties," 42; Hermaize, *Narysy*, 42.

89. Boshyk, "The Rise of Ukrainian Political Parties," 56–59, 74–78, 103–7. Chykalenko, *Spohady*, 296, gives the figures for the *hromada*, which was headed by Volodymyr Naumenko.

90. Hermaize, *Narysy*, 102, 182; Sadovs'kyi, "Students'ke zhyttia," 8–9; Boshyk, "The Rise of Ukrainian Political Parties," 152–53, 158, 179, 183; and *Istoriia Ukrains'koi RSR. Ukraina v periode imperializma (1900–1917)* (Kiev: Naukova dumka, 1978), 4:70.

91. "V provintsii," *Kievskoe slovo*, Mar. 22, 1905.

92. *Kievlianin*, Dec. 7, 8, and 14, 1905; *Kievskie otkliki*, Nov. 10 and Dec. 2, 4, and 12, 1905; and *Kalendar' "Pros'vita" na r. 1910* (Kiev, 1910), 93.

93. S. Efremov, *Kievskie otkliki*, Nov. 12, 1905, editorial.

94. "K Malorossiiskomu voprosu na Volyni," *Volyn'* (Zhitomir), Oct. 29, 1905.

95. "Ukraina. Ukrainskiia partii," in L. Martov, et al., eds., *Obshchestvennoe dvizhenie v Rossii v nachale XX-go veka* (St. Petersburg: Obshchestvennaia pol'za, 1914), bk. 5, 3:298, estimates that Spilka had 3,000 members, 500 of them in trade unions. Boshyk, "The Rise of Ukrainian Political Parties," 359, suggests its membership may have peaked at between 6,000 and 7,000.

96. Boshyk, "The Rise of Ukrainian Political Parties," 334.

97. Sadovs'kyi, "Students'ke zhyttia," 10.

98. S. Efremov, "Biurokraticheskaia utopiia," *Russkoe bogatstvo* 3 (1910): 82, 90, 100, 106–7.

99. Chykalenko, *Spohady*, 437–48. For the bribes, see p. 464.

100. Ibid., 468. For Hrinchenko's political activities, see Boshyk, "The Rise of Ukrainian Political Parties," 336, 341–42.

101. A good summary of the nature of the Ukrainian press, and data on printing runs, can be found in Shchegolev, *Ukrainskoe dvizhenie*, 173–85. See also Efremov, "Biurokraticheskaia utopiia," 82–84.

102. Shchegolev, *Ukrainskoe dvizhenie*, 191–96.

103. Ibid., 272–73. See also *Zvidomlennia tovarystva Prosvita u Kyivi za r. 1910* (Kiev, 1911), 41.

104. *Kievskaia mysl'*, Apr. 11, 1914. For the 1897 data, see *Pervaia vseobshchaia perepis'*, 16:98–99.

105. Shchegolev, *Ukrainskoe dvizhenie*, 272–73, 286, 291, 305–15. See also Thomas M. Prymak, *Mykhailo Hrushevsky: The Politics of National Culture* (Toronto: University of Toronto Press, 1987), 83.

106. Shchegolev, *Ukrainskoe dvizhenie*, 273, 294, 373–74.

107. Samiilenko, *Tvory*, 325–28.

108. *Utro*, Feb. 27, Mar. 1, 1911; Feb. 13, 1914. Shchegolev, *Ukrainskoe dvizhenie*, 322.

109. *Utro*, Feb. 26, 1911.

110. Osyp Hermaize, "Shevchenkyivs'ka demonstratsiia v Kyivi r. 1914," *Chervonyi shliakh* 3 (1924): 127ff. See also *Kievskaia mysl'*, Jan. 23 and Feb. 25–27, 1914; *Utro*, Feb. 25–28, 1914; and Shchegolev, *Ukrainskoe dvizhenie*, 416–18.

111. Prymak, *Mykhailo Hrushevsky*, 113–14.

112. Hermaize, "Shevchenkyivs'ka," 131.

CHAPTER V. JEWISH KIEV

1. For references to Jews in medieval Kiev, see Henrik Birnbaum, "On Jewish Life and Anti-Jewish Sentiments in Medieval Russia," in H. Birnbaum, ed., *Essays in Early Slavic Civilization* (Munich: Wilhelm Fink Verlag, 1971), esp. 227, 233; S. Ettinger, "Kievan Russia," in C. Roth, ed., *The World History of the Jewish People*, 2d ser., *Medieval Period*, vol. 2, *The Dark Ages* (Tel-Aviv: Massadah Publishing, 1966), 320.

2. Bernard D. Weinryb, *The Jews of Poland: A Social and Economic History of the Jewish Community in Poland from 1100 to 1800* (Philadelphia: The Jewish Publication Society of America, 1972), 62–63.

3. Zakrevskii, *Opisanie*, 319–20. According to "Kiev," *Encyclopaedia Judaica* (Jerusalem: Macmillan, 1971), 10:991–92, Kiev's Jews were expelled in 1495 but reestablished their community in 1503. See also Weinryb, *The Jews of Poland*, 83, 102.

4. Weinryb, *The Jews of Poland*, 123–25. Jews were not subject to the Magdeburg laws of the burghers, but to common Polish law and the laws of their own rabbinical courts.

5. Zakrevskii, *Letopis' i opisanie*, 113, provides the wording of the edict, citing a 1652 source. However, some Jews questioned whether such an edict had ever been issued, for the original document apparently was destroyed. One skeptic was M. I. Kulisher. See his "Evrei v Kieve," 1:357–58. "Kiev," *Encyclopaedia Judaica*, 992, notes that some Jews remained in Kiev even after 1619.

6. S. M. Dubnow, *History of the Jews in Russia and Poland*, trans. I. Friedlaender (Philadelphia: The Jewish Publication Society of America, 1916), 1:182–87. The number of casualties in the Uman massacre ranges from several hundred to 50,000 and more. See also Weinryb, *The Jews of Poland*, 122, 204–5.

7. Kulisher, "Evrei v Kieve," 1:250–52; Funduklei, *Statisticheskoe*, pt. 1, 250–52.

8. Ikonnikov, *Kiev*, 68. See also Richard Pipes, "Catherine II and the Jews: The Origins of the Pale of Settlement," *Soviet Jewish Affairs* 5, no. 2 (1975): 17–18.

9. Kulisher, "Evrei v Kieve," 2:419–22; I. V. Galant, "Izgnanie evreev iz Kieva po offitsial'noi perepiske (1828–1831)," *Evreiskaia starina* 7 (1914): 470; Funduklei, *Statisticheskoe*, pt. 1, 229; Kohut, *Russian Centralism*, 289, provides a figure of 1,411 for 1797.

10. Dubnow, *History of the Jews*, 1:268.

11. Galant, "Izgnanie," 470.

12. Zakrevskii, *Opisanie*, 317.

13. *KS* 9 (1884): 435; Kulisher, "Evrei v Kieve," 2:422–23.

14. "Obozrenie Kievskoi, Podol'skoi, i Volynskoi gubernii s 1838 po 1850 g.g.," *Russkii arkhiv* 3 (1884): 17.

15. Ikonnikov, *Kiev*, 184–85; Kulisher, "Evrei v Kieve," 2:425–27.

16. I. Galant, "K istorii Kievskago getto i tsenzury evreiskikh knig (1854–55 g.), *Evreiskaia starina* 6 (1913): 266, 276–78.

17. Funduklei, *Statisticheskoe*, pt. 1, 261.

18. Kulisher, "Evrei v Kieve," 2:427–29. Between 1797 and 1845, the number of merchants remained essentially the same in Kiev, while in Berdychiv the number of Jewish merchants grew by 1,934 between 1834 and 1845 alone. Of Berdychiv's midcentury population of 41,141, 35,707 were Jews, 3,749 were Catholics (Poles), and only 1,631 were Orthodox (Russians and Ukrainians).

19. Funduklei, *Statisticheskoe*, pt. 1, 404, 416, 419–36, 451, 463, 474; pt. 3, 368; I. Zhitetskii, "Evrei v iuzhnoi Rossii," *KS* 1 (1901): 15.

20. Zakrevskii, *Opisanie*, 319.

21. Dubnow, *History of the Jews*, 1:371, 409–11; 2:119–20, 124.

22. The body was discovered on March 20 by Lukianivka policeman Afanasii Shvets, a known anti-Semite. On April 9 *Zemshchina* (St. Petersburg) published the claim that Hasidic Jews had murdered the boy, and several other papers followed suit. See A. S. Tager, *Tsarskaia Rossiia i delo Beilisa. K istorii antisemitizma* (Moscow: Sovetskoe zakonodatel'stvo, 1933), 54–56. The Beilis Affair is discussed in the section of this chapter entitled "The Boy Who Knew Too Much."

23. Kulisher, "Evrei v Kieve," 2:430–31. *Russkii evrei* 19 (1881): 724; 20 (1881): 779, notes that many Jews in these districts, "where Jews lived like lords," were spared destruction by the pogrom mob in 1881. *Kievskaia gazeta*, Oct. 23, 1905, also makes note of the wealthy Jewish homes in Lypky.

24. Zakrevskii, *Opisanie*, 317.

25. *Kiev po perepisi 2 Marta 1874*, 138–53.

26. *Uezdy Kievskii i Radomysl'skii* (Kiev, 1887), 103. At this time it provided housing for five hundred workers.

27. *Kievskii telegraf*, Apr. 30, 1871. See also Pantiukhov, *Opyt*, 425–26.

28. Zhitetskii, "Evrei v iuzhnoi Rossii," 18–19.

29. Ibid., 21–33. The figures for Poltava Province are from 1881.

30. *Rech', proiznesennaia gorodskoi golovoi v zasedanii dumy 28 fevralia 1883 goda* (Kiev, 1883), 7, 17. As of 1870–1871 Jews were eligible to sit on the new city council, but apparently very few Jews won seats on the council in the 1870s and 1880s.

31. *Elizavetgradskii vestnik* (Elizavetgrad), Apr. 17–19, 21, 1881; "Umstvennaia i nravstvennaia fizionomiiu Elizavetgrada," *Zaria*, Apr. 21, 1881. See also Apr. 29.

32. "Deistvitel'naia kartina bezobrazii" and "Khronika," *Elizavetgradskii vestnik*, Apr. 29, 1881; "Vnutrennaia khronika. Kiev," *Russkii evrei* 20 (1881): 778, and "Bezporiadki na iuge," *Russkii evrei* 19 (1881): 724; 20 (1881): 768, 770, 778; 21 (1881): 825; 24 (1881), 955–56. According to a table published in G. Ia. Krasnyi-Admoni, ed., *Materialy dlia istorii antievreiskikh pogromov v Rossii* (Petrograd-Moscow: Gosudarstvennoe izdatel'stvo, 1923), 2:533, 896

Jewish families were victimized by the pogrom, 254 of which owned their own homes.

33. *Zaria*, Apr. 22, 23, 29, 30, May 9, 1881; *Russkii evrei* 18 (1881): 686–88; 19 (1881): 734–37; 20 (1881): 780.

34. Krasnyi-Admoni, *Materialy*, 532. Of the 379, 123 came from Kiev Province, 55 from Chernihiv Province. Twenty-six came from the Kaluga area, and 10 from around Orel. Forty came from the Minsk-Smolensk-Mogilev region. By occupation, 109 were listed as day workers.

35. Dubnow, *History of the Jews*, 2:252.

36. Omeljan Pritsak, "The Pogroms of 1881," *HUS* 11 (June 1987): 22, 30–31.

37. I. Michael Aronson, *Troubled Waters: The Origins of the 1881 Anti-Jewish Pogroms in Russia* (Pittsburgh: University of Pittsburgh Press, 1990), 128–31; Krasnyi-Admoni, *Materialy*, 397–99.

38. *Zaria*, May 5, 19, 23, and June 23, 1881.

39. Jonathan Frankel, *Prophecy and Politics: Socialism, Nationalism, and the Russian Jews, 1862–1917* (Cambridge: Cambridge University Press, 1981), 52.

40. Cited in Aronson, *Troubled Waters*, 206.

41. *Russkii evrei* 18 (1881): 687; 20 (1881): 768; 21 (1881): 824–25; 29 (1881): 1142.

42. *Russkii evrei* 29 (1881): 1142. Fifteen received sentences of one week to two months, thirty-nine of two to eight months, fifteen of one to four years, eleven of four to twenty years, and several were exiled to Siberia. Aronson, *Troubled Waters*, 149, argues quite plausibly that in 1881 "Russian law was underdeveloped and unprepared to deal with the unusual situation created by the anti-Jewish riots."

43. *Zaria*, May 20, 1881. There were 3,150 Jews still under the protection of military officials in May 1881.

44. *Kievskaia mysl'*, Mar. 25, 1914. There were 5,084 Jews in Demievka in 1914.

45. Starozhil, *Kiev*, 13, 27, and 36.

46. Ibid., 29–34, 106; Hamm, "Continuity," 92–93; and Kulisher, "Evrei v Kieve," 2:435–36. Dubnow, *History of the Jews*, 2:252, 276, 316–17, regards Drenteln as a vicious Jew-hater.

47. Starozhil, *Kiev*, 27, 36.

48. TsGIA, *fond* 1288, *opis'* 25, *delo* 29, pp. 25–50.

49. Władeldo, "Kiev," *Evreiskii mir* 12 (Mar. 25, 1911): 20–21.

50. *Kievskaia mysl'*, Apr. 18, 1914. There were 1,700 families officially registered with education permits.

51. *Poltavskaia rech'* (Poltava), Jan. 8, 1913. The city-funded schools apparently were similar to the one-room schools on the American frontier.

52. "Obo vsem," *Kievskoe slovo*, Mar. 15, 1905.

53. M. V. Ptukha, *Naselenie Kievskoi gubernii* (Kiev: Kievskoe Gubernskoe Statisticheskoe Biuro, 1925), 29, table 13.

54. *Kievskaia gazeta*, Sept. 20, 21, 23, and 25, and Nov. 17, 1904. See also the entry under "Brodsky" in *Encyclopaedia Judaica*, vol. 4.

55. *Zaria*, Apr. 29, May 28, 1881; *Russkii evrei* 19 (1881): 735–36.

56. *Kievskii i Odesskii pogromy v otchetakh senatorov Turau i Kuzminskago* (St. Petersburg: Letopisets, 1907), 44.

57. *Dvadtsatipiatiletie Kievskoi birzhi,* 152. The largest wheat mills were owned by Brodsky and Blinder, while two of the rye mills were owned by Grinshtein and Goldberg.

58. Data, from the city *uprava,* are cited in *Kievskaia gazeta,* Jan. 12, 1902. In addition, there was one first-guild Karaite and eight second-guild Karaites. Data were broken down only by categories of Christian, Jewish, and Karaite. See also Brower, *The Russian City,* 55–56.

59. A. Linden, "Gouvernement Kiew. Kiew," in *Die Judenpogrome in Russland* (Köln and Leipzig: Judischer verlag, 1910), 2:392.

60. "Kiev," *Encyclopaedia Judaica,* 10:994.

61. Tager, *Tsarskaia Rossiia,* 51–60, 78–79.

62. Ibid., 84, 87–90, 109–17.

63. Dubnow, *History of the Jews,* 3:165.

64. *Kievskaia mysl',* June 28, 29, 30, 1914.

65. Dubnow, *History of the Jews,* 3:19–20.

66. In 1913 Kiev taxed 9,288 income-producing real estate properties, 84 percent of which were owned by Orthodox Russians or Ukrainians. Only 7 percent of the city's income-producing property was owned by Poles, and only 6 percent by Jews. Berdychiv taxed 2,325 income-producing properties: 22 percent were owned by Orthodox; 17 percent by Poles; and 64 percent by Jews. Data are from TsGIA, *fond* 1288, *opis'* 25, *delo* 29, pp. 5–11; and *opis'* 5, *delo* 170 (1914), pp. 130, 143.

67. "Shalom Aleichem," *Encyclopaedia Judaica,* 14:1272–74.

68. Władeldo, "Kiev," *Evreiskii mir* 7 (Feb. 7, 1911): 19–20. There were some famous Jewish writers who lived in Kiev, including Shalom Aleichem, Moshe Zilberfarb, and Nahum Syrkin. With regard to the absence of Jewish theater in Kiev, Henry Abramson has pointed out in personal correspondence that Kiev is barely mentioned in M. Osherovitsh's study of Yiddish theater, "Der onhayb fun yidish teater in Ukrayne," *Yidn in Ukrayne* (New York, 1967), 2:67–102.

69. For the 1910 election, see *Kievskaia mysl',* Nov. 11, Dec. 1, 1910; I. Zubarev, *Gorodskoe delo* 18 (1910): 1278–80. Only twenty-one Nationalists were elected, and this election was viewed as a major defeat for the Nationalist cause. Even the Polish candidates, who fared poorly, got more votes than many Nationalists. Thirteen of the fourteen Nationalist candidates won in heavily Jewish Lybid District. The election was spiced with scandal. Attendance records of councilmen were published, including records of their committee participation. One Nationalist councilman, Nikolai Chokolov, had missed 314 of the 367 council meetings over the previous four years. "I couldn't work with the Kadets," he explained. Local councilmen were not allowed to use national political affiliations when running for office, and although some from the "Non-Party Group," which opposed the Nationalists, were apparently Kadets (the liberal Constitutional Democratic Party), most were said to be sympathetic to the moderately conservative Octobrists.

70. Dubnow, *History of the Jews,* 2:14.

CHAPTER VI. RECREATION, THE ARTS, AND
POPULAR CULTURE IN KIEV

1. Ikonnikov, *Kiev*, 295; Podhorodecki, *Dzieje Kijowa*, 133–35; Proko-povych, *Pid zolotoiu*, 39–40; *KES*, 365.

2. Cited in Ikonnikov, *Kiev*, 321. Bobrowski is cited in Podhorodecki, *Dzieje Kijowa*, 147. See also pp. 133–35.

3. Bagalei, *Istoriia Khar'kova*, 2:937.

4. Flaner, "Memuary," *Kievskaia gazeta*, Jan. 6 and 8, 1905.

5. Bagalei, *Istoriia Khar'kova*, 2:932, 951.

6. Ibid., 948–50.

7. "Starik," *Kievskoe slovo*, July 27, 1903.

8. Brower, *The Russian City*, 55.

9. For Kiev's *meshchane*, see *Kievskoe slovo*, May 9, 1905. For a good account of Kharkiv's *prikazchik* organization, with its ten-thousand-volume library, see *Utro*, Oct. 9, 1907.

10. Bagalei, *Istoriia Khar'kova*, 2:934.

11. Data on conveyance and the animal population may be found in Fun-duklei, *Statisticheskoe*, pt. 1, 390–91. For the 1880s see Starozhil, *Kiev*, 10–11.

12. Prokopovych, *Pid zolotoiu*, 46–48, 56–57.

13. Ibid., 41, 45.

14. Marta Pisetska Farley, *Festive Ukrainian Cooking* (Pittsburgh: University of Pittsburgh Press, 1990), 5.

15. M. G. Rabinovich, *Ocherki etnografii Russkogo feodal'nogo goroda* (Moscow: Nauka, 1978), 115–16.

16. Cited in "Kievskoe predstavitel'stvo prezhniago vremeni," 191. See also Podhorodecki, *Dzieje Kijowa*, 133–35; and Prokopovych, *Pid zolotoiu*, 42–44. Oleksa Voropai, *Zvychai nashoho narodu. Etnografichnyi narys* (Munich: Ukrains'ke vydavnytstvo, 1966), 2:236–37, cites the memories of Maccabeus of the legendary Kiev woman Kozeletska, reputed to be 120 years old in 1890.

17. Starozhil, *Kiev*, 16; Rabinovich, *Ocherki etnografii*, 136–37.

18. *Khar'kovskii listok*, May 23, 1905; *Iuzhnyi krai*, Oct. 1, 1905. For a list of the religious holidays, see *Kontraktovyi ukazatel'*, 81.

19. Hryhoryi Hryhor'ev, *U staromy Kyivi. Spohady* (Kiev: Radians'kyi pys'-mennyk, 1961), 65.

20. *Kievskaia gazeta*, Aug. 14, 15, 1904. For a description of St. Vladimir's Day, see *Kievskaia gazeta*, July 16, 1903. The reference to the electric lights is found in Paustovsky, *The Story of a Life*, 58. See also G. I. Shchetinina, *Studen-chestvo i revoliutsionnoe dvizhenie v Rossii. Posledniaia chetvert' XIX v.* (Moscow: Nauka, 1987), 95, for the reference to the 1884 event, which was used by students to stage a protest against the political reaction of the times.

21. *Kiev perioda pozdnego feodalizma i kapitalizma*, 105–6, refers to this festival in the eighteenth century. Shul'gin, "Iugo-zapadnyi," 6 (1879): 116–17, makes a brief reference to the disappearance of the parades on Epiphany and Maccabeus Days.

22. Starozhil, *Kiev*, 14–16.

23. *Kievskaia gazeta,* Jan. 1, 1905; *Khar'kovskie gubernskie vedomosti,* Dec. 24, 1900; Starozhil, *Kiev,* 13.

24. Pantiukhov, *Opyt,* 224, supplies data for the years 1866 to 1870, which indicate that the city's 2,944 Orthodox (Russian and Ukrainian) marriages occurred as follows: January, 376; February, 254; March, 0; April, 161; May, 264; June, 130; July, 351; August, 156; September, 362; October, 515; November, 375; December, 0.

25. Ibid., 207–8. In 1870, Kiev's population was fairly evenly balanced between men and women. Of the 69,410 Orthodox in the city, 59 percent were men, but this figure is largely explained by the presence of 9,035 Orthodox troops in the city (there were no female troops), and the fact that there were more monks than nuns.

26. Ibid., 225–29. For a good general account of marriage practices in old Russia, see Eve Levin, *Sex and Society in the World of the Orthodox Slavs, 900–1700* (Ithaca: Cornell University Press, 1989).

27. Rabinovich, *Ocherki etnografii,* 213–14.

28. Ibid., 220–21.

29. Pantiukhov, *Opyt,* 424. Pantiukhov points out that the data are not precise, in part because couples who married in one parish might reside in another. In the city as a whole during this period, marriages produced an average of 4.9 children.

30. *Kiev perioda pozdnego feodalizma i kapitalizma,* 170–72, 186. Eighteenth-century Kiev was also noted for *drzeworyt,* painted prints made from wooden or copper molds, and pencil drawings, often on Cossack themes, according to Podhorodecki, *Dzieje Kijowa,* 138–39.

31. *Kiev perioda pozdnego feodalizma i kapitalizma,* 106. The churches did not offer training in musical instruments because instrumental music was not a part of the religious service.

32. Ibid., 290. Zawadzki wrote nearly five hundred musical compositions.

33. Russell Zguta, *Russian Minstrels: A History of the Skomorokhi* (Philadelphia: University of Pennsylvania Press, 1978), 48.

34. Ibid., 86–87.

35. Sydorenko, *Kievan Academy,* 99. Discouraged by the authorities, these practices began to disappear in the eighteenth century.

36. There is an excellent museum of Ukrainian musical instruments on the grounds of Kiev's Cave Monastery. My thanks to Leonid Cherkassky, who assembled much of this collection, for the insights he shared with me during my December 1991 visit. See also Natalie O. Kononenko, "The Influence of the Orthodox Church on Ukrainian *Dumy,*" *Slavic Review* 50 (Fall 1991): 567, 571.

37. Starik, *Kievskoe slovo,* July 27, 1903.

38. Voropai, *Zvychai nashoho narodu,* 1:116–20.

39. Zakrevskii, *Letopis' i opisanie,* 40; Sydorenko, *Kievan Academy,* 99; and Rabinovich, *Ocherki etnografii,* 125, all make references to *vertepy.* I am also indebted to the curators at Kiev's State Museum of Ukrainian Theater, Musical Instruments, and Film Art for discussing this art form with me in great detail.

40. "Obo vsem," *Kievskoe slovo,* Sept. 2, 9, 10, 1903. See also Ikonnikov, *Kiev,* 339–41, and Funduklei, *Statisticheskoe,* pt. 1, 377.

41. For references to and reviews of Ukrainian performances, see, for example, *Khar'kovskii listok*, July 7, 1903; March 12 and 20, 1905. See also Mykola Bilins'kyi, "Z mynuloho perezhytoho 1870–88," *Ukraina* 2 (1928): 130–32.

42. *UCE*, 189–90. See also Samiilenko, *Tvory*, 405; and *Kiev perioda pozdnego feodalizma i kapitalizma*, 407–8.

43. Starozhil, *Kiev*, 2, 5–6; Hryhor'ev, *U staromu Kyivi*, 224–27.

44. Hryhor'ev, *U staromu Kyivi*, 148–50.

45. Sergei Berdiaev in *Kievskie otkliki*, Nov. 10, 25, 1905; Hryhor'ev, *U staromu Kyivi*, 150, 224–27, 270; Shchegolev, *Ukrainskoe dvizhenie*, 305–8.

46. E. K. Redin, *Narodnyi teatr* (Khar'kov, 1898).

47. For attitudes of Ukrainian activists toward Ukrainian theater, see Shchegolev, *Ukrainskoe dvizhenie*, 305–8. See also *Kievskie otkliki*, Nov. 10, 25, 1905; Hryhor'ev, *U staromu Kyivi*, 150, 224–27, 270.

48. *Kiev perioda pozdnego feodalizma i kapitalizma*, 412.

49. S. Ginzburg, *Kinemategrafiia dorevoliutsionnoi Rossii* (Moscow: Iskusstvo, 1963), 23, 42–43. See also Jay Leyda, *Kino: A History of the Russian and Soviet Film* (New York: Collier Books, 1973), 18, 31.

50. Leyda, *Kino*, 24–25; Ginzburg, *Kinemategrafiia*, 43.

51. Ginzburg, *Kinemategrafiia*, 31, 48, 58–60.

52. *Kiev perioda pozdnego feodalizma i kapitalizma*, 412.

53. *UCE*, 197. See also Ginzburg, *Kinemategrafiia*, 43; and *Istoriia Kieva*, 621–28. For one complaint about the impact of cinema on live theater, see *Kievskie vesti*, Dec. 20, 1907.

54. John Bushnell, "Urban Leisure Culture in Post-Stalin Russia: Stability as a Social Problem?" in T. Thompson and R. Sheldon, eds., *Soviet Society and Culture: Essays in Honor of Vera S. Dunham* (Boulder: Westview Press, 1988), 58–60.

55. Starozhil, *Kiev*, 9, 204–5.

56. *Deiatel'nost' obshchestva*, 51. Magnates such as N. I. Greter and N. A. Tereshchenko also supported these shelters, which taught various skills. The first opened in 1875. By 1911 five shelters were training 356 children. A shelter for Jewish children was opened in Podil in 1889. It was presumably financed by Jewish charity.

57. Gunther Barth, *City People: The Rise of Modern City Culture in Nineteenth-Century America* (New York: Oxford University Press, 1980), 156.

58. Ikonnikov, *Kiev*, 108–9.

59. Flaner, "Memuary," *Kievskaia gazeta*, Nov. 7, 9, 1904; Starozhil, *Kiev*, 8–9.

60. Ikonnikov, *Kiev*, 90–92; "Zapiski Ivana Matveicha Sbitneva," 654–55.

61. Ikonnikov, *Kiev*, 333–35; Starozhil, *Kiev*, 84–85.

62. Rabinovich, *Ocherki etnografii*, 211–12.

63. "Memuary," *Kievskaia gazeta*, Aug. 23, 30, 1904.

64. "Obo vsem," *Kievskoe slovo*, Aug. 31, 1903.

65. Shul'kevich and Dmitrenko, *Kiev*, 92; Hamm, "Continuity," 88.

66. Hryhor'ev, *U staromu Kyivi*, 41–44.

67. See Gusev, *Khar'kov*, 53, for a description of the transformation of the "*pan* rows" in Kharkiv into a high-fashion district.

68. *Khar'kovskii listok*, July 21, 1903; *Volna* (Kharkov), Jan. 21, 1906.

69. *Kievskoe slovo*, Nov. 25, 1905.

70. "Tolkuchnye rynki," *Kievskaia gazeta*, Nov. 7, 1904. See also Po-dhorodecki, *Dzieje Kijowa*, 180.

71. Funduklei, *Statisticheskoe*, pt. 1, 359.

72. Data are taken from *Obzor' Kievskoi gubernii za 1901 god* (Kiev, 1902); *Obzor' za . . . 1902* (Kiev, 1903); etc. It should be noted that in 1901 in Kiev *uezd*, the district immediately surrounding the city, there were sixteen murders, fourteen in 1902. In 1906 there were forty-seven murders in the *uezd* compared with twenty-two in the city. In 1913 there were fifty-eight in the *uezd* compared with forty-three in the city proper. The populations of the city and the surrounding *uezd* were very similar in size. Kiev had an estimated 319,000 people on Jan. 1, 1903, Kiev *uezd* 307,404. Both populations were evenly divided between males and females. For population data see *Obzor' za . . . 1901*, 85–87; *Obzor' za . . . 1902*, 97. *Obzor' za . . . 1906*, 94–95, lists a city population of 336,826, an *uezd* population of 349,196. See also *Prilozhenie: O nasil'stvennykh i sluchainykh smertiakh v Kievskoi gubernii za 1906 god. Obzor' za . . . 1913*, *vedomost'* 7, lists a population of 626,313 for Jan. 1, 1914.

73. "Otdykh," *Kievskoe slovo*, July 20, 1903.

74. "Memuary," *Kievskaia gazeta*, Jan. 27, 1905.

75. "Pogrom v Yalte," *Odesskie novosti*, Mar. 20, 1905.

76. *Khar'kovskii listok*, July 20, 1903. For Rostov-na-Donu, see "Pogromnye siluety," *Kievskaia gazeta*, Nov. 6, 1905.

77. Police data were published in "Kievskaia zhizn'," *Kievskoe slovo*, Mar. 12, 1905.

78. Joan Neuberger, "Stories of the Street: Hooliganism in the St. Petersburg Popular Press," *Slavic Review* 48 (Summer 1989): esp. 177, 193–94.

79. Starozhil, *Kiev*, 128.

80. For an excellent description of crime in Kharkiv, see "Na Kholodnoi Gore," *Utro*, Oct. 17, 1907. See also Starozhil, *Kiev*, 128.

81. *Kiev po perepisi 2 Marta 1874*, 248. See also Pantiukhov, *Opyt*, 352.

82. For St. Petersburg, see Richard Stites, "Prostitute and Society in Pre-Revolutionary Russia," *Jahrbucher für Geschichte Osteuropas* 31 (1983): 350–51. For Berlin see *Kievskie vesti*, Dec. 10, 1907.

83. *Khar'kovskie gubernskie vedomosti*, July 5, 1879.

84. Starozhil, *Kiev*, 187.

85. Hryhor'ev, *U staromu Kyivi*, 45–49.

86. *Khar'kovskii listok*, July 12, 1903.

87. *Kievskaia gazeta*, Nov. 28, 30, 1904.

88. "Kievskaia zhizn'," *Kievskoe slovo*, Mar. 12, 1905.

89. *Kievskie otkliki*, Dec. 8, 1905.

90. *Otchet' o deiatel'nosti voskresnykh shkol Kievskoi obshchestvennoi gramotnosti* (Kiev, 1900), 35–38. The report does not indicate the reasons for imprisonment.

91. Pantiukhov, *Opyt*, 418.

92. *Kievskie vesti*, Dec. 10, 1907. The nobleman Grebnev had earlier murdered a railway official.

93. Christine D. Worobec, "Temptress or Virgin? The Precarious Sexual Position of Women in Postemancipation Ukrainian Peasant Society," *Slavic Review* 49 (Summer 1990): 238.

94. Funduklei, *Statisticheskoe*, pt. 1, 392.

95. *Kiev perioda pozdnego feodalizma i kapitalizma*, 389–90.

96. V. Lebedev, "K istorii kulachnykh boev na Rusi," *Russkaia starina*, pt. 1 (July 1913): 103–10; pt. 2 (August 1913): 324–25, 333–34. The poem is cited in pt. 1, 123.

97. Bagalei, *Istoriia Khar'kova*, 2:954–56.

98. *Kievskii telegraf*, Apr. 9, 1871.

99. Cited in Rabinovich, *Ocherki etnografii*, 165–66.

100. Hryhor'ev, *U staromu Kyivi*, 65–66.

101. "Kishinevskii bomond," *Kievskaia gazeta*, July 7, 1903.

102. *Kiev po perepisi 2 Marta 1874*, 390–401.

103. *Istoriia Kieva*, 408; Pantiukhov, *Opyt*, 355.

104. Flaner in "Memuary," *Kievskaia gazeta*, Nov. 14, 1904.

105. Aronson, *Troubled Waters*, 113. For the reference to the Nazi executioners, see Joel E. Dimsdale, ed., *Survivors, Victims, and Perpetrators: Essays on the Nazi Holocaust* (Washington: Hemisphere Press, 1980), 345.

106. *Russkii evrei* 20 (1881): 725, 774.

107. This description is of the tearooms run in Kharkiv's Annunciation Bazaar. See *Khar'kovskie gubernskie vedomosti*, Dec. 18, 1900. For a general study of Russia's charitable institutions, see Adele Lindenmeyr, "Public Poor Relief and Private Charity in Late Imperial Russia," (Ph.D. diss., Princeton University, 1980).

108. *Izvestiia Moskovskoi gorodskoi dumy* 4 (1914): 36–38; Hamm, "Continuity," 108.

109. Hryhor'ev, *U staromu Kyivi*, 59–61, 234, 237–38. See also *Otchet' o deiatel'nosti Kievskago popechitel'stva o narodnoi trezvosti za 1905 g.* (Kiev, 1908), 8, 12–16.

110. *Kievskaia gazeta*, Sept. 26, 1904.

111. Barth, *City People*, 150–51.

112. *Kievskaia gazeta*, July 1, 1903. A second letter was published on July 16.

113. *Kiev perioda pozdnego feodalizma i kapitalizma*, 414. In 1913 seven soccer teams were competing, representing clubs with five hundred players.

114. *Kievskie otkliki*, Dec. 5, 1905.

115. *Kievskaia mysl'*, June 29, 1914; Hamm, "Continuity," 88.

116. *Otchet' o deiatel'nosti Kievskago popechitel'stva*, 22. This particular doss house was in Lukianivka.

117. *Obzor' deiatel'nosti Kievskoi gorodskoi dumy*, 14, 29–31.

118. One such advertisement ran in *Utro*, May 8, 1911. The Ford Runabout was advertised for 2,675 rubles; a four-cylinder Landolle Luxe cost 3,700 rubles. See also *Utro*, May 17, 1914.

119. *Kiev perioda pozdnego feodalizma i kapitalizma*, 395–96.

120. *World Who's Who in Science* (Chicago: A. N. Marquis, 1968), 1547.

121. *Utro*, May 10, 1911. On May 5, 1911, this paper carried a story on

Sikorsky. For Nesterov, see Hamm, "Continuity," 88; and *Kievskaia mysl'*, Mar. 20, June 8, 1914.

122. Cited in Ikonnikov, *Kiev*, 345.

123. *Pervaia vseobshchaia perepis'*, 16:198.

124. Pantiukhov, *Opyt*, 389–90, 412.

125. "Memuary," *Kievskaia gazeta*, Aug. 3, 1904.

126. Starozhil, *Kiev*, 92. See *Kontraktovyi ukazatel'* for the 1897 advertisements.

127. This particular supplement came with *Khar'kovskie gubernskie vedomosti*, May 1, 1900.

CHAPTER VII. THE PROMISE OF CHANGE: KIEV IN 1905

1. M. Popov, cited in V. Manilov, "Ocherki iz istorii sotsial-demokraticheskago dvizheniia v Kieve (80–90 g.g.)," *LR* 3 (1923): 122.

2. Subtelny, *Ukraine*, 288; Podhorodecki, *Dzieje Kijowa*, 185; *Kiev perioda pozdnego feodalizma i kapitalizma*, 215.

3. Manilov, "Ocherki," 3 (1923): 133–37; 4 (1923): 3; N. A. Bukhbinder, "K istorii sotsial-demokraticheskogo dvizheniia v Kievskoi gubernii. Kiev," *Krasnaia letopis'* (Moscow) 7 (1923): 263–64.

4. Manilov, "Ocherki," 5 (1923): 22–36; *Kiev perioda pozdnego feodalizma i kapitalizma*, 326–27.

5. Marakhov, *Kievskii universitet*, 88. University enrollment fluctuated between 613 and 1,012 during this decade.

6. Samuel D. Kassow, *Students, Professors, and the State in Tsarist Russia* (Berkeley and Los Angeles: University of California Press, 1989), 405–6.

7. Ibid., 390.

8. Ibid., 92, 96.

9. Ibid., 405.

10. Terence Emmons, "Russia's Banquet Campaign," *California Slavic Studies* (Berkeley and Los Angeles: University of California Press, 1977), 10:60–61, 85. See also V. M. Khizhniakov, *Vospominaniia zemskogo deiatelia* (Petrograd, 1916), 224. According to *Istoriia Kieva*, 510, Lenin's mother was released in June, his sister in July, and his brother in December. The Ulyanov family then left Kiev.

11. The exact date of the survey is unknown, but *Kievskaia gazeta* discusses it in its editorial of Aug. 30, 1904.

12. See the chronology of M. I. Mebel, ed., *1905 na Ukraine. Khronika i materialy* (Kharkov: Proletarii, 1926), 1:19–23.

13. Mebel, *1905 na Ukraine*, 1:22; V. Pravdin, "Epokha neslikhannoi smuty na Kievshchine," *LR* (March–April 1925): 105; *Kiev perioda pozdnego feodalizma i kapitalizma*, 343–44.

14. Boshyk, "The Rise of Ukrainian Political Parties," 219.

15. Other activists continued to pursue more modest cultural goals. In March V. B. Antonovych headed the creation of the Society to Assist Ukrainian Writers,

which hoped simply to raise enough money to provide financial assistance for Ukrainian writers and publish a journal. See *Khar'kovskii listok*, Mar. 6, 1905. For a good discussion of Porsh and his impact on the RUP, see Boshyk, "The Rise of Ukrainian Political Parties," 222–43.

16. Mebel, *1905 na Ukraine*, 1:45–47; *Kievskaia gazeta*, Feb. 25, 1905; *OIKGOPO*, 59–60.

17. *Kievskaia gazeta*, Feb. 24, 1905; *Kiev perioda pozdnego feodalizma i kapitalizma*, 113–15, 300.

18. Hermaize, *Narysy*, 118–19; Pravdin, "Epokha," 95.

19. Mebel, *1905 na Ukraine*, 53.

20. *Kievskoe slovo*, Feb. 27, 1905, carried the report on the secondary students, and reports of the organizational efforts of the other groups mentioned can be found in this paper throughout February and on March 6 and 8, 1905. See also Mebel, *1905 na Ukraine*, 47–48. For the *prikazchiki*, see *Kievskaia gazeta*, Feb. 22, 1905. See Boshyk, "The Rise of Ukrainian Political Parties," 229–33, for RUP efforts to organize students.

21. Kassow, *Students*, 195–96.

22. Mebel, *1905 na Ukraine*, 89.

23. N. A. Bukhbinder, "Evreiskoe rabochee dvizhenie v 1905 godu. 1 Maia," *Krasnaia letopis'* 7 (1923): 7–8, 11.

24. Frankel, *Prophecy and Politics*, 160–61.

25. *OIKGOPO*, 63; *Kiev perioda pozdnego feodalizma i kapitalizma*, 344. For the activities of the Bund, see Mebel, *1905 na Ukraine*, 47–48, 89–91.

26. Hermaize, *Narysy*, 118; *Kiev perioda pozdnego feodalizma i kapitalizma*, 344. *OIKGOPO*, 58, states that the Mensheviks were strongest in the workshops, the Bolsheviks in the large plants.

27. *Khar'kovskii listok*, June 24, 1905.

28. Mebel, *1905 na Ukraine*, 151; Hermaize, *Narysy*, 119; *1905. Profession'alnoe dvizhenie* (Moscow-Leningrad: Gosudarstvennoe izdatel'stvo, 1926), 257.

29. Pravdin, "Epokha," 93–97. See also the chronology of strikes and disturbances for June and July in Mebel, *1905 na Ukraine*.

30. *The American Jewish Yearbook 5667* (Philadelphia: The Jewish Publication Society of America, 1906), 46–47. The date given for the pogrom is July 23 (new style).

31. N. N. Leshchenko, *Ukrains'ke selo v revoliutsii 1905–07 r.r.* (Kiev: Naukova dumka, 1977), 206.

32. D. Antoshkin, *Professional'noe dvizhenie v Rossii* (Moscow, 1925), 127.

33. Hermaize, *Narysy*, 119. See also the chronology of disturbances for the summer months in Mebel, *1905 na Ukraine*.

34. Pravdin, "Epokha," 92.

35. Kassow, *Students*, 253.

36. Ibid., 254.

37. "Narodnye mitingi v Peterburge," *Proletarii* 25 (1905), cited in ibid.

38. "Vsepoddanneishii otchet o proizvedennom, po vysochaichemu poveleniiu, gofmeisterom dvora ego imperatorskago velichestva senatorom Turau izsledovanii prichin bezporiadkov, byvshikh v g. Kieve," in *Materialy k istorii*

Russkoi kontr'-revoliutsii. Pogromy po offitsial'nym dokumentam (St. Petersburg, 1908), 1:206–21. Hereafter cited as Turau, *Materialy*. Turau's report is also published in *Kievskii i Odesskii pogromy*. For the events of September and early October, see pp. 10–20. See also "Oktiabr'skie sobytiia 1905 goda v Kieve v izobrazhenii okhrannogo otdeleniia," *LR* (March–April 1925): 112–18.

39. Ascher, *The Revolution of 1905*, 204.

40. Boshyk, "The Rise of Ukrainian Political Parties," 306, notes the possibility that the first mass meeting of Ukrainians in Kiev may have occurred at this time. It was apparently organized by the RUP. Hermaize, *Narysy*, 119, suggests that a similar meeting took place in Kiev at the end of June. See also "Oktiabr'-skie sobytiia 1905," 118; Turau, *Materialy*, 215–16; *Kievskii i Odesskii pogromy*, 22.

41. Henry Reichman, *Railwaymen and Revolution: Russia 1905* (Berkeley and Los Angeles: University of California Press, 1987), 203–5, and chap. 7 in general.

42. F. E. Los, ed., *Revoliutsiia 1905–07 na Ukraine* (Kiev: Politicheskaia literatura, 1955), vol. 2, pt. 1, document 366. See also Turau, *Materialy*, 214; *Kievskii i Odesskii pogromy*, 19.

43. Los, *Revoliutsiia*, vol. 2, pt. 1, p. 466.

44. Ibid., 116–20.

45. *Kievskoe slovo*, Oct. 23, 1905.

46. Turau, *Materialy*, 222.

CHAPTER VIII. THE PROMISE SHATTERED: THE OCTOBER POGROM

1. *Kievskie vesti*, Jan. 15, 1908.

2. Los, *Revoliutsiia*, vol. 2, pt. 1, document 368.

3. The best accounts of the pogrom are found in *Kievskaia gazeta*, *Kievskoe slovo*, and *Kievskie otkliki* when they resumed publication on October 23. See also Los, *Revoliutsiia*, vol. 2, pt. 1, pp. 469–72; "Oktiabr'skie sobytiia 1905," 121–22; Turau, *Materialy*, 224–30; For an excellent account of the Odessa pogrom, see Robert Weinberg, "The Pogrom of 1905 in Odessa: A Case Study," in John D. Klier and Shlomo Lambroza, eds., *Pogroms: Anti-Jewish Violence in Modern Russian History* (Cambridge: Cambridge University Press, 1992), 248–90. The reference to the dogs is from p. 261.

4. Pravdin, "Epokha," 107–8.

5. The official report may be found in Los, *Revoliutsiia*, vol. 2, pt. 1, p. 472. Senator Turau's investigation also contends that soldiers were fired upon from four directions, including the balcony of city hall. See *Kievskii i Odesskii pogromy*, 39. See also *Kiev perioda pozdnego feodalizma i kapitalizma*, 347. For a typical press account, see *Kievskoe slovo*, Oct. 23, 1905.

6. *Kievskoe slovo*, Oct. 23, 1905.

7. *Kievskie otkliki*, Oct. 23, 1905, editorial.

8. Linden, "Gouvernement Kiew," 2:390. Official police figures, which represent the lowest estimate, state that 47 were killed (one-quarter of them Jews), and that 205 were injured (one-third of them Jews). Turau acknowledges that these

figures are low, noting that many victims had not been counted because they had been carried away privately. See *Kievskii i Odesskii pogromy,* 48.

9. F. Bogrov, "Evreiskaia zhizn' v 1907 g.," *Kievskie vesti,* Jan. 5, 1908.

10. Iu. Kernes, *Kievskoe slovo,* Nov. 3, 1905. On October 24 the paper reported that rumors about a pogrom had circulated in Podil.

11. Kh. Zafran, "Iz istorii rabochego dvizheniia na Volyni," *LR* 4 (1924): 115-16. Ten from Berdychiv were murdered by villagers in Troianov along the way, and some were decapitated.

12. *Kievskie otkliki,* Oct. 27, 1905. For Turau's account, see *Kievskii i Odesskii pogromy,* 47-48.

13. *Kievskaia gazeta,* Oct. 24, 1905. Turau, *Materialy,* 237-38, states that shots "came from many homes," in most cases "from members of self-defense." He adds, "certain witnesses contend that there were instances where Jews fired into patriotic demonstrations."

14. From reports in *Volyn'* (Zhitomir), Apr. 30, 1905; and *Kievskoe slovo,* May 1, 1905. *Volyn'* argued that public psychology in Zhytomyr had come to regard pogroms as relics of the past until rising tensions just before the Easter pogrom spurred the organization of resistance groups.

15. Komissiia TsIK SSSR, *1905. Evreiskoe rabochee dvizhenie* (Moscow-Leningrad: Gosudarstvennoe izdatel'stvo, 1928).

16. Pravdin, "Epokha," 109.

17. K. Basalygo, "Revoliutsionnoe dvizhenie v Khar'kove v 1905-06 g.g.," *LR* 1 (1924): 124; S. Brainin, "Oktiabr'-Dekabr' v Khar'kove," *LR* 5-6 (1925): 122-23. Boshyk, "The Rise of Ukrainian Political Parties," 307, notes that the RUP organized a small resistance group of students and telegraph operators in Kharkiv.

18. *Bessarabets* (Kishinev), Apr. 10, 1903. This paper was published by the notorious anti-Semite P. A. Krushevan.

19. According to *Krimskii kur'er* (Yalta), cited in *Odesskie novosti* (Odessa), Mar. 20, 1905.

20. "Evreiskii pogrom v Melitopole," *Kievskoe slovo,* Apr. 25, 1905.

21. Nora Levin, *The Jews of the Soviet Union since 1917* (New York: New York University Press, 1988), 1:37.

22. *Kievlianin,* Oct. 20, 1905. See also Los, *Revoliutsiia,* vol. 2, pt. 1, pp. 472-73.

23. See the letter by Pavel Kirilov in *Kievlianin,* Nov. 3, 1905.

24. See, for example, the letters to the editor in *Kievskie otkliki,* Oct. 26, 1905. On Oct. 24 and Nov. 9, *Kievskaia gazeta* linked Grigor'ev to the vandalism. Vasil'ev wrote a letter to *Kievskoe slovo* on October 28 vehemently denying that he had anything to do with the pogrom. See also *Kievskoe slovo,* Oct. 26, 1905; and *Kievskie vesti,* Dec. 6, 1907.

25. *Kievskii i Odesskii pogromy,* 61-67.

26. *Kievskaia gazeta,* Oct. 24, 1905; *Volyn',* Oct. 26, 1905.

27. *Kievskoe slovo,* Oct. 24, 1905; *Volyn',* Oct. 24, 1905, editorial; *Kievskie otkliki,* Oct. 24, 1905.

28. *Kievskie otkliki,* Oct. 23, Dec. 1, 1905.

29. *Volyn',* Apr. 30, 1905.

30. *Bessarabets,* Apr. 29, 1903.

31. *Donskaia rech'* (Rostov-na-Donu), Oct. 26, 1905.

32. For Uman, see *Kievskie otkliki,* Nov. 3, 1905; for the rumors in Kiev, see *Kievlianin,* Oct. 26; and *Kievskoe slovo,* Oct. 27 and 28, 1905.

33. Excellent accounts of the cholera riots in Saratov, Astrakhan, and elsewhere may be found in *Saratovskii listok* (Saratov), July 1, 3, 4, 7, 8, 1892. In Saratov the riots were confined to the city; surrounding villagers were said to display no hostility toward doctors. Interestingly, at about this time in the Ukrainian mining town of Iuzivka (Iuzovka), a cholera riot turned into an anti-Jewish pogrom. *Kievlianin* published the details of these riots together with a long article on the alleged ritual murder by Jews of a five-year-old Christian boy in Germany, perhaps trying to link the events in the public's eye.

34. *Saratovskii listok,* Oct. 25, 1905.

35. *Donskaia rech',* Oct. 24, 26, 1905.

36. See *Kievskoe slovo,* Nov. 3, 1905; and the letter from "Ivan Shevchenko" in *Kievskie otkliki,* Oct. 27, 1905.

37. *Kievskie otkliki,* Oct. 26, 1905.

38. *Volyn',* Oct. 26, 1905.

39. For Odessa, see Weinberg, "The Pogrom of 1905," 264. For Rostov-na-Donu, see *Donskaia rech',* Oct. 29, 30, 1905.

40. *Kievskoe slovo,* Oct. 23, 1905, editorial. For Rudoi's statement, see Turau, *Materialy,* 244.

41. *The Memoirs of Count Witte,* trans. Abraham Yarmolinsky (Garden City, N.Y.: Doubleday, Page & Co., 1921), 264.

42. Turau, *Materialy,* 267–69. Kleigels had apparently asked to leave his office in early October for reasons of ill health, but on October 15 had asked to remain in office until it could be ensured that order would be maintained. He was removed on October 18 anyway.

43. For the allegations against Tsikhotsky, see ibid., 254–55 and 293–95. For those against Bezsonov, see pp. 248–51 and 255–56. The allegations may also be found in *Kievskii i Odesskii pogromy,* 57–67.

44. See *Kievskoe slovo,* Oct. 27, 1905, and the letters to that paper on Oct. 30, 1905. For one discussion of Rafalsky, see Turau, *Materialy,* 240, 295.

45. *Kievskoe slovo,* Oct. 24, 1905; Turau, *Materialy,* 256.

46. Weinberg, "The Pogrom of 1905 in Odessa," 268.

47. *Kievskoe slovo,* Jan. 1, 1902, editorial.

48. See *Kievskoe slovo,* Mar. 14, 1902, for a biographical sketch of Eikhelman. Eikhelman often wrote for this paper, which was monarchist in sentiment. In 1903 it was apparently bought by individuals with more liberal leanings. It became openly supportive of the revolution in 1905.

49. *Kievskoe slovo,* June 21, 1905. Councilman Iasnogursky made this particular accusation.

50. *Kievskoe slovo* and *Kievskaia gazeta,* Oct. 24, 1905.

51. *Kievskaia gazeta,* Aug. 31, 1903.

52. "Starik," *Kievskaia gazeta,* Apr. 9, 1905.

53. *Donskaia rech',* Oct. 30, 1905.

54. *Saratovskii listok,* Oct. 19, 1905.

55. *Kievskaia gazeta*, Sept. 23, 1905.

56. Starozhil, *Kiev*, 150–51; *Kievskoe slovo*, Aug. 4, 1903.

57. Turau, *Materialy*, 233–35.

58. *Privolzhskii krai* (Saratov), Oct. 30, 1905.

59. "Dukhovenstvo i sobytiia poslednikh dnei," *Kievskaia gazeta*, Oct. 28, 1905.

60. Sergei Bulgakov, *Kievskie otkliki*, Oct. 25, 1905.

61. I. Petrovskii, *Russkii evrei* 20 (1881): 790.

62. Turau, *Materialy*, 235.

63. *Kievlianin*, Oct. 20, 1905, editorial. See also Oct. 27.

64. *Iuzhnyi krai*, Nov. 15, 1905.

65. "Po gorodam Podolii," *Kievskie otkliki*, Dec. 12, 1905; and "Pogromnye siluety," Nov. 6, 1905.

66. Anna Halberstam-Rubin, *Sholom Aleichem: The Writer as Social Historian* (New York: Peter Lang, 1989), 13.

67. *Kievskoe slovo*, Sept. 17, 1903.

68. *Donskaia rech'*, Oct. 29, 1905. See also *Kievskoe slovo*, Oct. 24 and Nov. 3, 1905.

69. Ascher, *The Revolution of 1905*, 130.

70. *Kievskoe slovo*, Oct. 27, 28, 1905.

CHAPTER IX. THE FINAL YEARS OF ROMANOV KIEV

1. *Kievskaia gazeta*, Nov. 6, 1905; *Kievskie otkliki*, Nov. 14, 1905.

2. *Kievskaia gazeta*, Nov. 8, 1905. See also *Kiev perioda pozdnego feodalizma i kapitalizma*, 347–49.

3. Twenty-four SRs were arrested in late November or early December, according to *Kievskaia gazeta*, Dec. 6, 1905, which got its information from *Kievlianin*. Most were peasants or university students from around the empire.

4. *Kievskie otkliki*, Jan. 17, 1906. See also V. Manilov, "Kievskaia voennaia organizatsiia RSDRP i vosstanie saper v noiabre 1905 goda," *LR* 5–6 (1925): 183. The influence of the Bolshevik-founded railway union appeared to be declining except at the Main Railway Shops, possibly because the flamboyant Shlikhter had been out of the city for long periods of time. According to Reichman, *Railwaymen*, 251–52, white-collar railway employees were "dividing into a more moderate, professional component" at this time.

5. *Kievskaia gazeta*, Nov. 8, 1905.

6. *Kievskaia gazeta*, Dec. 3, 1905. See also Komissiia TsIK SSSR, *1905. Sovetskaia pechat' i literatura o sovetakh* (Moscow-Leningrad: Gosudarstvennoe izdatel'stvo, 1925), 432–37.

7. For the Eikhelman affair, see *Kievskaia gazeta*, Nov. 7, 8, 1905. For the postal strike, see the Nov. 16 issue. Ascher, *The Revolution of 1905*, 326, reports the action of the city council.

8. Especially in November Kiev's press is full of notices about union organizational efforts. For the printers and bakers, for example, see *Kievskaia gazeta*, Nov. 9 and 14–16, 1905. For watchmakers, see *Kievskie otkliki*, Dec. 1, 1905.

9. *Kievskoe slovo*, Nov. 25, 1905.

10. *Kievskie otkliki*, Dec. 22, Jan. 15, 20, 1906; *Kiev perioda pozdnego feodalizma i kapitalizma*, 349. See also Komissiia TsIK SSSR, *1905. Professional'noe dvizhenie* (Moscow-Leningrad: Gosudarstvennoe izdatel'stvo, 1926), 203–7.

11. Iukhneva, *Etnicheskii sostav*, 157.

12. "Artel 'bosiakov' na Kievskoi pristani," *Kievskaia gazeta*, Oct. 10, 1904. See also *Zaria*, Apr. 19, 1881.

13. *Kievskoe slovo*, Sept. 10, 1903.

14. *Khar'kovskie gubernskie vedomosti*, May 11, 1881, notes that some Kiev artels and the 1,325 railway employees in Kharkiv spoke out against pogroms to set an example for other workers.

15. I found references to a metalworkers' artel that made and sold metal goods. It took orders from institutions or individuals, decided all of its disputes, and made all of its own decisions with regard to profit sharing, investment, and hiring. A six-man council selected its foremen. Men seventeen years of age could join for a one-hundred-ruble fee if they had a clean record. In 1903 it opened its forge and machine shop with a special ceremony and prayer meeting. Another artel of one hundred members, consisting apparently of railway guards, conductors, and city employees, bought about twenty acres of land and built forty private homes on it. The remaining sixty members sought to build homes and a school and petitioned the city council, hoping either to buy more land or to rent it cheaply. See *Kievskoe slovo*, Aug. 18, 1903.

16. Pantiukhov, *Opyt*, 308.

17. In 1905 Odessa needle workers sought to organize separate unions for those who sewed men's clothes and those who sewed women's clothes, for example. Those who made ready-to-wear clothes sought to remain separate from those who tailored custom-made clothes. Hatmakers and capmakers formed separate unions. Restaurant workers organized separately from cooks and waiters on the steamship lines. See Robert Weinberg, "Odessa, 1905: Workers in Revolt" (unpub. manuscript), chap. 8, pp. 10–11.

18. Ascher, *The Revolution of 1905*, 269–72.

19. Manilov, "Kievskaia voennaia organizatsiia," 192.

20. Ibid., 197–99.

21. *Kievlianin*, Nov. 20, 1905.

22. Manilov, "Kievskaia voennaia organizatsiia," 204–9.

23. *Kievskie otkliki*, Nov. 13, 18, 1905.

24. See, for example, *OIKGOPO*, 70.

25. "Kievskaia zhizn'," *Kievskoe slovo*, Nov. 30, 1905. See also reports in *Kievskie otkliki*, Nov. 22, 28, Dec. 1, 1905.

26. Ascher, *The Revolution of 1905*, 278.

27. Ibid., 301.

28. For the details of the strike, see *Kievskii vestnik* (Kiev), Dec. 12–18, 1905.

29. *Iuzhnyi krai*, Dec. 24, 1905; *Kievskie otkliki*, Dec. 14, 1905. At this time *Iuzhnyi krai* was a conservative paper and may have obtained its information from *Kievlianin*.

30. Based on reports in *Kievskie otkliki*, Dec. 10, 18, 21, 25, 1905, and Jan. 13, 15, 1906. See also *Kievlianin*, Dec. 17, 1905; *Kievskii vestnik*, Dec. 12–18,

1905; *Kiev perioda pozdnego feodalizma i kapitalizma*, 353–55; and Hermaize, *Narysy*, 116. *Iuzhnyi krai*, Dec. 29, 1905, carried the report on the arrest and "beating" of the secondary students.

31. Manilov, "Kievskaia voennaia organizatsiia," 217–19; *OIKGOPO*, 67.

32. Kassow, *Students*, 321–22.

33. A. Troianovskii, *Vosstanie v Kieve v 1907 g.* (Moscow, 1927), 5–8. Apparently, 102 soldiers from the 1905 mutiny were brought to trial in Kiev on March 23, 1907. Most were given long prison sentences. Few officers had participated in the revolt. Of the three who stuck it out until the end, two escaped abroad, and a third, Boris Zhadanovsky, was badly wounded. He ultimately died fighting against Symon Petliura in 1918. The Social Democrats began to agitate among Kiev's soldiers again in the spring of 1906 and managed to publish nine issues of *Golos soldat* (The voice of the soldier), which included information from a network of soldiers in the Kiev prison.

34. *Kiev perioda pozdnego feodalizma i kapitalizma*, 361, 366.

35. A. Rosnovskii, "Iz epokhi 'Zvezdy' i 'Pravdy' v Kieve," *LR* 6 (1926): 101–12. In all, the author estimates that Kiev's Social Democrats had about seven hundred members at this time, two hundred of whom were activists.

36. Ibid., 117–18.

37. *Kiev perioda pozdnego feodalizma i kapitalizma*, 370, 372; *Istoriia Kieva*, 555; P. A. Lavrov, *Rabochee dvizhenie na Ukraine v 1913–14 gg.* (Kiev: Politicheskaia literatura USSR, 1957), 9–33. Rosnovskii, "Iz epokhi," 129–40, profiles Bosh and the Bolshevik leaders, many of whom were students or print workers.

38. Hryhor'ev, *U staromu Kyivi*, 263–72.

39. *Kiev perioda pozdnego feodalizma i kapitalizma*, 376–79; Hryhor'ev, *U staromu Kyivi*, 272; Tikhon J. Polner, *Russian Local Government during the War and the Union of Zemstvos* (New Haven: Yale University Press, 1930), 193.

40. *Kiev perioda pozdnego feodalizma i kapitalizma*, 380. The print workers' strike of Sept. 5–16, 1916, led by the Bolshevik-dominated printers' union, was the main exception in that it had political demands.

41. *Kievskaia mysl'*, Feb. 24, 25, 1915, editorials. See also *Gorodskoe delo* 9 (1915): 498–99; 13–14 (1915): 725. By the late summer, three consumer societies had formed in the city and two others were in the process of organizing.

42. *Gorodskoe delo* 24 (1915): 1321; 7 (1916): 336–37. For the petition, see 8 (1916): 404–5.

CONCLUSION

1. Bushnell, *Moscow Graffiti*, 5.

2. Podhorodecki, *Dzieje Kijowa*, 180–84. *Kievskaia gazeta*, Aug. 12, 1904.

3. *Kievskaia mysl'*, May 4, 1914. Kiev also had a Gypsy Alley. *Pervaia vseobshchaia perepis'* (1897), 199, records 36 Gypsies in Kiev in 1897. According to O. P. Barannikov, *Ukrains'kyi tsygani. Vseukrains'ka akademiia nauk. Natsional'ni menshosti radians'koi ukrainiy* (Kiev: Akademiia nauk, 1931), bk. 2, p. 15, there were only 13,529 Gypsies in the Ukraine in 1926, 691 of whom lived in Kiev or its environs.

4. "Sredi bogomol'tsev," *Kievskaia gazeta*, Aug. 15, 1904. The data are from the August 16, 1903, edition.

5. Isaak Mazepa, cited in Bohdan Krawchenko, "The Social Structure of the Ukraine in 1917," *HUS* 14 (June 1990): 100.

6. This estimate is from Senator Turau in *Kievskii i Odesskii pogromy*, 47.

7. *Kievskie otkliki*, Oct. 23, 1905, editorial.

8. In 1904 the Society for the Defense of Women had organized a branch in the city for the purpose of helping working women "physically, morally, and legally." In 1905 the Union of Equal Rights for Women, with up to seventy affiliates, pushed for full political rights for women, equal educational and career opportunities, and the abolition of all laws on prostitution that demeaned the dignity of women. Although these organizations existed elsewhere, the fact that women were deprived of education in a city noted for its educational opportunity made Kiev a particularly important target for the empire's feminist movement.

9. *Istoriia Kieva*, 463. The figures are for 1912.

10. *Kiev perioda pozdnego feodalizma i kapitalizma*, 390.

11. Ibid., 398.

12. *Kievskie vesti*, Dec. 22, 1907. Cholera produced 2,908 illnesses and 1,376 deaths in 1872; 1,940 illnesses and 659 deaths in 1892; and 1,050 illnesses and 367 deaths in 1907.

13. "Otdykh," *Kievskoe slovo*, Aug. 31, 1903. See also *Khar'kovskii listok*, Mar. 4, 1905, editorial.

14. In 1905 about one-fifth of the city's comparatively small budget went to health and sanitation.

15. Kiev perioda pozdnego feodalizma i kapitalizma, 324.

16. Gorodskoe delo 11–12 (1914): 739.

17. Brian Ladd, *Urban Planning and Civic Order in Germany, 1860–1914* (Cambridge: Harvard University Press, 1990), 238. Spurred by political unification, German cities grew very rapidly. Between 1871 and 1914, for example, Berlin grew from 825,937 to 2,056,879; Hamburg from 300,504 to 1,039,697; and Munich from 169,693 to 646,000, according to Ladd, p. 14.

18. Titus D. Hewryk, *The Lost Architecture of Kiev* (New York: The Ukrainian Museum, 1982), offers a good account of the destruction of Kiev's treasures in the 1930s.

19. Marco Carynnyk, "The Killing Fields of Kiev," *Commentary* 90 (April 1990): 22, 25.

20. Levin, *The Jews in the Soviet Union since 1917*, 1:404. For a chilling recollection of this time, see Anatoly Kuznetsov, *Babi Yar: A Documentary Novel* (New York: Dell Publishing Co., 1966).

21. Levin, *The Jews in the Soviet Union since 1917*, 1:423.

22. Hewryk, *Lost Architecture*, 6.

BIBLIOGRAPHY

ARCHIVES

Tsentral'nyi gosudarstvennyi arkhiv Oktiabr'skoi revoliutsii (TsGAOR)
fond 102 Ministerstvo vnutrennikh del, Departament gosudarstvennoi politsii.
Tsentral'nyi gosudarstvennyi istoricheskii arkhiv (TsGIA)
fond 1263 Komitet ministrov.
fond 1284 Departament obshchikh del Ministerstva vnutrennikh del.
fondy 1287, 1290 Khoziaistvennyi Departament Ministerstva vnutrennikh del.
fond 1288 Glavnoe upravlenie po delam mestnogo khoziaistva Ministerstva vnutrennikh del.

NEWSPAPERS

Kiev

Kievlianin (1864–1916).
Kievskaia gazeta (1899–1905).
Kievskaia mysl' (1906–1916).
Kievskie gubernskie vedomosti (1893–1916).
Kievskie novosti (1905).
Kievskie otkliki (1903–1907).
Kievskie vesti (1907–1911).
Kievskii telegraf (1859–1876).
Kievskii vestnik (1905).
Kievskoe slovo (1886–1905).
Zaria (1880–1886).

Other Cities

(Cities of publication are listed as they appeared on the masthead.)
Bessarabets (Kishinev, 1897–1906).
Bessarabskaia zhizn' (Kishinev, 1904–1916).
Donskaia rech' (Rostov-na-Donu, 1899–1905).
Drug (Kishinev, 1905–1914).
Elizavetgradskii vestnik (Elizavetgrad, 1881).
Iuzhnaia zaria (Ekaterinoslav, 1906–1915)

Iuzhnyi krai (Khar'kov, 1880–1916).
Khar'kovskie gubernskie vedomosti (Khar'kov, 1838–1916).
Khar'kovskii listok (Khar'kov, 1901–1905).
Khar'kovskii spravochnyi listok (Khar'kov, 1905).
Odesskie novosti (Odessa, 1884–1916).
Poltavskaia rech' (Poltava, 1911–1913).
Privolzhskii krai (Saratov, 1903–1907).
Rech' (St. Petersburg, 1907–1917).
Saratovskii listok (Saratov, 1879–1916).
Severo-zapadnaia zhizn' (Minsk, 1913–1915).
Utro (Khar'kov, 1906–1916).
Utro Rossii (Moscow, 1907–1914).
Volga (Saratov, 1906–1916).
Volna (Khar'kov, 1905–1906).
Volyn' (Zhitomir, 1882–1906, 1908–1916).

BOOKS AND ARTICLES ON KIEV, 1800–1917

Belichko, Iu. V., and V. P. Pidgora. *Kriz' viky. Kyiv v obrazotvorchomu mystetstvi XII–XX stolit'*. Kiev: Mystetsvo, 1982.
"Bolsheviki v Kieve." *Letopis' revoliutsii* 4 (1925): 45–53.
Bukhbinder, N. A. "K istorii sotsial-demokraticheskogo dvizheniia v Kievskoi gubernii. Kiev." *Krasnaia letopis'* 7 (1923): 263–84.
Chevazhevskii, V. S. "Iz' proshlago Kievskago universiteta i studentskoi zhizni (1870–1875 g.). *Russkaia starina* (April–May–June 1912): 555–85.
Chizevskyi, A. M. "Vospominaniia o studentakh Kievskoi dukhovnoi akademii s 1819–1863 gg." *Russkaia starina* 1 (1917): 127–38; 2 (1917): 238–41; 3 (1917): 402–7.
Deiatel'nost' obshchestva dnevnykh priiutov dlia detei rabochego klassa za 1875–1911 g. Kiev, 1913.
Derenkovskii, G. M. "Uzlovoe biuro RSDRP Iugo-zapadnykh zheleznykh dorog v 1906–1908 g.g." In *Iz istorii rabochego klassa i revoliutsionnogo dvizheniia*, 371–97. Moscow, 1958.
Dolgorukii, Ivan. "Puteshestvie v Kiev v 1817 godu." *Chteniia v imperatorskom obshchestve istorii i drevnostei rossiiskikh pri Moskovskom Universitete* 2 (1870): 1–208.
Doroshenko, Dmytro. "Ukrains'kyi rukh 1890-ykh rokiv v osvitlenni Avstriis'-koho konsula v Kyevi." In *Z mynuloho. Zbirnyk. Pratsi Ukrains'koho naukovoho instytutu*, 48:59–70. Warsaw, 1938.
Dvadtsatipiatiletie Kievskoi birzhi, 1869–94 g. Kiev, 1895.
Eremeev, S. *Kiev i ego gorodovoe polozhenie.* Kiev, 1874.
Funduklei, Ivan. *Obozrenie Kieva v otnoshenii k drevnostiam.* Kiev: I Val'ner, 1847.
———. *Statisticheskoe opisanie Kievskoi gubernii.* St. Petersburg: Ministerstvo vnutrennikh del, 1852.
Galant, I. "Izgnanie evreev iz Kieva po offitsial'noi perepiske (1828–31)." *Evreiskaia starina* 7 (1914): 465–86.

———. "K istorii Kievskago getto i tsenzury evreiskikh knig (1854–55 g.)." *Evreiskaia starina* 6 (1913): 264–78.

Gorlenko, V. "Kiev v 1799 godu." *Kievskaia starina* 3 (1885): 581–92.

Hamm, Michael F. "Continuity and Change in Late Imperial Kiev." In M. Hamm, ed., *The City in Late Imperial Russia*, 79–121. Bloomington: Indiana University Press, 1986.

Hermaize, Osyp. "Shevchenkyivs'ka demonstratsiia v Kyivi r. 1914." *Chervonyi shliakh* 3 (1924): 121–47.

Hryhor'ev, Hryhoryi. *U staromu Kyivi. Spohady*. Kiev: Radians'kyi pys'mennyk, 1961.

Ikonnikov, V. S. *Kiev v 1654–1855 gg. Istoricheskii ocherk'*. Kiev: Imperatorskii Universitet Sv. Vladimira, 1904.

Institut istorii Akademii nauk USSR, *Istoriia Kieva*. Kiev: Akademiia nauk Ukrainskoi SSR, 1963.

Istoriia Kieva. See under Institut istorii, above, this section.

Istoriia mist i sil ukrains'koi RSR. Kyiv. Kiev: Akademiia nauk Ukrainskoi SSR, 1968.

Itenberg, V.S. *Iuzhno-rossiiskii soiuz rabochikh*. Moscow: Mysl', 1974.

Izvestiia Kievskoi gorodskoi dumy. Kiev, 1880–1915.

"K istorii Kievskikh monastyrei." *Kievskaia starina* 4 (1896): 9–11.

Kaminin, I. "Posledniaia samozashchita g. Kieva." *Kievskaia starina* 7 (1882): 186–88.

———. "Poslednie gody samoupravleniia Kieva po Magdeburgskomu pravu." *Kievskaia starina* 5 (1888): 140–68; 8 (1888): 157–95; 9 (1888): 597–622.

Khizniakov, V. M. *Vospominaniia zemskago deiatelia*. Petrograd, 1916.

Kholernaia epidemiia 1907 goda v g. Kieve. Kiev, 1908.

"Kiev." *Encyclopaedia Judaica*, 10:991–98. Jerusalem: Macmillan, 1971.

Kiev. Entsiklopedicheskii spravochnik. Kiev: Ukrainskaia Sovetskaia Entsiklopediia, 1986.

Kiev i ego sviatyni, drevnosti, dostopamiatnosti. Kiev: N. Ia. Oglobin, 1900.

Kiev perioda pozdnego feodalizma i kapitalizma. See under Kondufor, below, this section.

Kiev po perepisi 2 Marta 1874. Kiev: Universitetskaia tipografiia, 1875.

"Kiev v sorokovykh godakh." *Kievskaia starina* 5 (1899): 66–68.

Kievskii i Odesskii pogromy v otchetakh senatorov Turau i Kuzminskago. St. Petersburg: Letopisets, 1907.

"Kievskoe predstavitel'stvo prezhniago vremeni." *Kievskaia starina* 5 (1882): 177–92.

Klimko, A. I., and A. A. Shevchenko. "Dinamika etnicheskago sostava naselenie Kieva." In *Etnicheskie gruppy v gorodakh evropeiskoi chasti SSSR*, 72–81. Moscow: Akademiia nauk SSSR, 1987.

Konchakovskii, Anatolii, and Dmitrii Malakov. *Kiev Mikhaila Bulgakova*. Kiev: Mystetstvo, 1990.

Kondufor, Iu. Iu., ed. *Istoriia Kiev'a. Kiev perioda pozdnego feodalizma i kapitalizma*. Kiev: Naukova dumka, 1983.

Kontraktovyi ukazatel' v pamiat o stoletii kontraktov 1797–1897. Kiev: I. I. Chokolov, 1897.

Krasnyi-Admoni, G. Ia., ed. *Materialy dlia istorii antievreiskikh pogromov v Rossii. Vos'midesiatye gody, 12 aprel' 1881—29 fevral' 1882.* Vol. 2. Petrograd-Moscow: Gosudarstvennoe izdatel'stvo, 1923.

Kulisher, M. I. "Evrei v Kieve. Istoricheskii ocherk'. " *Evreiskaia starina* 3 (1913): 351–66; 4 (1913): 417–38.

Kupleba, G. I. "Pokazhchyk dokumentiv z istorii Kyeva." *Arkhivy Ukrainy* 4 (1981): 13–17.

Kyiv. Vchora, s'ogodni, zavtra. Kiev: Mystetstvo, 1982.

Lazarevs'ka, Kateryna. "Kyivs'kyi tsekhy v druhii polovyni XVIII ta na pochatku XIX viku." *Kyiv ta ioho okolytsia v istorii i pam'iatkakh. Zapysky Istorychnoi sektsii Ukrains'koho naukhovo tovarystva* (Kiev) 22 (1926): 275–308.

Levakovskaia, O. N. "Universitet piatidesiatykh godov." *Russkaia starina* (April–May–June 1917): 63–79; (July–August–September 1917): 110–18.

Levitskii, O. "Epizod' iz' pol'skago miatezha 1831 goda v Kievshchine." *Kievskaia starina* 4 (1899): 90–116.

———. "Trevozhnye gody. Ocherk' iz obshchestvennoi i politicheskoi zhizni g. Kieva i Iugo-Zapad. kraia v 1811–12 g.g." *Kievskaia starina* 10 (1891): 1–21; 11 (1891): 169–94; 11 (1895): 188–212; 12 (1895): 347–60.

Linden, A. "Gouvernement Kiew. Kiew." In *Die Judenpogrome in Russland*, 2:339–406. Köln and Leipzig: Judischer verlag, 1910.

M. K. "Bol'sheviki v 1905 v Kieve." *Letopis' revoliutsii* 4 (1925): 45–53.

Manilov, V. "Kievskaia voennaia organizatsiia RSDRP i vosstanie saper v noiabre 1905 goda." *Letopis' revoliutsii* 5–6 (1925): 176–225.

———. "Ocherki iz istorii sotsial-demokraticheskago dvizheniia v Kieve (80–90 g.g.)." *Letopis' revoliutsii* 3 (1923): 116–37; 4 (1923): 3–22; 5 (1923): 21–41.

Marakhov, G. I. *Kievskii universitet v revoliutsionno-demokraticheskom dvizhenii.* Kiev: Vishcha shkola, 1984.

Mebel, M. I., ed. *1905 na Ukraine. Khronika i materialy.* Vol. 1. Khar'kov: Proletarii, 1926.

Merder', A. "Gorodskoe opolchenie v Kieve 1863 g." *Kievskaia starina* 1 (1900): 2.

"Mery protiv kholery 1831 g." *Kievskaia starina* 11 (1903): 72–73.

Naumov, G. *Biudzhety rabochikh gor. Kieva.* Kiev: I. I. Chokolov, 1914.

1905 rik u Kyevi ta na Kyivshchyni. Zbirnyk statei ta spohadiv. Kiev: Derzhavne vyd-vo Ukrainy, 1926.

Obzor' deiatel'nosti Kievskoi gorodskoi dumy za chetyrekhletie 1906–1910 gg. Kiev, 1910.

Obzor' Kievskoi gubernii. Kiev, 1901–1913.

Ocherki istorii Kievskikh gorodskoi i oblastnoi partiinykh organizatsii. Kiev: Politicheskaia literatura, 1981.

"Oktiabr'skie sobytiia 1905 goda v Kieve v izobrazhenii okhrannogo otdeleniia." *Letopis' revoliutsii* 2 (1925): 112–24.

Otchet' Kievskoi gorodskoi ispoln. sanit. komissii za 1899 g. Kiev, 1900.

Otchet' o deiatel'nosti Kievskago obshchestva gramotnosti v 1905 g. Kiev, 1906.

Otchet' o deiatel'nosti Kievskago popechitel'stva o narodnoi trezvosti za 1905 g. Kiev, 1908.

Otchet' o deiatel'nosti obshchestva dlia bor'by s zaraznymi bolezniami v g. Kieve. Kiev, 1900–1914.

Otchet' o deiatel'nosti pervoi muzhskoi voskresnoi shkoly za vremia o 9 fevralia po 4 maia 1897 g. Kiev, 1897.

Otchet' o deiatel'nosti shkol Kievskago obshchestva gramotnosti. Kiev, 1898.

Otchet' o deiatel'nosti voskresnykh shkol Kievskoi obshchestvennoi gramotnosti. Kiev, 1900.

Otchet' otdela narodnago zdraviia Kievskoi gorodskoi upravy za 1910 g. Kiev, 1912.

Otchet' sanitarnago otdeleniia Kievskoi gorodskoi upravy. Kholernaia epidemiia 1907 goda v g. Kieve. Kiev, 1908.

Pantiukhov, Ivan. *Opyt sanitarnoi topografii i statistiki Kieva.* Kiev: Kievskii gubernskii statisticheskii komitet, 1877.

Parasun'ko, O. A. *Massovaia politicheskaia zabastovka v Kieve v 1903 g.* Kiev: Akademiia nauk Ukrainskoi SSR, 1953.

Pervaia vseobshchaia perepis' naseleniia Rossiiskoi imperii, 1897 g. Vol. 16. St. Petersburg: Tsentral'nyi statisticheskii komitet Ministerstva vnutrennykh del, 1904.

Podhorodecki, Leszek. *Dzieje Kijowa.* Warsaw: Książka i Wiedza, 1982.

Pravdin, V. "Epokha neslikhannoi smuty na Kievshchine." *Letopis' revoliutsii* 2 (1925): 91–111.

———. "Iiul'skaia stachka solidarnosti 1903 g. v Kieve." *Letopis' revoliutsii* 4 (1924): 66–94.

Prokopovych, Vyacheslav. *Pid zolotoiu korohvoiu.* Paris: U Paryzhi, 1943.

"Publichnyia uveseleniia i pozorishcha v Kieve sto let tomu nazad." *Kievskaia starina* 2 (1897).

Rech', proiznesennaia gorodskoi golovoi v zasedanii dumy 28 fevralia 1883 goda. Kiev, 1883.

Rosnovskii, A. "Iz epokhi 'Zvezdy' i 'Pravdy' v Kieve." *Letopis' revoliutsii* 6 (1926): 101–42.

Sadovs'kyi, Valentyn. "Students'ke zhyttia u Kyivi v 1904–1909 rokakh." *Z mynuloho. Zbirnyk. Pratsi Ukrains'koho naukovoho instytuta* (Warsaw) 49 (1939): 5–18.

Sbornik obiazatel'nykh dlia zhitelei g. Kieva. Postanovlenii iz Kievskago gorodskago dumy s 1871 po 9 fevralia 1887 goda. Kiev, 1887.

Shandra. V. S. "Pochatkova ta serednia osvita u Kyivi v pershii polovyni XIX st." *Arkhivy Ukrainy* 5 (1980): 63–67.

Shcherbyna, V. "Borot'ba Kyiva za avtonomiiu." *Kyiv ta ioho okolytsia v istorii i pam'iatkakh. Zapysky Istorychnoi sektsii Ukrains'koi akademii nauk* (Kiev) 22 (1926): 168–216.

Slavins'kyi, Maksym. "Spomyny" [Kyivs'ke ukrainstvo v rokakh 1877–1895]. *Ameryka* (Philadelphia) 95–98, 100–101, 106–11, 113–16, 118–21, 123–25, 128–31, 134–35, 138–39, 142–45, 147–50, 152–55, 157–59, 161–63, 165–66 (1960).

Starozhil. *Kiev v vos'midesiatykh godakh.* Kiev: Petr Barskii, 1910.

Stoletie Kievskago universiteta Sv. Vladimira. Belgrade: Komitet Kievskikh professorov v Liubliane, 1935.

Tabiś, Jan. *Polacy na uniwersytecie Kijowskim, 1834–1863.* Cracow: Wydawnictwo Literackie Kraków, n.d.

Troianovskii, A. *Vosstanie v Kieve v 1907 g.* Moscow, 1927.

Turau. *Materialy.* See under "Vsepoddanneishii . . . ," below, this section.

Uezdy Kievskii i Radomysl'skii. Kiev, 1887.

Umanov-Kaplunovskii, V. "M. L. Kropivnitskii i iuzhnorusskii teatr." *Istoricheskii vestnik* (April–June 1906): 523–31.

Vakar, V. V. *Nakanune 1905 goda v Kieve* (Khar'kov, 1925).

Ves' Kieva. Kiev, 1898–1905.

"Vsepoddanneishii otchet' o proizvedennom, po vysochaichemu poveleniiu, gofmeisterom dvora ego imperatorskago velichestva senatorom Turau izsledovanii prichin bezporiadkov, byvshikh v g. Kieve." In *Materialy k istorii Russkoi kontr'-revoliutsii. Pogromy po offitsial'nym dokumentam,* vol. 1. St. Petersburg, 1908.

Vychkov, A. "Delo o revoliutsionnykh kruzhakh v Kieve v 1879, 1880 i 1881 g.g." *Letopis' revoliutsii* 2 (1924): 39–62; 3 (1924): 161–74.

Zakharchenko, Mykhailo. *Kiev teper' i prezhde, 988–1888.* Kiev: S. V. Kul'zhenko, 1888.

Zakrevskii, Nikolai. *Letopis' i opisanie goroda Kieva.* Moscow: Universitetskaia tipografiia, 1858.

———. *Opisanie Kieva.* Moscow: V. Grachev, 1868.

Zvidomlennia tovarystva Prosvita u Kyivi za r. 1910. Kiev, 1911.

COLLATERAL WORKS

Abramson, Henry. "Jewish Representation in the Independent Ukrainian Governments of 1917–1920." *Slavic Review* 50 (Fall 1991): 542–50.

Adamovich, E. "Ianvar' 1905 goda na Ukraine." *Letopis' revoliutsii* 1 (1925): 150–93.

Alabin, P., and P. Konovalov. *Sbornik svedenii o nastoiashchem sostoianii gorodskago khoziaistva v glavneishikh gorodakh Rossii.* Samara: I. P. Novikov, 1889.

Alexander, John T. "Reconsiderations of Plague in Early Modern Russia." *Jahrbucher für Geschichte Ost Europas* 34, no. 2 (1986): 244–54.

The American Jewish Yearbook 5667. Philadelphia: The Jewish Publication Society of America, 1906.

Andrievskii, A. "Arkhivnaia spravka o sostave Kievskago 'obshchestva' v 1782–1797 godakh." *Kievskaia starina* 2 (1894): 192–203.

———. "Kievskie smuty srediny proshlago stoletiia." *Kievskaia starina* 12 (1886): 664–708.

Andriewsky, Olga. "*Medved' iz berlogi*: Vladimir Jabotinsky and the Ukrainian Question, 1904–1914." *Harvard Ukrainian Studies* 14 (December 1990): 249–67.

Anfimov, A. M. *Krupnoe pomeshchich'e khoziaistvo evropeiskoi Rossii (konets XIX–nachalo XX veka).* Moscow: Nauka, 1969.

Antonovich, Vladimir B. "Kiev, ego sud'ba i znachenie s XIV po XVI stoletie (1362–1569)." *Kievskaia starina* 1 (1882): 1–48.

———. *Monografiia po istorii zapadnoi iugo-zapadnoi Rossii*. Kiev: E. Ia. Fedorov, 1885.

Antoshkin, D. *Professional'noe dvizhenie v Rossii*. Moscow, 1925.

Aronson, I. Michael. *Troubled Waters: The Origins of the 1881 Anti-Jewish Pogroms in Russia*. Pittsburgh: University of Pittsburgh Press, 1990.

Ascher, Abraham. *The Revolution of 1905: Russia in Disarray*. Stanford: Stanford University Press, 1988.

Bagalei, D. I. *Istoriia Khar'kova za 250 let*. 2 vols. Khar'kov: Khar'kovskoe gorodskoe obshchestvennoe upravlenie, 1905.

Balabanov, M. *Ocherki istorii revoliutsionnogo dvizheniia v Rossii*. Leningrad: Priboi, 1929.

Baraboi, A. Z. "Khar'kovsko-Kievskoe revoliutsionnoe tainoe obshchestvo, 1856–60." *Istoricheskie zapiski* 52 (1955): 235–66.

———. "Pravoberezhnaia Ukraina v 1848 g." *Istoricheskie zapiski* 34 (1950): 86–121.

Barannikov, O. P. *Ukrains'kyi tsygani. Vseukrains'ka akademiia nauk. Natsional'ni menshosti radians'koi ukrainiy*. Kiev: Akademiia nauk, 1931.

Barth, Gunther. *City People: The Rise of Modern City Culture in Nineteenth-Century America*. New York: Oxford University Press, 1980.

Basalygo, K. "Revoliutsionnoe dvizhenie v Khar'kove v 1905–06 g.g." *Letopis' revoliutsii* 1 (1924): 119–36.

Bater, James H. *St. Petersburg: Industrialization and Change*. Montreal: McGill University Press, 1976.

Beletskaia, E., et al. *"Obraztsovye" proekty v zhiloi zastroike Russkikh gorodov XVIII–XIX vv*. Moscow: Literatura po stoitel'stvu, 1961.

"Berdichevskaia iarmarka." *Kievskaia starina* 6 (1893): 42–58.

Berlyns'kyi, M. F. *Istoriia mista Kyeva*. Kiev: Naukova dumka, 1991.

Bilins'kyi, Mykola. "Z mynuloho perezhytoho 1870–88." *Ukraina* 2 (1928): 117–32.

Birnbaum, Henrik. "Kiev, Novgorod, Moscow: Three Varieties of Urban Society in East Slavic Territory." In Barisa Krekič, ed., *Urban Society of Eastern Europe in Premodern Times*, 1–62. Berkeley and Los Angeles: University of California Press, 1987.

———. "On Jewish Life and Anti-Jewish Sentiments in Medieval Russia." In H. Birnbaum, ed., *Essays in Early Slavic Civilization*, 215–45. Munich: Wilhelm Fink Verlag, 1971.

Bobrowski, Tadeusz. *Pamietnik mojego życia*. 2 vols. Warsaw: Panstwowy Institut Wydawniczy, 1979.

Bojcun, Jaromyr Marko. "The Working Class and the National Question in Ukraine, 1880–1920." Ph.D. diss., York University, 1985.

Bonnell, Victoria E. *Roots of Rebellion: Workers' Politics and Organizations in St. Petersburg and Moscow, 1900–1914*. Berkeley and Los Angeles: University of California Press, 1983.

Boshyk, George Yury. "The Rise of Ukrainian Political Parties in Russia, 1900–07: With Special Reference to Social Democracy." Ph.D. diss., Oxford University, 1981.

Bradley, Joseph. *Muzhik and Muscovite: Urbanization in Late Imperial Russia*. Berkeley and Los Angeles: University of California Press, 1985.

Brainin, S. "Oktiabr'–Dekabr' v Khar'kove." *Letopis' revoliutsii* 5–6 (1925): 106–31.

Brooks, Jeffrey. *When Russia Learned to Read: Literacy and Popular Literature, 1861–1917.* Princeton: Princeton University Press, 1985.

Brower, Daniel R. *The Russian City between Tradition and Modernity, 1850–1900.* Berkeley and Los Angeles: University of California Press, 1990.

Bukhbinder, N. A. "Evreiskoe rabochee dvizhenie v 1905 godu 1 Maia." *Krasnaia letopis'* 7 (1923): 7–22.

———. "K istorii sotsial-demo. dvizheniiu v Kievskoi gubernii. I. Kiev." *Krasnaia letopis'* 7 (1923): 263–84.

Bushnell, John. *Moscow Graffiti: Language and Subculture.* Boston: Unwin Hyman, 1990.

———. "Urban Leisure Culture in Post-Stalin Russia: Stability as a Social Problem?" In T. Thompson and R. Sheldon, eds., *Soviet Society and Culture: Essays in Honor of Vera S. Dunham,* 58–86. Boulder: Westview, Press, 1988.

Callmer, John. "The Archaeology of Kiev to the End of the Earliest Urban Phase." *Harvard Ukrainian Studies* 11 (December 1987): 323–53.

Carynnyk, Marco. "The Killing Fields of Kiev." *Commentary* 90 (April 1990): 19–25.

Chykalenko, Evhen. *Spohady (1861–1907).* New York: The Free Ukrainian Academy of Sciences in the U.S.A., 1955.

Corrsin, Stephen D. "Language Use in Cultural and Political Change in Pre-1914 Warsaw: Poles, Jews, and Russification." *The Slavonic and East European Review* 68 (January 1990): 69–90.

———. *Warsaw before the First World War: Poles and Jews in the Third City of the Russian Empire, 1880–1914.* Boulder: East European Monographs, 1989.

Davies, Norman. *God's Playground: A History of Poland in Two Volumes.* New York: Columbia University Press, 1982.

Dimsdale, Joel E., ed. *Survivors, Victims, and Perpetrators: Essays on the Nazi Holocaust.* Washington: Hemisphere Press, 1980.

Domanyts'kyi, Viktor. "Akademichnyi tradytsii Kyievo-Mohyllians'ko-Mazepyns'koi Akademii." *Naukovi zapysky Ukrains'koho tekhinichnoho instytutu* 5 (1964): 3–21.

Dubnow, S. M. *History of the Jews in Russia and Poland.* Translated by I. Friedlaender. 3 vols. Philadelphia: The Jewish Publication Society of America, 1916–1920.

Efremov, S. "Biurokraticheskaia utopiia." *Russkoe bogatstvo* 3 (1910): 72–110.

Emmons, Terence. "Russia's Banquet Campaign." *California Slavic Studies,* 10:45–86. Berkeley and Los Angeles: University of California Press, 1977.

Ettinger, S. "Kievan Russia." In C. Roth, ed., *The World History of the Jewish People.* 2d ser., *Medieval Period.* Vol. 2, *The Dark Ages,* 319–24. Tel-Aviv: Massadah Publishing Company, 1966.

Evreiskii mir. St. Petersburg, 1909–1911.

Farley, Marta Pisetska. *Festive Ukrainian Cooking.* Pittsburgh: University of Pittsburgh Press, 1990.

Fedor, Thomas Stanley. *Patterns of Urban Growth in the Russian Empire.* Chicago: University of Chicago Department of Geography, 1975.

Flynn, James T. *The University Reform of Tsar Alexander I, 1802–1835.* Washington: Catholic University Press of America, 1988.

Frankel, Jonathan. *Prophecy and Politics: Socialism, Nationalism, and the Russian Jews, 1862–1917.* Cambridge: Cambridge University Press, 1981.

Gindin, I. F. *Banki i promyshlennost' v Rossii.* Moscow: Promizdat, 1927.

Ginzburg, S. *Kinemategrafiia dorevoliutsionnoi Rossii.* Moscow: Iskusstvo, 1963.

Gordon, Linda. *Cossack Rebellions.* Albany: State University of New York Press, 1983.

Gorodskoe delo. St. Petersburg, 1909–1918.

Grossman, Leonid. "Bal'zak v Rossii." *Literaturnoe nasledstvo* 31–32 (1937): 149–372.

Gupalo, K. N. *Podol v drevnem Kieve.* Kiev: Naukova dumka, 1982.

Gusev, A. N. *Khar'kov. Ego proshloe i nastoiashchee.* Khar'kov, 1902.

Halberstam-Rubin, Anna. *Sholom Aleichem: The Writer as Social Historian.* New York: Peter Lang, 1989.

Halperin, Charles J. "Kiev and Moscow: An Aspect of Early Muscovite Thought." *Russian History/Histoire Russe* 7 (1980): 312–21.

Hamm, Michael F. "Khar'kov's Progressive Duma 1910–1914: A Study in Russian Municipal Reform." *Slavic Review* 40 (Spring 1981): 17–36.

———, ed. *The City in Late Imperial Russia.* Bloomington: Indiana University Press, 1986.

———, ed. *The City in Russian History.* Lexington: University Press of Kentucky, 1976.

Henriksson, Anders. *The Tsar's Loyal Germans: The Riga German Community, Social Change and the Nationality Question. 1855–1905.* New York: Columbia University Press, 1983.

Herlihy, Patricia. *Odessa: A History, 1794–1914.* Cambridge: Harvard Ukrainian Research Institute, 1986.

Hermaize, Osyp. *Narysy z istorii revoliutsiinoho rukhu na Ukraini.* Kiev: Knyhospilka, 1926.

Hewryk, Titus D. *The Lost Architecture of Kiev.* New York: The Ukrainian Museum, 1982.

Hrushevskyi, M. *Ocherk' istorii Ukrainskogo naroda.* St. Petersburg: Obshchestvennaia pol'za, 1911.

Istoriia Ukrains'koi RSR. Ukraina v periode imperializma (1900–1917). Kiev: Naukova dumka, 1978.

Iukhneva, N. V. *Etnicheskii sostav i etnosotsial'naia struktura naseleniia Peterburga. Vtoraia polovina XIX–nachalo XX veka.* Leningrad: Nauka, 1984.

Izvestiia Moskovskoi gorodskoi dumy. Moscow, 1902–1913.

Kalendar' "Pros'vita" na r. 1910. Kiev, 1910.

Kamanin, I. "Kievliane i Bogdan Khmel'nitskii v ikh vzaimnykh otnosheniiakh." *Kievskaia starina* 7 (1888): 69–78.

Kanatchikov, S. I. *A Radical Worker in Tsarist Russia: The Autobiography of Semen Ivanovich Kanatchikov.* Translated and edited by Reginald Zelnik. Stanford: Stanford University Press, 1986.

Kassow, Samuel D. *Students, Professors, and the State in Tsarist Russia.* Berkeley and Los Angeles: University of California Press, 1989.

Keep, John L. H. *The Russian Revolution: A Study in Mass Mobilization.* New York: W. W. Norton, 1976.

"Kievskaia pochta v 1731 g." *Kievskaia starina* 1 (1898): 11.

Klier, John D. "The Ambiguous Legal Status of Russian Jewry in the Reign of Catherine II." *Slavic Review* 35 (September 1976): 504–17.

————. "*Kievlianin* and the Jews: A Decade of Disillusionment, 1864–73." *Harvard Ukrainian Studies* 5 (March 1981): 83–101.

Klier, John D., and Shlomo Lambroza, eds. *Pogroms: Anti-Jewish Violence in Modern Russian History.* Cambridge: Cambridge University Press, 1992.

Kohut, Zenon E. "The Development of a Little Russian Identity and Ukrainian Nationbuilding." *Harvard Ukrainian Studies* 10 (December 1986): 559–76.

————. *Russian Centralism and Ukrainian Autonomy: Imperial Absorption of the Hetmanate 1760s–1830s.* Cambridge: Harvard Ukrainian Research Institute, 1988.

Komissiia TsIK SSSR. *1905. Armiia pervoi revoliutsii.* Moscow-Leningrad: Gosudarstvennoe izdatel'stvo, 1921.

————. *1905. Evreiskoe rabochee dvizhenie.* Moscow-Leningrad, Gosudarstvennoe izdatel'stvo, 1928.

————. *1905. Professional'noe dvizhenie.* Moscow-Leningrad: Gosudarstvennoe izdatel'stvo, 1926.

————. *1905. Sovetskaia pechat' i literatura o sovetakh.* Moscow-Leningrad: Gosudarstvennoe izdatel'stvo, 1925.

Kondufor, Iu. Iu., ed. *Istoriia Kieva. Drevnii i srednevekovyi Kiev.* Kiev: Naukova dumka, 1982.

Koval'skaia, Elizaveta. *Iuzhno-Russkii rabochii soiuz, 1880–81.* Moscow: Vsesoiuznoe obshchestvo politkatorzhan, 1926.

Kramer, S. *1905 v Khar'kove.* Khar'kov: Proletarii, 1925.

Krawchenko, Bohdan. "The Social Structure of the Ukraine in 1917." *Harvard Ukrainian Studies* 14 (June 1990): 97–112.

Kubijovyč, Volodymyr. *Ukraine: A Concise Encyclopedia.* Toronto: University of Toronto Press, 1971.

————, ed. *Encyclopedia of Ukraine.* 2 vols. Toronto: University of Toronto Press, 1984, 1988.

Kubijovyč, Volodymyr, and Arkadii Zhukovsky. *Map and Gazeteer of Ukraine.* Toronto: University of Toronto Press, 1984.

Ladd, Brian. *Urban Planning and Civic Order in Germany, 1860–1914.* Cambridge: Harvard University Press, 1990.

Lavrov, P. A. *Rabochee dvizhenie na Ukraine v 1913–14 gg.* Kiev: Politicheskaia literatura USSR, 1957.

Lebedev, V. "K istorii kulachnykh boev na Rusi." *Russkaia starina* 8 (August 1913): 323–40.

Leshchenko, N. N. *Krest'ianskoe dvizhenie na Ukraine v sviazi s provedeniem reformy 1861 g.* Kiev: Akademiia nauk Ukrainskoi SSR, 1959.

————. *Ukrains'ke selo v revoliutsii 1905–07 r.r.* Kiev: Naukova dumka, 1977.

Leslie, R. F. *Polish Politics and the Revolution of November 1830*. London: Athlone Press, 1956.

———. *Reform and Insurrection in Russian Poland 1856–1865*. London: Athlone Press, 1963.

———, ed. *The History of Poland since 1863*. Cambridge: Cambridge University Press, 1980.

Levin, Eve. *Sex and Society in the World of the Orthodox Slavs, 900–1700*. Ithaca: Cornell University Press, 1989.

Levin, Nora. *The Jews in the Soviet Union since 1917*. 2 vols. New York: New York University Press, 1988.

Levitskii, O. "Arkheologicheskiia ekskursii T. G. Shevchenka v 1845–1846 g.g." *Kievskaia starina* 2 (1894): 231–44.

Leyda, Jay. *Kino: A History of the Russian and Soviet Film*. New York: Collier Books, 1973.

Lindenmeyr, Adele. "Public Poor Relief and Private Charity in Late Imperial Russia." Ph.D. diss., Princeton University, 1980.

Livshits, R. *Razmeshchenie promyshlennosti v dorevoliutsionnoi Rossii*. Moscow: Akademiia nauk SSSR, 1955.

Los, F. E., ed. *Revoliutsiia 1905–07 na Ukraine*. 2 vols. Kiev: Politicheskaia literatura, 1955.

Luchitskii, I. "Kiev v 1766 godu." *Kievskaia starina* 1–3 (1888): 1–74.

Maksimovich, Mikhail A. *Sobranie sochinenii*. Kiev: M. P. Frits, 1876.

Marakhov, G. I. "Iz istorii Pol'sko-Ukrainskikh revoliutsionnykh sviazei v 50-kh—60-kh godakh XIX veka." In *Revoliutsionnaia Rossiia i revoliutsionnaia Pol'sha*, 442–49. Moscow: Nauka, 1967.

———. *Pol'skoe vosstanie 1863 g. na pravoberezhnoi Ukraine*. Kiev: Kievskii universitet, 1967.

———. *Sotsial'no-politicheskaia bor'ba na Ukraine v 50–60-e gody XIX veka*. Kiev: Vishcha shkola, 1981.

Mezentsev, Volodymyr I. "The Emergence of the Podil and the Genesis of the City of Kiev: Problems of Dating." *Harvard Ukrainian Studies* 10 (June 1986): 48–70.

Miiakovskii, V. "'Kievskaia Gromada' (Iz istorii ukrainskogo obshchestvennogo dvizheniia 60-kh godov)." *Letopis' revoliutsii* 4 (1924): 127–50.

Miller, David B. "The Kievan Principality in the Century before the Mongol Invasion: An Inquiry into Recent Research and Interpretation." *Harvard Ukrainian Studies* 10 (June 1986): 215–40.

Nardova, V. A. *Gorodskoe samoupravlenie v Rossii v 60-kh— nachale 90-kh godov XIX v*. Leningrad: Nauka, 1984.

Neuberger, Joan. "Stories of the Street: Hooliganism in the St. Petersburg Popular Press." *Slavic Review* 48 (Summer 1989): 177–94.

"Obozrenie Kievskoi, Podol'skoi, i Volynskoi gubernii s 1838 po 1850 g.g." *Russkii arkhiv* 3 (1884): 5–42.

Obshchestvenno-politicheskoe dvizhenie na Ukraine v 1863–64 g.g. Kiev: Naukova dumka, 1964.

Obzor' Ekaterinoslavskoi gubernii. Ekaterinoslav, 1906–1913.

Obzor' Khar'kovskoi gubernii. Khar'kov, 1884–1914.

Ohloblyn, A. P. *Ocherki istorii ukrainskoi fabriki. Predkapitalisticheskaia fabrika.* Kiev: Gosudarstvennoe izdatel'stvo Ukrainy, 1925.

Olesnyts'kyi, Evhen. *Storinky z moho zhyttia.* Pt. 2. Lviv: Dilo, 1935.

Paustovsky, Konstantin. *The Story of a Life.* Translated by Joseph Barnes. New York: Pantheon Books, 1982.

Pipes, Richard. "Catherine II and the Jews: The Origins of the Pale of Settlement." *Soviet Jewish Affairs* 5, no. 2 (1975): 3–20.

Pogozhev, A. "Iz zhizni fabrichnago liuda v stolitse." *Russkaia mysl'* 6 (1885): pt. 2, 20–34.

Polner, Tikhon J. *Russian Local Government during the War and the Union of Zemstvos.* New Haven: Yale University Press, 1930.

Poltavets. "Pis'mo iz Poltavskoi gubernii." *Istoricheskii vestnik* (May 1902): 721–24.

Pritsak, Omeljan. "Kiev and All of Rus': The Fate of a Sacral Idea." *Harvard Ukrainian Studies* 10 (December 1986): 279–300.

———. "The Pogroms of 1881." *Harvard Ukrainian Studies* 11 (June 1987): 8–43.

Prymak, Thomas M. *Mykhailo Hrushevsky: The Politics of National Culture.* Toronto: University of Toronto Press, 1987.

Ptukha, M. V. *Naselenie Kievskoi gubernii.* Kiev: Kievskoe Gubernskoe Statisticheskoe Biuro, 1925.

Pushkareva, I. M. *Zheleznodorozhniki Rossii v burzhuazno-demokraticheskikh revoliutsiakh.* Moscow: Nauka, 1975.

Rabinovich, M. G. *Ocherki etnografii Russkogo feodal'nogo goroda.* Moscow: Nauka, 1978.

Rawita-Gawroński, F. *Włodzimierz Antonowicz.* Lwów, 1912.

Redin, E. K. *Narodnyi teatr.* Khar'kov, 1898.

———. *Professor Nikolai Feodorovich Sumtsov.* Khar'kov, 1906.

Reichman, Henry. *Railwaymen and Revolution: Russia 1905.* Berkeley and Los Angeles: University of California Press, 1987.

Russkii evrei. St. Petersburg, 1880–1884.

Ryndziunskii, P. G. *Krest'iane i gorod v kapitalisticheskoi Rossii vtoroi poloviny XIX veka.* Moscow: Nauka, 1983.

Samiilenko, Volodymyr. *Tvory v dvokh tomakh.* 2 vols. Kiev: Khudozhestvennaia literatura, 1958.

Saunders, David. *The Ukrainian Impact on Russian Culture.* Edmonton: Canadian Institute of Ukrainian Studies, 1985.

Schmidt, Albert J. *The Architecture and Planning of Classical Moscow: A Cultural History.* Philadelphia: American Philosophical Society, 1989.

"Shalom Aleichem." *Encyclopaedia Judaica,* 14:1272–86.

Shchegolev, S. N. *Ukrainskoe dvizhenie kak sovremennyi etap iuzhnorusskago separatizma.* Kiev: Izdatel'stvo avtora, 1912.

Shchetinina, G. I. *Studenchestvo i revoliutsionnoe dvizhenie v Rossii. Posledniaia chetvert' XIX v.* Moscow: Nauka, 1987.

Shevelov, George Y. "The Language Question in the Ukraine in the Twentieth Century (1900–1941)." *Harvard Ukrainian Studies* 10 (June 1986): 71–170; 11 (June 1987): 118–224.

Shul'gin, V. Ia. "Iugo-zapadnyi krai pod upravleniem D. G. Bibikova (1838–1853)." *Drevniaia i novaia Rossiia* 5 (1879): 5–32; 6 (1879): 89–131.

Shul'kevich, M. L., and T. D. Dmitrenko, *Kiev*. Kiev: Budivel'nyk, 1978.

Snytko, T. G. "K voprosu o vzaimootnosheniiakh i sviaziakh narodnichestva s pol'skim sotsial'no-revoliutsionnym dvizheniem v kontse 70-kh—nachale 80-kh godu XIX v." In AN SSSR, *Revoliutsionnaia Rossiia i revoliutsionnaia Pol'sha*, 209–314. Moscow: Nauka, 1967.

Solov'eva, A. M. *Zheleznodorozhnyi transport Rossii vo vtoroi polovine XIX v.* Moscow: Nauka, 1975.

Stites, Richard. "Prostitute and Society in Pre-Revolutionary Russia," *Jahrbucher für Geschichte Ost Europas* 31 (1983): 348–64.

Storozhenko, A. "Kiev trista let nazad." *Kievskaia starina* 2 (1894): 204–30; 3 (1894): 404–24.

Subtelny, Orest. *The Mazepists: Ukrainian Separatism in the Early Eighteenth Century*. New York: Columbia University Press, 1981.

———. *Ukraine: A History*. Toronto: University of Toronto Press, 1988.

Sydorenko, Alexander. *The Kievan Academy in the Seventeenth Century*. Ottawa: University of Ottawa Press, 1977.

Sysyn, Frank E. *Between Poland and The Ukraine: The Dilemma of Adam Kysil, 1600–1653*. Cambridge: Harvard University Press, 1985.

Tager, A. S. *Tsarskaia Rossiia i delo Beilisa. K istorii antisemitizma*. Moscow: Sovetskoe zakonodatel'stvo, 1933.

Teplyts'kyi, V. P. *Reforma 1861 roku i agrarny vidosyny na Ukraini*. Kiev: Akademiia nauk Ukrainskoi SSR, 1959.

Thurston, Robert W. *Liberal City, Conservative State: Moscow and Russia's Urban Crisis, 1906–1914*. New York: Oxford University Press, 1987.

Tolochko, P. P. *Drevnii Kiev*. Kiev: Naukova dumka, 1983.

Tsen. statis. kom. MVD. *Goroda Rossii v 1904 g.* St. Petersburg, 1906.

———. *Goroda Rossii v 1910 g.* St. Petersburg, 1914.

Tuchapskii, Pavel. *Iz perezhitogo. Devianostye gody*. Odessa: Gosudarstvennoe izdatel'stvo Ukrainy, 1923.

"Ukraina. Ukrainskie partii." In L. Martov, et al., eds., *Obshchestvennoe dvizhenie v Rossii v nachale XX-go veka*, bk. 5, 3:294–304. St. Petersburg: Obshchestvennaia pol'za, 1914.

Ukraine: A Concise Encyclopedia. Clifton, N.J.: Ukrainian Orthodox Church of the USA, 1987.

Ustynov, I. A. *Putevoditel' po g. Khar'kovu*. Khar'kov, 1881.

Voropai, Oleksa. *Zvychai nashoho narodu. Etnografichnyi narys*. Vol. 1, Munich: Ukrains'ke vydavnytstvo, 1958. Vol. 2, Munich: Ukrains'ke vydavnytstvo, 1966.

Weinberg, Robert. "Odessa, 1905: Workers in Revolt" (unpublished manuscript).

———. "The Pogrom of 1905 in Odessa: A Case Study." In Klier and Lambroza, *Pogroms: Anti-Jewish Violence in Modern Russian History*, 248–90.

———. "The Politicization of Labor in 1905: The Case of Odessa Salesclerks." *Slavic Review* 49 (Fall 1990): 427–45.

Weinberg, Robert. "Workers, Pogroms, and the 1905 Revolution in Odessa." *The Russian Review* 46 (January 1987): 53–75.

Weinryb, Bernard D. *The Jews of Poland: A Social and Economic History of the Jewish Community in Poland from 1100 to 1800.* Philadelphia: The Jewish Publication Society of America, 1972.

Weissman, Neil B. *Reform in Tsarist Russia: The State Bureaucracy and Local Government 1800–1914.* New Brunswick: Rutgers University Press, 1981.

Witte, Sergei. *The Memoirs of Count Witte.* Translated by Abraham Yarmolinsky. Garden City, N.Y.: Doubleday, Page & Company, 1921.

Worobec, Christine D. "Temptress or Virgin? The Precarious Sexual Position of Women in Postemancipation Ukrainian Peasant Society." *Slavic Review* 49 (Summer 1990): 227–38.

Zafran, Kh. "Iz istorii rabochego divizheniia na Volyni." *Letopis' revoliutsii* 4 (1924): 115–16.

"Zapiski Ivana Matveicha Sbitneva." *Kievskaia starina* 17 (1887): 439–68, 649–66.

"Zapiski P. D. Seletskogo." *Kievskaia starina* 10 (1884): 82–103.

Zguta, Russell. *Russian Minstrels: A History of the Skomorokhi.* Philadelphia: University of Pennsylvania Press, 1978.

Zhitetskii, I. "Evrei v iuzhnoi Rossii." *Kievskaia starina* 1 (1901): 57–80; 7–8 (1901): 1–45.

INDEX

number of, 54, 113, 157; and Jews, 127, 128; and language question, 62, 97–98, 99, 114; and Poles, 60–61; See also *gymnasia*; Kiev Commercial Institute; Kiev Polytechnical Institute; St. Vladimir University; students

science, 53

Second World War, 235

Senate, Russian, 15, 110

Senytovych, Ioaniky, 88–89

Serbia, 8

Serbs, 13, 146

serf orchestras, 145

serf theater, 147

Sevastopol: expulsion of Jews from, 119; mutiny at, 214

Shchedrin, Nikolai, 174

Shchekovitsa District, 31

Sherstiuk, G. P., 112

Shevchenko, Taras, 71, 73, 99, 107, 148; celebration of, 102, 114–16, 148; and Cyril and Methodius Society, 68, 95–96; streets named for, 115

Shlikhter, Alexander, 179, 180, 189–90, 193, 209, 218; importance of to Kiev labor movement, 178, 229–30; and railway strike in 1905, 187, 188

Shmakov, A. S., 132, 203

Shulgin, Vitaly, 62, 67

Shuliavka District, 27; crime in, 158; factories in, 33; neglect of its needs, 54; special significance of for socialists, 220; workers' republic in, 27, 216–19

Siberia, 64, 69

Sichevsky, Ivan, 15

Sigismund I (king), 117

Sigismund III (king), 14, 85, 117–18

Sigismund Augustus (king), 117

Sikorsky, Igor, 168

Sinkevich, Fedor, 132

Skarga, Piotr, 7

skittles, 152

Skrynnikov, A. A., 102

Skvyra (Skvir), 120

Skvyra District, 181

Slovaks, 166–67

smallpox, 46, 47

Smila (Smela), 84

Smolensk, 58

Smolensk Province, 93, 125, 256n.34

soccer, 167, 171

Social Democrats: initial appearance of in Kiev, 174–75, 229; and Jewish self-defense, 193; after 1905, 220; Polish, 78, 107, 180, 188; and Revolution of 1905, 109, 178, 179, 182, 183, 184; and Revolutionary Ukrainian Party, 107–8; and Shevchenko celebration, 116; and soldiers, 213–15, 270n.33; and Spilka, 180, 226; and students, 177; and trade unions, 209–10. *See also* Bolsheviks; Mensheviks; socialist movement

socialist movement: in Kiev, 78, 81, 107; and national issues, 107–9, 116, 126; and pogroms, 126, 170; and Polish question, 81, 225; reinforced by inequities of municipal order, 54, 233. *See also* Revolutionary Ukrainian Party; Social Democrats; Socialist Revolutionaries

Socialist Revolutionaries, 178, 183, 184, 187, 188, 208–9; and soldiers, 214

Socialist Zionist Labor Party (SSRP), 178

Society for the Defense of Women, 160, 271n.8

Society for the Dissemination of Enlightenment, 183

Society for the Education of Polish People, 72

Society for the Friends of the People, 97

Society for the Mutual Assistance of Clerks and Office Workers, 138

Society to Assist the Poor, 161

soldiers, 57, 127, 141, 259n.25; and epidemics, 45; and insurrection in Kiev (1905), 213–16, 230; and insurrection in Kiev (1907), 220; and Jews, 216; and pogroms, 125–26, 190, 195, 198–200, 202, 207, 213, 228; and public entertainment, 153; and Revolution of 1905, 219

Solomenka, 27, 54, 124, 126, 158; and pogrom, 195, 198

Solsky, Stepan, 38

soslovie (estate): and Jews, 120; and social life, 137–39, 169

South Russian Machine Works, 208; as citadel of revolution, 33; founded, 33, 231; and soldiers' insurrection, 215; strikes at, 175, 176, 178, 179, 180, 183, 187–88, 220, 229

South Russian Workers Union, 78, 126, 174

Southwestern Railway, 28, 35, 100. *See also* Main Railway Shops

Soviet, Kiev, 208–9, 216, 218–19

Soviet, Moscow, 209, 218

Soviet, St. Petersburg, 208, 209, 217–18